Bless the Pure and Humble

NUMBER EIGHT:
Kenneth E. Montague
Series in Oil and Business History
Joseph A. Pratt
General Editor

Discovery well, Mexia, 1921. Courtesy Vinson & Elkins Archives

Bless the PURE & HUMBLE

Texas Lawyers and Oil Regulation, 1919–1936

Nicholas George Malavis

Texas A&M University Press
College Station, Texas

Library of Congress Cataloging-in-Publication Data

Malavis, Nicholas George, 1951–
    Bless the pure and humble : Texas lawyers and oil regulation,
1919–1936 / Nicholas George Malavis.
        p.   cm. — (Kenneth E. Montague series in oil and business
history ; 8)
    Includes bibliographical references and index.
    ISBN 0-89096-714-8 (cloth)
    1. Petroleum law and legislation—Texas—History. 2. Vinson &
Elkins—History. I. Title. II. Series: Kenneth E. Montague series in
oil and business history ; no. 8.
KFT1458.A1M35   1996
343.764'0772—dc20   96-19245
[347.6403772]   CIP

I am eternally indebted to my parents,

George and Jennie Malavis,

for their love and devotion.

To them I dedicate this work.

Contents

List of Illustrations ix
Acknowledgments xi
Introduction xiii

CHAPTERS
1. Law of the Jungle in the "New Fuel" Age 3
2. Quest for Order and Stability in the Oil Patch 17
3. Sleeping with Strangers 30
4. To Have and Share Alike 45
5. In the Loving Arms of the State 62
6. The Long, Hot Summer 75
7. Sword or Constitution? 97
8. Play It Again, Texas 111
9. Oilmen Cry Wolf 132
10. New Deal for the Oil Patch 148
11. Déjà Vu: The Court Strikes Back 163

Epilogue 185
Notes 193
Glossary 283
Bibliography 287
Index 315

Illustrations

Discovery Well, Mexia, 1921 *frontispiece*

Colonel Albert E. Humphreys, 1920s 6

James A. Elkins, 1930s 51

Robert A. Shepherd, Sr., 1930s 53

Charles E. Francis, 1930s 159

Acknowledgments

The transition from lawyer to historian is a formidable challenge. I am forever grateful to Professor Harold Hyman for patiently undertaking what must have been a trying experience: honing a rough-edged criminal defense lawyer into a scholarly historian. Professor Hyman nurtured my growth and maturity as a historian and a person. His guidance and support facilitated the research and writing of this book.

I thank Professor John Boles for his painstaking efforts in helping me to improve my writing skills. My first published article was a product of his graduate seminar in Religion and Slavery in the Old South.

I thank Professor Chandler Davidson for his input and comments on this work.

I am also grateful to those members of Professor Hyman's graduate seminar in U.S. Legal and Constitutional History who read and commented on all or part of this manuscript: Charles Zelden, Jim Schmidt, Jon Singer, Barbara Rozek, Jeff Hooton, and Scott Dewey.

I am obliged to the law firm of Vinson & Elkins for allowing me access to primary research materials, for providing financial and logistical support, and for encouraging the production of a scholarly history. Numerous Vinson & Elkins attorneys and staff unselfishly and cheerfully assisted me in completing this work. I owe special thanks to Managing Partner J. E. Attwell; to Harry M. Reasoner, Jack Taurman, and the late Thomas B. Weatherly; to Mavis Epps and Gail Harper in the records and archives department; and to the personnel in human resources: Sandra Hickle, Judy Tucker, Tina Williamson, Penny Miller, Susan Morgan, and Wanda MacDonald.

Numerous other individuals facilitated the completion of this work.

They include Ferne B. Hyman, Sarah Bentley, and other librarians and staff of Rice University's Fondren Library; and faculty and staff of the Rice University History Department, including Professor Ira D. Gruber, Professor Edward Cox, Professor Martin Wiener, Irene Zisek, Sandy Perez, Nancy Parker, and Paula Platt.

For their tutelage and moral support, I owe a special debt of gratitude to Will Gray, a lawyers' lawyer; attorney Terry Gaiser; and Robert B. Merrifield, Chairman Emeritus of the Social Sciences Division of San Jacinto College–South. I also thank all of the lawyers, judges, coordinators, clerks, court reporters, bailiffs, process-servers, and other staff who serve the Harris County Criminal Courthouse and are like family to me.

Introduction

The problem of petroleum was rooted in an 1875 decision by the Pennsylvania Supreme Court. Lacking any legal precedents or knowledge of the peculiar nature of subterranean petroleum, the judges compared oil and gas to wild game. The analogy to animals *ferae naturae* was based mainly on the judges' individualistic conception of the ownership rights of adjacent landowners in a common oil reservoir, without concern for the public interest. Courts in other oil-producing states subsequently adopted this "rule of capture" to award title to whoever first appropriated underground oil and gas, without regard to conservation or to the uses made of the petroleum after its extraction. The capture theory was discredited and partially abandoned in the early twentieth century, but not before inciting the same ruthless exploitation that characterized the taking of wild animals where game laws were nonexistent. An inestimable amount of America's vital and unreplenishable oil and gas reserves were wasted in the process.

The rule of capture imposed no production restraints and merely required landowners to extract oil or gas through wells drilled on their land only. To secure their share and protect their property interests, landowners competed with one another to produce as much oil and gas as possible regardless of market demand. Excess supply was needlessly wasted, forcing prices down below operating costs. Scientific and technological advances in the early twentieth century debunked the capture theory by proving that subterranean petroleum did not migrate, like some wild creatures, but maintained its status until expelled by pressure through artificial openings in the reservoir. But this evidence outpaced the ability, or willingness, of legislators and judges to formulate adequate laws to sanction the application of scientific production methods so as to alleviate the inefficiency, waste, and instability wrought by the rule of capture.

Court decisions through the early 1930s did not embrace new scientific and engineering principles of petroleum production. Early twentieth-century jurists viewed evidence refuting the capture theory through the prism of their late nineteenth-century background and legal education. Efficient production methods could not be implemented without their legal sanction; therefore waste and instability were perpetuated in the petroleum industry. The discovery of several prolific oil fields in the late 1920s, climaxed by the East Texas field in October, 1930, brought the overproduction problem to a crisis. After failing to resolve the problem through voluntary cooperation, oilmen reluctantly opted for state and federal regulation.

Government regulation of petroleum production has been interpreted as an enlightened policy congruent with the national interest.[1] This theory recognized a paramount state interest in the conservation and proper utilization of petroleum resources to prevent waste. By the 1920s, petroleum had become strategically and economically vital and an important source of government tax revenue. From another perspective, oilmen supported conservation to rationalize their true objective of evading the pressures of competition. Government regulation was not perceived as a neutral force balancing the interests of consumers, independent producers, and major integrated oil companies. Public policy was allegedly constructed under the influence of large producers to restrict production in order to alleviate oversupply and raise prices.[2] Despite some variations, the foregoing interpretations have considered the petroleum problem from an economic perspective.

The problem of petroleum has also been analyzed from a political perspective. David F. Prindle has evaluated a half-century of public policy choices by the Texas Railroad Commission (TRC) and their effect on the state's oil and gas industry. He focused on the political processes that led to important TRC decisions and their effect on Texas and the rest of the United States. Robert Engler has attempted to show how the economic power of petroleum influenced the American political system, especially foreign policy. In a recent publication, Daniel Yergin portrayed oil as a commodity intertwined with national strategies and global politics and power.[3]

Previous studies thoroughly and adequately analyzed two interre-
lated issues of the problem of petroleum—economic and political—but
failed to address the legal concerns. Given the primacy of the rule of
law under the U.S. constitutional system, voluntary and state regulation of production of privately owned petroleum was subject to judicial
review. Although economic and political considerations influenced public
policy toward petroleum conservation, no regulation could be affected
without judicial sanction. Therefore, petroleum was primarily a legal
problem to be solved by lawyers.

The legal battle over petroleum illustrates the tension between the persistence of nineteenth-century concepts of law and economics and the
Progressive faith in the application of scientific solutions to political,
social, and economic problems. Issues entailing private versus public
interests, competition versus monopoly, states' rights versus national
power, and legislative versus executive power were inherent in the legality of state regulation of petroleum production during the 1920s and
1930s. The primacy of private property in Anglo-American jurisprudence made the conflict between private and public rights and states'
rights versus national power the two most contested legal issues involving petroleum. Landowners defended their vested, traditional, common law right to exploit privately owned petroleum against the exercise
of state police power to enforce conservation. They employed the doctrine of states' rights to resist national regulation of intrastate production even though this was an attempt to protect the national interest
in vital and unreplenishable petroleum reserves. These hotly contested
legal issues were ultimately decided by the courts based on lawyers'
arguments.[4]

James Willard Hurst, Stanley Kutler, and Morton Horwitz are among
legal historians who have argued that nineteenth-century judges
shaped public law doctrines to promote economic development. Hurst
and Kutler described the development of nineteenth-century American
law in terms of the "release of creative energy," meaning entrepreneurial energy, to facilitate economic growth and prosperity. Horwitz agreed
with Hurst and Kutler that courts gave preference to "dynamic" over
"static" property rights to encourage entrepreneurial activity and in-
novation, but he maintained that the release of creative energy enhanced the privileges of the wealthy and powerful instead of spreading
economic benefits among the greatest number of people.[5]

The legal contest over regulation of petroleum production fits the ideological interpretations of Arnold M. Paul and Herbert Hovenkamp more neatly than the instrumental thesis—that law is shaped to promote economic or social ends.[6] Paul argued that the judiciary emerged in the 1890s as the principal bulwark of conservatism and transformed the due process clause of the Fourteenth Amendment into a substantive check upon legislative regulation. It was part of a late nineteenth-century, conservative constitutional revolution that expanded the scope of judicial supremacy. He noted two main streams of legal conservative thought that influenced judicial decision making: laissez-faire, drawing heavily on the antipaternalism of Herbert Spencer and dedicated to the utmost freedom for economic initiative with the least legislative interference; and the desire to accord the highest protection to private property and to manage and control the forces of popular democracy. Late nineteenth-century conservative jurists seized upon the treatises of Thomas M. Cooley and Christopher G. Tiedeman, who argued that state regulation in the broad public interest was dangerously intruding upon vested property rights, individual liberties, and the right to conduct personal business with little governmental interference.[7]

Hovenkamp contended that classical economics dominated American economic thought from the Jacksonian era to the New Deal and that economic theory placed judicial decision making above interest-group politics. Classical economics pursued wealth maximization at the expense of redistributive concerns, thereby insulating itself from blatant political manipulation by interest groups. Hovenkamp emphasized that American judges were familiar with at least the rudiments of classical economics, which they consciously employed in their decision making. He explored the mounting tension between classical economic theory's abhorrence of redistributive state regulation and the late nineteenth-century economic phenomena that urgently demanded state regulation to deal with problems like monopolies. Judges incorporated dominant economic models into judicial decision making as long as they maximized wealth. When they ceased doing so, the judges shifted to emerging models that promoted wealth maximization. Contrary to Horwitz, Hovenkamp argued that all wealth-maximizing judicial decision making in the late nineteenth century was politically neutral and not influenced by any particular interest group.

Ideology, rather than economics or politics, guided judicial decision making regarding petroleum rights from the inception of the rule of capture in 1875 until the Connally Hot Oil Act of 1935. The courts that ultimately resolved conflicting legal rights to petroleum between 1875 and 1935 were dominated by jurists who received their legal training in the late nineteenth century. As Paul demonstrated, they were imbued with the predominate jurisprudential attitude of the era, which put a primacy on the protection of private property against unwarranted governmental intrusion. And as Hovemkamp suggested, they were guided more by the laissez-faire approach of classical economic theory than by interest group politics. Throughout the legal battle over regulation of petroleum production, from the rule of capture through the New Deal petroleum code, the courts consistently favored the private over the public interest.

Lawyers became key players in the legal contest over regulation of petroleum production. In arguing for or against production controls, lawyers either defended traditional common law property rights against unwarranted governmental interference or advocated the exercise of state police power to regulate privately owned petroleum in order to promote the public interest in conservation. The effects of judicial decisions in key petroleum cases, especially during the early 1930s, illustrated how judges were guided more by ideology than economics or politics. By overturning state and federal production controls, judges protected traditional private property rights against what they perceived to be unreasonable and dangerous state interference, regardless of the political consequences or the economic cost in terms of wasted petroleum reserves. In this context, lawyers and judges shaped the law which, more so than economics and politics, determined the outcome of the petroleum problem.

Law firm records offer the most primary and illuminating evidence of the role of lawyers in defining legal issues, influencing the outcome of lawsuits, and shaping the development of law. Leading law firms, such as Baker & Botts and Vinson & Elkins of Houston, have recently afforded historians access to their archives. Yet, the problem of client confidentiality remains the biggest obstacle to scholars' access to the archives, lawyers, and staff of law firms. Lawyer-client confidentiality is one of the lawyer's most important professional responsibilities. The confidentiality rule applies not only to matters communicated in confidence by a client to the lawyer, but to all information relating to the lawyer-client relationship regardless of its source. Lawyers are ethically and legally responsible to shield clients' interests from intrusive third parties, including historians. Failure or negligence in upholding this fiduciary duty to clients subjects lawyers and law firms to serious sanctions by the bar and malpractice suits by clients. Legal and professional liabilities justify lawyers' and law firms' denying historians unrestricted access to their records and staff.[8]

Several proposals have been set forth for reconciling the mandate of lawyer-client confidentiality with historians' need to gain a better insight into the legal process. One proposal suggests that attorneys obtain waivers from clients to permit third-party access to relevant records. Another proposes that lawyers distinguish between open and closed cases and living and deceased clients. With the passage of time, after some cases have been adjudicated to finality, issues become moot and clients have either died or no longer possess a legitimate claim to sensitivity. The American Law Institute (ALI) has recommended that lawyers be allowed to open clients' files to historians after passage of a "long and discreet interval" of time as long as there is "no reasonable likelihood of risk" to clients or counsel.[9]

The legal history of lawyers and law firms such as Vinson & Elkins shows how lawyers assume a plurality of roles, legal, economic, and political, in serving both private and public interests. Subject to precautions required by current rules on confidentiality, Vinson & Elkins generously afforded access to all of the Pure Oil Company files I requested. These files contained important correspondence between lawyers and clients, memoranda of law on vital legal issues, briefs of landmark court decisions, transcripts of TRC hearings, and other information relating to all aspects of the petroleum industry. This material provided a "magic mirror" revealing the critical legal issues affecting regulation of petroleum production and the multifaceted roles lawyers played in shaping oil and gas law.[10] It illuminates the historian's understanding of how lawyers influenced solutions to marketplace and legal problems petroleum posed. Further, this data allows researchers to revise and expand past interpretations which have analyzed these complex interactions primarily from economic and political perspectives to the exclusion of law. Even more important, it suggests a broader, multidimensional perspective of the function of lawyers in lieu of the stereotype of lawyers as hired guns who serve clients' narrow economic dictates. Lawyers are pressured by clients. But attorneys' professional duties and responsibilities also simultaneously shape lawyers' defense of their clients' interests as they try to influence and shape court decisions, legislative law-making, and legal and political ideology.[11]

Bless the Pure & Humble

CHAPTER 1

Law of the Jungle in the "New Fuel" Age

The good old rule . . . the simple plan,
that they should take who have the power,
and they should keep who can.

—Samuel B. Pettengill

"Petroleum has revolutionized industry and transportation . . . created untold wealth . . . and has altered man's way of life throughout the world," testifies the inscription on a monument commemorating the fabulous Spindletop gusher near Beaumont, Texas. Spindletop ushered in an oil boom that transformed the predominantly agrarian Texas economy into an industrial one. It spurred technological innovations and improvements in petroleum exploration, production, transportation, and refining that boosted the oil industry into the forefront of manufacturing. Petroleum production soared from 69 million barrels in 1901 to over a billion barrels in 1929. Spindletop also fueled the vertical growth of independent producers such as Humble, Gulf, Phillips, and the Texas Company into wholly integrated oil companies that challenged the dominance of the grand dame of American petroleum, Standard Oil, in the "new fuel" age.[1]

In the decade following World War I, two factors accounted for the petroleum industry's rapid ascendence: the automobile and the strategic importance of oil to the nation. Gasoline-powered automobiles quickly (and relatively inexpensively) reduced distance as a factor in America's drive for industrial supremacy, forever reshaping its landscape and reordering its society. Petroleum also fueled tractors and motor-driven farm equipment, locomotives, seagoing vessels, airplanes, factories, and plants. A fourfold expansion in domestic motor fuel sales, a two-and-one-half-fold increase in fuel oil distribution, and a 75 percent rise in the production of lubricants all testified to petroleum's emergence as a major energy source.[2]

Greater convenience and lower cost accounted for a shift from coal to fuel oil in maritime transportation. In 1904 the U.S. Navy Fuel Oil Board recommended that American war vessels convert to oil. Ten years later, Secretary of the Navy Josephus Daniels reported that all American battleships and destroyers were burning fuel oil. Maritime fuel oil consumption rose from 41 million barrels in 1919 to nearly 106 million barrels in 1929. Annual sales to the U.S. Navy increased from 5.8 million to 7.4 million barrels between 1919 and 1929. Petroleum products comprised approximately two-thirds of the cargo shipped from the United States to Europe during World War I. The Allies used 39,000 barrels of gasoline daily as they "floated to victory upon a wave of oil." The U.S. Navy was entirely oil-burning by the early 1930s, attesting to petroleum's vital role in modern warfare.[3]

As the petroleum industry grew in size and significance, so did its complexity. Some matters, especially legal problems, came to be handled by specialized professionals. Legal issues involving property rights, patents, corporate organization, antitrust regulations, and taxation required the advice and assistance of lawyers. Both the petroleum industry and the lawyers' role therein underwent a transformation during the two decades after World War I. From the industry's inception in the mid-nineteenth century until the 1920s, disputes over land titles constituted the bulk of oil-related litigation. This changed in the late twenties, when overproduction forced lawyers to focus on government regulation instead. Throughout the entire period lawyers blazed new trails through the wilderness of oil and gas law.[4]

The initial legal problem facing the petroleum industry was the validity of titles. Oil producers had to get permission from landowners to drill. Poor Texas farmers, who struggled to eke out a bare existence from unforgiving soil, could hardly resist strangers offering cash advances with the promise of a one-eighth profit, or royalty, of all the oil produced in exchange for simply letting them drill a well on their land. These rather simple and crude transactions became known as drilling leases. Land titles of prospective leases had to be examined to assure oil producers, refiners, and retailers that they were dealing with legitimate landlords so as to avoid liability for wrongful conversion of crude oil to third parties claiming rightful ownership of the property. Lawyers played an instrumental role in this, since determination of the legitimacy of land titles entailed property law.[5]

Large producers and major oil companies could afford to retain prestigious legal counsel. For example, the Texas Company retained the Houston law firm of Baker & Botts beginning in 1917 to examine land titles and to prepare leases and contracts for oil exploration and drilling. By the early 1920s, Baker & Botts was amassing an impressive oil-related clientele including the Sinclair, Atlantic, Continental, and Standard oil companies. Preoccupied with major oil company clients, Baker & Botts had no time to represent those young, unestablished, and unrespectable pioneers of the Texas oil industry known as wildcatters. These rugged individualists who gambled their future in pursuit of black gold turned to smaller local law firms, such as Vinson & Elkins in Houston.[6]

The history and growth of Vinson & Elkins paralleled the rise of petroleum in Texas and illustrates the significant role lawyers played in shaping oil and gas law. Founded in 1917 by William A. Vinson and James A. Elkins, popularly called the "Gold Dust Twins," Vinson & Elkins was a young law firm when the oil boom struck Texas in the 1920s. The firm initially represented primarily local lumber and insurance businesses. That soon changed. In keeping with Texas tradition, Vinson & Elkins lawyers realized that hard work and persistence were the only ways that country boys with heavy drawls could beat Ivy Leaguers in the courtroom. Their determination appealed to mavericks such as Colonel Albert E. Humphreys, an independent oil producer with considerable lease-holdings in the Mexia field in North-Central Texas' Limestone County. The Colonel's oil business had outgrown the capacity of a local small-town, solo practitioner, and Humphreys wanted to retain a respectable law firm. By chance, he met Elkins in 1921 in Houston and told him about his difficulties in getting the Texas Company to pay him for crude oil purchases. Elkins persuaded the Texas Company to pay Humphreys that same day. Impressed, Humphreys retained Vinson & Elkins to represent the Humphreys–Mexia Oil Company. The

Colonel Albert E. Humphreys, 1920s.
Courtesy Vinson & Elkins Archives

relationship blossomed into a marriage that ultimately made Vinson & Elkins Texas' premier oil and gas law firm.[7]

Vinson & Elkins was immediately put to test. Numerous lawsuits had been filed contesting the validity of Humphreys's oil leases in Limestone County. Elkins and a team of Vinson & Elkins lawyers, including Clyde Sweeton and former Texas attorney general Claude Pollard, handled these cases. The oil boom had far outstripped available office space in little Mexia, forcing the legal legion from Vinson & Elkins to bivouac in a barn outside of town. Here, they labored over the tedious task of examining land titles amid the noise and scent of their four-legged roommates.[8]

Land-title litigation had been virtually nonexistent in Limestone County before 1921. But the drilling rigs in Mexia unearthed skeletons from the past along with the oil. Distant relatives claiming to be heirs of the original landowners in the Mexia oil field bombarded the Limestone County Courthouse with lawsuits attacking the validity of existing claims. After the Civil War, emancipated slaves had acquired much of the land in question. A legal determination of their legitimate heirs hinged on the legality of slave marriages. Though Texas law had prohibited slave marriages, some masters had encouraged their slaves to marry so as to promote strong family ties, presumably making the slaves more obedient and industrious—and less likely to run away. The legitimacy of slave marriages became the crucial issue in many of the Mexia land-title suits to be untangled by lawyers.[9]

Vinson & Elkins defended Humphreys in a suit involving forty acres of land in the Mexia oil field originally owned by a slave couple, Felix and Mattie Dancy. After the discovery of oil on the Dancy land, several individuals alleging to be "forgotten" children of Felix's "other wives" claimed a share of the estate. John Lindley swore that he was Felix and Marzella Brown's son. Ella Baker claimed to be the daughter of Felix and Julie Whittaker. She contended that Felix had acquired the forty acres during his marriage to Julie, making it community property and entitling her, as their daughter, to a share. The Limestone County Courthouse had burned down in 1873, leaving no surviving records of this marriage. Marvin Johnson claimed that Julie had given birth to him out of wedlock in 1882, entitling him to a one-fourth undivided interest in the estate.[10]

Sweeton spent many long, hot Texas days taking depositions. Humphreys stood to lose some $1.5 million in damages for wrongful conversion to the rightful heirs if they proved that the company had obtained leases from and paid royalties to illegitimate landowners. Pure Oil Company also stood to lose between $250,000 and $400,000 in damages, since it had acquired an ownership interest in Humphreys in 1922. The case went to trial on March 9, 1925.[11]

Contradictory testimony, based largely on depositions, turned the trial into a circus-like spectacle. Witnesses testified that Marzella Brown and Julie Whittaker were "bad women" who had run around with "a lot of men." Willis Medlock, a local minister, testified that a "colored man" and a white man had offered him money to lie on the witness stand, and that he had refused their offer for fear of going to hell. He accused Julie Whittaker of having "loose morals" and described Marzella Brown to be "as bad a woman as ever lived in this county and she died that way." Sam Medlock testified that had never known Felix to be married to anyone else but Mattie until the discovery of oil in Mexia. Ella Baker testified that, at Felix's funeral, Mattie had assured her that she would never inherit any of the estate.[12]

The jury decided the case by answering several special issues.[13] It determined that Felix and Marzella Brown had never been married and that John Lindley was not their child. The jury further found that Felix and Julie Whittaker had never been married, but that Ella Baker was their daughter. It decided that the forty acres was the community property of Felix and Mattie. Felix had died intestate (without a written will) in 1902, leaving as his surviving heirs his wife Mattie and three children Celester Bluitt, Enes Carter, and Ella Baker, who were awarded the estate. The verdict, upheld on appeal, was favorable to Humphreys and Pure, since their leases had been acquired from the legitimate heirs. Humphreys and Pure escaped liability through the efforts of Vinson & Elkins lawyers.[14]

There was nothing novel in the laws governing land titles. Sweeton and the other Vinson & Elkins lawyers had simply slogged through a thicket of legal complexities involving the family relations of slaves. Sweeton had painstakingly located and questioned ex-slaves, who were likely illiterate or semiliterate, to determine the rightful heirs of the Dancy estate. Their depositions were crucial in influencing the verdict and in persuading other litigants to settle out of court for substantially less than they had demanded. These settlements saved Humphreys and Pure substantial money in legal fees and in potential damages had they lost the cases. The outcome enhanced Vinson & Elkins's reputation in Texas oil and gas circles.[15]

♦ ♦ ♦

The rapid growth of the petroleum industry in the 1920s led to new and more complex legal problems because of the unworkable laws governing oil production. During the first two decades of the twentieth century, speculation grew among oil industry leaders and public officials that this new fuel would soon run out. The gap between consumption and production in the United States widened from 9 million barrels in 1915 to 78 million barrels in 1920. Even though the importation of Mexican crude had narrowed the margin, domestic production had not kept pace with demand. In 1919, U.S. Bureau of Mines director Van H. Manning warned the Council of National Defense that drastic measures, including governmental intervention, might be necessary to assure adequate production and avert an oil shortage. Prairie Oil and Gas Company president J. E. O'Neal forecast imminent shortages unless abundant new oil reserves were discovered. Standard Oil of New Jersey president Walter Teagle mused that pessimism over crude supplies had become a chronic malady in the oil business. But new discoveries in California, Oklahoma, and Texas during the twenties doubled proven oil reserves and swelled annual production from 442.9 million to nearly a billion barrels.[16]

Behind this decade of expansion lay the dynamics of flush field development.[17] Leading experts, including petroleum economist Joseph E. Pogue and Bureau of Mines official F. G. Cottrell, recognized that the steady depletion of oil reserves did not preclude periodic gluts when production would exceed demand. Short-term oversupply was to be expected with improved recovery techniques and new refining technologies.[18]

A vicious cycle was set into motion. Concerns about running out of petroleum gave way to worries over overproduction and cheaper prices. Cheaper prices encouraged consumption and demand, which raised prices and stimulated production until the market was again glutted and prices fell. Free-market forces did not respond quickly enough to ensure a prompt and smooth transition during periodic fluctuations between supply and demand. Oilmen wanted to keep production in line with demand to stabilize prices; the federal government wanted to conserve unreplenishable petroleum resources vital to national defense; and the public demanded a cheap and reliable source of petroleum products. Because oilmen could not agree over whether or how to control production, government regulation seemed the next logical step. But government regulation of privately owned American petroleum reserves had to be reconciled with due process restraints and traditional notions of free enterprise. For this reason, regulation of petroleum production became primarily a legal problem to be resolved by lawyers.[19]

The "rule of capture," which had defined legal rights in subterranean petroleum since the late nineteenth century, encouraged unrestrained production regardless of market demand. Absolved of liability by the capture theory, lessors, lessees, royalty owners, and drillers all raced to beat their neighbors out of all the oil they could get. The rule's genesis lay in the medieval common law of property, which put a premium on an owner's undisturbed and peaceful enjoyment of his land. The concept had originated in a feudal, agrarian environment in which all available land was either in use or assigned to particular owners. English common law allowed landowners to use their estates as they desired with one limitation: *Sic utere tuo ut alienum laedus*—that they inflict no irreparable harm on neighboring landowners' respective property rights.[20]

Traditional English common law rules were gradually transformed in America. A vast, resource-laden frontier afforded opportunities for continent-wide expansion and industrialization, which in turn demanded a more dynamic concept of law. Land and water usage illustrate how American courts generally ruled in favor of development, balancing the economic good of the community against the inconvenience or injury to individual landowners. In a static agrarian society, the "first in time, first in right" principle protected certain activities that were natural to the land and initiated by one property owner against interference from projects subsequently begun by a second landowner. *Natural* meant the normal use of land and its appurtenances, such as water. The courts employed a balancing test to retard or advance new uses of land or water made possible by technological innovations. A priority rule gradually supplanted the natural use doctrine, as first illustrated in the legal controversies generated by the use of water power for economic development.[21]

Under traditional common law, water flowing in its natural channel was held to be inviolable, and any interference with it was unnatural. All riparian landowners (those owning land abutting a flowing stream) could use the water as they desired, as long they did not diminish their neighbors' corresponding rights. A riparian owner could divert as much water as necessary for irrigation, mill dams, and so forth without liability if the diversion had been established prior to a neighboring landowner's use. The priority doctrine proved impractical in America, where the drive to develop a vast frontier and exploit abundant resources called for the release of creative energy.[22]

In 1783, the Supreme Judicial Court of Massachusetts held in *Shorey v. Gorell* that a landowner who had not established his rights through long usage could not prevent a newcomer from obstructing a stream to build a mill dam. In *Palmer v. Mulligan* in 1805, the New York Supreme Court upheld an upstream owner's right to dam the stream, noting that riparian owners had to suffer little inconveniences for the sake of the greater good. Thirteen years later, in *Platt v. Johnson*, the New York Supreme Court first introduced the principle that the right to develop land for commercial purposes was an inherent right of land ownership. The court balanced the traditional doctrine of *sic utere* against the benefits that accrued to the community through economic development.[23]

Some jurists disapproved of this departure from common law tradition. Joseph Angell severely criticized the *Palmer* decision in his 1824 treatise on *Watercourses*. Three years later, U.S. Supreme Court Justice Joseph Story's circuit court opinion in *Tyler v. Wilkinson*, while somewhat ambiguous, seemed to confirm traditional limits on water diversion. Developmental-minded judges used Story's criterion of "reasonable use" as a permissive departure from strict common law rules to justify extensive diversions.[24]

The riparian cases illustrated how nineteenth-century American courts transformed traditional English common law rules of property to meet local economic conditions. They also show how Americans adapted the common law to a unique and peculiar problem never before encountered: the reconciliation of competing private property rights in petroleum. Colonel Edwin L. Drake's discovery well at Titusville, Pennsylvania, in 1859 spurred the commercial exploitation of petroleum. The rising demand for oil enhanced its value and instigated more lawsuits among landowners asserting competing claims to common petroleum reserves underlying their estates. There were no direct legal precedents to guide lawyers and judges, since ownership disputes over oil and gas had been virtually nonexistent prior to the mid-nineteenth century. As a result, lawyers and judges grappled for an analogy in other areas of property law to support their respective arguments and decisions.[25]

Some of the earliest oil litigants based their ownership claims on the common law rule that recognized a landowner's absolute dominion over everything above and below his landed estate, including the underlying minerals. They argued that oil and gas were minerals constituting part of the physical aggregate of the land. But the absolute ownership theory did not apply neatly to petroleum. Unlike solid minerals, such as coal and iron, oil and gas are fugacious. Undisturbed in its natural state, petroleum is held stationary within the pores and crevices of the surrounding rock strata by natural gas pressure. The confines of an oil-bearing rock structure make up a petroleum reservoir. In this natural state, petroleum cannot move or "migrate" unless the reservoir is punctured, releasing the gas pressure. The force of the escaping gas propels the oil through the puncture opening. Under ideal production methods, natural gas pressure can be harnessed to recover 90 to 95 percent of the oil. Conversely, flush production is akin to removing a cap from a well-shaken bottle of carbonated beverage. The gas pressure dissipates before most of the liquid is expelled from the bottle. This unique physical attribute rendered the absolute ownership theory unworkable for oil and gas, and posed a dilemma for those lawyers and judges who struggled to reconcile competing ownership claims to subsurface petroleum.[26]

By the late 1920s, petroleum's growing economic importance was stymied by the legal question of ownership. Until the law settled overlapping title claims, America's vital petroleum resources could not be exploited without potential legal liabilities. A landowner held absolute title to the subsurface petroleum if the courts applied the traditional common law. But petroleum's fugacious nature prohibited one landowner from exercising his absolute right to extract his petroleum without infringing on a neighbor's respective right. The courts had to find a way to allow two or more landowners to enjoy their property rights in petroleum without destroying these rights.[27]

If the law classified oil and gas as minerals constituting part of the realty, one landowner could not exercise his right to use them without interfering with a neighbor's correlative right to do likewise. By classifying petroleum as *res communes*,[28] the law would have discouraged production of a newer and cheaper energy source to fuel America's burgeoning industrial base. Yet by pursuing an instrumentalist approach in order to facilitate petroleum production, the courts unwittingly opened up a Pandora's box of competing legal issues, including private property versus the public interest, competition versus monopoly, states' rights versus national power, and legislative versus executive authority.[29]

In 1875, the Pennsylvania Supreme Court had addressed the first in a trilogy of cases that culminated in the rule of capture. James E. Brown had leased a 30-acre tract to J. J. Vandergrift to produce oil. Noncompliance with any of the lease provisions constituted a forfeiture, allowing the lessor to eject the lessee. Brown sued to eject Vandergrift on the grounds that the latter had forfeited the lease by failing to commence drilling within a stipulated time period. Vandergrift responded that he had avoided a forfeiture by paying a monthly rental fee in lieu of drilling.[30]

The court ruled that petroleum's fugitive nature made its precise location and quantity uncertain, making drilling speculative and requiring new methods of leasing land. Landowners leased as much of their land as possible to enhance the probability of striking oil. Since the oil might be here today and gone tomorrow, landlords added lease provisions requiring lessees to drill without delay or face forfeiture and ejectment. The court classified oil and gas as minerals *ferae naturae* which, like wild animals and unlike other minerals, have the power and the tendency to escape without the volition of the owner.[31]

The Pennsylvania Supreme Court had previously upheld lease forfeiture clauses on the ground that lessees had no ownership rights to the oil and gas *in situ* since their fugitive and wandering nature rendered them incapable of being owned until captured and reduced to possession. The court sidestepped the inconsistency of this ruling with its decision in *Funk v. Haldeman,* which recognized a landowners' title to petroleum *in situ,* by confining *Brown* to the validity of lease forfeiture clauses. Since time was of the essence in oil leases, equity protected a lessor against the harm inflicted by a lessee's indifference and delay which could not be alleviated by payment of a monthly rental fee. The court decided that Vandergrift had forfeited the lease and could thereby be ejected from Brown's property.[32]

In the second case, in 1889, Westmoreland Natural Gas Company sought to restrain a Mr. DeWitt from producing gas from one of its leases. DeWitt claimed that the lessor had leased the land to him after Westmoreland forfeited its rights by failing to drill or pay monthly rental fees. Westmoreland maintained that it had complied with the lease terms by drilling a well that only needed "a turn of the control valve" to start producing gas. On appeal the Pennsylvania Supreme Court decided two legal issues: whether Westmoreland had forfeited the lease, and who was entitled to the gas.[33]

The court had already, in *Brown v. Vandergrift,* qualified its previous ruling that oil and gas *in situ* were minerals that constituted part of the real estate. It now determined that petroleum's fugacious nature rendered it unamenable to legal precedents governing property rights in solid minerals, and fashioned a new rule. The court held that oil and gas belonged to the owner of the land, and were subject to his control as long as they remained there. But when the oil and gas escaped into other land, or came under another landowner's control, the former owner lost his title. Ownership of the land therefore did not necessarily imply title to the underlying petroleum. If an adjoining or distant owner drilled on his own land and tapped a neighbor's petroleum reserve, he gained title to the oil and gas captured through his well. By way of analogy, the Pennsylvania Court applied legal precedents governing ownership of wild animals and underground water to oil and gas, *in situ,* to fashion a new rule that actual possession was the only valid ownership claim to petroleum. Consequently, the court determined that DeWitt did not own the gas until he captured it, and that Westmoreland had not forfeited its lease since it had already drilled a well which simply needed to be turned on to allow gas to flow. Since this gave Westmoreland possession of the gas, the court awarded the company title thereto.[34]

In *Barnard v. Monongahela Gas Company* in 1907, the Pennsylvania Supreme Court decided that there was no way to ascertain the precise amount or location of oil and gas under any given land-tract. It acted on the mistaken assumption that petroleum migrated through porous rock strata, thereby "fully justifying" a rule giving every proprietor an opportunity to drill and produce wherever he pleased on his own land. The court in essence admonished aggrieved litigants who complained of drainage, "Go thou and do likewise." (Subsequent scientific discovery, however, proved that petroleum was held inert by gas pressure, and did not migrate until a drill tapped the reservoir and the escaping pressure propelled oil out the puncture.) Conceding that this was not the best rule, the court invited the legislature or some "higher court" to do better, and refused to impose the equitable remedy of injunction to stay any potential harm. The Keystone State's high judicial priests admittedly applied the law of the jungle to petroleum. So came to pass the rule of capture.[35]

Courts in other oil-producing states subsequently adopted Pennsylvania's novel capture theory, and permitted landowners to produce at will without liability. So long as landowners drilled within the parameters of their acreage, courts deemed any resulting harm to their neighbors' oil rights as *damnum absque injuria.* The strained comparison of petroleum with water and wild animals could only be rationalized as a judicial compromise. Late nineteenth-century judges had to reconcile the historical primacy of private property rights in Anglo-American jurisprudence with the widespread desire to develop this new energy source to fuel the ever-expanding American economy. Without established legal precedents or advanced scientific and technological knowledge, nineteenth-century judges grappled to resolve competing ownership claims to petroleum. Logically, and by habit, they scoured the common law for some analogy to apply to oil and gas. They settled upon the law of wild animals and water as a convenient solution to their dilemma. By attempting to weave petroleum into the fabric of traditional common law, the Pennsylvania Supreme Court legalized the caveman instinct. "The extension of the Rule of Capture to oil and gas flunked," said Judge Richard Posner, "and was replaced [albeit through legislative rather than judicial action] by efficient rules."[36]

Whether late nineteenth-century jurists intended the rule of capture to protect private property rights in petroleum or to release creative energy, or both, is debatable. Petroleum's novelty as a commercial commodity and the lack of legal precedent dealing with the subject made it ripe for an equitable remedy. Judges could have utilized equity to resolve competing ownership claims and balance private versus public interests in petroleum. But existing technology had not convinced the judges that shares in a petroleum reservoir could be fairly divided among common tenants. Overproduction was not then a problem, and oil and gas litigation in the late nineteenth century concerned neighbors' competing claims to a common supply source rather than government regulation of private property. The capture theory was the easiest way to protect private property interests in a manner that encouraged production and fit the instrumentalist theme of law promoting economic development.

But the instrumentalist view fails to explain why most judges in the early twentieth century adhered to the rule of capture after it had encouraged wasteful overproduction and been debunked by contemporary scientific and engineering advances. Contrary to instrumentalism, the petroleum problem illustrates how judges were guided by ideology in sanctioning the release of destructive rather than creative energy to protect sacrosanct private property rights against government intrusion.[37]

The rule of capture served its purpose at a time when America was concerned about finding and producing enough petroleum to fuel its future. With its help, petroleum toppled mighty King Coal from his throne as the world's major power source. Petroleum contributed substantially to the Allied victory in World War I and laid the basis for America's postwar transformation into a hydrocarbon-based society. As it rose to preeminence, petroleum moved beyond a simple past, in which the rule of capture settled disputes between neighboring landlords, toward a multifaceted legal, political, and economic struggle pitting rugged individualists against monopolists and governments, and states' rightists against advocates of national power. Under the American constitutional system, which made law the final word, lawyers played a key role in fashioning new rules to dictate the future of petroleum. Harry G. Berenger, director of France's Comite General du Petrole, prophesied in 1918, "As oil had been the blood of war, so it would be the blood of the peace."[38]

CHAPTER 2

Quest for Order and Stability in the Oil Patch

An oil man is a barbarian with a suit on.
—Edward L. Doheny

Spectacular new oil discoveries in Texas, Oklahoma, California, and New Mexico between 1920 and 1930 transformed the problem of petroleum from one of scarcity to abundance. Prolific production led to a chronic imbalance between supply and demand. As stocks increased, the price of crude oil declined from a per-barrel high of $3.50 in 1920 to $1.25 in 1930. The rule of capture forced operators to produce regardless of market demand in order to protect their property rights. Wasteful production went unabated. Oilmen who thrived on the competitive spirit and the lure of new fortunes rode roughshod over weaker neighbors' rights and resisted any attempts to restrain their right to produce when and where they pleased.[1]

Waste in petroleum production had captured the attention of scientists and engineers sooner than most oilmen. In the 1920s, scientific study of the behavior of underground oil made possible more efficient production methods which also reduced uncertainty in the search for new reserves, supplanting the "mere hunch" practice that had persisted since Drake's discovery well in 1859. In 1917, the U.S. Bureau of Mines established an experimental station at Bartlesville, Oklahoma, to study new ways of improving production methods. Station director James O. Lewis's significant study emphasized the importance of natural gas as an energy drive in crude oil production. In 1919, the Bureau of Mines estimated that 80 percent of the recoverable underground petroleum was being lost under flush production methods.[2]

The use of geophysical science to search for new petroleum reserves aroused the oil industry's interest in scientific approaches to production. During the 1920s, a growing number of independents and major oil companies added geology departments and geophysical units to their operations to minimize risk and enhance success at finding new deposits. The majors seized any opportunity to ascertain beforehand the probability of finding oil in a given location before risking heavy capital investment. They initially welcomed improvements and innovations in exploration and drilling, which contributed to additional oil discoveries and production at a time when scarcity was their main concern. But by the late 1920s, technological progress had invited rapid growth and expansion far beyond market demand. As supply exceeded demand and prices fell, production control became necessary to restore stability and profitability.[3]

Wasteful recovery practices and the presumed diminution of domestic reserves, along with attendant periods of glut, fluctuating prices, and the growing economic and strategic importance of petroleum, underlay conservation efforts in the twenties. The National Petroleum War Services Committee, established during World War I to mobilize the petroleum industry behind the war effort, carried over into peacetime as the American Petroleum Institute (API). The API became the oil industry's leading representative organization.[4] One of its directors, Cities Service Company president Henry L. Doherty, hammered away at the rule of capture, warning that the oil industry was operating in a way that undermined its own future.[5]

Doherty criticized "extremely crude and ridiculous" production methods, which prematurely exhausted reservoir pressure and trapped oil underground that might otherwise be recovered. He cited petroleum's strategic importance as ample legal authority for federal intervention to eliminate waste. "If the federal government has no power to conserve oil and prevent waste," Doherty argued, "then our plan of government is defective, because the power is not vested any place for us to do that which may be necessary for our national defense." He advocated federally sanctioned cooperative development, or unitization,[6] of American oil fields as a solution to the overproduction problem. As an alternative, Doherty suggested the passage of state laws patterned after irrigation and drainage districts that regulated water allocation in western states, and requiring unit development of oil fields under the supervision of oil districts staffed by landowners. All land or lease owners in a common field would agree to combine their resources and jointly develop the reservoir. Expenses and profits would be divided according to the size of individual land or lease holdings. Doherty emphasized how unitization reconciled science and law by circumventing the rule of capture to promote the greatest economy in lieu of irrational and wasteful flush production.[7]

Texas Company president Amos L. Beaty, an attorney and API officer, responded that compulsory unitization violated the due process and contract clauses of the U.S. Constitution. He argued that oil districts would interfere with lease provisions obliging producers to exercise due diligence in drilling and capturing the lessor's oil before a competitor did. Beaty considered Doherty's proposal a radical threat to private enterprise—one that would convert the oil industry into a public utility. The conservative lawyer agreed with the pragmatic oilman that production had to be stabilized, but disagreed about the means. Doherty viewed Beaty's plan as a half-hearted approach, depending as it did on voluntarism by oilmen. He believed that only state or federal laws would force a majority of oilmen to control production.[8]

Some API directors shared Doherty's views, while others regarded him as a "crazy man" who would betray his colleagues. Most of the directors held the attitude prevalent among oilmen, abhorring any compulsion—especially by the federal government. Oilmen had an idealized conception of laissez-faire capitalism and believed the state should not interfere with private enterprise. Experienced oilmen viewed with contempt politicians who lacked practical knowledge of the petroleum industry they sought to regulate.

Doherty fought back. In a letter to President Calvin Coolidge on August 11, 1924, he recommended federal regulation of the petroleum industry if the individual oil-producing states failed to enact conservation laws. Petroleum engineer Mark Requa, who had served as federal oil czar during World War I, supported Doherty's position.[9]

On December 19, 1924, Coolidge created the Federal Oil Conservation Board (FOCB) to formulate a plan to safeguard national security through oil conservation. Though the conservative Coolidge shared oilmen's distaste for government regulation of business, he noted that "present methods of capturing our oil deposits is [sic] wasteful to an alarming degree." The FOCB conducted public hearings in 1926. Virtually every oilman, with the exception of Doherty, denied that anything was radically wrong with the industry, opposed government intervention, and demanded immunity from antitrust prosecution to facilitate industrial cooperation. Professional experts recommended unitization as the most efficient way to curb wasteful overproduction. To the chagrin of oil industry leaders, in contrast to the API's finding that waste had been "negligible," the FOCB determined that flush production and uncontrolled escape of natural gas prematurely dissipated reservoir pressure, leaving too much underground oil unrecovered.[10]

The API's position had been formulated by its Committee of Eleven. Established in 1925 to investigate conditions in the oil industry and forestall possible federal oil legislation, the committee, headed by New Jersey Standard president Walter Teagle, was composed mostly of major oil company executives. To allay fears of an imminent oil shortage, the committee issued a report in May, 1925, citing new discoveries in California, Oklahoma, and Texas, in addition to one billion unexplored acres in the nation containing some 30 million barrels of petroleum. The API report, which noted only negligible waste in petroleum production and emphasized letting free market forces and competition dictate policy, lacked conservationist sentiment and remained faithful to traditional laissez-faire economics.[11]

On May 27, 1926, former U.S. Supreme Court Justice Charles Evans Hughes, now representing the API, offered the FOCB a strict constructionist critique of the petroleum problem. "The Government of the United States is one of enumerated powers and is not at liberty to control the internal affairs of the states . . . such as production," he argued, " . . . through assertions by Congress of a desire either to provide for the common defense or to promote the general welfare." Hughes doubted that the federal government possessed legal authority to control petroleum production, and questioned the legality of any statute authorizing a majority of producers to negotiate a unitization agreement that would be binding on the minority. He recommended relaxation of antitrust laws to permit voluntary cooperation among producers without governmental interference as the best solution to the oil industry's problems. Hughes maintained that the evils wrought by the rule of capture either were exaggerated or could not be remedied under existing constitutional law.[12]

Critics of the API's position charged that existing production rates painted a false picture of great abundance when oil reserves were actually limited and irreplaceable. Scientists and engineers accused the API of narrowly measuring waste against short-term business profits. The Rocky Mountain Association of Petroleum Geologists unanimously questioned the API's findings. E. J. Fohs, a consulting engineer and member of the American Institute of Mining and Metallurgical Engineers (AIMME), argued that excessive waste typified domestic petroleum production operations. D. N. Killefer, secretary of the New York section of the American Chemical Society, predicted the exhaustion of gasoline supplies within twenty years. George Otis Smith, head of the U.S. Geological Survey and technical advisor to the FOCB, criticized the API's claim as "a gross exaggeration" and warned that without conservation, the nation would soon face an oil shortage. The American Association of Petroleum Geologists echoed Smith's view. While many oilmen publicly denied that wasteful production occurred, they privately conceded its existence but blamed the rule of capture for retarding the application of new production methods and technologies.[13]

In a report to the president on September 6, 1926, spokesmen for the FOCB stated that federal authority to regulate petroleum production was limited to public lands unless the states failed to prevent waste to a degree that imperiled national defense. The FOCB rejected compulsory unitization in favor of relaxing antitrust laws to permit voluntary unit agreements. The Coolidge administration never seriously contemplated intervening in the oil industry, preferring that it regulate itself through the medium of trade associations. During the 1920s conservatives lauded industry self-regulation through trade associations as a rational model of enlightened competition and a panacea to the primitive practices of cutthroat competition.[14]

In August, 1927, U.S. Secretary of the Interior Hubert Wok addressed the Mineral Law Section of the American Bar Association. He diagnosed the oil industry as "sick," and proposed the creation of a Committee of Nine—consisting of three representatives each from industry, the federal government, and the legal profession—to explore ways to circumscribe antitrust laws to permit cooperative agreements among oil producers to limit output during times of overproduction. The federal government already required unit development of petroleum reserves in public lands.[15]

Attorney James A. Veasey addressed the issue of private versus government control of petroleum production. Veasey argued that U.S. Supreme Court decisions in the Child Labor cases erased doubts concerning congressional power, through the indirect route of the commerce clause, to regulate matters local to the states such as mining, manufacturing, or other production. The court had held that federal regulation of a purely national matter such as interstate commerce did not destroy local powers reserved to the states by the Tenth Amendment. Since the power to regulate oil production resided within the states' police power, Veasey explained, it had to be determined at what point state regulatory statutes must yield to the private property guaranties of the Fourteenth Amendment.[16]

He cited an Indiana Supreme Court decision, *State v. Ohio Oil Company*, in which the state's attorney general had sought to restrain the Ohio Oil Company from wasting natural gas in permitting it to escape into the open air during oil production operations. An Indiana statute passed in 1893 prohibited the escape of oil or gas into the open air for a period longer than two days, after which the oil and gas had to be safely and securely confined in wells, pipes, or other receptacles. The legislature cited the critical economic importance of natural gas to the welfare of the state's citizens. Ohio Oil claimed that it could not produce oil without wasting gas and that compliance with the statute constituted a taking of property without due process.[17]

The Indiana Supreme Court upheld the constitutionality of the statute on the grounds that it did not unduly interfere with private property because title to oil and gas did not vest in anyone until the substances had been reduced to possession. It found an absolute analogy between natural gas, wild animals, and fish, and that the state, in its sovereign capacity, owned the gas before it was reduced to possession. The court based its decision squarely on the proposition that the statute had been designed to promote the public welfare, ignoring the issue of correlative rights and obligations among owners in a common pool. It rebuked anyone who "recklessly, defiantly, persistently, and continually" wasted a vital natural resource like gas as an "enemy of mankind." The court deemed Ohio Oil's economic interest to be of "small consequence" compared to the "calamity which it mercilessly and cruelly held over the heads of the people of Indiana" by telling them that the gas "is my property to do as I please . . . [and] help yourselves if you can." Its ruling implied that the state had unlimited power to regulate the taking of natural gas to abate a public nuisance.[18]

The decision was appealed to the U.S. Supreme Court. Justice Edward Douglas White delivered the majority opinion repudiating the Indiana Supreme Court's position that the statute had been designed to abate a public nuisance. Owing to the fugacious character of oil and gas, White held that the surface owners had a co-equal right in the common source of supply. He upheld the statute as a proper exercise of state police power to abate a private, rather than a public, nuisance by protecting the surface owners from waste of their common oil and gas property.[19]

White rejected the analogy between petroleum and things *ferae naturae* which underlay the rule of capture. He distinguished between things *res communes*, such as wild animals, and private property, such as petroleum. The state could either forbid or permit the capture of things *ferae naturae*, which are owned by no one, but not so with oil and gas because only the surface owners, not the public, had an exclusive right to reduce them to possession. Accordingly, government could not regulate the capture of petroleum, as it did wild animals or water, without infringing on private property rights. White held that the state could regulate oil and gas production only to abate a private nuisance by protecting the correlative rights of all surface owners against the unfair taking or destruction of their property by another owner in a common pool.[20]

The *Ohio Oil v. Indiana* decision provided precedent supporting the exercise of state police power to abate a private nuisance such as protecting a landowners' property rights in petroleum from an unfair taking or destruction by another. The federal Supreme Court, however, had not yet developed satisfactory rules governing state regulations, such as petroleum conservation laws, designed to abate public nuisances.

By the early twentieth century, the Supreme Court had established a pattern of reviewing the particular facts and circumstances of each state regulation of private property to determine if it bore a direct and reasonable relation to a legitimate and compelling public interest. If not, the court found that the intrusion offended the due process clause of the Fourteenth Amendment. The differing attitudes of the justices toward such issues made it difficult to predict how they would rule in any particular case involving the constitutionality of police measures designed to promote the public welfare. Generally, however, conservative justices were inclined to favor due process, while their more "progressive" brethren tended to rule in favor of the public interest.[21]

To survive judicial scrutiny, Veasey believed that petroleum conservation statutes intended to prevent wasteful production or protect reservoir pressure had to be designed to safeguard either landowners' correlative rights or a legitimate and compelling public interest. He predicted that the courts would strike down conservation statutes of a broader scope.[22]

No one at the time seemed to notice that, in the case of petroleum, the effect would be the same whether a conservation statute had been designed to abate a private or public nuisance; i.e., production could be limited to prevent waste. By 1927, two distinct immediate solutions to the evils of overproduction had emerged: the exercise of state police power to restrict output or voluntary operators' agreements. Veasey preferred unitization because the oil business was "too individualistic [and] too technical to be controlled by statute," but he warned oilmen that if they failed to put their house in order, there would be an insistent and irresistible demand for government control of the petroleum industry.[23]

In January, 1928, the Committee of Nine recommended revising state and federal antitrust laws to permit cooperative agreements between producers; state enforcement of compulsory unitization in the event voluntary agreements failed; and creating an interstate compact to assure common state action. These findings mirrored the views of the API and most major oil company executives—hardly surprising since most of the committeemen represented major oil company interests. Independents, as expected, blasted the committee's report, particularly the recommended relaxation of antitrust laws.[24]

The accumulation of research conclusions convinced more and more oilmen that Doherty was not so crazy after all. Humble Oil & Refining Company president William S. Farish[25] had scorned Doherty's ideas in 1925, but thanked him three years later for opening the industry's eyes to improved production methods. Farish became a zealous crusader for petroleum conservation and unitization. But Doherty, Farish, and other conservationists were ahead of the game. Tradition-minded colleagues such as Sun Oil Company president J. Howard Pew and Gulf Oil Company president G. S. Davidson clung to classical economics, preferring self-regulation without governmental interference. Pew boasted that "timber reserves would be depleted and the world's rivers would change course" before petroleum ran out, and noted that oil shortages had been predicted ever since he was a small boy. Spectacular new oil discoveries in Oklahoma and Texas in 1926 had washed away gloomy predictions of a shortage, making Pew a more credible prophet than Doherty. But the stock market crash of 1929 and the subsequent economic depression soon humbled many diehard individualists.[26]

The oil boom unleashed a production frenzy; this in turn led to an unprecedented glut that, ironically, shifted support toward Doherty's conservationist views. An increasing number of oilmen converted to conservation not to save oil but to alleviate the ruinous overproduction that had violently shaken crude oil prices. They still disagreed on the topic of voluntary solutions versus government regulation. Walter Teagle favored voluntary controls, while Farish considered the oil industry powerless to help itself. Teagle advocated intra-industry cooperation and elimination of federally imposed obstacles to industrial growth such as the antitrust laws. He feared that the oil industry would become a scapegoat if a joint-cooperative plan between business and government failed, further politicizing the issue of government regulation. Farish countered that "no one in the industry today . . . has sense enough or knows enough" to solve the problem.[27]

Although federal regulation seemed reasonably out of the question, most oil industry leaders realized by 1929 that the cutthroat competition engendered by the rule of capture had incurred waste and instability. API president E. W. Clark challenged his peers to accept the "ideals of coordination, of cooperation, of understanding, [and] of confidence rather than suspicion." Oilmen's options had narrowed to three possibilities: self-help, state regulation, or federal control. Whichever one they finally settled upon, it would assuredly be challenged in the courts, adding another wrinkle to be ironed out by lawyers.[28]

Without legal sanction or precedent, Humble took the first step in setting a course toward the unitization of Texas oil and gas fields. With Humble's legal staff, headed by Edgar E. Townes,[29] as his crew, William Farish piloted unitization through the shoals of Texas antitrust law. Townes warned of rough sailing ahead unless the Texas legislature immunized unitization agreements from existing state antitrust laws. He doubted that the state could compel landowners to pool their properties for oil and gas development and could therefore only sanction voluntary unitization agreements. Without legislative approval, Townes advised that separate ownership interests would have to be merged before developing an oil and gas field as a unit to avoid the strictures of antitrust law. With Farish's blessing, Humble's legal department drafted a pooling agreement for "exploration only," with operations to be unitized only should oil be discovered. Townes assured that this was antitrust-proof, as separate ownership interests would be merged before the land proved to contain oil. Humble's stratagem became a model for subsequent unitization agreements in Texas oil fields.[30]

Townes did not simply produce Humble's unitization scheme as a magician pulls a rabbit from his hat. It had been developed, slowly and tediously, through years of study and debate by experienced attorneys. Hines H. Baker had chief responsibility within Humble's legal staff for studying conservation law. Rex G. Baker, who did title and contract work, assisted in the discussions and debates. Humble's legal department worked closely with private practitioners who specialized in oil and gas law, such as attorneys Robert E. Hardwicke and John E. Kilgore, as well as corporate lawyers including Lewis Foster of Sun Oil, W. O. Crane of the Texas Company, W. P. Z. German of Skelly Oil, and James A. Veasey of Carter Oil. Humble lawyers also worked closely with operators and engineers to gain a better understanding of the practical and scientific problems of petroleum production.[31]

"There was a lot that wasn't known about the producing business in the oil industry . . . everything was in a developing stage," Hines Baker recalled, and "the question of conservation . . . producing at high rates, dissipating the gas energy pool, and lowering the final recovery from the reservoir . . . were [all] tied into the law." He blamed the rule of capture for prodding oilmen into a mad rush to secure an advantage in production regardless of market demand or waste. As the fugacious nature of oil and gas could not be changed, and vested property rights could not be constitutionally eliminated, Baker considered unitization the best legal and practical solution to the problem. He preferred voluntary unitization agreements, but realized the improbability of securing unanimous cooperation and consent among all landowners in a common oil pool. He expected them to disagree over the relative value of their respective properties and particular production techniques, and to fear antitrust prosecution. Baker suggested the removal of antitrust barriers and enactment of a compulsory unitization statute to force recalcitrant landowners to respect their neighbors' correlative rights as well as the public interest in eliminating waste in petroleum production. He favored state laws rather than federal control.[32]

Baker also called for an interstate compact among the oil-producing states to determine the nature and extent of overproduction, assign production quotas to each state (to keep supply in line with demand), and provide a channel through which the states might agree to remove antitrust barriers to unitization. He hoped that Congress would ease federal antitrust restrictions to facilitate development of oil fields as single units, similar to the mining and manufacturing businesses, to promote conservation by permitting more efficient production of vital and unreplenishable petroleum resources. To supplement the interstate compact, Baker recommended enactment of state oil conservation laws authorizing a regulatory agency to enforce production quotas designed to eliminate waste. Ideally, he hoped that the oil industry and the states would cooperate in working out a practical solution to the problem with minimal government interference.[33]

Humble's lawyers had formulated a legal cure to remedy the crippling effects of the rule of capture on the oil industry. It contained three significant ingredients: the exercise of state police power, rather than federal regulation, to control petroleum production; the restriction of production to market demand; and the creation of an interstate compact as the most practical and equitable method of distributing total production among individual states. Farish endorsed the antidote, warning that otherwise the oil industry would someday "have to answer for the uneconomic and wasteful way in which oil and gas are being used."[34]

In 1927, Oklahoma oilman Ernest W. Marland joined Humble's conservation crusade, telling producers and refiners that if they could not overcome the negative effects of overproduction through "the ruthless and inexorable law of supply or demand working through the price factor," then to do so "by [the] intelligent curtailment of output." National Organization of Independent Producers president H. H. Gray wanted to limit output by curtailing exploration and imposing some system of production controls. Teagle thought that Farish and Humble were moving too quickly. He supported conservation as long as industry regulated itself without any governmental interference. F. C. Proctor, Gulf Oil Company's spirited legal counsel and a confirmed individualist, denounced Humble's unit plan as a "nostrum worthy of a blatter skite politician, but not of the leaders of a great industry." API legal counsel Hughes doubted that overproduction could be solved without better educating oilmen and obtaining consensus support from the oil indus-

try. He believed that the states lacked both the constitutional authority and the ability to curb overproduction. Hughes opposed governmental interference in private business, but preferred federal over state
regulation as a last resort. He agreed with Farish that the oil industry
was "powerless to help itself" and needed "government help, permission to do things we cannot do today [unitization], and perhaps government prohibition of those things [waste] that we are doing today."[35]

Despite his convictions, Farish realized that many oil industry leaders needed a great deal of education before they could be persuaded to
agree on a single conservation plan. Disillusioned, he concluded "that
there are more individual fools in the petroleum business . . . [who] do
not know the meaning of cooperation and teamwork." Farish relaxed
his efforts to affect petroleum conservation legislation in Texas and
settled for more popular alternatives such as voluntary unitization,
which appealed to oilmen's individualism and distaste for government
control. Petroleum engineers had praised unitization as the most efficient means of producing oil. Unitization not only afforded neighboring landowners a legal method to improve the efficiency of their oil
production operations and lessen costs, but also protected them against
the "carefree wildcatter" who exhibited little concern for the market's
capacity to absorb more oil.[36]

Certain difficulties with voluntary unitization had to be overcome.
Owners of land tracts with natural structural advantages were unlikely
to agree to a plan that reduced the value of oil and gas they could recover by going it alone. Confident that oil would continue migrating
toward their tracts, these landowners could use delay in negotiating a
unitization agreement to improve their bargaining position. Some landowners would assuredly remain skeptical of the plan's profitability.
Holdouts could get a free ride without sharing the costs of unit development because more efficient operation would increase reservoir pressure and force more oil to migrate toward their land tracts. Farish and
other proponents wanted compulsory unitization laws to eliminate this
kind of profitable obstructionism. They cited eminent domain as one
source of legal authority to support state laws compelling reluctant
landowners to join a unit development plan in return for a fair share
of the profits.[37]

The lack of widespread support from oil industry leaders and public
officials stymied the implementation of voluntary unitization. Up until 1928, the post–World War I demand for petroleum boosted crude oil

prices as high as three dollars a barrel, confirming oilmen in their confidence of unending economic prosperity and in their indifference toward conservation. Oilmen also remained skeptical from scientific, technological, and legal standpoints about the soundness of restricting production. During the late 1920s, Humble and other progressive-minded oil companies such as Pan-American (Indiana Standard), Roxanna (Shell), and Marland became convinced that improved production techniques lowered operating costs, enhanced ultimate recovery, and helped adjust output to market demand.[38]

Farish touted unitization as "the only method of reducing costs to a point where we can meet the competition of cheap foreign oil, itself the product of oil pools owned and operated as individual units." Many oilmen still worried that unitization agreements were vulnerable to prosecution under antitrust laws. Speaking not "as a lawyer, but as a businessman," Gulf's Proctor—who opposed any government interference in business affairs—dared Farish and other unitization enthusiasts to disregard legal uncertainties and risk prosecution. Farish accepted the challenge. In West Texas' hot, desolate, rattlesnake-infested Pecos County, Farish undertook a bold and extralegal exploit, gambling that it would remain beyond the reach of the law long enough to vindicate what he and other forward-thinking oilmen had been saying: that cooperation was the key to the future viability and success of the American petroleum industry.[39]

CHAPTER 3

Sleeping with Strangers

If you've got a big [oil] field and . . . a whole bunch
of different ownerships . . . [cooperation] becomes
an enormously complicated thing.

—Robert A. Shepherd, Jr.

On November 9, 1927, "Judge" James A. Elkins presided over a general partnership meeting of his Houston law firm, Vinson & Elkins.[1] Among the topics of discussion was a proposal that one of the firm's most important clients, Pure Oil Company, form a partnership with several other oil companies to consolidate and manage production in the Yates oil field in Pecos County, Texas. Humble owned the only pipeline in that part of West Texas, and agreed to extend it into the Yates field and purchase 30,000 barrels of oil daily if producers unitized their operations. An advocate of unitization, Farish lectured the Yates oilmen on the evils of overproduction, the high costs of storing production in excess of market demand, and the attendant waste for producers lacking storage facilities. Farish also warned that uneven withdrawal would permit intruding water to bypass and trap much of the oil underground, inflicting financial loss on producers and depriving the public of vital petroleum resources. Humble had large quantities of oil in storage, which would decline in value if overproduction at Yates drove prices lower. The Yates oilmen asked for time to ponder unitization.[2]

Farish's unitization dream coincided with a chaotic boom era in American petroleum history. The discovery in late 1926 of the Yates oil field, the "Queen of the Pecos," further aggravated already dire overproduction. But the discovery of black gold underlying the barren soil also dealt a winning hand to some humble West Texas ranchers and to the University of Texas, which owned 184,960 acres in Pecos County. Thanks to wildcatter and UT alumnus Robert R. Penn, the Pecos field was spewing 192,000 barrels of crude oil a day by September, 1927. But there was no pipeline outlet to carry all that oil to refineries. Penn never had to deal with the problem because a gun in his car "accidentally" discharged, ending his short career in oil. So Farish stepped in and made his conservation pitch to a throng of surly West Texans.[3]

At a meeting in Fort Worth on September 2, 1927, Farish offered to buy and transport 30,000 barrels of oil each day if the Yates producers, who lacked a pipeline and an adequate market, agreed to unitize their operations. A committee of Yates oilmen appointed three attorneys— James Elkins, Hines Baker, and Tom Knight—to go to Austin and solicit the Texas attorney general's opinion concerning the legality of unitization. The attorney general refused to make any pronouncement for or against the plan, but promised not to prosecute the Yates operators "without notice" should they proceed by its terms. Experience, however, had taught Elkins not to bank on prosecutors' promises. He thought unitization violated Texas antitrust law and advised Pure Oil against joining the Yates operators' agreement. Elkins also believed that Pure's share of unit production would be inadequate to meet its existing contractual obligation to supply purchasers with a specified amount of crude oil.[4]

On September 8, the Yates operators' committee adopted a unitization plan that allocated a share of total pipeline capacity and market demand to each partner according to "well potential."[5] A general committee was created to represent unit members and administer the plan, and a three-member executive committee to supervise unit operations. On a designated date, representatives of unit operators jointly gauged production from each individual lease to determine potential production. The representatives signed "gauge tickets," which were forwarded to the chairman of the executive committee. On the fifteenth and last day of every month, each operator notified the chairman of the quantity of oil he intended to store or dispose of other than delivery to a pipeline. The executive committee then assigned production quotas to each operator. Operators could appeal their quota assignments to the general committee.[6]

The unit partners shared operating expenses and profits in proportion to their respective production quotas. Ironically, the operators expressed their intent not to limit or fix the amount of oil each one could produce, store, or market. The unitization agreement expired ninety days after October 1, 1927, and could be renewed for successive 90-day periods. All the Yates operators signed the agreement with the conspicuous exception of the Gulf and Pure Oil companies.[7] Gulf vice-president Underwood Nazro and company attorney F. C. Proctor had already opposed unitization. Instead of basing quotas on individual well-potential, Proctor complained, the Yates plan allocated production to each producer according to the ratio of output his acreage bore to the entire field. He pointed out that even a fool realized he could increase his quota by drilling more wells, thereby defeating the object of the plan. But the Yates unit partners feared that tighter production controls would trigger antitrust prosecutions. Gulf likely held out because it needed to produce additional crude oil to feed its refineries.[8]

B. S. SoRelle, manager of Pure's Texas Producing Division, solicited Elkins's advice about legal problems such as antitrust violations. Though Elkins did not expect the attorney general to prosecute, he warned that this official's policy "would not be binding upon his successors in office and the statute of limitation does not run against violation of the antitrust laws," indefinitely subjecting the unit partners to prosecutions, fines, and penalties. SoRelle thanked Elkins and assured him that Pure would not join the Yates unit. He offered Elkins his houseboat on Sweet Lake, "where you will have a cook to take care of your physical needs and a good boatman to take you around over the lake to the best places for fishing . . . . You will be clear out of touch of everything."[9] The Yates unitization agreement, however, did not remain in force long enough to face any legal tests, for on July 1, 1928, the Texas Railroad Commission (TRC) for the first time exercised its authority, under a 1919 statute, to regulate oil production in the state.

The TRC was the product of agrarian discontent in the late nineteenth century. Angry farmers and merchants complained that railroads were discriminating against them by charging exorbitantly high freight rates.

The Texas Farmers' Alliance, organized in 1875, spearheaded the drive for state regulation of railroad rates. Congress had already responded to alleged railroad abuses by enacting the Interstate Commerce Act in 1887. Meeting in Houston in 1890 for its annual state convention (popularly called the "Farmers' Alliance Picnic"), the Texas Democratic Party included in its platform a plank calling for the creation of a state railroad commission to regulate freight and passenger rates. The delegates to that convention also nominated James Stephen Hogg for governor. As state attorney general, Hogg had successfully prosecuted the railroads to recover excessive land grants, which were then used to support public education. Hogg's campaign for governor included a pledge of support for a railroad commission. On November 5, 1890, Texans elected Hogg governor and ratified a state constitutional amendment authorizing the legislature to create a railroad commission. The Texas legislature established the three-member TRC in April, 1891.[10]

From its inception, the TRC was mired in legal troubles. During the debates over its creation, lawyers argued that regulatory commissions were unconstitutional because they unduly interfered with private property rights. On April 3, 1892, the Farmers' Loan and Trust Company, acting as trustee for the bondholders of five Texas railroads, sued to enjoin the TRC from enforcing its railroad rates. Farmers' alleged that the TRC's rates were too low to allow the railroads to recoup operating costs and pay interest on bonded indebtedness, thereby forcing them into default and decreasing the value of the bonds. John F. Dillon, legal counsel for the railroads, argued that the act creating the TRC was unconstitutional because it empowered a state regulatory agency to confiscate private property without due process of law, in violation of the Fourteenth Amendment of the U.S. Constitution. The Texas attorney general responded that the trustees had conspired with the railroads to create a fictitious financial loss as a way to defraud bondholders and then discredit the TRC's rates as unreasonably confiscatory. U.S. Circuit Judge A. P. McCormick issued an injunction restraining the TRC and the Texas attorney general from regulating railroad rates. The U.S. District Court in Austin upheld the order on August 23, 1892. State authorities appealed to the U.S. Supreme Court.[11]

On May 26, 1894, Justice David J. Brewer announced the court's decision, upholding the constitutionality of the state act delegating legislative regulatory power to a commission. Brewer cited the *Railroad Commission Cases* in validating the exercise of state police power to regulate railroad rates, subject to judicial review to determine whether such regulations or rates unreasonably confiscated private property without due process of law. Brewer struck down the TRC's rate schedules as unreasonably low and depriving the bondholders of their private property without due process of law.[12]

Instead of offering evidence to prove a conspiracy between the trustees and the railroads, the Texas attorney general demurred to the unreasonableness of the TRC's rates and rested the state's case on the constitutionality of the enabling act. Had he proven that the trustees had collaborated with the railroads to create a false debt, the Supreme Court might have upheld the TRC's rate schedules as reasonable. The attorney general apparently believed that the case hinged on the constitutionality of the enabling act since the Supreme Court had never before struck down regulatory rates established under legislative fiat. Despite the attorney general's miscalculation, the state achieved a moral victory in getting the nation's highest legal tribunal to bestow its blessing upon the TRC.[13]

In 1899, the Texas legislature passed the state's first petroleum conservation act in an attempt to prevent physical waste of oil and gas by regulating drilling and production methods. It required that oil and gas wells be cased off to prevent the intrusion of water into the oil sand (or oil and gas into fresh-water sands), provided for the plugging of all abandoned wells, forbade the flambeau burning of escaping gas, and prohibited the escape of natural gas into the open air.[14]

The development of Spindletop and subsequent oil fields elevated Texas to the world's foremost petroleum-producing region by 1929, as total production surpassed two billion barrels.[15] This dramatic increase further accentuated the need for conservation. The Texas legislature followed the 1899 act by enacting statutes in 1905, 1913, and 1917.[16] The 1917 statute empowered the TRC to administer state petroleum conservation laws. Texans also approved in 1917 a constitutional amendment declaring "that conservation and development of all of the natural resources of this State . . . are each and all hereby declared public rights and duties, and the Legislature shall pass all such laws as may be appropriate thereto." The 1917 amendment furnished the legal authority for state enforcement of petroleum conservation.[17]

There was little opposition to or litigation against these early oil conservation statutes since they pertained purely to the mechanics of production and were aimed solely at prevention of physical waste. Moreover they applied equally to everyone, and did not deprive any one individual or group of rights and privileges to the advantage of others. Petroleum-related litigation at this time dealt primarily with disputes over ownership rights, like the 1911 Texas case in which William H. Thomas sought to prevent George H. Herman from drilling on an adjacent land-tract. Since he could not afford to drill an offset well, Thomas alleged that Herman was confiscating some of his oil. On appeal, the Texas Fourteenth Court of Civil Appeals in Galveston applied the rule of capture and held that the oil belonged to whoever first appropriated it.[18]

The court's ruling overlooked a conflict in Texas law. Texas courts recognized landowners' absolute title to oil, gas, and other minerals underlying their land while, at the same time, applying the rule of capture.[19] The U.S. Supreme Court, in *Ohio Oil v. Indiana,* recognized that things *ferae naturae* could not be owned by anyone. Texas courts failed to recognize the contradiction between upholding a landowner's absolute title to petroleum and then ruling, as it did in *Herman v. Thomas,* that oil and gas belonged to no one until captured. Intermediate appellate courts in Texas had uniformly held that production leases did not pass title to the minerals in place, despite language to the contrary in the instrument of transfer. In 1915, the Texas Supreme Court decided otherwise.[20]

W. H. Daugherty had leased land in Wichita County to the Texas Company to produce oil and gas. In the lease agreement, Daugherty specifically conveyed his ownership interest in the oil, gas, and other minerals to the Texas Company for valuable consideration and royalties. He deducted the value of the minerals from the tax he owed on his land. The state factored in the underlying petroleum in assessing land values for tax purposes. State tax officials determined that Daugherty had conveyed ownership of the minerals in the lease and levied a tax on the Texas Company for the value of the oil and gas. The Texas Company argued that oil and gas were incapable of being owned until captured and reduced to possession. If damages for draining oil and gas *in situ* could not be proven, then how could state authorities determine the value of underlying petroleum for tax purposes?[21] The Texas Company claimed that it held a mere license to extract petroleum from Daugherty's land in return for a share of the profits.[22]

The Texas Supreme Court attempted to reconcile the rule of capture with the absolute ownership theory by deciding that oil and gas *in situ* were part of the realty and that, when conveyed in that condition, an ownership interest in them likewise passed. A purchaser of oil and gas *in situ* assumed the risk of their escape, but this possibility did not alter the property interest in them. The court reaffirmed a landowner's absolute title to oil in gas *in situ,* which could be conveyed to another. It ruled that Daugherty had conveyed an ownership interest in his oil and gas to the Texas Company, making it liable for applicable taxes. Texas courts conveniently applied the rule of capture to deny damages or injunctive relief to landowners who complained of losing their oil to neighbors' drainage, while applying the absolute ownership theory for tax purposes.[23]

The court cited Justice White's opinion in *Ohio Oil v. Indiana* that, unlike things *ferae naturae,* which were public property, oil and gas were private property belonging to the owner of the overlying surface land. Landowners sharing a common reservoir owed a duty to respect each others' correlative rights and not extract more than a fair share of the underlying oil and gas. White, however, had tried to emphasize the difference between petroleum and wild animals to show that the rule of capture and the absolute ownership theory were irreconcilable, thereby exposing the fallacy of the analogy between petroleum and things *ferae naturae.* This was a vital point, one the Texas Supreme Court either overlooked or misread in citing White's opinion as support for its attempt at reconciling the capture and absolute dominion theories.[24]

The obvious ambiguity of Texas law governing ownership rights in petroleum had little effect on production. By 1919, new oil discoveries at Burkburnett, West Columbia, Ranger, Desdemona, and other Texas fields accentuated the overproduction problem necessitating more stringent measures to prevent waste. In response, the Texas legislature enacted that same year a comprehensive petroleum conservation act which specifically prohibited waste of oil and gas and conferred broad regulatory powers upon the TRC to enforce the statute. UT law professor George C. Butte organized and supervised the TRC's oil and gas division as it studied petroleum production and conducted public hearings to gather evidence concerning the development of specific rules and regulations. Butte's experience and reputation as an expert in oil and gas law had been a prime consideration in his selection for the task, attesting to lawyers' significant influence in shaping petroleum regulation policies. He and Commissioner Clarence Gilmore, an advocate of the "New South," infused the TRC with progressive administrative values during the Jazz Age. [25]

Based on the oil and gas division's recommendations, the TRC issued 38 rules and regulations designed to minimize waste in oil and gas production. The most notable of these was Rule 37, which prohibited the drilling of wells within 150 feet of one another or closer than 300 feet to the lease boundary line. Prior to this rule's promulgation, operators could drill as many wells they pleased and produce each well to capacity. Rule 37 was generally endorsed by large land and lease owners who wanted to produce their oil at a minimum expense of drilling wells. Small land and lease owners opposed the rule because it deprived them of the opportunity of drilling additional wells to produce as much as the larger tracts. They argued that the rule of capture gave each operator the correlative right to drill as many wells as one pleased to recover as much oil as possible. After a lengthy legal battle, Texas courts upheld Rule 37. But Rule 37 did not engender any serious opposition from most majors and independents as it did not limit oil production from any well or field—and because the TRC generously granted exception permits where the rule affected a substantial hardship.[26]

Against this background, the TRC assumed responsibility for regulating petroleum production in Texas. Rule 37 did not apply neatly to the Hendrick oil field in Winkler County. The predominance of 5- to 10-acre tracts leased to small independent producers, who far outnumbered the major oil companies' lease-holdings operators, forced the TRC to grant numerous exception permits, which resulted in excessive drilling. Daily production in the Hendrick field reached 50,000 barrels by December, 1927. By March, 1928, Hendrick crude oil was selling for ten cents a barrel. In addition to falling crude oil prices, the Hendrick field faced another problem: Over half the wells became saturated with water. Engineers employed by major companies to study the situation were shocked to find that small independents systematically pumped as much oil as possible to beat the onrushing water. The engineers argued that increased production would only hasten water intrusion by prematurely decreasing reservoir pressure. As the water crept forward, the independents finally succumbed and realized that it was in their best interest to curtail production.[27]

In conjunction with the TRC, the Hendrick operators formed a six-member committee, chaired by TRC member Richard Denny Parker, that hammered out a proration[28] plan in April. Due to the predominance of small land holdings, the Hendrick field was divided into 40-acre units. Half of the field's total allowable production, as established by the TRC, would be apportioned equally to each unit while the remaining half would be allocated according to each unit's percentage of the total production. Unit shares would then be divided among individual operators therein. With the exception of minor revisions to the allocation formula, the plan had been modeled after the Yates operators' agreement. The TRC appointed a "field umpire" to administer and supervise the plan; he was to be assisted by an advisory committee composed of operators. At the end of April, the TRC issued its first proration order, limiting production in the Hendrick field to 150,000 barrels a day.[29]

Prorationing held back the tide of Hendrick oil, but failed to silence West Texas wildcatters. The TRC had restricted Hendrick production to one-fifth of the field's capacity output. Small producers crowded on single 40-acre tracts complained that their quotas were too small to enable them to profit. Their only recourse under existing regulations was to drill more wells to enhance unit potential and qualify for a bigger allowable. But the costs of that option were prohibitive for small operators. The TRC's order also disturbed larger independents such as Tom Cranfill, who had contracted to deliver specific quantities of crude oil to major company purchasers. With their production cut, they stood in possible breach of contract. Despite these complaints, after a year of prorationing in the Hendrick field, the price of West Texas crude oil stabilized, and engineers estimated that the reservoir-life had been prolonged by 20 to 50 percent.[30]

Some Hendrick wildcatters defied TRC orders and continued producing at will. They argued that the TRC lacked legal authority to regulate the use of their private property and to prevent them from selling their oil at whatever price they pleased. As long as independents could market their oil, Cranfill asked, where was the waste? Under protection of two injunctions restraining the TRC from enforcing its proration order, Dallas-based Murchison Oil Company continued to pump 5,400 barrels of oil daily from its Hendrick wells. Regulation of petroleum production, voluntary or enforced, was still in its infancy and without judicial blessing. Neither the 1917 pipeline law nor the 1919 conservation act specifically authorized prorationing. The TRC could only beseech producers to comply with its regulations. The problem was further complicated by the diverse attitudes of oilmen. Major oil companies generally supported conservation, though some, such as Gulf, did not. The views of independents toward production controls varied with their size, business interests, strategy, and financial position. The variety of reactions to prorationing in the Hendrick field not only demonstrated the lack of consensus in the oil industry; it indicated that size alone did not determine on which side of the conservation fence an oilman lined up.[31]

With mixed results at Hendrick, the TRC hoped to fare better in the Yates oil field, where operators had been voluntarily controlling production through unitization. Although they detested government interference, Yates producers probably welcomed TRC regulation as a means of maintaining the relative stability they had so far achieved without the risk of antitrust prosecution. In addition, the unit's initial plan, which allocated production according to well potential, encouraged each producer to increase his share by boosting potential output. Yates operators revised the formula in January, 1928, to determine allowables according to the amount of each producer's proven acreage within the field. But this plan benefitted large companies such as Humble, which held larger tracts, while smaller producers lost out on the scheme. The new formula also encouraged more drilling on the perimeter of the field where operators attempted to produce their undeveloped leases to increase their allowables. For these reasons, the TRC banked on smooth sailing when it divided the Yates field into 100-acre units and based production quotas one-fourth on acreage and three-fourths on well potential.[32]

The regulation of oil production in the Yates field, initially through operators' voluntary cooperation and later by TRC proration order, marked a watershed in the legal history of petroleum. The Yates unitization agreement, though less than ideal, was the earliest attempt by individual oilmen to regulate production voluntarily. From a scientific and engineering perspective, it demonstrated the feasibility of employing more efficient production methods to conserve reservoir energy and maximize ultimate recovery. The Yates experiment also illustrated the economic advantage of limiting output to market demand. One petroleum engineer credited unitization with allowing Yates operators to profit by producing oil at four cents a barrel and selling it at ten. Despite its questionable legal status, the Yates unit plan offered the most equitable method of regulating oil production, protecting both the public's interest in conservation and landowners' correlative property rights. Moreover, the Yates unitization experiment afforded the TRC some justification for prorating production under the 1919 act. Voluntary unitization still remained susceptible to sudden death under Texas antitrust law.[33]

◆ ◆ ◆

By 1929, the regulation of petroleum production, whether voluntary or enforced, was gaining momentum in both the private and public sectors owing to a growing interest in conservation. The API urged oil-producing states to limit their 1929 production to a level matching output during the last nine months of the preceding year. It established five regional committees (Pacific Coast, Interior, Atlantic Seaboard, Gulf Coast, and Mexico–South America) to study the feasibility of unitization and the kind of regulation best suited to each region. The API also formed committees to ascertain the need (and if so, of what type) for federal intervention. In June, 1929, President Herbert Hoover summoned the governors of oil-producing states, major oil company officials, and trade association representatives to Colorado Springs to discuss uniform state legislation for petroleum conservation. The idea of an interstate oil compact was ultimately shelved, however, because independents from Texas and Oklahoma refused to sanction a "super commission."[34]

Speaking on behalf of the Southern Oklahoma Oil and Gas Association, Wirt Franklin feared "that in the name of conservation a compact may [vest] absolute authority in a commission, which might fall under the domination of the major[s]." Small independent Tom Slick thundered, "No state corporation will tell me how to run my business." Major oil companies with large overseas production operations opposed the independents' call for an oil tariff and the exclusion of imported oil. Disunity and ill-will among majors and independents broke up the conference, leaving nothing accomplished except the creation of the Independent Petroleum Association of America (IPAA), under Franklin's leadership. The IPAA soon became a leading voice for independent oilmen.[35]

The fiasco at Colorado Springs epitomized the oil industry's disunity in the face of impending crisis. This did not deter Farish from continuing to tout unitization. Humble promoted passage of a bill in the Texas legislature to amend the 1919 oil conservation statute, giving the TRC authority to enforce voluntary unitization agreements endorsed by a majority of field operators. A tough legislative battle ensued, marked by fierce opposition from small independents, who feared that large independents and majors would use their size to dominate unit operations. They also opposed unitization because it tied up capital for longer periods and delayed payoffs. Supporters of the measure wanted to add a provision granting antitrust immunity to unitization agreements. The legislature did pass a bill in March, 1929, authorizing the TRC to prevent waste in petroleum production, but omitted any provision for unitization. Although it did not define *waste*, the new act specified that it not be construed to mean economic waste, clearly implying that the TRC could not limit production to market demand.[36]

The 1929 law reflected the legislature's desire to conserve petroleum while avoiding any confrontation with the industry. Small independents' unfairly accused Humble and other majors of seeking their monopolistic aims under the guise of unitization. Humble, a low-cost producer, would have outlasted small independents through any prolonged period of low crude oil prices. Higher prices would arguably encourage more drilling and production, which would defeat Humble's aim of achieving order and stability. Farish believed that consumers would accept the increased costs resulting from controlled production if it promoted conservation and guaranteed a reliable, long-term supply at a reasonable price. He argued that "the public interest and the correlative rights of all parties operating in a pool [justified] intelligent controlled production." By limiting production to conserve reservoir pressure and enhance ultimate recovery, unitization promoted the same end as the 1929 Act in alleviating physical waste.[37]

Humble's failure to secure legislative sanction for unitization did not dampen Farish's enthusiasm for stability in the oil patch. At a meeting of the AIMME's Petroleum Division in October, 1929, he assured engineers that unitization would solve the overproduction plaguing the oil industry. But fear of antitrust prosecution still prevented many majors and large independents from supporting unitization. Farish nevertheless forged ahead, staking Humble's fortunes and reputation, as well as his own, on unitization. He rolled the dice again; this time his gaming table was the rolling prairies of Van Zandt County, in North-Central Texas. The major oil company executive ironically found himself playing the wildcatter's tune.[38]

Farish hoped to unitize an oil field near Van, a small town about twenty miles northwest of Tyler. The Van field had been discovered in the summer of 1927 by a Pure Oil Company seismograph crew. Pure acquired extensive lease-holdings in the field and struck oil on October 14, 1929. Daily production averaged 144,000 barrels. The Van discovery set off yet another Texas oil boom, luring wildcatters and every other breed of fortune-seeker. Pure possessed production rights to four-fifths of the 5,800-acre Van field, while Humble, Sun, Shell, and the

Texas Company held most of the remainder. A crusty old farmer named J. A. Bracken, whose property lay in the middle of the prolific oil field, spurned repeated lease offers, as high as $500,000, from the major companies. Bracken, standing his ground like a lone wolf found out on the prairie, had ideas of his own. He managed to sink a few wells and became a rich man overnight. Bracken's new financial status had little noticeable effect on his disposition; much to his corporate neighbors' consternation, he remained as stubborn and surly as ever. Unitization was not a word in Bracken's vocabulary. Farish ultimately gave up on Bracken, but had better luck peddling his ideas to the majors.[39]

Amid the stock market's Great Crash, cost-conscious major oil company executives sought more than ever to avoid the added expense of competitive leasing and drilling. With general economic depression looming, the czars of Sun, Shell, and the Texas Company overcame their antitrust phobia and agreed to try Farish's unitization schemes. Baker teamed up with Vinson & Elkins attorney Robert A. Shepherd, Sr., to transform Farish's dream into reality. The two legal brain-trusts employed Townes's formula for eluding antitrust prosecution. As most of the Van field had not yet been explored and drilled, they drafted a unitization agreement to take effect only after it became *generally known* that the remainder of the field contained oil.[40]

Under the agreement, the five unit partners—Humble, Pure, Sun, Shell, and the Texas Company—consolidated their Van lease-holdings and agreed to share expenses and profits in proportion to the size of their leases. They conveyed their lease-rights to one another and created a joint-partnership giving each partner an undivided interest in the whole unit. Pure owned the lion's share, with 81.7 percent, followed by Humble (7.75 percent), the Texas Company (4.51 percent), Sun (3.57 percent), and Shell (2.47 percent). Production would be allocated to each partner according to the size of its respective lease-holdings during an initial period of two and one-half years. An engineering and geological study of the reservoir would then be conducted to determine the production potential of individual leases and wells. Based on those findings, a new and more equitable allocation formula would be devised. As the partner with the largest interest, Pure managed the unit operation.[41]

Pure vice-president R. W. McIlvain solicited Elkins's advice about possible antitrust violations. Elkins believed that the Van agreement could pass antitrust muster because all the unit partners had transferred and assigned their respective interests to one another to become tenants in common. "While this specific fact situation has not heretofore been presented to our appellate courts, similar fact situations have been presented and," Elkins advised, " . . . our higher courts have held that the right to convey property in whole or in part, or to impose restrictions upon its use, are inherent rights incident to the ownership of property and do not transgress the antitrust statute." Based on these precedents, Elkins assured McIlvain that the Van unitization agreement did not violate Texas antitrust laws.[42]

Elkins believed that the Van unitization agreement not only avoided antitrust problems but operated in harmony with state oil conservation policy by promoting efficiency in petroleum production and minimizing waste. He told McIlvain that "no single subject [had] demanded or received so close study from the legislature as the conservation of oil and gas," which had been "a matter of paramount importance to the whole state." Elkins pointed out how the legislature had vested the TRC with broad and comprehensive powers to restrict oil and gas production so as to prevent waste. He viewed the Van unit plan as accomplishing the same purpose and benefitting the public interest without government intervention.[43]

With Elkins's blessing, the Van unitization agreement took effect on November 1, 1929. Farish's dream had come to fruition with the indispensable assistance of the expert and innovative legal talent at Humble and Vinson & Elkins. Baker and Shepherd forged a cooperative alliance of five highly competitive major oil companies, showing the rest of the industry how to achieve and maintain order and stability without government interference. The tireless efforts of the legal teams from Humble and Vinson & Elkins, along with Farish's persistence, saved the Van oil field from the instability, waste, and lawlessness that plagued other Texas oil fields. Thanks to unitization, fewer dry holes were drilled and Van's reservoir pressure was adequately conserved, prolonging production in paying quantities by another decade.[44]

The alliance's lawyers had a bit of luck come their way when the TRC issued its first statewide proration order on August 27, 1930. Van's antitrust worries were soon buried beneath a pile of lawsuits challenging the legality of the TRC's order. The ensuing litigation consumed a decade, touching upon a multitude of fundamental constitutional rights. With injunctions restraining enforcement of TRC proration orders pending the outcome of litigation, other Texas oil fields ran amuck, but peace and stability reigned at Van due to unitization, which had negated any need for TRC regulation. To stave off future TRC control, the Van unit partners made every attempt to conduct their operations in ways that met with the TRC's approval. SoRelle assured TRC oil and division supervisor R. D. Parker "that our men will be glad to accord you every courtesy and render you every service in making an inspection of our operations." In true wildcatter fashion, Farish had won a high-stakes poker game.[45]

Voluntarism at Yates and Van had made an impression on many oilmen. Self-help appealed to those rugged individualists who detested outside authority, especially that of the government. Most significant, oilmen came to see that uncontrolled production was wasteful, and that the state government would step in if they failed to curb it. They also noticed how unitization at Yates and Van had kept excessive crude oil from flooding the market and driving prices down at the worst possible time. Unitization advocates such as Farish hoped that the relative success of Yates and Van would encourage more oilmen to voluntarily control production, averting government regulation. But rough waters lay ahead.[46]

CHAPTER 4

To Have and Share Alike

The public will be obliged to bear the cross carried
so long upon the shoulders of the independent producer.

—Joseph C. Danciger

The 1930s would prove a trying decade for the American petroleum industry. Until 1928, the post–World War I demand for petroleum had boosted the price of crude oil to three dollars a barrel. Confidence in the permanence of the Roaring Twenties' economic boom had contributed to producers' laxity about conservation. And, in fact, crude oil prices did not follow the precipitous decline of other commodity prices in 1929, prompting both the industry and government to leave well enough alone. But the ill effects of the market crash soon caught up with the oil industry. Few oilmen perceived the effects of unrestrained competition. The early thirties witnessed a critical transition era in American petroleum as oilmen battled government officials to preserve their absolute dominion over privately owned petroleum. Issues including traditional private property rights versus the public interest, monopoly versus competition, states' rights versus national power, and legislative versus executive authority all intertwined in the ensuing legal battle over petroleum.[1]

Economic self-interest remained the primary motive for oilmen's support of conservation. Regulation of petroleum production also promoted the public interest by diminishing waste of an essential and unreplenishable natural resource. Spearheaded by Farish, the Yates unitization plan showed a practical way to control production, conserve reservoir pressure, and, ultimately, achieve stability and conservation—to the benefit of both producers and the public. But too many oilmen refused to follow this example. The rule of capture still fed their fierce competitiveness, bringing the American oil industry to the brink of economic disaster. The ensuing drama was packed with enough frontier-style action to make Texas an appropriate setting.[2]

In January, 1930, Humble cut its posted price for crude oil purchases in an attempt to force other producers to curtail output. Farish attributed the price cut, which came soon after he had denied the existence of overproduction, to excessive stocks that had forced a drop in gasoline prices. Those independent producers who had banked on Humble's promise to maintain the posted price of crude oil if they reduced production were confused, upset, and downright angry. Farish released company records to the Mid-Continent Oil & Gas Association[3] in an attempt to convince independents that "competing units operating on the seaboard," not Humble, were the culprits. Humble even agreed to purchase more West Texas oil, at the expense of reducing its own production, but its reputation among independents, never high, was further tarnished. Many independents became more convinced than ever that Humble was selfish, unscrupulous, ruthless, and untrustworthy, and they retaliated by seeking regulatory legislation.[4]

The IPAA and the Mid-Continent Oil and Gas Association blamed overproduction on excessive imports of crude oil by majors such as New Jersey Standard. Independents of all sizes and shapes found common ground in their support of a one dollar per barrel oil tariff. The Independent Petroleum Association of Texas (IPAT), organized in Fort Worth on February 22, 1930, proudly proclaimed in its newsletter, *The Texas Independent,* that it had "no major company affiliations" and was strictly "an organization of the 'little man.'" IPAT pledged to wage an offensive against major oil companies and to resist prorationing.[5]

Although they favored higher prices and stabilization, independents viewed any form of production control as a ploy to allow large integrated companies to import more oil from their overseas connections. They argued that domestic production cuts would not alleviate overproduction without reducing imports. By eliminating competition, independents warned, the majors would monopolize the oil business and control prices to their advantage. IPAT asked the Texas legislature to pass a common purchaser law to reclassify pipelines as public carriers, thus compelling their owners to purchase or transport a ratable share of oil from all producers without discrimination. Independents viewed the measure as a means of forcing the majors to buy more domestic oil in lieu of imports.[6]

On March 30, 1930, the Texas legislature enacted the Common Purchaser Act. As the independents had sought, the law designated owners and operators of oil storage facilities and pipelines as public utilities, and required them to buy crude oil ratably from all producers and fields. The law was designed to prevent major companies from using their monopoly over pipeline transportation to take unfair advantage of smaller operators by denying them equal access to the market. In signing the bill, Governor Dan Moody stated that artificially low oil prices injured the public interest by decreasing tax revenues and royalties in the public school fund. Although independents viewed the measure as punishment for Humble, Farish regarded it as providing better legal machinery for controlling ruinous production. By requiring common purchasers to purchase ratably, he believed that production would have to be prorated to give each producer a fair share of the market. Since Humble had been purchasing more oil ratably than other companies, Farish thought that the new act would permit it to shift some of its excess connections to other purchasers. Despite the high expectations of independents and majors alike, the TRC exerted little effort in enforcing the act.[7]

As legal counsel to large independents such as Humphreys and Pure, Vinson & Elkins kept busy staying abreast of new changes in Texas oil and gas law. The TRC had asked Texas producers to appoint a six-member committee to propose rules and regulations under the pipeline act for TRC approval. Vinson was especially concerned over Section 6 of the new act, which required common carriers to file monthly reports with the TRC detailing the amount of petroleum stored, received, or delivered, and available storage space. Though the TRC was making little effort to enforce the act, Ben H. Powell, an Austin attorney and former judge who kept Vinson & Elkins apprised of state legislative matters, advised Vinson to urge his firm's oil clients to comply with the new regulations.[8]

To goad the TRC into action, Humble dropped a bombshell shortly before the Common Purchaser Act was to take effect in June. Farish announced that, effective July 1, 1930, Humble would discontinue purchasing crude oil in seven North Texas counties. By this act, described by the *Oil and Gas Journal* as an "unprecedented move for a major oil company," Farish gambled that the TRC would get serious about enforcing the new law and prorate production so that output would not exceed Humble's pipeline capacity. Representatives from various oil and gas associations petitioned the TRC to prorate production under the Common Purchaser Act. Convinced of their sincerity and good faith, Humble resumed purchasing North Texas crude. But the action came too late to quell a pack of angry wildcatters, one of whom reminded Farish, "God still rules the Universe."[9]

With tempers flaring hotter than the July sun in Texas, representatives of the IPAA, the Mid-Continent Oil and Gas Association, and other large independent groups met and called upon the state government to use "every means possible" to deal with this "grave emergency." The delegates warned that delay in implementing equitable statewide restrictions would inflict substantial physical and economic loss. Implicit in their plea was a conviction about conservation's beneficial effect on the price of crude oil. Large independents, unlike their smaller counterparts, recognized that some form of production control was necessary to stabilize the oil industry. Voluntary solutions notwithstanding, they accepted state regulation as preferable to federal controls.[10]

The differences among various Texas oil fields made state regulation more feasible than cooperative solutions. Voluntary unitization could be employed in an oil field like Van, in which the majority of leases were owned by majors and large independents, all sharing common attitudes toward conservation. But it was virtually impossible to persuade the multitude of small independents who controlled the East Texas field to become unit partners of the majors and large producers they mistrusted and despised, or to teach them sound conservation practices. Unitization was also seen as highly susceptible to antitrust prosecution. State-enforced prorationing, pioneered by Oklahoma and experimented with in Texas' Yates and Hendrick oil fields, appeared to be the only legally defensible alternative to voluntary production controls, which had neither legislative nor judicial sanction.[11]

Texas independents formed a central prorationing committee, chaired by Dallas oilman Robert R. Penn, to alert the TRC that "petroleum is one of the great natural resources of the State of Texas . . . [whose] production . . . has been . . . in excess of the ready market demand." It noted how the "development of geophysical devices and new and improved drilling machinery . . . [had] hastened the transformation of the business of producing oil from a gambling basis to a scientific basis." The committee beseeched the TRC to implement and enforce rules and regulations adequate "to take care of . . . future generations . . . and to prevent the actual waste through reckless and prolific production of this great natural resource."[12]

The TRC held a hearing in Austin to solicit data from producers regarding the number of producing wells, drilling activity, storage facilities, oil in storage, and market outlet. Two hundred Texas oilmen gathered in the state capital and voiced opinions as varied as the state's landscape. Each pleaded his case with the ferocity of a Texas twister. Penn summed up the views of many independents in accusing the major oil companies of trying to "exterminate" them. "If the pipeline law is a failure," Penn testified, "find it out now [and] have the governor and the state legislature . . . make a law to help the oil situation."[13]

IPAT member Claude Wilde called for an investigation to determine who was responsible for excessive drilling and the level of oil imports. Phillips Petroleum executive Don Emory proposed that producers in each field select their own proration committees to advise the TRC. T. D. Strong, of the Yount-Lee Oil Corporation, argued that Gulf Coast production was being marketed without waste, and that it was unfair for "anybody or any commission . . . to take advantage of one area and give to another area" which could not market all of its oil.[14]

Most of the witnesses testified that any fair proration plan had to apply equally to all Texas oil fields. Even though independents generally detested production controls, an increasing number seemed willing to suffer a little now to keep the bottom from falling out later. Barnsdall Oil Company president R. F. McArthur urged fellow independents to form local prorationing committees that would in turn appoint field umpires to cooperate with Penn's central committee and the TRC in devising a fair and acceptable proration plan. Farish pledged Humble's support, warning that it would be "Texas' own fault if proration fails and we suffer." He assured independents that Humble's parent company, New Jersey Standard, had reduced its imports of foreign oil. Representatives of Gulf and Shell also testified that their companies had cut oil imports.[15]

Austin attorney Charles L. Black told the TRC that his client Big Lake Oil Company, a West Texas independent producer, opposed any proration plan designed to do anything but prevent physical waste. He argued that West Texas producers deserved special consideration since the University of Texas derived royalties from the sale of their oil. But that university's Board of Regents chairman, R. L. Batts, told the TRC, "The Texas University is a permanent institution and it matters little whether the oil is recovered now or one hundred years from now."[16]

Independent producers operating in the Pettus oil field were particularly concerned about prorationing's effect on the production, storage, and marketing of their oil. Each producer was asked to propose a fair and equitable method of curtailing production to eliminate physical waste and promote conservation. On August 14, 1930, a committee of Gulf Coast producers petitioned the TRC to limit any reduction in Gulf Coast production to 15 percent pending further study of individual tracts, to avoid injustice and unfair discrimination to any producer.[17]

Houston independent J. S. Abercombie and the Harrison Oil Company challenged the TRC's constitutional authority to prorate oil production. They alleged that any regulation designed to curtail output deprived them of their private property without due process of law. Claiming that they could market all the oil they produced without waste, Abercombie and Harrison objected to any proration plan designed to fix prices, and criticized the TRC for "wasting time."[18]

The TRC planned to issue its first statewide proration order by the end of August, 1930. Vinson & Elkins assumed an active interest in prorationing as its major client Pure stood to gain or lose by the order. Proration notwithstanding, the Common Purchaser Act was the only state regulation that potentially affected Pure's Texas production. Even though Pure had production and pipeline operations in Texas, Elkins believed that Pure was immune from the act because it was not a common purchaser, since it did not purchase oil from any other Texas producers. Pure had the pipeline capacity and the market to handle additional Van production to supply an expanded market.[19]

Vinson & Elkins attorney Robert A. Shepherd, Sr., briefed Elkins on the legal, economic, and scientific aspects of prorationing, unaware that he was creating ammunition for the subsequent legal battle over oil production controls. Proration was a novelty. Neither the lawyers nor the courts had ever heard of it. There were no legal precedents or rules to guide lawyers in advising their clients. Hence, lawyers such as Shepherd were blazing trails in petroleum law. He noted technological advances in exploration and the development of scientific instruments, such as the torsion balance and the seismograph, that permitted drill-

James A. Elkins, 1930s. Courtesy Vinson & Elkins Archives

ing to unprecedented depths and thus contributed to overproduction. Shepherd explained that prorationing could be enforced either through voluntary operators' agreements or by TRC orders. He preferred TRC enforcement for the following reasons: First, Texas' strict antitrust laws might adversely affect voluntary production controls; second, it would be difficult to obtain the consent of all operators to limit their output; and third, TRC proration orders would shield operators from liability for breach of contract to royalty owners for failing to drill and produce leases to the utmost.[20]

Shepherd dispelled doubts over the TRC's authority to prorate oil production. He believed that prorationing was inherent in the TRC's statutory power to conserve the state's oil and gas resources and to prevent purchasers from discriminating against producers. State courts had not yet construed the meaning and extent of the TRC's authority under the conservation or common purchaser acts. To survive judicial scrutiny, Shepherd believed, TRC proration orders could eliminate only physical, not economic, waste.[21]

According to TRC guidelines, no proration order could issue without ten days notice to all affected parties and a public hearing. The TRC recommended the appointment of field umpires to handle the details of administration and enforcement in each oil field. Field operators selected an eleven-member committee to advise and assist the field umpire. The TRC's limited financial appropriations forced operators to pay field umpires' salaries. Advisory committees or producers could appeal any decision of the field umpire to the TRC. Because the TRC willingly appointed as field umpire any qualified candidate recommended by the operators, Shepherd underscored the importance of selecting the "proper person," for on that person's shoulders rested the success or failure of prorationing.[22]

The TRC's statewide proration quota had to be allocated among individual oil fields and further distributed among individual producers. Individual leases within each field were divided into 20-acre units, with fractional units to handle any remaining acreage. Larger units were utilized in areas such as West Texas, where land tracts were sectionalized while smaller units were employed where tracts had been cut up into small leases. The next step involved gauging selected oil wells in each field to determine potential production. Shepherd believed that, from an engineering standpoint, it would be more practical to allow advisory committees and field umpires to devise a method for gauging wells in their respective oil fields than to impose a uniform formula.[23]

Robert A. Shepherd, Sr., 1930s. Courtesy Vinson & Elkins Archives

Shepherd's memorandum and the legal uncertainty of prorationing heightened Elkins's anxiety. Elkins appreciated the significance of advisory committees and field umpires in affecting producers' interests. Pure had just completed in July a new 10-inch pipeline some 211 miles long to transport its crude oil from Van to its Gulf Coast refinery at Smith's Bluff and to a storage terminal near Nederland. Six pumping stations had been constructed along the pipeline, with three more in the planning stages. The Pure–Van Pipeline could carry up to 45,000 barrels of crude oil a day. But the TRC could stymie Pure's expansion plans by reducing Van production. Pure stood to lose a substantial amount of money unless Van production was at least maintained at its existing level. Yet all the other producers at Van would also be seeking to maintain their own production levels. Pure could hardly expect them to suffer a bigger cut so to permit Pure to maintain its existing output. For these reasons, Elkins was concerned over prorationing as well as the selection of advisory committeemen and field umpire.[24]

Elkins suggested the appointment of J. S. Young, an independent oilman from San Antonio, as Van field umpire. Richard D. Parker, supervisor of the TRC's oil and gas division, told Shepherd that the TRC would appoint whoever the operators wanted as their field umpire. Based on his personal conversation with Parker, Ben Powell assured Elkins that "an umpire will be named in line with [your] recommendation." On August 15, Powell notified Elkins of Young's appointment as Van field umpire and of the selection of an advisory committee in accord with his recommendations. After Young was disqualified for lack of experience, Elkins's second choice, R. E. Andrews, got the nod.[25]

On August 14, 1930, the TRC issued its first statewide proration order, to take effect as of August 27 at 7 A.M. The order would remain effective for 90 days, during which time total oil production in Texas would be limited to 750,000 barrels a day. The TRC cited its legal authority under state oil conservation statutes to restrict production in order to prevent physical waste and denied any intent to raise crude oil prices. Acknowledging its "keen interest in the economic welfare of the large group of . . . citizens whose capital is devoted to the production of oil," the TRC refused to "be the guardian of their pecuniary interests." Since "the functions assumed by our government cannot include that of an economic dictator," the TRC disclaimed its authority to "limit the production of oil . . . through any proration order upon any other basis than . . . necessary to insure conservation of the resources." The TRC was dancing a Texas two-step around the statutory proscription against restricting oil production to prevent economic waste.[26]

Texas producers lost no time in protesting the TRC's new order. The objectors fell into three general categories: small producers who believed that marginal wells should be exempt from prorationing; producers who could market all of their oil and opposed any restraints; and producers who opposed any kind of regulation. Houston attorney Elwood Fouts, representing Abercombie and Harrison Oil, denounced the TRC's order. Attorneys George E. B. Peddy and Will Orgain argued that their Gulf Coast producer-clients should be exempt from prorationing because their oil had a unique quality and supplied a special market not affecting, and unaffected by, other Texas oil markets. Orgain explained that the Yount-Lee Oil Company had reduced its production from 3,150,000 to 1,350,000 barrels a quarter during the past sixteen months and any further reductions would jeopardize the company's ability to fulfill contractual obligations to purchasers.[27]

Pure appeared content with the TRC's order. "The order as finally entered announces exactly the rules which we submitted," Powell informed Elkins, and "the umpire you suggested has been appointed as well as the advisory committee." Not all Van producers shared Pure's elation. C. Andrade accused Pure and its unit partners of monopolizing production at Van. "We have spent a lot of time and money [fighting] . . . Pure . . . and Humble . . . before your Commission," Andrade told Parker, and "then we spend a lot of money fighting them in court." He complained that the major companies at Van had "used . . . 'bull-dozing' tactics . . . to keep the few independents, who have several small strips, from developing them." Andrade claimed that the majors "have it in for me" and that a Pure representative had told one purchaser "not to fool with my [Andrade's] oil." He explained how the "major companies are going ahead with their development work [while] hollering" about overproduction. "What chances had a man got with a strip 80, 90, 100, or 200 feet wide?" Andrade asked. "I am not a 'curbstone' broker or a 'shoe-string' trader," he insisted, "and have never failed to carry out a contract that I have made."[28]

A. J. Broderick, George Calvert, and other small Van producers echoed Andrade's protest. Rumblings resounded from the Pure camp as well. Elkins was upset that "someone" on the TRC had recommended the appointment of Gene Germany and Tom Cranfill to the Van advisory committee. "I cannot see that they have any place on this committee as neither of these gentlemen are producers," Elkins told Powell.

"They have been the greatest nuisance and disturbing element we have had," and "if there is any way you can keep them off the advisory committee please do so." Elkins feared that Germany and Cranfill would give control of the Van field to small operators like Andrade who owned less than one percent of the leases. To assure control of the Van field by Pure and its unit partners, he recommended the appointment to the committee of B. S. SoRelle, Pure's Texas production manager; F. C. Sealy, of the Texas Company; John R. Suman, of Humble; M. B. Sweeney, of Sun; and M. G. Allen, of Shell.[29]

To ensure its future growth, Pure petitioned the TRC to increase Van's daily production quota from 35,000 to 50,000 barrels. Powell advised Elkins that Pure had to prove that additional production would not damage reservoir pressure, that its wells were being "pinched in"—becoming clogged—under existing levels of output, and that it had a market outlet for additional oil. Small producers were expected to protest Pure's request at a TRC hearing, scheduled for December 10. Powell assured Elkins that they could "never defeat us in the courts," but the difficulty would be in "getting the commissioners to see that we are not selfish in wanting to increase our production while everybody else is striving so hard to get along on a decreased allowance." Even though he expected opposition from Governor Pat Neff, Powell believed that they could "straighten him out . . . without any trouble." Texas Company president Ralph C. Holmes warned Pure president Henry M. Dawes to go slow. Sensing a major battle in the brewing, the TRC mercifully postponed the hearing until January 10, 1931, so that everyone could first enjoy Christmas.[30]

Storm clouds gathered over the Texas oil patch as the new year approached. The TRC discovered that it was one thing to issue orders, quite another to enforce them. The mere idea of government regulation to achieve some semblance of stability aroused the suspicion and ire of small independent producers. They viewed prorationing as nothing more than a conspiracy between government and the majors to drive them out of business and foster monopoly. Local federal judges apparently shared the same suspicions as they freely granted injunctions restraining enforcement of TRC proration orders. Some operators simply ignored the TRC's orders and continued producing at will.[31]

The situation had been further aggravated by the surge of drilling and production activity that followed in the wake of Columbus M. "Dad" Joiner's discovery of oil on the Bradford farm near Kilgore, in East

Texas, on October 3, 1930. Joiner had unwittingly opened a Pandora's box. East Texas' yellow pine forests were instantaneously transformed into thickets of wooden oil derricks towering above a 140,000-acre oil reservoir that stretched 45 miles north to south and 12 miles east to west. Estimated to contain approximately 5.5 billion barrels of crude oil, the East Texas field was the world's largest known petroleum reservoir at the time, and accounted for a third of the nation's total oil production. This was good news to many local inhabitants, who had been hard hit by the Depression. The discovery of oil under their drought-stricken land offered economic salvation to the many small East Texas farmers who could no longer adequately supplement their income from cotton production by raising and selling poultry, fruit, and truck crops. Now they could pay their debts, keep their land, perhaps even escape their economic misery.[32]

The roaring gushers in the leviathan East Texas field lit the arid countryside with excitement. Land agents, petroleum prospectors, speculators, machinery merchants, well drillers, pipeline constructors, and others came in a stampede, seeking their fortunes in oil. People who had never possessed more than a few dollars purchased new clothes and paid off mortgages and other debts. After years of suffering from overextended credit in the declining cotton market, banks gained new leases on life. Real estate values skyrocketed, rents doubled and tripled, new hotels and merchandise stores sprang up, and builders scrambled to keep pace with soaring housing demand. By the spring of 1931, East Texas Baptists were inundated by gamblers, prostitutes, and profit-seekers. When a well sunk in a local churchyard struck oil, the minister gathered his flock to thank and praise the Lord, who was beseeched for "oil, more oil!"[33]

The East Texas oil boom arrived at an opportune time for local residents, but spelled economic disaster for the petroleum industry. Convinced that the area contained no oil, major companies had initially shown little interest in East Texas. Humble and Mid-Kansas Oil were the only majors with leases in the East Texas field, and even they were not in a dominant position to control production as they had done at Van. Small operators had an unparalleled opportunity to corner leases and shoot for the big time. Overproduction soon glutted an already saturated crude oil market. Crude oil selling for $1.10 a barrel in October, 1930, plummeted to 25 cents in early 1931. Declining prices hurt oil fields throughout the country. Small farmers could not be persuaded to cut back production. Much like late nineteenth-century farmers, small oil producers could not comprehend and adjust to the paradox of a market economy in which a more bountiful harvest often reaped lower prices and reduced family income. The problem was further complicated by the diversity of opinions, attitudes, philosophies, and personalities among independents and majors alike, which hindered voluntary and cooperative efforts. The TRC, upon which responsibility for alleviating overproduction had fallen, hoped that prorationing would succeed where voluntarism had failed. State government regulation of private property interests in petroleum (unique to the United States) was legitimized as a necessary exercise of police power to protect the public interest in a vital and strategically important natural resource. Small independent producers were unimpressed.[34]

Oil-starved independents, depression-ridden cotton farmers, and the chambers of commerce of struggling towns organized groups such as the East Texas Lease, Royalty and Producers Association—backed by Carl Estes, a fiery newspaper editor from Tyler—to voice their vociferous opposition to production controls. Small independents gathered in Fort Worth on January 15, 1931, and blamed Texas' lack of pipeline and storage facilities for forcing them to sell their oil at any price just to get a connection. The majors took advantage of the situation to buy up cheap oil for their refineries. Some independents started refining their own oil into cheap gasoline, which competed with the majors' more expensive premium grades. The majors deplored this practice, which undercut their market and further depressed prices.[35]

Humble again seized the initiative in trying to restore stability to the scene. Farish announced that Humble would lay the first major pipeline in East Texas and purchase ratably from all producers, provided they agreed to divide the field into 20-acre units, each sharing a ratable portion of total production. "In the absence of any orderly program of development and production," Farish explained, "it would be foolish for the Humble company to attempt to serve the area generally." Humble held nearly 16,000 acres of leases in the East Texas field, containing 13 percent of the field's proven oil reserves. A Humble research team had gauged the bottom-hole pressure (pressure at the bottom of an oil well) of selected East Texas field sites to determine the ideal productive capacity in terms of efficiency and conservation. Farish believed that the only way to prevent waste was to control production; and the only way to do that fairly was to allocate output for individual wells according to their productive potential and acreage. Humble had successfully employed this formula in the Yates, Hendrick, and Van oil fields.[36]

Farish failed to rally a majority of small East Texas operators behind Humble's proposal. Caught in the middle, the TRC hesitated to wield its authority against such overwhelming and vociferous opposition in the region. East Texans proved to be less cooperative than the Yates and Hendrick operators, who had welcomed TRC assistance in maintaining the order and stability they had already achieved voluntarily. Baker believed the TRC had "yielded to political pressure" in exempting the East Texas field from its proration order and freely granting exception permits to the spacing rule. It allowed small East Texas operators to "drill a well on an acre or a tenth of an acre," Baker complained, "and get as much allowable as a man who drilled on the twenty acre" tract. He criticized the TRC's policy as "outrageous" and held it responsible for "the drilling of a great number of unnecessary wells and the taking of oil in vast quantity by the fellow who had wells on closely spaced acreage compared with a man who had one well on twenty acres." Farish announced that Humble would not enter the East Texas field as a common purchaser and would construct its own private facilities for handling the company's East Texas field production.[37]

The legal uncertainty of prorationing fomented a spirited debate between small producers, who opposed any controls, and large independents and major companies, who supported any oil conservation program that respected the correlative rights of all operators in a common reservoir. Opponents of conservation argued that every oil well was a problem unto itself, to be handled individually. Some wells produced more than others, but the imbalance could not be corrected without hurting someone. For that reason, anti-conservationists believed that well-spacing and prorationing were impractical and unfair. Conservationists responded that operators in a common pool shared an interest in regulating production to guarantee each a fair share of the total output.[38]

Baker likened the problem to a bunch of kids sticking their straws into a shallow, sloped bowl filled with soda pop. Straws near the bowl's outer edge drained it faster than straws in the middle. Kids on the shallower outer edge of the bowl ran out of soda before those in the middle. The latter got more. Situated on a subterranean incline, the East Texas field presented a similar situation, except that it drained from the bottom up because of underlying water, which pushed the oil to the surface. Producers on the shallower outer edges of the field drained their oil leases before those in the deeper middle section. "The fellow at the top can take oil as long as there is any oil being pushed up," Baker explained, "It's just the reverse of the soda pop." He believed that existing technology was sophisticated enough to formulate a more equitable method of production, but that too many diehard independents, protected by the rule of capture, insisted upon their right to produce as much oil as they pleased to keep their neighbors from getting it.[39]

Baker theorized that there was no irreconcilable conflict between the common law absolute ownership doctrine and the rule of capture. Landowners "still owned the oil and gas in place beneath [their] land," he explained, but could not get to it without drilling and producing. He viewed the rule of capture as simply a convenient tool, auxiliary to the absolute ownership theory, to give landowners the means to protect their correlative property rights in oil and gas in the absence of state police power. The state regulated production, Baker maintained, only to ensure that each landowner did not take advantage of the capture theory to destroy his neighbors' rights by grabbing an unfair and inequitable share of petroleum. "I don't see why we have to argue with that," Baker insisted, "but that's been the subject of more antagonism, more bitterness, and more trouble in the business than most anything connected with the production of oil."[40]

The legal issues generated by the crisis in the Texas oil industry in the 1930s embodied what historian Morton Keller has identified as a tension between the persistence of nineteenth-century laissez-faire ideology and the growth of a Progressive faith in governmental intervention as a means of maintaining a stable economy during the first three decades of the twentieth century. The tensions—between equality and liberty, between the desire for freedom and demands for social order, between hostility to the state versus dependence on government, between localism and nationalism—that Keller found to persist from the late nineteenth century through the early twentieth-century American polity can all be found in the legal battle over oil prorationing in Texas during the early 1930s.[41]

Scientific and technological advances during the 1920s and 1930s were transforming the American petroleum industry into a more highly organized and complex business dominated increasingly by professionals. Relationships were strained between older, more traditional, independent oilmen hewing to a classical economic ideology, and younger, more "progressive" oilmen, petroleum engineers, and scientists, who believed the latest knowledge and technology would solve what they considered counterproductive tendencies (such as overproduction), which free market forces inadequately balanced and corrected. Small independent oilmen decided to take a stand against what they perceived as an unpatriotic attempt by "liberal reformists" to undermine established Anglo-American rights and liberties, especially private property rights, in the name of "order" and "efficiency."[42]

Mutually distrustful and uncompromising, conservationists and anti-prorationists in 1930 experienced another "impending crisis" leading to civil war.[43] Joseph C. Danciger fired the first shot in this long and costly conflict—one, fortunately, fought in the courtroom rather than on the battlefield, and using words rather than bullets, thereby illustrating the critical role played by lawyers in this classic confrontation between old and new values.

CHAPTER 5

In the Loving Arms of the State

Oil men are no better or worse than the average run
of humanity. We can't expect a man, who has every
reason, from a selfish standpoint, to want the prisoner
at the bar to decrease his production, to give fair
consideration to his claims for an increase.

—Henry M. Dawes

Joseph Danciger, a North Texas independent oil producer and refiner, fired the first shot in the legal war over prorationing when he filed suit in the State District Court of Travis County to restrain the TRC from limiting production from his wells. He argued that the TRC's proration order bore no reasonable relation to the prevention of physical waste, but aimed to curtail production in order to raise crude oil prices, in violation of state law. Danciger claimed that he could market all the oil he produced and that the TRC's proration order deprived him of his private property without due process of law.[1]

State District Judge George Calhoun granted a temporary injunction restraining the TRC from prorating Danciger's production in the Panhandle oil field until a trial on February 2, 1931. Danciger amended his petition to attack the TRC's revised proration order of January 23, which reduced statewide daily production from 750,000 to 644,253 barrels, and cut daily production in the Panhandle field from 64,616 to 40,000 barrels. Danciger had 42 wells, each capable of producing 5,200 barrels a day. His lawsuit posed a critical legal challenge to the exercise of state police power to regulate production of privately owned petroleum.[2]

The trial took place in Austin before State District Judge Charles A. Wheeler. Danciger's legal team comprised attorneys Charles L. Black of Austin, S. A. L. Morgan of Amarillo, and I. J. Ringolsky of Kansas City. Hines Baker represented Humble, which intervened in the suit as a pipeline carrier for some of Danciger's oil. Fort Worth attorney Robert E. Hardwicke, Jr., and John E. Kilgore of Wichita Falls assisted Texas attorney general James V. Allred in defending the TRC. They were joined by assistant attorney generals Maurice Cheek and Fred Upchurch.[3]

Black argued that the TRC lacked statutory authority to restrict production to market demand, and that none of the oil Danciger produced created fire hazards or was being wasted or stored. He reiterated that the TRC's order deprived Danciger of his property without due process of law by preventing him from producing enough oil to fulfill outstanding contractual obligations, making him liable for breach of contract. By operating his wells at capacity, Allred countered, Danciger had forced other Panhandle producers to drill offset wells, resulting in needless and wasteful overproduction. He maintained that prorationing promoted conservation and protected producers' correlative property rights by preserving reservoir pressure that enhanced ultimate recovery.[4]

Judge Wheeler upheld the constitutionality of the 1929 Act and the TRC's proration orders. He agreed with Allred that prorationing bore a reasonable relation to the prevention of physical waste, and that any effect on the price of crude oil was merely incidental to the undisputed power of the state to enforce conservation.[5]

Danciger's appeal put a damper on conservationists' victory celebrations, and prolonged the legal uncertainty of prorationing in Texas. Small independents continued producing at will, further aggravating overproduction in the feverish East Texas field, where most wells pumped some 15,000 barrels a day. Economic depression impelled small East Texas farmers to extract as much oil from their land as possible. The legality of an equitable prorationing program based on sound engineering principles had to await the outcome of the Danciger appeal, which hinged in large part on whether the court accepted recent scientific advances in petroleum production techniques as more than theory and speculation. "The East Texas field," according to Henrietta M. Larson and Kenneth W. Porter, "had, perhaps, been discovered too early for the normal processes of democracy to have prepared the ethical codes and institutional methods capable of dealing with so large and important a field."[6]

Danciger had thrown a potent first punch on behalf of those small independents who believed that the majors and large independents had manipulated the TRC into increasing their production allowances at small operators' expense. The situation resembled present-day professional sports, in which ball club owners must satisfy the salary demands of individual athletes while keeping their total team payroll within a prescribed budget. No single player can receive a raise without cutting another athlete's salary. The result often produces antagonism and disunity. An analogous situation confronted the TRC as it attempted to allocate a limited amount of oil production among individual producers. One Texas independent suggested that small producers were being treated like "slaves ready to go the slaughter house," adding, "You have as bold and as blood thirsty a set of pirates running these big oil companies as ever scuttled a ship."[7]

By limiting Van production to 35,000 barrels a day, the TRC's proration order adversely affected Pure, Van's largest lease-holder. With 92 wells in the field, Pure was allocated 27,500 barrels of the 35,000-barrel allowable. This was hardly enough oil to enable Pure to supply its own refineries in Texas and Pennsylvania and to fulfill its contractual obligation to sell 15,000 barrels of crude oil daily to Humble, which in turn delivered it to a huge Standard refinery recently constructed in Baton Rouge. Humble had built a 10-inch pipeline running 93 miles from the Van field to Standard's pipeline at the Louisiana border. By 1931, Humble's pipeline network reached into all of Texas' oil-producing regions, enabling it to move large quantities of crude oil to its Gulf Coast loading terminals at Texas City and Ingleside; to refineries at Baytown and Baton Rouge; and to smaller refineries, both company-owned and independent, throughout the state. Without at least 50,000 barrels a day production, Pure could not supply Humble and Standard and expand its own operations. The TRC could not raise Pure's production quota without increasing the statewide allowable, thus disrupting the entire oil conservation program, unless it cut smaller producers' shares. As elected officials, TRC members recognized the powder keg on which they sat.[8]

Pure had the option of pursuing its quest through the TRC's administrative hearing process or, like Danciger, through the courts. Neither option offered Pure great probability for success—the first because of Texas' volatile political situation, the second due to the legal uncertainties of prorationing. Pure turned to its vaunted legal counsel, Vinson & Elkins, for advice. James Elkins, who was not only an able attorney but a skilled political fixer, in this instance preferred the mayhem of politics to the uncertain outcome and cost of protracted litigation.

Elkins had become a leader of the Houston business community, and a figure of political power statewide, by promoting a stable, conservative political climate that fostered economic growth and prosperity. As both a banker and a lawyer, Elkins offered his clients a range of financial, legal, and political services. This versatility enabled him to win concessions from the TRC for Pure that other Texas producers had failed to obtain during the initial prorationing struggles in the early 1930s. Elkins's representation, which proved of immeasurable value to Pure's growth and prosperity, illustrates the complex roles lawyers played in shaping petroleum law.[9]

Elkins instructed Powell to petition the TRC for an increase in Pure's Van allowable at the January 10 hearing. Powell expected most opposition to the petition to come from outside producers. But Elkins knew better. Pure had a contractual obligation to obtain the agreement of its Van unit partners—Humble, Shell, Sun, and the Texas Company—to increase and share production. Pure held leases on fourth-fifths of the unit, while its four partners collectively held the remainder. Pure would therefore receive by far the greater share of any additional production. Its unit partners would obtain only meager gain, but they would receive equal shares in the fury of the already hostile small independents at Van and the wrath of the TRC. Major oil companies that had been decrying overproduction and advocating prorationing would appear hypocritical if they now pleaded for an increased allowance.

"I rather think that we work against our own interests" in seeking to increase production, Texas Oil Company president Ralph C. Holmes warned Pure president Dawes, "I am only hopeful that . . . compromises can be worked out . . . [to] make it possible for us to continue working together for improvement and stability in the general situation." Dawes responded that Pure had "left nothing undone to protect the industry and [has] subjected [itself] to every conceivable form of harassment and

... will receive support not simply because we deserve it, but because it is in the best interests of industry."[10]

Sun vice-president J. Edgar Pew opposed outright increasing the Van allowable. If "the industry is to escape utter demoralization," he explained, "it must adhere to a program of some kind, and the larger producing companies must make such sacrifices as are necessary to accomplish this." Pew feared that raising Pure's allowable would upset the entire oil conservation effort since other operators would demand like consideration. "I do not agree with you that there is any injustice being done to Van over other similar fields of the same age [and] I do not think the royalty interests at Van are being discriminated against," he told Pure vice-president R. W. McIlvain, "but on the other hand I believe if you were to open this thing wide they would be very much the losers because of the less amount they would get for their oil." Pew warned McIlvain, "Don't do it now."[11]

Pure's in-house lawyers believed that they could secure an injunction permitting the company to produce 50,000 barrels a day at Van should the TRC deny the company's petition. Elkins advised Dawes to be firm with the TRC but to be prepared for a lawsuit if necessary. So advised, Dawes informed Pew that "the proration movement [could] not be sustained solely on the basis of emotional appeal," and he vowed to pursue Pure's "present application to its ultimate logical conclusion." Pure asked "for nothing in return for the sacrifices [it had] already made," Dawes explained, and the industry would "be better served by reasonable cooperation . . . on the part of those with whom we are not only associated in this field but with whom we have cooperated to the limit of our abilities in the general interests of the industry."[12]

Elkins cautioned Dawes that, even though legal action was an option, "I do tremble sometimes when I think about the [Pure Oil] Company taking the responsibility of breaking up and destroying proration." Elkins concluded that Pure should not sue "except where the Company's demands are such to absolutely require this action."[13]

New Jersey Standard, Humble's parent company, supported Pure's position because it relied on 15,000 barrels of Van crude oil daily to feed its Baton Rouge refinery. E. J. Sadler, Standard's vice president for production, believed it "entirely reasonable to accord the [Van] field such an outlet as it will now receive through the Pure Oil Company line and the [Humble] line just completed to Shreveport" and that he considered "any other view . . . entirely unsound." Elkins discounted protests by small independents such as Andrade, and could not "conceive of a place where a small increase would be less disturbing . . . except sentimentally . . . [and] when it comes to sentiment, there is a very strong feeling that reasonable equity must be observed as between producers." Small independents must have been pleased to hear Elkins echo their cries to observe "reasonable equity."[14]

Shell refused to back Pure. Shell president U. de B. Daly reminded Dawes that Van production was already equivalent to that of other Texas fields of similar size and potential. He predicted that other producers would demand higher quotas if the TRC increased Pure's Van allowable, undermining prorationing and encouraging overproduction. Daly asserted that additional production would exhaust the natural gas pressure of the Van field and induce excessive water intrusion, and recommended deferring increases until the industry got "on its legs again" so that greater profits could be derived from higher prices.[15]

And so of Pure's four unit partners at Van, Sun and Shell opposed its petition, while the Texas Company was leery at best. Humble was forced to go along with its parent company's support for Pure's petition. This cleavage among the Van unit partners signified a crack in the majors' solid front behind prorationing. New Jersey Standard was encouraging Pure to increase production at a time when other majors were arguing that output should be reduced to alleviate waste and stabilize prices.

From its perspective, Standard had expended considerable capital constructing a huge new refinery at Baton Rouge to process high volumes of crude oil. To realize an adequate return, Standard had to ensure a steady flow of oil to the refinery. Standard and its subsidiary, Humble, had built pipelines connecting the Baton Rouge refinery to the Van field. The negative effect of additional production on crude oil prices was not Standard's immediate concern, as most of its capital was tied up in petroleum transportation and refining. To the contrary, an adequate supply of cheap crude would benefit Standard far more than scarce, high-priced oil. In this context, Standard's position is understandable.[16]

The Texas Common Purchaser Act of 1930 also increased the odds against Pure's gaining an increased allowable. In part, the act guaranteed every Texas oil producer a fair market share by prohibiting crude oil purchasers who owned pipelines from discriminating against operators who lacked their own transportation facilities. The act required companies such as Pure and Humble, which produced and shipped oil through their own pipelines, to purchase and transport a fair portion (or ratable share[17]) of oil from smaller operators. Small independents argued that Pure lacked adequate pipeline capacity to transport additional Van production without discriminating against them by buying and shipping less of their oil. Elkins responded that the Common Purchaser Act required purchasers in a single field to take ratably from all producers in that field, and common purchasers throughout the state to take ratably from all oil fields. He claimed that this latter provision did not apply to Pure, as it purchased only Van oil ratably from all producers in that field.[18]

As the TRC hearing approached, Powell kept Elkins apprised of events in the state capital. Richard Parker of the TRC's oil and gas division opposed Pure's request for additional production at a time when the TRC expected other Texas producers to sacrifice. Parker suggested that Pure instead purchase additional oil from marginal producers, which would also rescue them from certain ruin.[19] He accused Pure of disguising what he considered its true intention—to produce more oil to sell to Humble in order to supply Standard's Baton Rouge refinery. If Pure quit this practice, Standard itself would be forced to purchase more oil from small marginal producers. Powell told Parker that he was unaware of what Humble did with the crude it purchased from Pure, but that in any case the TRC lacked jurisdiction over oil once it left the state. He asked Elkins to come to Austin to persuade Parker to see things the Pure way. Powell noted that Elkins should be prepared, first, to prove that Pure could produce 50,000 barrels daily at Van without incurring subsurface or aboveground waste; next, to procure a geologist who would testify to the danger that Pure would lose wells due to clogging and declining profits when daily production was less than 100 barrels; next, to show that Pure had not purchased oil from any other Texas fields except Van; and, finally, to demonstrate, as a matter of equity, that even with an increased allowance Pure would still be producing much less of its potential at Van compared to production in other Texas oil fields. "I want us to insist on this allowance," Powell concluded, "even if we have to go to court . . . to teach these people a lesson."[20]

By rejecting an increased allowance, the TRC would jeopardize Pure's oil shipments to Standard's Baton Rouge refinery, Dawes warned Parker, and therefore "would simply be robbing the State of Texas of [an] outlet for that oil without in any way affecting conditions in the West," penalizing Texans to the benefit of other oil-producing states. Without additional Van production, Pure would have to purchase oil outside of Texas or be forced to shut down its refinery in Smith's Bluff,

Texas. Dawes said he did not understand how the TRC could "put it-self in the indefensible position of robbing its own people of markets in favor of any indefinite ideas they may have of remedying world condi-tions."[21]

At the same time, land and royalty owners at Van had retained state senator Tom Pollard as legal counsel to fight for their interests. A sec-ond group, composed of Fort Worth land and royalty owners, had re-tained the law firm of Trammel, Sizzum & Price to defend their Van interests. They accused Pure of cheating them out of higher profits by failing to produce more oil from their Van properties. Unless Pure in-creased its Van production, Elkins warned Dawes, it would face "un-desirable litigation" having "far reaching effects" on the future of prorationing in Texas.[22]

Such a situation offered a mixed blessing for Pure. The litigation would be moot if the TRC increased Pure's Van allowable. If not, Elkins planned to use the TRC's rejection as a defense to the lawsuit. Antici-pating a heated contest, the TRC again postponed the hearing, this time to January 22.[23]

Dawes tried to use the land and royalty owners' threatened lawsuit to win Sun's support for the Pure petition. He assured Pew that Pure desired merely to put Van in a position of "measurable equality" with other Texas oil fields. "You know what we have to combat in this effort," Dawes said, and "if the people in this field, through the indifference or weaknesses of the operators, feel that they are being discriminated against, they will take the matter in their own hands." He warned Pew that "five different persons or corporations . . . are prepared to bring suit in case" the TRC denied Pure's petition. "It is the Pure Oil Com-pany who, so far, [has] prevented this and kept the situation in hand," Dawes reminded Pew, "but I am obliged to say to you, as one of our associates in the unit, that we have come to the end of our string."[24]

The outlook seemed bleak for Pure as the hearing neared. On January 21, Vinson & Elkins attorney George Peddy sent Elkins a scouting re-port from the state capital indicating that Pure could "get the increase [only] with the influence which has been and is now being exerted upon those in authority against granting [the] same."[25] Peddy's dispatch cast a shadow over the Pure camp, which faced foes more formidable than it had anticipated. In desperation, Pure management leaned on their ace legal strategist to outmaneuver the enemy.

Pure's fate rested with Elkins. In turn, the outcome of its confrontation with the TRC held great significance for both the relatively young Houston law firm (founded in 1917) and for the future of prorationing in Texas. A loss would not only stifle Pure's growth but undermine Elkins's ambition to transform Vinson & Elkins into a regional legal powerhouse. But odds were that even Elkins could not salvage what appeared to be a lost cause.[26]

Assuming personal command of Pure's legal forces, Elkins sped to the Austin battleground. On January 22, he reported to Pure headquarters that "conditions [had] crystallized against any increase whatever until this morning" when the central proration committee, headed by Dallas oilman R. R. Penn, discovered that some royalty owners had employed former Governor Dan Moody to represent them in the hearing. Desperately, Elkins forged a last-minute alliance with Penn's committee in order to reinforce Pure's position in the pending showdown against the formidable force led by a former Texas governor. As the opposing forces lined up for battle, Penn volunteered to lead the new alliance of majors and independents into combat. Back at company headquarters, Pure management anxiously awaited the results.[27]

As chairman of the central proration committee, representing an allied group of independents and majors, Penn had hailed the TRC's proration program as an "achievement of pride." Asking the TRC to clamp down on producers in the Big Lake oil field, where the University of Texas owned substantial acreage, Penn claimed that wasteful overproduction at Big Lake was costing the university thousands of dollars weekly. He also urged the TRC to reduce production in East Texas while recommending that it increase Van's daily allowable by 5,000 barrels each month until total output reached 50,000 barrels a day. Penn assured the TRC that additional Van production would not be wasted due to the expected rise in gasoline demand with the opening of the tourist season and farm work in April.[28]

The climax came when Elkins quietly rose in the rear of the hearing chamber and asked for an opportunity to be heard. He demanded that Pure be permitted to produce 50,000 barrels of Van oil at once, citing the company's ready market for the additional oil. It would not be needlessly stored or wasted. Noting that the TRC's proration order of August 14, 1930, had limited Pure's 92 Van wells to 27,500 barrels per day despite a daily productive potential of a million barrels, Elkins specified that on November 1, 1930, Pure had 194 wells at Van with a daily productive potential of 2,775,000 barrels. Further pointing out that the 27,500-barrel allowable divided among Pure's 194 Van wells reduced the ratio of each well's output to less than a third of the allowable of wells in other Texas oil fields, Elkins complained that this was "not right when there is an open market." Posturing now as a defender against the oil giants, he asserted that Pure "refused to pinch down some of the smaller fellows because it would ruin their wells." Elkins predicted that by April 1 there would be some 233 wells at Van without a barrel of additional allowable making it "wrong, . . . unsound and unjust" to limit each one to an "average of 110 barrels" a day. "We are producing with tubing and choke on all wells . . . [with] . . . so much back pressure . . . that the gas escapage is large," Elkins explained. He offered to pay the TRC's expenses to "make a personal inspection [of the Van field] and hold hearings on the ground to get the facts.[29]

The TRC acquiesced. Effective January 23, and until April 1, statewide production would be limited to 644,253 barrels per day. Yet though the TRC reduced output in all Texas oil fields, it actually increased Van's daily production by 5,000 barrels per month until it reached 50,000 barrels a day, and scheduled a special hearing for February 24 to determine the East Texas allowable.[30]

Pure's management greeted the victory with understandable enthusiasm. McIlvain elatedly thanked Elkins for "the most welcome and . . . best news we have had in many a day," adding, "This had gotten to be so serious, and the strain, both inside and out, was so great that we are all very glad it is over . . . hope you take a week's vacation." He attributed Pure's success to Elkins's presentation, which "forestalled completely any inquiries into our basic facts supporting our claimed potential."[31] Dawes also expressed his gratitude to Elkins for "fight[ing] a lone battle [with] nothing on your side except a just cause and your own natural abilities" in defending "a vital matter to the Company, and it is a great relief to have it definitely out of the way."[32] Elkins received many accolades for his personal role in saving the day for his corporate client. By "sending . . . Judge Elkins to Austin," influential East Texas newspaper editor Carl Estes wrote, "Pure's action is . . . indeed commendable and merits the appreciation of us all and other corporations might well emulate it."[33]

Thirteen Pullman carloads of East Texas operators, represented by Moody, did not fare as well on their arrival in Austin on February 24 for the special TRC hearing. Fisticuffs were certain to erupt whenever majors and independents came within arm's length of one another. Penn refused to answer Moody's question about his connections with major oil companies. "It's necessary to tell the truth!" Moody admonished

Penn. Penn retorted, "You mean to insinuate that I'm not?" Estes
shouted in reply, "If you want to fight somebody, fight me, you big bully!"
The gallery cheered as emotion and irrationality prevailed.[34]

Distressed that overproduction in Texas threatened to upset the entire domestic oil conservation effort, oil industry representatives from
Texas, Oklahoma, Louisiana, Arkansas, Kansas, California, New
Mexico, Colorado, and Wyoming, including several governors, met in
Fort Worth on March 9, 1931, to discuss ways to correlate their respective state regulatory efforts to establish fair production quotas and restore crude oil prices to a profitable level. They formed an Oil States
Advisory Committee (OSAC), and called for immediate market-demand
prorationing in the East Texas field. At a Washington, D.C. meeting in
April, Colorado's representative accused oilmen of being "short-sighted,"
"selfish," and incapable of visualizing "the public interest." The OSAC
recommended the restriction of unnecessary drilling and unitization
to protect the interests of both independent producers and the public.[35]

Amidst stormy protests, the TRC issued a proration order for the East
Texas field to take effect on April 10. It limited daily production to
90,000 barrels, to be increased by 15,000 barrels every two weeks until 130,000 barrels were reached by July 1, when the order expired.
Moody and Estes persuaded State District Judge J. D. Moore to issue a
temporary injunction restraining enforcement of the order. Assistant
Attorney General Upchurch advised that Moore's injunction decree
applied only to Estes's 72 acres in the East Texas field. The TRC revised its order twice, on April 22 and 29, and delayed its inception until May 1 to mollify angry independents. But many East Texas operators
simply ignored the TRC and continued their own way, drilling 317 more
wells while producing at capacity from the 817 wells already extant.
Humble reacted by lowering its posted price for crude from the East
Texas field by 20 cents a barrel. Farish warned that "the price of East
Texas oil will control the price of all competitive crudes." One report
noted, "East Texas is the independent spirit in its most violent expres-
sion; and violent is not too strong a word to describe the most vocal
leader, Carl Estes, an eccentric and tempestuous newspaper man." As
editor of the *Tyler Courier-Times,* Estes voiced the sentiments of the
local "plain folk," denouncing the "big boys" and "slick lawyers" who
were moving in to steal their oil.[36]

A "Red Scare" added further to the chaos, excitement, and anxiety of the East Texas field. In a "confidential" letter addressed to the executives of 38 oil companies operating in Texas, Texas Ranger Frank Hamer (renowned as the nemesis of the bank robbers Bonnie and Clyde) warned of an imminent Communist plot to blow up refineries, pipelines, and storage tanks in East Texas. Hamer refused to divulge his sources, and became upset when the letter's contents were leaked to the public, but insisted that it was his duty to warn oil company officials. He claimed that saboteurs had stolen a large quantity of nitroglycerine from oil field storehouses.[37]

East Texas production soared as the TRC's regulatory authority stalled in the courts. "It takes time to finally dispose of those cases, sometimes six months and often one or two years," TRC chairman C. V. Terrell complained, "so these operators who bring suit can with impunity run their wells wide open, get neighbors' oil and soon bring in water and soon ruin the field." The mere filing of numerous injunction suits stifled the TRC's ability to impose some semblance of orderly production in the East Texas field. "No matter how far the Railroad Commission stretches allowances," the *New York Times* suggested, "it appears to be impossible to satisfy oil-thirsty East Texans . . . [who] demand all their oil and will not listen to the old adage about eating one's cake and having it too."[38]

With the courts as battlegrounds and law as the weapon of choice, lawyers were soldiers for the warring factions that skirmished over oil. Pure had found a capable general in the co-founder of Vinson & Elkins. By the 1930s, Elkins's influence as a leader of the Houston business establishment with ties to influential patrons (such as banker Jesse Jones, a close friend) was unsurpassed. Elkins's performance before the TRC hearing in January, 1931, illustrated his ability to sway politicians and businessmen alike to further his clients' interests—without resorting to uncertain, slow, and expensive litigation such as Moody and his East Texas clients were forced to undertake. In a single day, Elkins had journeyed from Houston to Austin and back, turning impending defeat into victory. His power derived largely from his magnetic personality, his endless political connections, and the legal ability he and other Vinson & Elkins lawyers wielded.[39]

Elkins drew upon his charisma and charm to forge an alliance with Penn, thereby gaining for his client the support of the powerful central proration committee. He then used shrewd arguments and his compelling manner to sway the TRC into agreement. The impact of Elkins's alliance with Penn's committee, and of his personal testimony before the TRC, can be gauged by the bleakness of Pure's situation prior to his arrival in Austin. Elkins obtained for Pure all that it had wanted. In this context, he fulfilled what he believed to be a lawyer's ethical obligation: to serve a client's needs to the client's satisfaction. Moreover, Elkins's service to his client had a substantial effect on broader issues, such as oil depletion and public regulation of the oil industry in the region. The role played by Elkins and his firm on Pure's behalf attests vividly to the impact of Texas lawyers on petroleum law and politics in early twentieth-century America.

CHAPTER 6

The Long, Hot Summer

To legalize proration, with all its inequities . . .
would be most unwise and would be beneath the
dignity, judgment and good common sense
of any legislator of this State.

—Joseph C. Danciger

By the summer of 1931, Texas' first experiment in prorating petroleum production had run into a legal stone wall. Lower federal courts had enjoined enforcement of TRC orders, permitting small operators throughout the state to drill and produce with impunity. As lawyers and judges wrangled with relevant constitutional issues, Texas' production exceeded twice the limit set by the TRC. Statewide production reached a million barrels a day and crude oil prices plummeted to 10 cents a barrel. Production from the East Texas field alone could supply a third of the nation's domestic demand for petroleum, forcing down prices in other oil-producing regions of the country. Small independents operating on borrowed capital felt pressed to produce more oil, regardless of price, to pay off their debts. Cheap oil enabled small Texas operators, never enamored of big business and monopolies, to compete with the better-capitalized major companies.[1]

Joseph Danciger epitomized the frontier-style rugged individualism of the small independents, who exhibited a penchant for hard work, upward mobility, and resistance to authority. Law enforcement officials in East Texas labeled some independents as "the worst criminals in the United States," allegedly committing "three or four robberies with firearms every night . . . and . . . a murder out in the woods." Texas Rangers were dispatched to Kilgore to quell the rampant lawlessness and to round up "underworld characters" who made it perilous to walk the streets or travel the highways after dark. Daring gunmen robbed work crews on oil rigs. Nicknamed "The Law," Texas Ranger Manuel T. Gonzaulles, brandishing a pair of fancy revolvers, patrolled the area atop his shiny black horse. Shouts of "Here comes 'The Law'!" reportedly sent the bad guys fleeing.[2]

Vice, too, was rampant. Attorney Olga Lapin recalled being awakened at 2:30 A.M. on one occasion to arrange bail for 25 naked women, who had been arrested during a raid on a dancehall performance titled the "Midnight Rambler." Some 30 prostitutes regularly lodged in the Kilgore jail. Unscrupulous operators cheated many poor and illiterate landowners, bewildered by complex oil and gas leases, out of their "royal tea." The oil bug even infested church congregations, which compromised their godliness by literally praying for more oil. One observer noted that everyone, "caught in the maelstrom of boomtime confusion, found themselves working on Sunday, or if not at work, so worn and weary from the long and strenuous days of the week past that they were compelled . . . to take the day for rest."[3]

Despite hardships and crime, the East Texas oil boom offered opportunity for poor farm youths, who found employment in the numerous stores, hotels, and cafes that sprang up to meet the needs of many new customers. A local resident recalled, "Those were the days when people worked. . . . They didn't mooch or march." Another recalled how much fun it was "just to drive around over the country . . . and see the derricks." One observer was awestruck by the glowing gas flares that lit the pine forests at night. Kilgore newspaper publisher Tom E. Foster described the East Texas field as the "California gold rush and Alaska thrown into one." Streets in downtown Longview were congested with vehicles and pedestrians some 15 to 18 hours a day. "It was just a sight to see," the Gregg County sheriff said. "People were everywhere and the cars were stacked." After striking oil on her land, one elderly lady boasted, "Now I can go to town and buy all the chewing gum and bacon I want." Many East Texans looked forward to going to the post office to pick up royalty checks instead of bills.[4]

Not all East Texas field producers shared the boom mentality. Those not compelled by poverty or immediate financial pressure to produce more oil at any price understood the long-term advantages of restricting output to conserve reservoir pressure, thereby enhancing ultimate recovery and profits. Local businessmen recognized that a "feast today, famine tomorrow" approach undermined long-range prosperity. Even many consumers realized that a lot of cheap gasoline today meant less and more expensive gasoline tomorrow.[5]

Overproduction in the East Texas field became a national issue. Its oil at 10 cents or less per barrel depressed crude prices through the country. Fear and demoralization gripped the American petroleum industry as crude oil prices fell far below production costs. Shell Oil director Frederick Godber described senior managers of major oil companies as "very depressed, almost panicky, and . . . nervous." Teagle of New Jersey Standard was "very pessimistic." Godber attributed the oil industry's problems "to known causes over which individuals have little or no control and which cannot be remedied until laws are passed in various producing states permitting enforcement of laws preventing waste and excessive drilling." But, he concluded, "There is much prejudice to overcome, particularly in Texas."[6]

The TRC blamed the "many suits . . . contesting orders especially as to the East Texas field" for preventing the imposition of "penalties . . . for violations . . . [while] operators are producing as they please." It "took months before the Supreme Court [could] decide the legal questions involved." The TRC warned Governor Ross Sterling, "The time will come when our oil and gas reserves will be greatly depleted or exhausted," and "if no cheap substitute is available, the calamity will be too serious to contemplate."[7]

Although the TRC was one of the state's most significant and enduring agencies, the uncertain legal status of prorationing undermined its ability to enforce production controls. The ease with which producers obtained injunctions further undermined its authority, encouraging many operators to simply ignore all regulations and produce at will. Politics also eroded the TRC's power. By the 1930s, the commission had become a sinecure for politicians at the twilight of their careers. A seat on the TRC allowed them to retain political influence and kept patronage at their disposal. Customarily, the governor would appoint one of the senior Democratic Party faithful to any vacancy on the commission, giving the appointee the advantage of incumbency in the next election. This process was standard fare in the one-party politics then prevalent in the South, ensuring maintenance of the status quo, since compliant incumbents were generally assured of a return to power. Most of the electorate remained disenfranchised. This explains, in part, why C. V. Terrell, Lon A. Smith, and Pat Neff—the commissioners in 1931— were indifferent to the pandemonium of the East Texas field.[8]

The TRC's lackadaisical pace was compounded by the traditional spoils system endemic to Texas politics. The three commissioners each hired a third of the TRC staff, often on the basis of personal acquaintance rather than merit. Ability to pull the right strings helped ensure employment. Usually, a father would ask a friend in public office—such as a judge, legislator, or commissioner—to help procure a job for a son recently graduated from college or law school. This entrenched process illustrates the persistence of antebellum Southern social customs such as paternalism, patronage, and *noblesse oblige* in early twentieth-century Texas. The spoils system was also evidenced in the hiring practices of Texas law firms such as Vinson & Elkins, and contributed to the kind of power and influence that Elkins wielded to benefit clients like Pure. Although patronage opened the door to upward mobility for many young aspirants, it did not always push the best and brightest to the top. For example, in 1930, the TRC employed only one engineer, and not a single geologist, to evaluate the technical data submitted by staff experts of major companies. Underpaid field inspectors earned less than $200 per month. Some accepted bribes. Incompetence and corruption eroded the respect the TRC needed to command before it could hope to enforce state oil-conservation laws. As elected politicians, railroad commissioners walked a thin line between political suicide and popular opinion. The TRC's precarious position was aggravated by the commissioners' refusal to part with the patronage that undermined their claim on general public confidence.[9]

Concern mounted as the price of East Texas field crude fell to 2 cents a barrel. Farish attributed the problem to the lack of market-demand prorationing. Large East Texas independents such as Charles F. Roeser, Tom Hunter, and J. S. Bridwell cooperated with the majors in endorsing a bill (H. R. 1052), introduced in the Texas House near the end of the regular session of the Forty-first Legislature, to legalize market-demand prorationing.[10]

East Texas Lease, Royalty & Producers' Association chairman Carl Estes attacked the bill, alleging that it would make the TRC "the executioners of every little independent operator in Texas." San Antonio

Independent Petroleum Association president Harry Pennington denounced the bill as an "economically unsound attempt at price fixing." Independent Tom Cranfill voiced the same concern on behalf of IPAT. And Joseph Danciger declared it "inconceivable" that "the oil industry . . . harbor[s] any members who could have got so dumb in so short a time as to believe that House Bill No. 1052 is a good thing for the independent producer." Strong opposition prevented the bill's passage during the waning days of the regular legislative session.[11]

Flagrant violations of TRC proration orders continued. Low crude oil prices spoiled the "easy money" dreams of many diehard antiprorationists. Disillusioned, they joined IPAA president Wirt Franklin in appealing to Governor Sterling to call a special session of the legislature to enact a more stringent oil conservation statute.[12] Sterling hesitated in order to give East Texas operators a chance to work out a voluntary solution. In a last-ditch attempt to stave off more government control, Cranfill promoted a "Texas Plan," which would limit East Texas field production to 200,000 barrels a day, to be increased up to 500,000 barrels daily as market demand permitted. Each 20-acre tract would be allowed to produce 300 barrels a day regardless of the number of wells on it. To help small producers, wells completed before June 10, 1931, could produce 300 barrels a day regardless of acreage, except on tracts under 20 acres, which would be limited to 600 barrels per day. A seven-member East Texas Oil Arbitration Committee would supervise the plan.[13]

Advocates touted the Cranfill plan as a way to allow East Texans to regulate themselves. However, the plan never received enough support to ensure its long-term success. Operators with tracts of 5 acres or fewer refused to trust in an arbitration committee. Producers favoring lower production allowables demanded a market-demand prorationing statute. Charles Roeser pointed out that the largest lease-holder in the field, Arkansas Fuel Company (a Cities Service subsidiary), refused to comply with the plan. Texas Oil Emergency Committee chairman W. L. Todd argued that the plan violated state antitrust laws. Roeser, Todd, and Penn called for a special session of the legislature to deal with the problem.[14] Penn told the API's Division of Petroleum Production, meeting in Dallas on June 7, "We have come here to sit at the bedside of a very sick patient." Discussion focused on whether Sterling should call a special legislative session. Anti-conservationists wanted to produce as much oil as they pleased, confident that they could still earn a profit despite low prices. Conservationists argued that state government had to stop the reckless waste of unreplenishable petroleum resources that formed the nation's "economic backbone."[15]

Despite mounting pressure to call a special session of the legislature, Sterling believed it politically imprudent to take precipitate action, since he had amassed a "great fortune" as past president of Humble. The matter was further complicated by what one observer called "the unrelenting passion for quick money that seems to rule among some people in Texas." Emotions ran high among thousands of small producers and land, royalty, and lease owners, who resisted any attempt to restrict their oil production. They were especially suspicious of the major oil companies, which had entered the East Texas field only after the wildcatters had discovered oil where the corporate geologists had insisted none existed. Estes turned their cause into a moral crusade. It was "high time" that independents "had their inning," he declared, and in a democracy, a landowner could use his property as he pleased without governmental interference. "Every one of you to a man," Estes reminded Texas politicians, "was bawling around from every stump in this state, preaching the doctrine of retrieving the little man, the home, and small farmers and busting the trusts. Well, this is your opportunity to make good on those sweet-sounding promises."[16]

On July 2, the TRC issued a new proration order embodying many features of the Cranfill plan. The East Texas field allowable was increased to 250,000 barrels a day, to be distributed among individual producers according to acreage. Forty-acre units, as utilized in the Van field, were essentially substituted for 20-acre tracts.[17]

How the substitution came about is unclear, but probably Elkins had a hand in the change. At Elkins's request, Powell had asked Parker to approve a change in the size of production units at Van from 20 to 40 acres. It is uncertain why Elkins wanted the change, but Parker soon notified him that the TRC had approved it, saying, "I hope that the amended rules are just what you wanted." Elkins possibly hoped that larger production units would reduce the proliferation of wells on smaller tracts, which had undermined the stability of Pure's unit operation at Van by necessitating costly offset drilling. The TRC likely acceded to Elkins's request without question because, by this time, it was willing to try anything to reduce drilling and production. The matter illustrated Elkins's ability to further his clients' interests without resorting to the protracted and costly litigation by others that added to the instability in the East Texas field.[18]

◆ ◆ ◆

While the Van field remained relatively stable and calm, Alfred E. MacMillan carried the fight of small East Texas producers into a lower federal court in Austin, where he filed suit to restrain enforcement of the TRC's proration order. MacMillan probably chose a federal rather than state forum because the state district court in Travis County, which had sole jurisdiction over suits against the TRC, had already upheld a TRC prorationing order in the Danciger case. Since MacMillan challenged the constitutionality of the state oil conservation statute, a three-judge federal court had to be impanelled. The trial took place in Austin on June 24.[19]

On behalf of MacMillan, Austin attorney Charles L. Black argued that the TRC's proration order deprived MacMillan of his property without due process of law, in violation of the Fourteenth Amendment; impaired MacMillan's obligations under contracts; unduly interfered with interstate commerce; and bore no reasonable relation to the statutory intent to prevent physical waste in oil production. Black maintained that the TRC had arbitrarily restricted production to market demand, in violation of state law, to raise the price of crude oil. He also alleged that prorationing had hurt market conditions in the East Texas field, and asked the court to enjoin enforcement of the TRC's orders against all operators there. The court recessed for 30 days.[20]

With the outcome pending, Humble on July 8 cut its posted per-barrel price for crude from the East Texas field to 10 cents. The next day, Shell slashed its price to 6 cents, a move followed by Sinclair, Stanolind, and Indiana Standard. Anti-prorationists denounced the price cuts as a conspiracy by major oil companies to achieve monopolistic control. Sterling instructed Texas Land Commissioner James H. Walker to refuse any royalty payments owed to the state that were based on the reduced crude oil prices. Declining oil prices wrecked state tax revenues and posed a budget deficit, a prospect that finally persuaded Sterling to call a special session of the legislature to convene on July 14.[21]

Conservationists urged the legislature to pass a market-demand prorationing statute. Pennington encouraged majors and independents to work out a voluntary solution, and warned Sterling that passage of another conservation law would set off an "avalanche" of lawsuits. Estes pressed his anti-prorationing crusade by asking Attorney General Allred to investigate the "real" causes of falling crude oil prices, reminding Allred that he "was elected on a platform as a 'trust-buster' and the current situation should give him some food for thought." All sides in the controversy prepared to wage heated battle in the special legislative session.[22]

The legislative battle broadened the debate over prorationing. Now the contest aimed to win legislators, lawyers, judges, and the general public—many of whom were not well versed in the problems peculiar to oil—to support a more disciplined approach to production. Their ignorance posed a serious obstacle to the oil industry's effort to gain legislative sanction for some kind of production controls. Suspicions as to the real intent of oil conservation had not been allayed. Anti-conservationists played upon Texans' traditional hostility to big business and government regulation. Historically, Texans as a group had rarely welcomed government intervention. Farmers in non-oil-producing regions opposed anything that would raise gasoline prices so long as wheat and cotton prices remained depressed. In short, classical economics remained popular, especially among small independent oilmen. They responded to the warning that unrestrained competition would eventually kill them off by proudly proclaiming, "not as long as a single independent lives and breathes."[23]

This highly emotional state of affairs greeted the Texas legislature when it convened in special session on July 14. One poll indicated that a majority of legislators favored more stringent oil conservation laws, but disagreed over the specifics. Sterling wanted a new conservation commission armed with broad powers to enforce state regulations in all natural resources. Senator Walter C. Woodward and Representative R. M. Wagstaff Bill introduced identical bills that provided for a new natural resources commission and specifically authorized market-demand prorationing. The Woodward and Wagstaff bills were supported by large producers and major companies such as Humble, which took the position that market-demand prorationing was essential to any sound and effective oil conservation program. Small independents attacked the bills as a mere monopolistic, price-fixing scheme to promote the interests of large producers.[24]

Pure, with a vested interest in the pending legislation, continued to rely on Vinson & Elkins for advice. Robert Shepherd, in briefing James Elkins on the matter, summed up the legislative proposals as "entirely too drastic, and giving the Railroad Commission too much power over private business interests," such as the authority "to issue practically any order and assume practically any power with reference to the production, transportation, and marketing of oil and gas." Shepherd specifically objected to provisions allowing the TRC "to inquire into market requirements in . . . determining how much production shall be allowed," which effectively empowered it to "fix the price of oil and gas" and to regulate "the refining and manufacturing ends of the business." He was particularly concerned about another provision protecting marginal wells. Shepherd warned Elkins that the TRC could use this power to cut Pure's Van allowable in half to allocate more production to small producers on the ground that it would "not hurt the [larger producing] wells to cut down their production and keep the oil in storage underground, while if the small pumpers are shut in, they will be ruined or abandoned and the oil which could have been recovered from them will be lost forever."[25]

Shepherd was also concerned about a proposed law to prevent the filing of a *supersedeas* bond staying the effect of any TRC rule or order, upheld by a trial court, pending the outcome of an appeal. He believed such a law would give a trial court judgment the effect of an injunction pending the appellate court's final decision. The proposed bills further required that production in excess of any TRC order subsequently upheld by the courts must be deducted from the violator's future allowable. Shepherd feared that one provision giving operators the right to sue one another for violating TRC orders "would certainly increase the hazard of vexatious litigation . . . against any operator who . . . was thought to have violated any rule of the Railroad Commission." Regardless of how hard operators tried to comply with TRC orders, it was often impossible to keep from violating them, he explained, and "any operator . . . could give any other operator a world of trouble and put them to considerable expense."[26]

A majority of legislators appeared to favor market-demand prorationing. The minority opposition successfully employed the old tactic of calling for an investigation, thus delaying action and clouding the issues. On July 16, the legislature adopted a resolution directing the attorney general to investigate all phases of the Texas petroleum industry for possible antitrust violations. The House, acting as a committee of the whole, conducted its own investigation, and summoned oil industry leaders for questioning. Alvin Richards, Pure's in-house legal counsel, asked Elkins to advise him as to "what is actually going on as distinguished from what is reported in the press." Elkins assured Richards that he was "keeping in close touch with legislative matters relative to proration" and that "the Governor has informed leaders of the Senate and House that he is utterly opposed to any bill which has the effect of price-fixing." He also told Richards that "little can be done by the legislature . . . except to strengthen the penalties for violation of our present law unless the legislature in effect repeals the antitrust laws of this state," which he did not think it would do. Elkins predicted that the legislature would "throw as many safeguards as possible around the prevention of actual waste with the provision that it is not contemplated that such bill shall relate to or affect economic waste." Richards reminded Elkins that "the oil industry wants only such legislation as will protect it in times of distress and leave it free during ordinary times."[27]

The legislative probe, as expected, was filled with emotion and prejudice. One legislator referred to Farish, a keynote witness, as "the little boy of the Standard Oil Company of New Jersey." Farish, denying that major oil companies had conspired to fix prices and monopolize the industry, stated his support for the creation of a new conservation commission comprising businessmen and technicians with experience in the oil business. Danciger reiterated his opposition to prorationing, and belittled engineers and geologists as mere "theorists and fourflushers."[28]

In the midst of the brouhaha over oil, Judge Joseph C. Hutcheson, Jr., announced the decision of the three-judge panel in the *MacMillan* case on July 24. "When a subordinated body like the railroad commission of Texas undertakes to deal in a broadly restrictive way with the right of the citizen to produce oil which under the laws of the state he owns," Hutcheson held, "it must be prepared to answer the imperious query: 'Is it not lawful for me to do what I will with my own?'" Under the "thinly veiled pretense of going about to prevent physical waste," he found the TRC had, "in cooperation with persons interested in raising and maintaining prices of oil and its refined products, set on foot a plan . . . to control the delicate adjustment of market supply and demand, in order to bring and keep oil prices up." Hutcheson struck down the TRC's proration order for the East Texas field as bearing no reasonable relation to the prevention of physical waste and as usurping undelegated legislative power to arbitrarily "control the output, price, and market for crude oil by reducing the supply of oil to the demand for it."[29]

Sidestepping the constitutionality of the state oil conservation statute, Hutcheson's ruling, was in effect premised on Charles Black's contention that the state could enforce conservation laws as long as it did not unreasonably interfere with the mechanics of the free market. Hutcheson's opinion was not closely reasoned. Acknowledging the chaotic condition of the oil industry as evidenced "in hearing after hearing before committees, public bodies, and courts in oil-producing states . . . and daily appearing in countless articles and interviews," Hutcheson added, "Indeed, so importantly has . . . proration as the cure for market glut been advanced, so currently and so widely debated as a matter of public concern has the necessity for its adoption been, so known to every man, that this court could fairly take judicial cognizance of the matters disclosed by the evidence." Yet, despite taking judicial notice of the peculiar problem of oil, and of scientific and technological advances in petroleum production that prevented physical waste by prolonging reservoir life and enhancing ultimate recovery, Hutcheson dismissed such evidence as "largely theory and speculation." How did he arrive at such a contradictory conclusion?[30]

Hutcheson was "in many ways a man of the nineteenth century, believing implicitly in the importance of the individual and individual rights." Admitted to the bar in 1900, Hutcheson became a lawyer at a time when, according to Arnold M. Paul, the judiciary had emerged as the principal bulwark of laissez-faire conservatism. "By the 1890s . . . in a time of social crisis, when rampant populism might threaten the established order," Paul wrote, the judiciary acted as a counterweight to increasing legislative power and as defender of minority rights against majority will, protecting individual private property against the overreaching arm of the state. Due process of law, once primarily procedural, became a substantive check against government regulation and "promot[ed] the advancement of judicial supremacy and . . . the enshrinement of laissez-faire philosophy in constitutional law." In Paul's view, the neo-Federalism of the 1890s paved the way for judicial obstructionism in succeeding decades.[31]

The Supreme Court's landmark decision in *Swift v. Tyson* in 1842 had permitted federal judges to decide cases, absent state statutes, according to the common law. Federal judges thereby gained the power to shape decisions according to their own ideologies and conceptions of the common law. Hutcheson's ruling in the *MacMillan* case is easier to understand in this context. Although he took judicial notice of the severity of oil overproduction and the state's power to enforce conservation, Hutcheson's judicial ideology obligated him to scrutinize the TRC's regulations strictly. They must impose no unreasonable governmental restraints on the use of privately owned petroleum. Generally, jurists such as Hutcheson favored private property over the public interest in regulation, except in dire emergencies.[32]

The situation illustrated the classic tension between constitutional guarantees of private property rights and government action to safeguard the public welfare. Judges such as Hutcheson recognized and respected both doctrines as protecting basic rights, and fashioned the "rule of reasonableness" to reconcile conflicts between the two. They struck down any regulations they believed arbitrarily and unreasonably interfered with private property. There being no statutory definition of what was reasonable, the judges had broad leeway to resolve conflicts between private and public rights according to their own ideology. Hutcheson's *MacMillan* decision illustrates how often judicial attitudes used the power of judicial review to the detriment of the public interest. In *MacMillan*, Hutcheson's ideology, and possibly his ego, led him to dismiss scientific and technological progress as theory and speculation. But he took judicial notice of evidence to the contrary, in a costly example of the way judicial arrogance and vanity facilitated the waste of an inestimable amount of vital and unreplenishable petroleum natural resources.[33]

Texas Company attorney Jacob F. Wolters noted that Hutcheson had not ruled that market-demand prorationing was invalid, but only that state law had not authorized the TRC to consider economic factors in regulating production. Wolters believed that Hutcheson's ruling clearly implied that the Texas legislature could revise the state oil conservation statute to authorize market-demand prorationing. "Such a provision does not provide for the fixing of price, it merely endeavors to prevent an economic waste as the result of which thousands of small oil wells must shut down with consequent permanent loss of oil," he pointed out. Also ensuing would be "the bankruptcy of producers, the loss of millions of dollars in revenues of the State, and the consequent increase of taxes on other sources in order that the public schools, higher institutions of learning, eleemosynary institutions and the departments of the State may continue to function."[34]

With the dog days of August approaching, the *MacMillan* decision did nothing to cool flaring tempers in the legislature. As runaway production continued in the East Texas field, Governor Sterling took his cue from Hutcheson and threatened to veto any market-demand prorationing bill. "If our laws permit the Railroad Commission to prohibit the production of oil in excess of market demand," the governor declared, "it would tend to bring about a condition where the oil interests in this state might create a monopoly." Sterling realized that his veto threat ran counter to the philosophy he shared with his former colleagues at Humble. Major oil company executives had long advocated market-demand prorationing as the only viable way to limit production so that supply did not exceed demand and result in waste. They countered charges of price-fixing with the argument that any effect on prices was incidental to the more important goal of conservation. Moreover, Humble had advanced Sterling a $175,000 bonus on a lease and $250,000 in deferred royalties right before his election campaign in 1930.[35]

The fortunes of the entire petroleum industry were riding on the outcome of the special legislative session, a worrisome thought given the legislature's reputation for infighting and delay. Deep and bitter divisions in both houses killed the Wagstaff-Woodward bill. The Senate adopted a substitute measure, submitted by Senator Frank Rawlings, that omitted market-demand prorationing and reduced the TRC's enforcement powers. Wagstaff predicted that passage of the Rawlings bill would invite continued lawlessness in the East Texas field.[36]

Exasperated, Sterling hinted that he might declare martial law in the East Texas field "to protect the oil people from having the conservation laws trampled under foot." He threatened to veto the Rawlings bill as being too weak and "wholly unacceptable." Sterling reminded legislators that they had been called into special session to strengthen, not weaken, state conservation laws, and that "the nation is looking anxiously to Texas to remedy the chaotic situation existing within her borders." He produced a hundred telegrams, bearing the signatures of 500 oilmen and chambers of commerce throughout Texas, opposing the Rawlings measure in favor of the Wagstaff-Woodward bill and commending his promise to restore order in the East Texas field through martial law if necessary.[37]

J. F. Cunningham of Abilene, whose son Oliver was a state senator, raised the lone cry as to the constitutionality of invoking martial law to control oil production. Independent oilman Sam Kruger of Wichita Falls asked Sterling to "stop [the] thieving of East Texas oil." Oklahoma governor Murray sent Charles West, a former attorney general of that state, to ask Sterling what he planned to do to stop the reckless overproduction. Murray had imposed martial law in the Oklahoma City and Seminole oil fields on August 4. West advised Sterling that the common law, along with implied executive powers, furnished adequate legal authority to declare martial law. Joseph M. Dixon, acting U.S.

Secretary of the Interior, blamed the oil industry's problems entirely on "Texas, its Legislature, and selfish and irresponsible interests operating in the East Texas pool."[38]

As pressure and criticism mounted, the legislature referred the Rawlings bill to a conference committee for resolution. Wagstaff warned that the bill would undermine the TRC's authority and relegate Texas oil fields to "those dissipating gas into the air in incredible quantities." Wolters told legislators that if they refused to permit proration against overproduction "Texas will see dark days . . . [and] 120 counties will default their bonds." Gulf general counsel John E. Green reiterated his company's opposition to government regulation of the industry.[39]

Lawyers, advancing the interests of their oil clients in the legislature, accentuated existing prejudices and emotions, ensuring that the drama over production controls would be played out in stereotypical Texas brawling style. As legal counsel to a group of independents opposed to prorationing, Moody labelled conservationists such as Penn as stooges of the major oil companies. Penn challenged Moody to a fistfight. Carl Estes, undeterred by his age and an ulcerated stomach that had left him on crutches, waved a crutch at Penn and shouted, "Come on, you son-of-a-bitch, I'll knock your brains out!"[40]

Pure Oil general counsel Alvin Richards confided to James Elkins his fears that market-demand proration would clothe the TRC with absolute authority "to control and run the oil business for some time to come." Government meddling in the oil industry had convinced Richards of the need to eliminate political influence as soon as possible. He believed that legislative investigations diverted lawmakers' time and attention from considering the actual problems of the industry.[41]

During this same period, Attorney General Allred tentatively investigated Pure's Van unit operation for possible antitrust violations. Voluntary unitization agreements, *per se*, violated the Texas Antitrust Act, which had not been revised since its enactment in 1889. Elkins turned over copies of the Van unitization agreement, explaining that it neither limited production nor attempted to affect or influence crude oil prices, but merely guaranteed each partner a proportionate share of the production allowable assigned by the TRC. Elkins also offered to furnish Allred with the minutes of the Van unit operating committee's proceedings. Allred thanked Elkins for his cooperation, declined the proffered minutes, and pursued his investigation no further. Elkins had saved the day again for Pure.[42]

Other companies were not so fortunate. On November 12, 1931, Allred filed an antitrust suit against 15 major oil companies operating in Texas. He charged that these companies had conspired to systematically acquire all independent filling stations in Texas by fixing the prices of wholesale gasoline and service station equipment, in an attempt to eliminate competition and monopolize the marketing branch of the petroleum industry. Allred alleged that the "code of fair practices" under which the companies operated, though approved by the Federal Trade Commission (FTC), was illegal.[43]

Although company executives scoffed at the suit, accusing Allred of seeking publicity to further gubernatorial ambitions, many Texans were pleased by his attacks on the big oil companies. Allred declared that the FTC had no authority to approve violations of Texas antitrust laws, and suggested that this was not the first time that a "bunch of Republicans in high federal office" had sanctioned illegal activities, reminding his audience of the "looting of Teapot Dome." *New York Times* correspondent Irvin S. Taubkin opined that Allred was merely following traditional Texas politics in "shaking the big stick at the 'trusts.' "[44]

Though the major companies eventually won the lawsuit (in November, 1932), Allred's decision not to include Pure in his suit was significant. Pure had been supplying crude oil to Standard's subsidiary Humble, which was also one of Pure's Van unit partners. Pure likely escaped antitrust prosecution because Allred's suit was aimed at marketing activities, of which Pure had none in Texas. Elkins's political ties to Allred probably played a role in influencing the attorney general's actions. Elkins would be a formidable ally or enemy in Allred's quest for the governorship. In this context, Allred's suit provides another example of Elkins's subtle influence.[45]

As lawyers and legislators exchanged blows over proposed oil conservation laws, conditions in the East Texas field continued to degenerate. One observer was appalled by "shyster lawyers, two-bit politicians, and other home-grown scalawags" who cheated and connived gullible East Texas farmers out of their croplands and fortunes, and "framed, maligned, and even plotted the murder of anyone bold enough to stand up to their unprincipled drive for wealth and power." With each passing day and each new well, crude oil prices dropped as small operators produced ever more in a self-defeating attempt to stay financially afloat.[46]

On August 11, 1931, the legislative conference committee hammered out a compromise oil conservation bill that passed both houses and was signed by Governor Sterling. The so-called Anti-Market Demand Act eliminated the Wagstaff-Woodward provision for a new conservation commission and strengthened the TRC's authority to eliminate virtually every kind of physical waste in petroleum production. It defined physical waste to include excessive gas-oil ratio, underground waste caused by water intrusion, waste of natural gas, and waste incident to inequitable utilization of the natural gas and water drive resulting from inequitable production. But the new act specified that waste "shall not be construed to mean economic waste, and the Commission shall not have the power to attempt, by order or otherwise, directly or indirectly, to limit the production of oil to equal the existing market demand for oil, and the power is expressly withheld from the Commission." It retained the maximum $1,000 per day fine for violations.[47]

The Anti-Market Demand Act provided that any violation of a TRC order sustained by the courts subjected the violator to receivership. Any party suffering harm could sue a violator for damages. To alleviate the judicial backlog of proration cases, the new act prohibited injunctions against TRC orders without notice, and provided for a court hearing at which the judge would set bond for a complainant sufficient in amount to indemnify all persons who might suffer damages. Suits against the TRC and appeals from its judgments would be advanced for trial as expeditiously as possible. Elkins advised Pure management that the new provision requiring notice to all interested parties before enjoining any TRC order had obviously been designed to prevent small operators from securing injunctions from local elected judges in *ex parte* hearings.[48]

The extent to which the *MacMillan* decision and Sterling's veto threat influenced the anti-market demand feature of the new act is uncertain. To be sure, the Anti-Market Demand Act acceded to both Hutcheson's ruling and Sterling's desire to eliminate economic considerations from regulating petroleum production. Sterling never comprehended the relationship between limiting oil production to market demand and preventing physical waste, despite recent rulings by Oklahoma and Texas courts that had found such a nexus. Market-demand advocates were pessimistic about the probable success of the new law unless judges changed their skeptical view of scientific and technological progress. They hoped that appellate courts would review TRC orders by the same standard as other cases with conflicting evidence, and accord any benefit of doubt to the TRC.

Major oil companies viewed the Anti-Market Demand Act as a mixed blessing. While less stringent than they had hoped, it was also less susceptible to invalidation in the courts. One anonymous major oil executive hailed the new act as "the most helpful single item toward stabilizing the oil industry that has taken place this year," adding, "It seems reasonable to expect that within the next thirty days we should have fairly satisfactory prices for both crude oil and refined products." East Texas field production was expected to be reduced by a much as 300,000 barrels a day, while total state production would be cut 20 percent.[49]

Farish denigrated the Anti-Market Demand Act for failing to provide "direct authorization . . . to effectively prorate any individual field." His concern was well-founded. The new act not only prohibited statewide prorationing but annulled all prior oil conservation statutes. Until the TRC issued new rules and regulations under the guidelines of the new statute, Texas fields were free from all production controls. During the week of August 16, 1931, Texas production exceeded a million barrels a day, and the TRC did not expect to issue new proration orders before September 1. Still, Farish and other leading oilmen were willing to give the new law a chance to succeed.[50]

Pure management was less optimistic. Texas production manager B. S. SoRelle expressed concern over the legal status of field umpires and advisory committees under Section 18 of the Anti-Market Demand Act. Assistant Attorney General Upchurch advised Richard Parker of the TRC that Section 18 mandated the use of regular state employees to enforce TRC rules and regulations in the field. This meant that the TRC would no longer rely on privately subsidized field umpires and advisory committees to enforce prorationing. Parker doubted that the state-employee pay scale was sufficient enough to retain existing umpires and committeemen. As the TRC had not yet formulated a hiring policy, he suggested that existing umpires and committeemen continue as usual. Oilmen were upset at losing their influence over those responsible for administering and enforcing prorationing, who were about to become paid agents of the state. This loss of influence, individual oilmen feared, would hurt their respective production allowables. Elkins's apparent silence on the topic may indicate that he sensed some advantage for Pure under the new law.[51]

By mid-August, East Texas field production averaged one million barrels a day, a third of the nation's domestic needs. On August 15, there were 1,600 oil wells on 93,000 proven acres in the East Texas field. The *MacMillan* decision had eased producers' fears of incurring legal liabili-

ties and penalties for violating TRC proration orders, and they ran their
wells wide open. Major oil companies quit posting prices for East Texas
field crude, but American producers could boast of one accomplishment:
Domestic oil was now cheap enough to undersell Russian crude in foreign markets. No immediate relief was in sight, and oilmen anxiously
awaited issuance of new TRC orders under the Anti-Market Demand
Act. As the August heat wore on, tempers flared. Threats proliferated
of dynamiting oil wells and pipelines. One disgruntled operator complained, "Hell, I sell a barrel of oil at ten cents and a bowl of chili costs
me fifteen."[52]

The glut exacerbated a difficult situation in Oklahoma. Governor
Murray announced that martial law would remain in effect in the Oklahoma City and Seminole fields until crude oil rose to a dollar per barrel. A group of East Texas producers congratulated Murray, lamenting
"that the same fine character of leadership and courage has not been
shown in the State of Texas." They were joined by many other operators, who were alarmed over increasing threats that their wells, pipelines, and storage tanks would be blown up.[53]

On August 14, some 1,200 petroleum producers and land, lease, and
royalty owners gathered in Tyler for what acting chairman Captain J.
F. Lucey hailed as the most important oil industry meeting ever held
in Texas. They debated whether to ask Sterling to invoke martial law
in four East Texas oil-producing counties: Gregg, Rusk, Smith, and
Upshur. A heated discussion degenerated into outbursts of disorder and
violence. S. A. Guiberson, Jr., the "shutdown movement" steering committee chairman, denounced the sale of millions of barrels of East Texas
field crude at ridiculously low prices as the "largest steal in the history
of the industry." He listed three alternatives for controlling production:
by law; through state administrative regulation; or "by a governor with
a backbone." API executive vice-president W. R. Boyd, Jr., warned East
Texas field producers that persistent overproduction would wreck the
entire industry and bankrupt 95 percent of the nation's independents.
Judge W. N. Stokes, whose Slick Oil Company had voluntarily shut down
111 oil wells in the Oklahoma City field, urged Texas producers to do
likewise until crude oil prices recovered.[54]

Mexia district attorney Sam McCorkle advised producers to form
partnerships to market their oil collectively at higher prices. He assured his audience that this arrangement would not violate Texas
antitrust law. Dallas oilman H. L. Hunt, who was chairman of the cur-

tailment committee (though not yet the colorful, controversial public figure he would eventually become), opposed use of martial law to shut down the East Texas field. (Hunt possessed substantial lease acreage there.) Despite Hunt's plea to give the TRC a chance to restore order under the new oil conservation statute, the convention unanimously adopted a resolution asking Sterling to invoke martial law in the East Texas field.[55]

As pressure mounted on Sterling to act, the TRC held hearings in Austin to solicit information and advice on formulating a new proration plan for the East Texas field. The OSAC postponed a meeting, scheduled for August 24 in Denver, until the TRC issued a new order. While the TRC deliberated, a flood of petitions from inside and outside the state convinced Sterling to declare martial law in the East Texas oil field. As of 6 A.M. on August 17, 1931, all oil wells in Gregg, Rusk, Smith, and Upshur counties were to be shut down. The Texas National Guard's Brigadier General Jacob F. Wolters (who was also the Texas Company's legal counsel) would command a 1,300-man militia unit in taking charge of the East Texas field.[56]

Sterling defended his act on the grounds that "a state of insurrection, tumult, and riot and breach of peace exist [in East Texas] . . . which threaten to spread to other oil and gas fields where operators are still obeying the law." He cited the existence of "an organized and entrenched group of oil . . . producers in East Texas oil field . . . who are in a state of insurrection against the conservation laws of the state" and "in open rebellion against the efforts of constituted civil authorities . . . to enforce such laws." Sterling displayed 19 petitions, signed by a thousand East Texas oilmen, requesting martial law. Local sheriffs had complained to the governor about the lack of legal authority and manpower to enforce prorationing. Sterling hoped that martial law would buy the TRC time to issue a new proration order.[57]

Wolters wasted no time. At 7:16 A.M. on August 17, the first contingent of 1,104 soldiers and 99 officers in Texas National Guard Troop A of the 124th Cavalry marched into the anxious town of Kilgore. They bivouacked outside of town on "Proration Hill." There were no reported hostilities as the word spread like prairie fire across the 2,815 square miles of oil country that all wells had to be shut down by noon on August 18. "It's jail for those who haven't quit," Wolters warned a crowd of protesting producers, reminding them that "ignorance of the law was no excuse" for disobeying the shutdown order. Wolters boasted that his authority was "beyond the courts," and vowed to arrest and incarcerate violators until the lifting of martial law since "it would be folly to release prisoners of war and let them go back to the firing line."[58]

As a goodwill gesture, Wolters ordered a military band to entertain the residents of local towns and oil camps, saying, "I trust our wives and sweethearts are busy at home knitting sweaters and making fudge." He was disturbed by certain "painted women" gallivanting around in "beach pajamas" and distracting militiamen, who had "their duties" to perform. Wolters banned the attire, pointing out that the nearest beach was over a hundred miles away. Young lovers who courted near the Tyler airfield complained about gawking soldiers, who were supposed to be guarding military aircraft. Wolters informed them that "the war could not bend itself to the whims of the lovelorn."[59]

Sterling claimed that a majority of letters, telegrams, and petitions from oilmen commended the imposition of martial law. API vice-president Boyd lauded the governor's action as "that of a statesman . . . He is to be congratulated." API president E. B. Reeser told Sterling, "The personal feelings and selfish interests of a comparatively few operators had completely demoralized the industry, resulting in great physical as well as economic waste." Elkins also congratulated Sterling, assuring him of his support and cooperation. Standard executive Teagle insisted that martial law was necessary to curb overproduction in the East Texas field and reverse its impact on petroleum prices.[60]

Small independents vehemently expressed a different view. The lost income from the shutdown barred them from drilling additional wells that might offset the majors' and large independents' greater production on their larger acreage. Landowners missed royalty payments. Wolters banned protest meetings, which were then held in secret. Hundreds of defiant operators gathered near Palestine to hear a speaker protest, "[With] the national guard on duty . . . like watchdogs . . . the major companies are drilling night and day to sink new wells into the pool that the independents discovered and developed." State Representative Bailey Hardy of Dallas introduced a resolution in the Texas House demanding that Sterling cite legal authority for his decree. He hinted at possible impeachment proceedings. Representative Pat Dwyer of San Antonio accused Hardy of "just trying to get newspaper notoriety" as the House voted down his resolution amidst a chorus of noes.[61]

With the East Texas field under military occupation, the TRC issued a new proration order on September 2, limiting production to 400,000 barrels a day there. Individual wells were allocated a maximum of 225 barrels production per day. Commissioner Neff opposed the per-well allocation formula, fearing it would "start a race to see who could drill wells the fastest" and result "in an orgy of drilling day and night." Sterling stated that the TRC's order would put "the little fellow out of business because he hasn't the money like big operators to drill more wells," and vowed the order would not go into effect without his approval. The governor had been informed that some 250 new wells per week would be added to the existing 1,750 wells in the East Texas field should the TRC's order take effect.[62]

Despite Sterling's opposition, the TRC order took effect at 7 A.M. on September 5, and was enforced by military rule. The valves on some 1,800 East Texas field wells were turned, and oil flowed once again, but at a reduced rate of 225 barrels per well each day. Under controlled conditions, the per-barrel price of crude from the East Texas field rose from a low of 2 cents to 85 cents. A similar trend was experienced throughout the country as crude oil prices rose while total stocks declined.

But the calm and order did not last long. As critics predicted, the TRC's flat per-well allocation formula, which omitted consideration of acreage and well-potential, unleashed a wild drilling spree. The TRC tried to correct the problem by issuing one revised proration order after another, reducing the daily per-well allowable first to 185 barrels on September 18, then to 165 barrels on October 13. Despite the troops, defiant operators managed to produce oil in excess of TRC orders.[63]

The TRC's authority and prestige had been tarnished by past allegations of corruption. In compliance with the new regulation classifying field umpires and advisory committeemen as state employees, the TRC sent special investigators into the East Texas field to search for violators. Small operators suspected these investigators of being bribed by the majors. Honest investigators noticed some of their colleagues "riding around in big cars and carrying substantial bank accounts." One TRC investigator felt "like a dumb cluck" until "the next hot oil runner [i.e., bootlegger] who asked me to look the other way and slipped me a big bill found me looking the other way. From then on my income was never less than five hundred a month." Majors and independents accused one another of bribing officials. Though some independents were unquestionably defying production quotas, the majors' hands were not clean either. Tired of charges of corruption, the TRC in December abdicated responsibility for enforcing production controls to the military.[64]

Complications in the East Texas field had overshadowed conditions in other Texas fields, where operators—who realized that overproduction would only worsen a bad situation—appeared to be obeying TRC orders. Despite corruption and enforcement problems, martial law had curtailed production in the East Texas field sufficiently to halt the decline in reservoir pressure and boost crude oil prices. Most Texas oilmen applauded the results, though they looked forward to the end of military occupation and a resumption of TRC control.[65]

Others, less accommodating, would soon take the TRC, the governor, and the military to court. Depressed and dispirited by the proration battle, an independent seeking solace in church dozed off, only to be awakened by the preacher's exhortation, "Oh, Lord, bless the *Pure* and *Humble*." The startled independent jumped up and shouted, "Hold on there, parson! Us independents are still in this fight, and I want you to put in a word for us."[66]

CHAPTER 7

Sword or Constitution?

*Whatever the final judgment of legal technicians
may be, public sentiment is disposed to react favorably
to its rulers who regard the obligations to observe
the functions of the State of greater moment
than forms and technicalities of law.*

—Earl Oliver

The year 1932 threatened to prove as bleak as its predecessor for the petroleum industry. Irreconcilable differences between large and small producers had led to martial law in the East Texas field, with the legal status of prorationing still uncertain. Overproduction would have been easier to solve had most American petroleum resources been state-owned. But under the U.S. constitutional and legal system, due process of law protected life, liberty, and property—including petroleum—against overreaching by the state. Judicial review of legislative and executive actions made regulation difficult and slow to effect, especially where it intruded on private property rights. Americans nevertheless preferred this system to the dictatorships they read and heard of elsewhere on the globe as they relied on lawyers to guide them through the maze of due process.[1]

The social disorder and waste of resources attendant upon the East Texas field's acute overproduction in 1931 was comparable to the great 1871 Chicago fire, Galveston's hurricane of 1900, and San Francisco's 1906 earthquake, but—being less spectacular—went unnoticed by most of the populace. Public interest was not broadly aroused by natural gas escaping into the open air, or by the daily loss of underground oil equivalent to a thousand burning gushers. This disaster, though it squandered natural resources, had been largely manmade. Confounded by unique legal and technical issues, lawmakers had imposed inadequate solutions. The problem had been further complicated by numerous lawsuits, filed by producers who objected to governmental interference in their business affairs. Ensuing litigation hindered state legislative efforts to alleviate overproduction. Ultimately the problem, and the ensuing social chaos, had gotten so out of hand that Governor Sterling had been compelled in August to call out the militia to restore order in East Texas.[2]

An increasing number of oilmen and public officials realized that existing laws dealt inadequately with the magnitude and uniqueness of the petroleum problem. New laws would be subject to review by judges who had to balance conflicting public and private interests. Yet, though scientific and engineering advances in production technology filled the pages of trade and legal journals and local newspapers, they failed to impress many judges, such as Hutcheson, who chose to maintain the status quo. With the East Texas field under martial law, oilmen wondered whether the sword or the constitution would rule their household.[3]

Attorney Earl Oliver pointed to communism and fascism as "mere present day examples of the direct action that society takes, and has always taken, to correct its ills when the regular established procedure becomes too slow and cumbersome." The crisis in the East Texas field demonstrated the necessity for action to avert complete chaos and the destruction of vital petroleum resources. "Before we condemn indiscriminately all assumptions of dictatorial power," Oliver said in reference to martial law in East Texas, "it is well that we ascertain whether there are in fact existing due processes of law by which grave crises might be avoided." He asked, "What is a chief executive to do when faced with such a situation?"[4]

In lieu of the finders-keepers law occasioned by the rule of capture, Dawes suggested, production in all oil fields should be unitized as Pure had successfully done at Van. Continental Oil president D. J. Moran complained that too many oilmen were living in the past—not realizing, or refusing to admit, that petroleum had "passed through a revolution . . . in which brains and science [had] vanquished luck and brawn." API president E. B. Reeser advocated prorationing because free-market forces did not apply neatly to petroleum. It could not be renewed, as cotton, wheat, sugar, and rubber could be even if an entire crop was wasted or destroyed.[5]

"If an inhabitant from Mars . . . were to visit us," William Farish chided, "he could hardly escape a feeling of bewilderment if not actual dismay at the manner we earthlings carry on this great enterprise, so essential to our convenience and welfare." He called for adequate laws "requiring the performance of those things which science and engineering have found to be essential to conservation, to efficient oil production, and to the protection of the correlative rights of the common owners of an oil pool."[6]

Anyone who assumed "that by ruthlessly crushing the weaker units the excesses of production can be curbed is tragically mistaken," Sun vice-president J. Edgar Pew argued. "It would drive out all those splendid forces of adventure, initiative, individual effort, and bull-necked courage on which the industry depends for finding the hidden stores of crude." He added, "To seek salvation that way, would be about as wise as Noah would have been if, instead of building the Ark, he had started work on an irrigation system."[7]

The theory that demand determines supply, and that the two eventually balance each other, was, according to Pew, "a good enough generalization for the economist thinking in the absolute zero of a perfect vacuum." He believed the oil industry had been straddled by statutes and injunctions that were as responsive to supply and demand "as Sir Isaac Newton's apple was to the gravitational pull of the planet Neptune." The time was ripe for an alternative to the rule of capture since science had proven that "the only 'rivers of oil' in motion under a property [were] those created by the extraction of oil itself." Pew could not understand how reasonable contemporary oilmen could countenance "legalized piracy." Game laws restricted hunters to preserve wildlife. "Should not the game hog in oil, who is destroying hundreds of millions of dollars in value, likewise be controlled?" Pew likened the rule of capture to Dr. Frankenstein's monster, a creature "which bids fair to ruin its creator and destroy a most important national resource."[8]

Claiming to speak for a majority of large and small independents,

J. R. Parten, who succeeded Tom Cranfill as IPAT president in 1932, insisted "that the only way to the return of prosperity and normalcy in the oil business is through the medium of free operation of that time-honored economic law that supply and demand must govern." Although they favored higher prices and stabilization, Parten and his independent followers opposed state and federal production controls, fearing they would lead to monopoly by the majors. IPAT, portraying itself as the protector of the "little man" against corporate wealth and power, drew the line at production controls.[9]

In response, the newly formed Texas Oil and Gas Conservation Association (TOGCA) represented Texas independents who supported the majors' demand for market-demand prorationing. Organized in Dallas on September 12, 1931, TOGCA attracted from across the state small and large independents who blamed their economic woes on overproduction in the East Texas field. They had become disenchanted with IPAT, which was by now a voice of resistance to market-demand prorationing and compulsory unitization. Through its bimonthly newsletter, the *Conservationist,* TOGCA condemned the TRC for "writing the worst law possible" for the East Texas field, and called for the creation of a new, appointed oil and gas commission. IPAT and TOGCA were soon embroiled in a free-for-all as to who was the voice of independents. TOGCA president Charles Roeser viewed the fight not as a struggle of majors versus independents, but as between independents and majors who desired order and stability versus those who opposed any form of conservation.[10]

"Now is the time to stop preaching," declared Robert Penn; it was time to change the law to permit market-demand prorationing. He attributed the industry's plight to the rule of capture. "With the unwise practices of men as with the convulsions and disaster of nature," Penn quoted from John Stuart Mill's *Principles of Political Economy,* "the longer they remain unrepaired the greater become the obstacles to repairing them."[11] Penn argued that the law should afford as much protection to the public interest in petroleum as it did to private property.[12]

Tulsa attorney Henry M. Gray blamed the petroleum problem on greed, ignorance, and an inadequate legal system. He charged that state judges, "perhaps more concerned with local crowd emotion and the next election than with the correctness of the law, or the good of the state, and nation," were thwarting efforts to enforce conservation. "Were it not for the doubtful wisdom of men long since dead," Gray mused, "society could protect itself by any measures believed to be expedient."

Judges had wide latitude to interpret constitutional restraints, framed in broad and general language, according to their ideologies. As Hutcheson had demonstrated in *MacMillan*, the more novel the remedy, the less likely it would survive judicial scrutiny. Gray believed that experimentation was as essential to the progress of law as anything else.[13]

Prior court decisions sustaining municipal zoning laws, Gray insisted, offered legal precedents sustaining governmental restriction against the use of private property in a way that harmed the public interest. Because petroleum was vital to the nation's defense and economic well-being, Gray argued, the oil industry affected a public interest, and was subject to government regulation.[14]

Gray hoped that "society [was] not so helpless against the local judge menace that it [could] not prevent legitimate power from degenerating into a matter of arbitrary license." He advocated compulsory unitization as the most effective and practical remedy to overproduction, and believed its constitutionality could be sustained on the same basis as irrigation, drainage, and municipal public improvement districts. Supreme Court rulings in *Ohio Oil Company v. Indiana* (upholding use of state police power to protect owners' correlative property rights in a common pool) and *Munn v. Illinois* (sustaining government regulations designed to protect a public interest) gave ample authority for regulating petroleum production. Moreover, in *Marrs v. City of Oxford,* the Eighth Circuit Court of Appeals had upheld a Kansas city ordinance permitting only one oil well on each city block, and providing for the division of royalties among individual lot owners and lessees. The ordinance clearly required unit development to protect the public interest in conservation rather than the private property interests of individual lot owners.[15]

W. P. Z. German, general counsel of the Skelly Oil Company in Tulsa, Oklahoma, argued that prorationing could be justified as an exercise of state police power to protect the public interest in petroleum conservation and to safeguard private property rights by ensuring an equitable distribution of a common pool among individual owners. Washington attorney Peter Q. Nyce encouraged engineers and lawyers to cooperate in formulating a viable oil conservation policy. Humble engineer John Suman stated that prorationing and unitization offered the best means of eradicating a rule that awarded oil "to the man who reduced it to possession."[16]

Fort Worth lawyer Robert E. Hardwicke, Jr., maintained that American oil and gas law had not kept pace with scientific advances. He blamed inconsistent and contradictory petroleum laws, "replete with property rules based upon assumptions of fact which had been disproved," for the instability in the oil industry. Unlike the wild animals to which nineteenth-century jurists had likened to petroleum, oil and gas remained stationary until penetration of the reservoir released natural gas pressure and caused movement. Hardwicke pointed out that the analogy between petroleum and water was inappropriate because water movement was not affected by gas pressure, and, unlike oil and gas, water was replenishable.[17]

Hardwicke portrayed the rule of capture as a legal anomaly inspired by nineteenth-century judges' inability to ascertain the precise location and quantity of underground petroleum. Yet these same judges had accepted proof of the source and extent of subterranean oil and gas, virtually to the barrel or cubic foot, in awarding damages to lease and royalty owners against producers for delinquent drilling. To criticism that prorationing was a price-fixing scheme, Hardwicke responded that it was "perfectly obvious" that limited production would affect price. He cited a Supreme Court decision upholding a Wyoming statute, banning the use of natural gas to produce carbon black, to show that states could regulate production of an important natural resource as a way to raise the price and discourage consumption or less beneficial uses.[18]

Hardwicke posed a hypothetical situation to illustrate why states should be able to regulate petroleum production to market demand regardless of the economic consequences. Suppose a refiner or retailer, by evading payment of gasoline taxes, gained an advantage of four cents a gallon over a competitor who paid the tax. The tax evader could thereby cut prices and still earn a profit. To remain competitive and not lose business, the taxpaying retailer would have to reduce prices; therefore, he would insist that the tax law be strictly enforced. "Surely a court would not be justified in declaring the law unconstitutional on the ground that [the taxpaying retailer's] economic motives were involved," Hardwicke argued, "or because the enforcement officers gladly stopped the tax evasion knowing that the price of gasoline would likely be increased by such act."[19]

Opinions and attitudes concerning the causes and solutions of the petroleum problem varied like the Texas landscape. Yet, most oilmen and lawyers agreed that legal issues—especially the rule of capture—were the main obstacle to alleviating wasteful overproduction. The courts now refused to sanction the kind of radical state action they had sustained in putting down labor strikes a few decades earlier. The failure of the legal system to respond quickly enough to change resulted in the same ruthless exploitation of America's petroleum as had occurred to its wildlife and other precious natural resources during the late nineteenth century, restricted in this instance only by the maxim that the hunter must stay on his own land.[20] Unlike many state and federal judges in Texas, however, Sterling admitted that existing laws were inadequate to cope with the magnitude of destruction in the oil patch. For this reason, in part, Sterling had concluded that martial law was the only viable course of action.

America's vital petroleum resources became hostage to a legal duel between rugged individualists, who adhered to the notion of survival of the fittest, and those professionals who believed that twentieth-century industrialization demanded a new *modus operandi* to ensure peace, order, and stability. Efforts by scientists and engineers to educate judges and laymen about the need to achieve efficient and stable oil production had been muddied by propaganda. Anti-conservationists defined the issue as a struggle involving individual liberty, private property rights, competition, and states' rights versus national power. Conservationists responded that "nothing . . . will destroy [the individual] more quickly than perpetuation of the law of the jungle under which the industry is now being operated." By the 1930s, both sides had grown to appreciate the significant role of law in promoting their agenda, and realized that ultimately the courts would decide this aspect of the petroleum industry.[21]

While the debate raged, the continued military occupation of the East Texas field stemmed the violence that had become as commonplace on country roads as mob warfare on Chicago streets. Fortunately, words were exchanged more often than gunfire. The Gladewater *Gusher*, a local newspaper that lasted only a week, took verbal potshots at "the pompous jelly-bellied representatives of this terrible thing called the oil industry," and accused Sterling of "high treason" and of being "a tyrant and an enemy to constitutional law." It called for an end to martial law and Sterling's impeachment even though the shutdown of the East Texas field had helped raise crude prices to nearly a dollar per barrel.[22]

Sterling warned East Texas field operators of "the folly of sinking more wells . . . causing the allowable in wells already completed to be reduced" as low as fifty barrels apiece to keep total field production within the 400,000-barrel daily allowable. Martial law failed to intimidate some small independents from bootlegging oil out of the area. Tank trucks of the day carried from up to a thousand gallons, and drivers willing to incur the risk could earn as much as a hundred dollars a night hauling bootleg gasoline. Runners devised elaborate tactics to elude roadblocks and military patrols. Decoy trucks distracted guards while convoys of tank trucks proceeded unmolested to their destination. Independent oilman Tom G. Patten earned notoriety for outmaneuvering authorities. He drilled three oil wells on a quarter-acre lot along the main street of London, Texas. Patten erected a one-room penthouse of sorts atop one of the wells, declared it his legal homestead under state law, and obtained an injunction to keep soldiers away, boasting, "It's my oil, and if I want to drink it, that's none of your damned business."[23]

Patten, needing an outlet for his oil, negotiated a deal with Jack D. Wrather, a small independent refiner in Kilgore. Under cover of darkness, he laid an underground pipeline to Wrather's refinery. Militiamen discovered the pipeline with a metal detector and severed it. Patten defiantly constructed another pipeline using firehose of nonmetallic fabric. The militiamen eventually discovered and destroyed it, too. Patten then laid another subterranean pipeline that remained undetected for four months, allowing him to run about a million barrels of bootleg oil to Wrather's refinery. Tired of his war with the military, Wrather and his partner, Eugene Constantin, filed suit in federal district court on October 13 against the TRC, the military, the governor, and other state officials, alleging that the latter had conspired with major companies, under color of enforcing oil conservation, to arbitrarily limit production to raise prices, which deprived the plaintiffs of their property without due process of law. Sterling responded that the issue involved states' rights, and that the federal courts should not "throttle the will of the people."[24]

Federal District Judge Randolph Bryant, sitting in Tyler, issued a temporary injunction restraining the militia from interfering with Constantin and Wrather's production until a hearing before a three-judge panel on October 29. Under protection of the injunction, the pair resumed full-scale production of some 5,000 barrels per well daily. Confident that the court would grant a permanent injunction, other East Texas field operators ran their wells wide open. Sterling, unnamed in Bryant's injunction decree, boasted, "They enjoined the wrong fellows," and ordered Wolters to continue enforcing the 165-barrel per well daily limit on everyone except Constantin and Wrather. Bryant held Wolters in contempt of court, but delayed further legal action until the three-judge panel could hear the case. But TRC engineer E. O. Buck impatiently took matters into his own hands and ordered cement poured into a pipeline feeding Wrather's refinery, knocking it out of commission for sometime thereafter.[25]

Judge Hutcheson presided over the three-judge federal court that heard the *Constantin* case on October 29.[26] On behalf of Constantin and Wrather, Dallas attorney Joseph Bailey, Jr., argued that the TRC's authority contravened the contracts clause of Article I, Section 10 of the Texas Constitution and the due process clause of the Fourteenth Amendment of the U.S. Constitution. TRC restrictions had inflicted at least $1,500 a day in irreparable damages on Bailey's clients, who insisted that they could market all the oil they produced without waste.[27]

During the trial, the militia attempted to restrain Constantin, Wrather, and other East Texas field operators from resuming full production under the aegis of Bryant's injunction. Sterling claimed that the war powers of the Texas Constitution authorized use of military force to put down insurrection and riot. Likening the situation to a state of war, he issued Special Order 48, appointing a board of inquiry, composed of military officers, to investigate violations of proration orders. A special military court would try violators under military law. Constantin and Wrather attacked the martial law decree as an arbitrary and tyrannical deprivation of their property rights without due process of law.[28]

In defense of Sterling, attorneys Paul Page, E. F. Smith, and Dan Moody responded that state constitutional and statutory law authorized the martial law decree. Sterling had not suspended any laws or the writ of habeas corpus, and civil authorities in the four East Texas counties (Gregg, Rusk, Smith, and Upshur) affected by martial law continued to function. Page argued that Sterling's martial law decree was unlike the situation in *Ex Parte Milligan,* in which military authority had been asserted in a peaceful locality where no executive, pursuant to constitutional and statutory authority, had proclaimed a state of riot or insurrection. He explained that the insurrection in the East Texas field had been "as real as if every pine tree in that [field] hid an armed man and every derrick stood above a dead one." Page cited Supreme Court Justice Oliver Wendell Holmes's declaration, "Public danger warrants the substitution of executive process for judicial process."[29]

Moody and Smith argued that state constitutional and statutory provisions empowered the governor, not the courts, to take action necessary to protect public peace and safety. The public interest was vitally concerned or affected in no way more than by the oil industry. As the power governing America's largest crude oil– and natural gas–producing region, the State of Texas derived substantial revenue from various forms of petroleum taxes and royalties from state-owned oil-producing lands.[30]

Sterling's lawyers cited U.S. Supreme Court Chief Justice Joseph Story's refusal, in *Martin v. Mott,* to substitute his judgment for a governor's in determining the existence of an emergency and the need to use military force to restore order and peace. Citizens claiming injury from abuse of executive discretion could sue for damages after the emergency had passed and military operations had ceased, Moody and Smith noted. They maintained that frequent elections allowed citizens to remove offending public officials and that the Guarantee Clause of the Constitution protected the people from "a tyrant who fills the office of chief executive officer . . . and by his acts and conduct deprives the state of a republican from of government."[31]

"Would any court have attempted to substitute its judgment for that of the President [Grover Cleveland]," they asked, "as to what steps were necessary to suppress the insurrection and outlawry that existed during that great [Pullman] strike?" They compared the East Texas crisis to that in *Luther v. Borden,* in which Supreme Court Justice Roger B. Taney refused, during the Dorr Rebellion of 1842, to question the government of Rhode Island, which had "deemed the armed opposition so formidable . . . as to require the use of its military force and the declaration of martial law." Moody and Smith also cited Judge Thomas M. Cooley's pronouncement, in *Weimer v. Bunbury,* that "nothing . . . implies that due process of law must be judicial process," and "much of the process by means of which the government is carried on and the order of society maintained is purely executive or administrative," sometimes necessitating temporary deprivations of liberty or property by ministerial or executive officers. They insisted that Sterling had acted within his constitutional and statutory powers in invoking martial law after determining the existence of a state of insurrection, riot, tumult, and breach of the peace.[32]

Judge Hutcheson announced the court's decision on February 18, 1932. Invoking the federal courts' chancery jurisdiction, "exercised uniformly throughout the nation unaffected by statutes, usages, or customs of the several states," he interpreted Article I of the Texas

Constitution as expressly forbidding the governor from suspending constitutional law, even in an emergency, as long as the civil courts remained open and functioning. "Martial law, the law of war, in territory where courts are open and civil processes run," the judge held, was "totally incompatible" with constitutional provisions written by "men who had suffered under the imposition of martial law, with its suspension of civil authority, and the ousting of the courts during reconstruction in Texas" and by those who in 1689 "wrote limitations upon the power of the crown to suspend laws."[33]

Conceding a governor's power to invoke martial law in times of emergency, Hutcheson explained that this power derived from the civil law making the governor and militia civil officers, whose conduct never rose above judicial review. "Ours is a government of civil, not military, forces," he noted, in which "soldier and citizen stand alike under the law," and "both must obey its commands and be obedient to its mandates." Citing *Ex Parte Milligan,* Hutcheson reiterated that "martial law and civil law are mutually contradictory; they may not coexist," and that martial law could never supplant the judicial process except under dire circumstances—and then only to rehabilitate, not destroy or usurp, the courts. He noted that *Luther v. Borden* arose before passage of the Fourteenth Amendment, and involved a damage suit over an arrest made under the authority of a legislative act declaring martial law during a rebellion and civil war in Rhode Island. Without the Fourteenth Amendment, the Supreme Court had been bound by the law of Rhode Island. Hutcheson believed that Louisiana judge Rufus Foster, while sitting in the Southern District of Texas, had incorrectly ruled that a governor, in addition to possessing power to declare martial law, could set aside the laws and institute a military government in lieu of civil law.[34]

Hutcheson concluded that Sterling and Wolters had, "without warrant of law," illegally deprived Constantin and Wrather of their private property. He found no proof of insurrection, riot, and tumult in the East Texas field, with the exception of producers trying to get their oil out of the ground. Hutcheson suspected that the militia might have been taking orders from major oil companies since its actions, which raised crude oil prices, fit their needs. That Governor Sterling had once been president of Humble did nothing to ease the judge's suspicion. Hutcheson issued an injunction restraining enforcement of martial law against Constantin's and Wrather's properties.[35]

The injunction did not apply to the TRC, however, since Constantin and Wrather had not pressed their case against the agency. Hutcheson took judicial notice of the enormous production capability (and potential for waste) of the East Texas field, as well as of the TRC's authority to enforce state conservation laws. He implied that producers could not resume full production until the TRC had an opportunity to determine how much oil could be produced without waste and issue new proration orders. Sterling and Wolters appealed to the U.S. Supreme Court.[36]

Railroad Commissioner C. V. Terrell announced that the TRC would temporarily withhold issuance of a new proration order for the East Texas field pending the outcome of the appeal. Sterling had fifteen days to secure a stay of the injunction decree. Considerable confusion abounded. Smith had advised Sterling to restrain the militia from interfering with production on the Constantin-Wrather properties. Hutcheson told Smith that "any fourteen year old child could understand that no injunction" would take effect until Constantin and Wrather had presented an order for the court to sign. Until then, no court decree was in effect. Sterling immediately ordered the militia to seize control of Constantin's and Wrather's wells.[37]

On February 25, 1932, the TRC resumed regulation of the East Texas field, limiting daily production to 75 barrels per well. The TRC retained its flat per-well allocation formula, which only encouraged additional drilling. Sterling announced that martial law would continue, except on the Constantin-Wrather properties, since the court finally signed the injunction order on February 26. Sterling ordered the militia to refrain from enforcing prorationing but to remain in East Texas to maintain peace.[38]

Rebellious operators took advantage of the uncertainty and ambiguity of protracted litigation and resumed full-scale production. The TRC's flat per-well allocation formula dissatisfied many producers because it failed to account for variations in the productive potential of individual wells or acreage. Some operators simply ignored the TRC and continued producing at will; others filed lawsuits (nineteen in all), attacking the validity of the new proration order on the ground that it violated the Anti-Market Demand Act, and challenging the per-well allocation formula as discriminatory. The Anti-Market Demand Act reinforced the legal position of its opponents, who argued that market-demand prorationing bore no reasonable relation to physical waste. It also provided a convenient way for jurists such as Hutcheson to avoid overturning legal precedents in the face of scientific and technological advances that had rendered past decisions obsolete.[39]

As a large independent with production and refining operations in Texas, Pure had an interest in the upcoming lawsuit. If the courts upheld market-demand prorationing, the Texas legislature could revise the Anti-Market Demand Act accordingly. Market-demand prorationing foreshadowed reductions in production quotas, depending upon consumptive demand. Pure had to maintain a 50,000-barrel daily allowable at Van to service existing outlets, and wanted to increase production to expand its market-share. Market-demand prorationing would have a detrimental impact on Pure's expansion aims unless Elkins again finessed the TRC, as he had done the year before. This was highly unlikely, given the state of affairs in East Texas. Without an increased allowable, Pure might benefit from market-demand prorationing—if the TRC held its competitors' allowables to existing levels, and if crude oil prices stabilized. Pure needed all the allies it could muster to achieve its goal.

As if by divine intervention, a potential ally appeared at an opportune time and from a wholly unexpected direction. In February, W. F. Bryan, Presiding Elder of the Tyler District of the Texas Conference of the Methodist Episcopal Church, reminded Pure management that a majority of the company's Van leases were on land belonging to Methodists. Because of an error in drawing and ratifying the original Van leases, it was necessary to secure new leases on certain properties. In return for Pure's $1,000 contribution to each of the two Methodist churches in Van, the ministers had induced parishioners to ratify the original leases, though they were being offered more money by others to repudiate them. Bryan indicated that a "substantial donation" would ensure the continued happy union between religion and oil.[40] Elkins advised McIlvain to make the requested contribution, as the church members' cooperation had enabled Pure to avoid costly litigation.[41] Even though he appreciated the church's standing behind the deal, McIlvain protested, "It seems rather strange that we are asked to contribute to the church on the basis of their having done the right thing." He grudgingly, but prudently, heeded Elkins's counsel and approved the donation.[42] The two Baptist churches in Van subsequently consolidated and asked Pure to donate a more modest $400 towards constructing a new church. McIlvain suggested that Pure work out a budget for all the churches in Van then prorate it equally, adding, "This church business can get to be a very heavy burden."[43]

The TRC failed to command as much respect as the Methodist church from small producers, who charged that the TRC's flat per-well allocation formula discriminated against them. This alleged inequity exposed the TRC's orders to lawsuits. Regulation of petroleum production, whether to prevent physical waste or to stabilize prices, seemed impossible without statutory authority for limiting output to market demand. But the legislature had already taken its crack at the problem during the long, hot summer of 1931, and now the ball bounced back into the courts. While lawyers wrangled with the problem, hot oil continued to pour out of East Texas' piney woods. Thieves and outlaws even stooped to stealing oil from the First Baptist Church of Gladewater.[44]

By 1932, the 50-year reign of the rule of capture had brought the oil industry near collapse. The courts invited state legislatures to do better, but they had the final word, and what they gave they took away. Legislators and jurists knew little or nothing about the physical characteristics of petroleum or oil reservoirs, and too many of them, moored by their nineteenth-century roots, failed to absorb scientific and technological discoveries that had proven the absurdity of the capture theory. Local federal judges persistently thwarted legislative attempts to alleviate the inefficiency and waste in petroleum production occasioned by judge-made law. Judicial obstinacy relegated the oil patch to the law of the jungle, and so a younger generation helplessly witnessed the plunder of an inestimable amount of their natural inheritance through legalized piracy. Farish mused, "We can never grow a new crop of this commodity." The problem of petroleum bounced back and forth like a ping-pong ball between the legislatures and the courts, but remained a legal issue to be worked out by lawyers and judges.[45]

Meanwhile, chaos continued to plague the East Texas field as lawyers prepared to argue the *Champlin* case in the U.S. Supreme Court on March 23, 1932. At issue was the validity of Oklahoma's market-demand act. Questions from the bench indicated that the Supreme Court might uphold the Oklahoma statute. March 23 also marked the announcement of the decision by the Texas Court of Civil Appeals at Austin in the *Danciger* case. These two decisions bore significant legal implications for prorationing and regulation of petroleum production. The Ides of March had descended upon the crisis-wracked oil industry.[46]

CHAPTER 8

Play It Again, Texas

*The men who have spent their lives in . . . oil
production best know how to conduct their business.
The law should assume only the function of seeing
that the game is fairly played.*

—Joseph C. Danciger

The arrival of spring did not thaw the icy relationship between the TRC
and small East Texas independents in 1932. The latter secured 19 injunctions from local federal judges, including Hutcheson and Bryant,
who rejected newer production methods and applied strict constructionist interpretations of the Anti-Market Demand Act of 1931. These
jurists found that market-demand prorationing bore no reasonable relation to conservation and regarded it as a thinly veiled scheme for price-
fixing.[1]

Not all was gloom. March brought two significant victories for conservationists. On March 23, the U.S. Supreme Court heard arguments
in the *Champlin* case concerning the validity of Oklahoma's market-
demand proration statute. On the same day, the Texas Court of Civil
Appeals in Austin announced its decision in Danciger's appeal from a
trial court verdict sustaining the TRC's proration orders for the Panhandle field.[2]

The *Danciger* case challenged TRC orders issued under the 1929 oil conservation act, which prohibited consideration of economic factors in regulating production but did not single out market demand. The Anti-Market Demand Act specifically forbad market-demand prorationing, but it antedated and was irrelevant to Danciger's suit. Contrary to Hutcheson's ruling in *MacMillan,* the state appellate court rendered a broad and expansive interpretation of the 1929 statute. In upholding the TRC's order, the Texas court found that market demand bore a reasonable relationship to the prevention of physical waste.[3]

The court accorded "great deference and regard" for Hutcheson's *MacMillan* decision, but refused to dismiss recent scientific and technological advances as "mere theory and speculation." It was convinced that substantial physical waste of petroleum in the Panhandle field justified reasonable production controls. Noting that market-demand prorationing had been recognized and authorized by the legislatures of California, Oklahoma, and Kansas, the court did not feel bound by federal court interpretations of state statutes where no federal question was involved. It ruled that regulations reasonably calculated to prevent physical waste fell within the TRC's "implied" authority to enforce petroleum conservation laws in the absence of express statutory power.[4]

Danciger appealed to the Texas Supreme Court. However, the court did not hear the case until after enactment of the Texas Market Demand Act of November, 1932. The court dismissed the case as moot. Its decision had little immediate practical importance, and the Texas Supreme Court subsequently accorded the TRC wide latitude in enforcing petroleum conservation laws. But the battle over prorationing had ensnared the Texas courts with a local federal district court. Until the U.S. Supreme Court resolved the conflict, the legality of prorationing remained in limbo.[5]

Relief came on May 16, 1932, when the Supreme Court rendered its decision in the *Champlin* case. The Champlin Refining Company had appealed a federal district court ruling sustaining the Oklahoma Corporation Commission's proration order for the Oklahoma City field. Champlin complained that the restriction deprived the company of property without due process of law by forcing it to purchase oil from other producers to keep its refinery operating. The Supreme Court upheld Oklahoma's proration statute as a proper method of limiting production to reasonable market demand, which was merely incidental to preventing physical waste. Its decision added weight to the *Danciger* ruling and the validity of market-demand prorationing while undermining Hutcheson's opinion in *MacMillan*. Hardwicke predicted that the "bug-a-boo of market demand [would] be overthrown."[6]

The legal assault against prorationing was not confined to the courtroom. Some disgruntled producers challenged proration orders through the TRC hearing process. Statutory law required the TRC to conduct public hearings to allow interested parties—meaning operators, landowners, lawyers, engineers, geologists, politicians, and just about anyone else—to testify, ask questions, or express their views about proposed rules and regulations. After the hearing, the TRC could issue a proration order, normally effective for 90 days. TRC hearings were recorded and interested parties could appeal any finding or order in a court of law which conducted a trial *de novo*.[7]

Van royalty owners A. J. Broderick and George Calvert attacked the TRC's orders through the hearing process. They complained that Pure was not producing enough oil from land they had leased to it, and condemned the TRC's prorationing program as entirely unsound. "Since October 1931, under the new proration plan for Van . . . tracts of royalty which we own show a loss in production of 76,347.54 barrels," they explained, adding that "instead of our income being at an even keel, we are suffering large financial losses." Broderick and Calvert were particularly irked at the TRC for penalizing producers for past violations by deducting from future production.[8]

Carl Estes forwarded to Elkins a copy of a letter that Broderick and Calvert had sent him for publication in his newspaper, the *Tyler Courier–Times,* in hopes of embarrassing Pure and rallying other dissatisfied royalty owners and producers to their cause.[9] Estes headed a group of East Texas operators who had vowed not to become sacrificial lambs by acceding to further reductions in their allowable without similar sacrifices by producers in other Texas oil fields. W. E. McKinney, president of the Irish Oil Company in Tyler, informed Elkins that several Van royalty owners had tipped him off about a scheme to secure an increased allowable from the TRC. McKinney was concerned as the TRC was being pressured to curtail overproduction in the East Texas field. As vice-president of the Independent Petroleum Association of East Texas, "with a substantial membership and with a number of men who have their votes paid who I might have some influence over," McKinney offered to use his leverage with various politicians in Van Zandt County on behalf of his and Elkins's mutual interests.[10]

Powell advised Elkins to prepare to defend Pure's Van interests at a TRC hearing scheduled for March 30. Elkins intended to petition the TRC to maintain the 50,000-barrel daily allowable at Van without the 10 percent readjustment penalty.[11] He was caught between unhappy Van royalty owners, who wanted their production increased, and East and West Texas producers, whose allowables had been cut by the TRC. Elkins's willingness to maintain the status quo undermined Pure's relations with Van royalty owners, but strengthened its hand against the TRC by gaining Estes's support. Estes and an increasing number of East Texas field producers and royalty owners had begun to realize that, instead of profiting from additional production, they were losing money because of low prices, premature exhaustion of reservoir pressure, and a general decline in property values wrought by chaotic conditions. By 1932, the East Texas field's deterioration threatened to eliminate small independents and leave the majors in control, converting many anti-prorationists into conservationists. Estes considered Elkins's stance a reasonable compromise: Elkins was not asking for more oil, and never accused East Texans of getting too much. East Texas needed all the friends it could get, and Elkins's silence would help that region while Estes's support would in turn enhance Pure's position. Estes told the TRC that West Texans' demands to reduce the Van allowable were "unfair and disastrous." He recommended that Van production be maintained at 50,000 barrels a day, in accord with Elkins's desire.[12]

At the TRC hearings, which ran April 5–7, Calvert, Tyler attorney Tom Pollard, and geologist David Donoghue (a technical advisor to the central proration committee) testified on behalf of Van royalty owners demanding more oil. Calvert asked the TRC to increase Van production to 55,000 barrels a day and to adopt a uniform proration plan for all Texas fields. Elkins invited him to propose a specific plan. Calvert replied, "I do not assume to take the role of suggesting to the Commission some pet plan of my own," adding, "I am a practical man, all these technical things do not appeal to me, they are mystic, confusing and get away from the practical production of oil."[13]

Pollard asked the TRC to increase the Van allowable by between 5,000 and 15,000 barrels a day.[14] Donoghue testified that the additional production would not result in waste and that any proration scheme which "pretended to be fair" had to consider soil porosity and permeability. He explained that Van production had been prorated according to porosity without consideration of well-potential, giving an advantage to leases in the middle of the field.

Elkins asked what percentage of production should be allocated according to porosity as opposed to permeability. Donoghue responded: 25 percent to porosity, 75 percent to permeability. "How do you arrive at 75 percent value of permeability?" Elkins asked. "There is no way to arrive at it definitely, is there?" "No," Donoghue replied. When Elkins asked whether porosity and saturation were uniform throughout the Van field, Donoghue stated, "I don't think they are, but I could not testify to it."[15]

Pure production engineer R. B. Kelley testified that the porosity of the Van field was remarkably uniform. He believed that it was impossible to apply a uniform proration plan to all Texas oil fields and that Pure had employed the fairest method of developing the Van field. Humble engineer John R. Suman and TOGCA president Charles Roeser agreed that the Van field had been operated in a just and equitable manner and opposed any additional production.[16]

Elkins warned the TRC that it would be "a serious mistake" to increase Van production, as the existing allowable distributed a fair and equitable share to each royalty owner. He was willing to adopt a more equitable plan if one could be devised, and assured the TRC that Pure's principal interest was to develop the Van field in a manner that guaranteed all royalty owners a rightful share of oil. Elkins asked the TRC to repeal the 10 percent readjustment rule. It was unfair given the instability of oil prices, Elkins argued. Commissioner Neff agreed.[17]

After the hearing, Elkins told Pure management how Donoghue had "assumed a very dictatorial and arbitrary stand," but made a "very sorry showing . . . owing to his utter lack of knowledge relative to conditions at Van," thereby undermining his credibility with the TRC and the public. He described how Calvert's initial mild manner had become increasingly tense towards the end of the hearing. Elkins denied Calvert's charge that Pure was producing more oil on company-owned land than on leases procured from others. Commissioners Neff and Terrell refused to permit further insinuations, which, according to Elkins, "ended this unpleasant feature of the controversy." Elkins predicted that the TRC would maintain Van's 50,000-barrel daily allowable without the 10 percent readjustment.[18]

On April 9, the TRC vindicated Elkins's prediction. Powell congratulated Elkins for scoring a "complete victory," trusting that the outcome would be "entirely satisfactory" to Pure. McIlvain thanked Elkins for handling "the matter well and I am glad the boys gave you the necessary support." Elkins thanked Estes for furnishing him a copy of

Broderick's and Calvert's letter. "Of all the people in the world," he told Estes, "[Broderick and Calvert] have the least cause for complaint relative to the operation of the Van field," where they have "a very meager claim to two acres of land" upon which they had drilled a well. "The Pure Oil Company paid these gentlemen, in money and oil, the sum of $168,000 for this land, which was an outrageous price," Elkins quipped, "but they were the only independents within the unit area and we thought it would be worth the money to get rid of them." After they got their money, he complained, the pair had resorted to every means to "shake us down." Elkins asked Estes to attest in his newspaper to Pure's fair and equitable development of the Van field.[19]

Elkins had once more rescued Pure, again without resorting to a long and costly lawsuit. In contrast, lacking legal counsel with Elkins's finesse, East Texas field operators fought their legal battle in the courts, where the far-reaching *Danciger* and *Champlin* decisions came too late to aid their cause. People's Petroleum Company became the lead plaintiff in a series of lawsuits, filed in federal court, attacking the TRC's order for arbitrarily and unreasonably depriving property without due process of law in violation of the Fourteenth Amendment and the 1931 Anti-Market Demand Act. Texas assistant attorney general Fred Upchurch responded that the TRC had issued the order pursuant to its statutory authority to prevent physical waste.[20]

While the case was pending, the TRC revised the East Texas field allowable to 325,000 barrels a day. But disorder continued as shotgun-wielding operators barred TRC inspectors from their property. A total of 213 suspects were indicted for stealing oil—including some belonging to the First Baptist Church of Gladewater—but lack of proof and sympathetic juries resulted in few convictions. Elkins complained of thieves and vandals "slipping into the [Van] field at night, breaking oil valves and doing other destructive acts," causing a waste of oil and property damage.[21]

On June 27, the TRC substituted a 51-barrel per well daily limit for the 325,000-barrel daily allowable in the East Texas field. Lessees of state-owned land petitioned the TRC to reinstate the 325,000-barrel field allowable; otherwise the state would suffer a $3 million revenue loss from an expected 50-cent a barrel drop in crude oil prices.[22] Commissioner Ernest O. Thompson[23] agreed to "go with the people of Texas" as far as possible in resolving the problem. He believed the important

issue was not majors versus independents, but whether future generations of Texans would "be forced through a lack of opportunity to work
for some big oil company in a chain filling station."[24]

Several independents and major company executives feared that the
per-well allowable, without a field limit, would encourage more drilling and exacerbate overproduction. Farish protested that there were
already too many wells without pipeline connections, and that Humble
was "already purchasing far in excess of [its] needs and . . . cannot take
on any additional commitment." Some operators accused the TRC of
favoring the Van and Yates fields over the East Texas field by maintaining their daily allowables at 50,000 barrels and 65,000 barrels respectively while reducing East Texas' quota. The TRC's defenders
responded that strict proration rules had been easier to enforce at Van
and Yates, where major companies and large independents such as Pure
controlled a majority of the producing acreage. Tensions eased on June
28, when 90 percent of the East Texas field operators and landowners
asked the TRC to reinstate the 325,000-barrel daily field allowable.
Thompson praised their action as "proration of the highest type."[25]

Elkins asked Estes about a "new movement, instigated by a certain
major oil company and assisted by some of the operators in east Texas,"
to reduce the Van allowable. "We have given the Railroad Commission
less trouble than any other operators in Texas," Elkins said, and "a reduction would be manifestly unfair to the operators who have conducted
this field in the systematic manner which will ultimately result in the
recovery of a greater amount of oil . . . than from any other area in the
state." He vowed not "to permit a reduction of the 50,000 barrels which
we are now producing . . . without any waste." Elkins expressed doubt
that "any court will enter an order requiring us to produce less than
50,000 barrels, but court proceedings are the last measure we wish to
take." He solicited Estes's cooperation in maintaining the Van allowable in return for his promise not to oppose an increase in East Texas
field production.[26]

Estes assured Elkins that he "unalterably opposed . . . a reduction
in the Van field allowable" and would "continue to exert every effort
humanly possible to prevent it." He agreed that Van operators had never
been allowed to produce as much as they deserved and opposed those
East Texans—"a great number . . . resid[ing] in Tyler"—who wanted to
reduce the Van allowable. Estes promised Elkins that he would "do
everything within my power to resist further unfair treatment of the
royalty owners at Van."[27]

Elkins expected some East Texas field producers to petition the TRC to reduce the Van allowable, while some Van royalty owners would seek a change in the proration formula to include consideration of well-potential and sand thickness. Van royalty owners supported Pure's fight to maintain the 50,000-barrel daily allowable, but, unlike Pure, wanted to change the allocation formula. Elkins asked Pure management to furnish him with documentation of the amount of oil the company was producing, storing, and selling overseas, and any other information refuting allegations that Pure was storing 12,000 to 15,000 barrels of oil daily (produced in other fields) while marketing its own production from Van. Critics were arguing that the Van allowable could be reduced without jeopardizing Pure's contractual obligations because it could sell the oil purchased from other fields instead of storing it.[28]

Dawes told Elkins that Pure produced an average of 63,375 barrels a day and had refined 66,193 barrels per day during the last two weeks of June. Pure's inventory of 5,307,000 barrels on April 1, 1931, had declined to 3,615,000 barrels in June, 1932. Dawes cited this as evidence to prove that Pure was not storing oil, but had been forced to purchase crude to supply its refineries. He explained that Van production was insufficient to adequately supply Pure's two refineries at Smith's Bluff, Texas, and Marcus Hook, Pennsylvania. Dawes claimed it was impossible to supply Pure's Texas refineries with any of its production from outside the state. The demands of Pure's Texas refineries had reduced inventories of Van crude by 767,000 barrels, leaving only 12 days' supply. Even with the 50,000-barrel a day Van allowable, Dawes claimed, Pure had purchased 5,000 barrels of oil daily to keep its refineries operating. Regarding Pure's crude oil sales to Humble, Dawes reminded Elkins to "please bear in mind that this is not essentially a sale to them but an exchange of Van oil for which they give us Oklahoma oil."[29]

At a hearing in Austin on July 11, East Texans demanded that the TRC measure all Texas oil fields by the same yardstick. Thompson assured them that the TRC was making every effort to "stop all this talk about someone running too much oil," and had ordered meters installed on selected wells to gauge production. He praised oil-purchasing companies for their cooperation in hooking up 64 of 91 East Texas field wells that lacked pipeline connections and expressed hope that the remaining wells would be connected soon. The TRC concluded that the evidence was too indefinite to issue a new order, and appointed its own engineers to gather data before the next hearing, on August 29.[30]

Powell advised Elkins to "get in the good graces of whoever [the TRC] sent" to investigate the Van field. Even if the engineer's findings were unfavorable, the TRC might still be persuaded to leave the Van allowable alone. If not, Powell was confident that Pure would prevail in court. Elkins suspected that the API and New Jersey Standard had instigated the agitation to reduce Texas production in order to increase crude oil prices by 25 cents a barrel. East Texas producers had incorrectly assumed that the 100,000-barrel reduction would come from other oil fields. Elkins hoped to sway East Texas field operators to Pure's side by telling them that Van and East Texas field production would be reduced by 10,000 and 40,000 barrels a day respectively. The East Texas Chamber of Commerce repudiated its resolution supporting the cut and endorsed Elkins's position that the TRC lacked authority to reduce production in any field without proving actual physical waste of oil and gas.[31]

Elkins was annoyed by the opposition among Pure's Van unit partners (Humble, Texas, Shell, and Sun) to a production increase at a time when Van royalty owners were asking the TRC to raise the daily allowable to 75,000 barrels. Humble took the position that, without a reduction in statewide production, crude oil prices would continue to fall. Elkins could not predict which way the TRC would lean, but trusted that its engineers would be fair, as they were familiar with the Van field and considered Pure's operating method fair. "The Commissioners are only human," he said, but "I think at the present time the Commission is against any reduction." Powell told Elkins to notify the TRC that it would be pressed to raise the Van allowable. "If they [the TRC] feel like they are going to have a battle against a considerable raise in the allowable," Powell advised, "they might be all the more willing to let our present allowable alone."[32]

Fort Worth attorney Rice M. Tilley, who represented groups of Van and East Texas field operators and royalty owners, supported Elkins's stance. He told the TRC that Pure had developed the Van field fairly and that some East Texans had "gone mad in pursuing a disastrous and unjustified drilling campaign." Tilley assured Elkins that he had "some pretty good friends" in the East Texas field crowd, whom he had warned to "lay off" the Van field. He assumed that Elkins would resist attempts to decrease Van production, and noted that his Van clients had been satisfied with the 50,000-barrel allowable (although ideally they wanted more) and were content with Pure's operation of the field.[33]

Pure could "very easily take ten or fifteen thousand barrels [of] additional oil out of [the Van] field and, in fact, it would be to the company's interest to do so," Elkins told Tilley, adding that Pure had accepted the 50,000-barrel per day limit to cooperate in the conservation movement, but would not acquiesce to any further reduction. Independents were "digging their own graves" by pursuing a "disastrous and unjust drilling campaign in subdividing large tracts of land into small tracts and drilling wells on each tract." He suspected that some royalty owners would ask the TRC to increase the Van allowable to 75,000 barrels a day. Although Pure would comply with TRC orders, Elkins believed that an increase was unadvisable at the time.[34]

Amidst the furor, on July 19, Hutcheson denied People's application for an injunction. He refused "to conjecture" whether the TRC's proration order was "beyond necessity," and that another oil conservation program "would accomplish the permissible purpose without trenching upon the impermissible one." People's had limited its proof to the condition of its own wells, without showing the status of other wells in the East Texas field. Hutcheson intimated that, upon presentation of more convincing evidence, he might find the TRC order in conflict with the 1931 Anti-Market Demand Act and the flat per-well allocation formula to be arbitrary and inequitable. A trial on the merits was scheduled for October. By hinting at the invalidity of the TRC order, Hutcheson encouraged operators to ignore it, and gave them confidence that it would be overturned or that they would not be penalized for violations incurred while the suit was pending, even if the order were ultimately upheld.[35]

"Lord only knows what will happen," Elkins mused as TRC hearings resumed in Austin on August 29.[36] East Texas field operators pressed the TRC to limit production of all Texas oil wells to 200 barrels a day. They claimed that it was unfair to limit the 7,580 wells in the 114,000-acre East Texas field to 43 barrels per well a day while allowing the 324 wells in the 4,300-acre Van field to produce 153 barrels apiece daily. Elkins responded that East Texans had no reason to complain, as the average formation thickness in the Van field was 270 feet, compared to 60 feet for the East Texas field. With a 4½-to-1 ratio in favor of Van, Elkins argued, Van's per-well allowable should have been 4½ times that of the East Texas field, or 193 instead of 153 barrels per day.[37]

On August 31, the TRC issued a new proration order limiting daily East Texas field production to 375,000 barrels and restricting existing wells to 50 barrels a day. The TRC planned to cut production in other Texas fields, including a 5,000-barrel per day reduction at Van, after a separate hearing on September 21 in Fort Worth. Elkins advised Pure management that the TRC would probably reduce the Van allowable by 5,000 barrels a day, forcing Pure to buy oil elsewhere, possibly outside of Texas, to supply its Philadelphia and Beaumont refineries.[38]

Soon after the TRC's order took effect on September 1, a group of East Texas field operators led by Tom Cranfill, whose motto was "Peace and Plenty," realized that their relatively high allowable would drive the price of crude oil down to 30 cents a barrel. Cranfill's group petitioned the TRC for a 10 percent reduction of production in all Texas oil fields. A federal district court in Austin enjoined enforcement of the TRC's order. McIlvain wrote Elkins, "The atmosphere down in Texas seems thoroughly charged with dynamite. What will happen next?"[39]

The prorationing issue brought royalty owners on the outer edge of the Van field into conflict with those in the middle. Elkins anticipated that owners on the fringe would procure geologists and engineers to testify to the irregular permeability, saturation, porosity, and thickness of oil-bearing sands underlying the Van field, while centrally located owners would try to show uniformity. He asked the TRC to appoint its own engineers to check sand uniformity at Van, and offered access to Pure's records "in order to assist in arriving at a fair and just conclusion." Elkins insisted that Pure was endeavoring to ensure that each royalty owner received a fair share of oil.[40]

At a TRC hearing in Fort Worth on September 24, Elkins offered testimony by Pure production engineer R. B. Kelley to refute allegations concerning inequalities in Van production. Small royalty owners near the outer edge of the Van field demanded a higher allowable than those in the center, on the ground that their leases were drained sooner and filled with water more quickly, allowing operators in the middle to recover more oil. Broderick and Calvert accused Pure of producing more oil on its own land in the middle of the field than from leases on the outer edge. Water encroachment would be uniform throughout the field if soil permeability was uniform, Kelley testified. He admitted that Pure had not conducted tests to determine the uniformity of soil permeability at Van, and that wells in the center of the field could produce twelve times as much oil as those on the perimeter. Elkins asked, "That is what happens in every field . . . The Pure Oil Company cannot change it?" "No, sir," Kelley answered. J. S. Hudnall, a consulting geologist from Tyler, testified that no avoidable or unnecessary waste had occurred at Van.[41]

The TRC issued a new order on October 10 limiting statewide production to 805,000 barrels per day and reducing allowables in all Texas oil fields. Production at the East Texas and Van fields was cut to 335,000 and 42,500 barrels a day respectively.[42] Pure wanted to maintain the existing 50,000-barrel daily allowable, but accepted a 10 percent statewide reduction. Elkins's strategy had been to cooperate with the TRC in stabilizing Texas production and stay in its good graces to avoid any dramatic increases or decreases in the Van allowable. In addition, "this course . . . would have the endorsement of the other members of the unit," Elkins explained, "and it has occasioned less disturbance than we had anticipated from the royalty owners who are . . . the most difficult element in the situation to handle." In this context, Elkins achieved a partial victory by averting two extreme and undesirable outcomes.[43]

As noted earlier, some Texas oilmen opted to sue the TRC rather than pursue their interests through the hearing process. On September 17, a three-judge federal court in Houston heard petitions by East Texas field producers, who alleged that the TRC's proration order violated the 1931 act by limiting production to market demand and that the per-well allocation formula, when combined with a maximum field allowable, contributed to physical waste. Because these lawsuits raised the same legal issues, the court consolidated them into the *People's* case to clear its docket of all East Texas field proration cases.[44]

The contradictory testimony of equally reputable engineers and geologists left the court in a quandary. Petroleum engineers and geologists testified on behalf of People's that natural gas pressure, rather than that of water, was the chief propulsive force of oil reservoirs. They stated that water could not be the main driving force in the East Texas field, noting that the water table had risen only two feet since the field opened. The witnesses suggested that closer well spacing than existing regulations permitted would enhance ultimate recovery, by allowing drilling in tight sand areas to extract oil that could not be reached by more widely spaced wells.[45]

On October 24, the court struck down the TRC's order as arbitrarily and unjustly depriving People's of its property without due process of law. In accord with his ruling in *MacMillan,* Hutcheson held that "under a thinly veiled pretense of going about to prevent physical waste," the TRC, "in cooperation with other persons interested in raising and maintaining the prices of oil and its refined products," had attempted to limit production of crude oil to market demand in violation of the 1931 Act. He found that the TRC's per-well allocation formula, which made no distinction between well potential and acreage, discriminated against some producers by arbitrarily cutting their quotas in favor of others.[46]

The *People's* decision left the TRC virtually powerless to enforce prorationing. Hutcheson clearly implied that he would not countenance "unreasonable" government interference with private property. By comparison, the *Danciger* and *Champlin* decisions were more in line with scientific and engineering findings indicating a nexus between market-demand prorationing and conservation. Enforcement of a practical and successful petroleum conservation program in Texas seemed impossible unless the TRC devised a proration order that satisfied federal judges, who had the final word.[47]

Outraged by the *People's* decision, 1,500 oilmen convened in Tyler on September 27 to avert a catastrophe which would "plunge [Texas] back into the economic pit of despair." Estes chaired the meeting, which was also attended by state senator Thomas G. Pollard of Tyler and TOGCA president Roeser. Proponents and opponents of production control met on common ground "to thwart the minority that would destroy their birthright." In a radical shift of position, Estes labeled opposition to prorationing as an "umbrella" employed by those who wanted cheap oil. "When you declared martial law in the East Texas oil field in August, 1931," Estes told Sterling, "many major oil groups had millions of barrels of oil in storage; now they have less than 24 days' supply on hand." He stated his fear that majors would take advantage of the *People's* decision to purchase oil at deflated prices. Roeser found "no reason for alarm" in that ruling, and advised East Texas field operators to continue business as usual until the situation could be "worked out satisfactorily." The delegates adopted a resolution urging Sterling to call a special session of the legislature to save "the natural resources of Texas."[48]

TRC chairman Terrell announced that only a special session of the legislature could remedy the defects in regulation cited by the court in the *People's* case. "We have saved the producers of oil in East Texas millions of dollars," he said, "and we do not intend to let that pool be lost if we can prevent it." Commissioner Thompson called a special session "highly important" to sustain proration in Texas oil fields. Parker received reports that some East Texas field wells had been operating wide-open as a result of the *People's* decision. Terrell asked Sterling to use whatever means necessary to assist the TRC in enforcing prorationing, as TRC field agents were not armed peace officers. The TRC scheduled a hearing in Austin on November 3 to give East Texas field operators an opportunity to air their views. Commissioner Smith predicted that the evidence would "show the court that there is such a thing as physical waste."[49]

Houston attorney Clarence Wharton argued that the *People's* decision confirmed the inadequacy of Texas oil and gas conservation statutes. He claimed that the legislature had neither devised an "intelligent conservation code" nor delegated adequate enforcement power to the TRC. "It is well recognized that the production of oil, a limited natural resource and a highly perishable product, in excess of market demand is waste," Wharton declared, citing Oklahoma's market-demand statute upheld by the Supreme Court. "If our statute were similarly drawn," he suggested, "it would be relieved of the necessity of undertaking to balance production with demand in an underhanded way, as it has had to do in the past." Wharton noted that virtually every state except Texas recognized and enforced the correlative rights of common pool owners. "The legislature could easily adopt this common sense rule in Texas," he advised, to give the courts and the TRC power to issue appropriate orders regulating correlative rights.[50]

Vowing to "swim or sink on the proposition that the state has no business enforcing laws that would fix prices or permit consideration of market demand," Sterling refused to call a special legislative session. He disagreed with the argument that the *People's* decision would upset the state's oil conservation program, and threatened to shut down the East Texas field again under martial law if violations continued. Assistant Attorney General Maurice Cheek, who handled oil litigation involving the TRC, asked the lower federal court to delay implementation of its *People's* decree until the Supreme Court announced its decision in the *MacMillan* appeal. The Supreme Court had agreed to hear arguments in the appeal of the *Constantin* case on November 14, followed by *MacMillan* the following week. Until then, the TRC announced, it would continue enforcing its proration order in the East Texas field and instructing its inspectors to report violators for prosecution.[51] Sterling dispatched additional militia to ensure that the East Texas field would "not . . . run wild again."[52]

The virtual impossibility of devising a proration plan without reference to market demand in light of *MacMillan* and *People's* convinced Sterling to change his mind, and he called the Texas legislature into special session on November 3, 1932. He warned legislators that a "grave crisis confronts the state in the conservation of its natural resources," which were being dissipated in an "orgy of disorderly production." Sterling stressed the urgency of protecting revenue derived from the state's gross production tax on oil to avoid a budget deficit that would hurt taxpayers, government services, and the public schools.[53] Even though he doubted that human ingenuity could devise an oil conservation statute that would withstand judicial scrutiny and save Texas from ruin, TRC chairman Terrell told legislators that they owed a duty to their fellow Texans to prevent federal judges from destroying the East Texas field. He denied that the TRC had attempted to fix prices, but failed to see how "any man could close his eyes at the price."[54]

Senator Tom Deberry asked what influence price played in determining market demand, and whether the TRC considered the price of refined products such as gasoline, recalling, "I came down to this legislature on 14-cent gasoline one time lately and four months later, I was obliged to pay 19 cents." Terrell responded that "if the prices of refined products become oppressive, we shall consider increasing the crude allowable." "Do you think a person should pay 19 cents for gasoline," Deberry retorted, "while a cattleman is obliged to sell his product at Fort Worth for 75 cents per hundred?" Terrell refused to "say that 19 cents per gallon for gasoline is too high."[55]

Pandemonium in the Texas Senate rivaled the disorder in the East Texas field. A fracas erupted when Senator George Purl requested that TRC Oil and Gas Division chief Parker be expelled from the chamber for prompting Terrell's testimony. Senators Walter Woodward and Walter Woodul objected to expelling anyone from a public hearing. Some senators then cheered Terrell's answers to Purl's questions.[56]

Danciger assailed market-demand prorationing as "bunk," a plot by major oil companies to fix the price of oil. He spoke of "a competitive right to exist" and refused "to surrender my rights for a few dollars." Danciger admitted that low crude oil prices would hurt him, but added that it wouldn't be long until orders came in from world markets for East Texas oil and the price went back up. If the East Texas field had not been closed, he mused, "the greatest oil refining center in the world would have been built there, with independent pipelines carrying oil to the gulf for distribution in the world market." Danciger surmised that open and competitive operations in East Texas would afford independents four or five outlets for their oil instead of only one—to the majors.[57]

Gulf's Underwood Nazro reiterated his opposition to "interfering with the laws of supply and demand under the guise of waste." He cautioned senators, "You have a law already under which the Railroad Commission can do everything that is necessary" to prevent physical waste in petroleum production. Nazro suspected that market-demand pro-rationing was unconstitutional since it essentially amounted to government price-fixing. He noted how attempts by other governments to fix commodities prices had "all failed with absolutely disastrous results." The imposition of such a task on the TRC in view of its past track record, Nazro argued, would be comparable to asking it to figure a calculus problem when it could not handle simple arithmetic.[58]

The divisiveness in the Texas Senate carried over into the House, where considerable opposition developed against a market-demand statute. Representative Gordon Burns asked Terrell, "Would you summon officers of the Standard Oil Company of New Jersey to your hearings to determine how much oil they were importing and what they thought the market demand ought to be?"

"No," Terrell answered, adding that the amount of imported oil could be ascertained from other sources, such as the U.S. Department of Commerce. Representative P. L. Anderson asked Terrell if the TRC or "someone in New York" would determine market demand. Terrell replied that the TRC would consider all available information relevant to market demand in order to establish a fair and reasonable allowable.[59]

Commissioner Thompson denied that the TRC would use market-demand prorationing to fix prices, but admitted that it had an indirect effect on prices. Carl Estes, in an about-face, testified in favor of a market-demand bill. Asked by San Angelo representative Penrose Metcalfe if the bill was a price-fixing scheme, Estes shot back, "What if it is?" Metcalfe retorted, "You're dodging the question; I am asking you if it is."

"Why certainly it is," Estes replied heatedly, "and it doesn't make me mad. Wouldn't you rather have the price of oil fixed by honest men than by the Capones of the oil industry?"

"Don't you know," Representative Burns asked, "that this bill would turn the oil industry over to the major companies?"

"It suits me fine if it helps the industry and the state," Estes replied, adding that it would be "criminal" for the legislature "to sit idly by" and allow the state's oil industry "to go on the rocks."[60]

Estes accused Danciger of fomenting disorder in the Texas oil industry. Danciger responded that he could not understand why Estes had abandoned the fight, and asked, "Is the businessman of today justified in surrendering his most priceless heritage?" He warned, "Let them get the output as low as they want it, and then see how much you will be obliged to pay for your gasoline." Danciger vowed to fight prorationing "as long as there is a court where I can get justice." He expressed doubt that there was a "man in the world who [had] enough brains to fig-ure . . . out" what market demand was and apply it "in a way that would do justice to all in the industry."[61]

John Kilgore, attorney for the North Texas Oil and Gas Association testified that, in *Champlin*, the Supreme Court did not equate market-demand prorationing to price-fixing. He noted that crude oil had dropped from $2 to 75 cents a barrel during the pendency of the case.[62] Baylor University law professor T. E. McDonald stated his belief that, although the Oklahoma market-demand act had been upheld, a simi-lar law would not necessarily work in Texas, where the state constitu-tion defined property rights in minerals differently. "Inasmuch as the U.S. Supreme Court has held that the oil industry is not a public util-ity," he stated, "the government does not properly have power to regu-late petroleum to the extent of fixing prices." McDonald opposed market-demand prorationing because it encouraged monopoly, and suggested instead a graduated production tax to control petroleum production.[63]

To Houston attorney Steve Pinckney, "fundamentally, a market de-mand law is wrong," and, "governmentally, it is silly." Houston attor-ney Elwood Fouts advocated producers' legal rights to govern their own private business affairs and produce as much oil as they pleased.[64] "There are plenty of forums ahead of us," Dallas attorney Luther Nickels warned, and "no warrant in law for proration in any form." He disagreed with the notion that *Champlin* provided legal precedent supporting a Texas market-demand act, because Texas had ceded its mineral rights to public lands sold to individuals whereas Oklahoma had reserved partial title thereto.[65] James Elkins, however, stated his belief that the legislature would enact a market-demand bill patterned after the Okla-homa law.[66]

On November 12, a market-demand act passed both the House (105 to 22) and Senate (23 to 5) and was signed by Governor Sterling. The Market Demand Act differed from the Anti-Market Demand Act, which it superseded, in that it authorized the TRC to consider economic waste or reasonable market demand in regulating petroleum production. To satisfy the courts, the new statute specified that production, transpor-tation, or storage of crude oil in excess of reasonable market demand

constituted waste. It also provided for TRC hearings to determine excess production and reasonable market demand.[67]

"From now on there will be none [i. e., oil and gas] taken without
the consent of the state," Sterling proclaimed, congratulating the legislature for "a most wonderful piece of work." API president Amos L.
Beaty hailed the Market Demand Act as "the most outstanding achievement of the year." Dawes predicted the new law would "be of inestimable value to the industry." Passage of the act was a bitter defeat for
a small but vocal minority of Texas independents, who were expected
to challenge it in the courts. IPAT president Parten predicted dire consequences from the act, pointing out that "utilities have feasted well
at the expense of the public and under semblance of regulation of
profits."[68]

A TRC hearing in Austin on November 26 to promulgate a new proration order under the Market Demand Act occurred the same day that
Moody and Smith urged the U.S. Supreme Court, in the *Constantin* case,
to set aside the injunction restraining the governor from invoking martial law in the East Texas field.[69] They argued that federal courts lacked
jurisdiction to interfere with a governor's power to take action necessary to restore peace and order, including the restriction of oil production. Constantin and Wrather's counsel responded that there had been
no riot or insurrection in the East Texas field to justify martial law,
and that Sterling had exceeded his legal authority.[70]

While the justices deliberated, at the TRC hearing petroleum
engineer E. O. Buck proposed that two-thirds of the 325,000-barrel East
Texas field allowable be based on well-potential and the remaining
third on acreage and bottom-hole pressure.[71] The field would be divided
into zones according to relative bottom-hole pressures. A larger allowable would be assigned to wells in the western third or half of the field,
which had been affected by water intrusion sooner than the central or
eastern sections. Although the plan omitted consideration of sand thickness, Buck still considered it better than the TRC's flat per-well formula. A drop in bottom-hole pressure would reveal excessive production
from any well. Bottom-hole pressure in all zones of the field could be
continually monitored to revise allowables according to changing
conditions.[72]

The TRC adopted Buck's formula and issued a new proration order
on November 29, setting the statewide allowable at 845,625 barrels a
day. It retained the 325,000-barrel daily East Texas allowable (which

worked out to about 37 barrels per well), to discourage additional drilling. Many small operators objected to the new order because, unlike
the well-staffed majors, they lacked technical personnel to gauge
bottom-hole pressures and collect other engineering data. The TRC responded that there were many well-qualified consulting engineers and
geologists who would work for small operators at a fee that would enable them to derive all of the benefits and avoid the penalties. It expressed hope the new plan would appease the disparate oil factions and
satisfy the federal courts.[73]

On December 12, the U.S. Supreme Court unanimously struck down
Sterling's martial law decree. Chief Justice Charles Evans Hughes chas-
tised Sterling for infringing on Constantin's and Wrather's federal due
process rights, rejecting the contention that federal courts lacked jurisdiction because the suit was one by citizens against the state. State
officials who interfered with rights secured by the U.S. Constitution
remained subject to judicial review even when they purported to act
under legal authority.[74]

Hughes agreed with the lower federal court that "there was no exi-
gency or state of war which justified the Governor in attempting to
enforce by executive or military order the restriction which the District Judge had restrained pending proper judicial inquiry." As long as
the courts and civil processes continued to function, the chief justice
cautioned, a governor could not, by executive fiat, override rights secured by the U.S. Constitution or substitute dictatorship for the rule of
law. Although Hughes did not define "martial law" or the permissible
scope of military rule in all conceivable emergencies, he clearly held
that judicial control was not deferred until an emergency or exigent
circumstance had passed.[75]

The *Constantin* decision affected a significant though little-noticed
trend in American public law. Governors had invoked martial law before, but only once since adoption of the Fourteenth Amendment had
their actions been reviewed by the Supreme Court. In *Moyer v. Peabody,*
the court had denied relief to a union leader who had filed a writ of
habeas corpus contesting his arrest and detention; he had been held
for 76 days under martial law in an attempt to suppress labor-related
strife. The court had sustained preventive detentions made in good faith
to reasonably accomplish a governor's constitutional duty to suppress
insurrection. In *Constantin,* however, the Supreme Court rejected *Moyer*
as well as subsequent lower court rulings supporting the proposition

that judges would not question a governor's determination of the existence of an emergency and the need to invoke martial law. Although it recognized that state governments must be accorded wide latitude in maintaining law and order, the Supreme Court clearly emphasized that such discretion was not absolute, and was subject to judicial review for reasonableness.[76]

The TRC praised Hughes's ruling as a "just one." Sterling refused to comment, but indicated that he would not immediately revoke martial law or withdraw the 46 remaining militiamen from the East Texas field. API president Ames pointed out that the decision did not impair a governor's authority to use military force to enforce valid state laws or court orders, and that the Court had merely held that a governor could not forcefully override determinations made by the courts.[77]

On the same day that the Supreme Court handed down its decision in *Constantin,* the TRC reduced statewide production by 60,000 barrels, to 789,745 barrels a day, and cut the East Texas field allowable from 325,000 to 310,000 barrels per day. It cited the need to adjust production to purchasers' actual requirements and to stimulate pipeline connections to wells lacking outlets.[78] But the reduction failed to bring production into line with market demand, and the price of East Texas field crude fell. Major purchasers such as Humble lowered their offering price for East Texas field crude from $1 to 75 cents a barrel. Shell and the Texas Company slashed their prices to 65 cents a barrel. Bootlegged oil sold for 50 cents a barrel. Small operators blamed Humble for instigating the price drop just before Christmas and "robbing Santa Claus."[79] Faced with overproduction, lower crude prices, and complaints from small operators about the inclusion of bottom-hole pressure as a factor in determining allowables, the TRC ordered a complete shutdown of the approximately 9,300 East Texas field oil wells on December 17. The shutdown would remain in effect until January 1 to provide a breathing spell before the TRC determined a future strategy. On December 21, after 16 months of occupation, national guardsmen withdrew from the East Texas field, leaving 9,300 silent oil wells in the hands of the TRC and the courts.[80]

A year and a half of litigation and military rule left the East Texas field in disarray. Small independents had persistently defied both voluntary and state-backed efforts to alleviate overproduction. They had been aided and abetted by judges such as Hutcheson and Bryant, whose injunctions reflected their ideology more than sympathy for the underdog. Though they did not uphold private property rights as absolute, Hutcheson and Bryant refused to countenance "unreasonable" governmental restraints on individuals' rights to use their property as they desired. After implying that they would uphold TRC market-demand prorationing orders if expressly authorized by state law, Hutcheson and Bryant struck them down as "unreasonable." Their rulings demonstrated how local federal judges stymied efforts by state regulatory agencies to alleviate the abuses of the rule of capture. With the courts having the final word, petroleum remained a legal problem, to be worked out by lawyers and judges. The Texas Market Demand Act offered the oil industry a last opportunity to avoid what it dreaded most: federal regulation.

CHAPTER 9

Oilmen Cry Wolf

We know of no calamity that could befall our state more disastrous than the failure by our courts to enforce our orders of proration and to destroy them by the route of injunction . . . It is unwise, nondemocratic and was never intended by those great patriots who so wisely founded our government and established our judiciary in both State and Nation.

—Texas Railroad Commission

The year 1933 boded ill for oil conservation in Texas. Producers who had sacrificed to obey proration orders became discouraged when vast quantities of illegally produced oil in Texas and Oklahoma triggered price-gouging.[1] East Texas field crude at 25 to 40 cents a barrel was refined into gasoline at 2 cents a gallon. Small operators employed illegal production, cut-rate prices, and injunctions to gain an edge over larger competitors, who argued that it was suicide to abandon production controls. With so much oil in sight, anti-prorationists urged the removal of regulations to allow producers to compensate volume for low prices.[2] Pew lamented that "the patience of everyone is about exhausted," as the desire for stability in the oil patch shifted attention

from state to federal regulation.[3] The law was the primary stumbling
block to effective enforcement of state regulations. Federal court injunctions had emasculated the TRC's proration orders destabilizing production and forcing prices down.[4]

On December 28, 1932, the TRC conducted what it hailed as the most
important proration hearing ever held in Texas. It disallowed the usual
side-door arguments whereby oilmen lobbied commissioners. The TRC
warned everyone not "to attempt either orally or in writing, to influence this commission when it is not in session." To avoid frequent
clashes between witnesses and spectators, the TRC vowed to conduct
an orderly and civilized hearing, governed by law, without the usual
abuse, insults, and demonstrations.[5]

The TRC's first prorationing order under the Market Demand Act,
effective January 1, 1933, limited East Texas field production to 290,000
barrels per day, or 28 barrels per well, until TRC engineers could gauge
bottom-hole pressures from 365 "key" wells.[6] Again the TRC's order
angered some producers, who threatened lawsuits. Dawes complained
that reduction in the Van allowable from 42,500 to 41,500 barrels a day
jeopardized Pure's $16 million investment in refineries at Smith's Bluff
and Marcus Hook.[7] With eight refineries requiring 70,000 barrels of
crude daily, Dawes told Elkins, "Texas oil is available only for the Beaumont and Philadelphia refineries which . . . we will be compelled to close
down . . . unless . . . we secure oil." Regardless of Pure's disposition "to
lighten the burdens of the industry," Dawes saw "no other alternative
except to exhaust every legal recourse available to protect our obligations to our customers, the public, and our stockholders," adding, "We
have come to the end of the road." Elkins advised Dawes against push-
ing for an increase the Van allowable at a time when East Texas field
producers were pressing the TRC to cut production in other Texas fields.[8]

API president C. B. Ames noted that Texas produced more oil than
any other state, and double the value of its cotton crop. Oil affected the
livelihood of banks, merchants, and other businesses, and the state
government derived more than half its revenue from petroleum taxes.
Ames warned that abandonment of prorationing would inflict incalcu-
lable harm. Instead of receiving an eighth of a 75-cent barrel of oil, with
the prospect of more, royalty owners would get an eighth of a 10- or
5-cent barrel of oil, with the prospect of less. Local banks which had
loaned money on the basis of a 75-cent barrel would find borrowers
unable to repay with crude at 10 cents a barrel. The oil trade of local
merchants would be adversely affected. State revenues derived from

the gross production tax on oil would plummet, leading to an increase in ad valorem taxes.[9]

Commissioner Thompson suggested that the comparative novelty of Texas' oil conservation laws compelled experimentation to find out what worked best. "People have so long thought that it was their proud privilege to do whatever they desired with whatever they owned," Thompson said, "that it is hard . . . to get them to understand that . . . to do as one pleases with one's property carries with it the correlative duty to . . . do no violence to the rights of others." He cited recent engineering advances as "sufficient testimonial for any fair-minded person to justify the use of scientific methods in the development of our natural resources."[10]

On January 12, 1933, the TRC opened hearings in Tyler to investigate proration violations in the East Texas field. Investigators G. M. Cosby and K. M. Knox disclosed that a well owned by the P & G Oil Company of Gladewater had been fortified by concrete walls equipped with iron doors. This "fortress of Gladewater" gave its owner time to shut off control valves before TRC inspectors could gauge the wells' flow rate. Knox testified that 98 producers had committed most of the violations, and that the majority of the 700 to 750 East Texas field operators were obeying TRC orders.[11]

Allred subpoenaed pipeline company representatives to question them about "hot" (illegally produced) oil shipments from East Texas. He asked William Irish, III, the head of Atlantic Oil Producing Company's crude oil purchasing department, about his company's dealings with Golding & Murchison of Dallas and the American Liberty Oil Company. Atlantic had "loaned" money to East Texas field producers to entice them to sell $1.5 million of their oil for 43.5 to 80 percent of the posted price. Thompson accused Atlantic of abetting a practice which struck "at the very heart of the whole situation in East Texas." Irish responded that it was not illegal to loan money or to purchase oil at a discount price.[12]

Atlantic had also loaned 500,000 barrels of oil to Golding & Murchison for delivery to tankers on the Gulf Coast. Golding & Murchison reimbursed Atlantic from their East Texas field production. An audit of Atlantic Pipe Line Company's transportation and storage records revealed a discrepancy of over a million barrels of oil received between September 1, 1931, and January 1, 1933. Atlantic's attorney, S. M. Leftwich, argued that the oil had been procured under protection of a federal injunction. The hearings concluded on January 14.[13]

When they resumed on January 19, the investigation focused on illegal pipeline shipments. The TRC required pipeline operators to submit "E-N forms," showing the specific origin of all oil shipments. The
E-N forms were designed to reveal illegal production.[14] Witnesses from
the Pure Van Pipe Line Company and the Liberty Pipe Line Company
testified that E-N forms did not cover East Texas field oil that they had
transported during 1932. Pure Van Pipe Line vice-president W. W.
Averill admitted that his company had run some of Liberty's oil, but
only on Liberty's assurance that it was legal.[15] Liberty vice-president
Mills Cox testified that his company presumed that oil accepted from
the Tyler Pipe Line Company under protection of a federal court injunction was legal. "Pure . . . does not wish to transport this oil if it is
injunction or illegally produced oil," Elkins assured the TRC, "and we
will cooperate with you in every way to prevent [its] transportation."[16]

The Texas House Committee on Oil, Gas, and Mining launched its
own probe of the TRC on January 19. Representative C. M. Turlington
accused TRC employees of having "their hands behind their backs" and
being "Al Capones of the oil industry." Representative Gordon Burns
disagreed and referred to a previous legislative investigation of the TRC
which had resulted in nothing more than "hearsay" evidence. Turlington
responded that East Texas field land and royalty owners had not been
organized before, but had now amassed valuable information that would
aid the legislature in passing remedial laws. Representative Bob Long
claimed to possess sufficient proof to impeach the TRC for "dereliction
of duty." Representative O. F. Chastain defended the TRC for doing its
best in the face of federal court injunctions and urged his colleagues
"to clothe [the TRC] with authority that will stand in the courts."[17]

Thompson refuted "such wild statements as Bob Long's," saying it
was "strange . . . that he should have waited so long to take a crack at
us . . . when we are engaged in a thorough investigation of the amount
of [illegal] oil . . . [coming] out of the East Texas field." He insisted that
Long "had nothing but a lot of hearsay and gossip" and was confident
that the legislature would not countenance further investigation of the
TRC. On January 26, 1933, the House voted 76 to 56 to investigate the
TRC.[18] As the inquiry heated up, 23 lawsuits were filed in the federal
district court in Tyler to restrain the TRC from prorating production
in the East Texas field. The cases were consolidated for trial under
Rowan & Nichols Oil Company on January 27.[19]

Confident that the federal court would again restrain the TRC, many
East Texas field operators continued producing at will, driving East

Texas field crude down from $1 to 50 cents a barrel. Hardwicke criticized the TRC's 290,000-barrel daily East Texas field allowable as "ill-advised, especially in view of the attitude of the federal courts toward an allowable of approximately 400,000 barrels a day, much less a smaller one."[20] Both honest and dishonest producers could not understand why the TRC had restricted flowing wells, which required no artificial pumping to lift oil to the surface, to only 28 to 31 barrels a day, while permitting marginal wells[21] to produce 40 barrels per day. Logic dictated that a good well should be allowed to produce at least as much as a bad one. The problem lay with the Marginal Well Act, enacted prior to the discovery of the East Texas field, which exempted wells with potential production of less than 40 barrels a day from regulation. Too many marginal wells in the East Texas field, exempt from prorationing, consumed a substantial share of the field allowable, with little left over to allocate to more productive, high-flowing wells.[22]

Pure also filed suit in federal court to restrain the TRC from restricting its Van production below a level for which it had a ready market demand. Elkins preferred to avoid costly and uncertain litigation, but the TRC had refused to increase the Van allowable by 10,000 barrels a day, suggesting instead that Pure purchase additional oil from East Texas field producers. Pure claimed that its refineries were set up at considerable expense to refine a particular grade of crude oil available only from Van.[23] Judge Bryant issued a temporary injunction on January 24 permitting Pure to produce an additional 8,000 barrels of Van oil daily pending the outcome of its lawsuit.[24]

Dawes congratulated Vinson & Elkins attorneys Clyde Sweeton and J. Hart Willis for securing the injunction and expressed his "great satisfaction [of having] our legal affairs in Texas in such capable hands." Elkins replied, "When one is doing his dead level best to serve a client, it is not only encouraging but it is a real inspiration to know that the client appreciates the value of such services." He added, "We have always had such appreciation from the officers of the Pure Oil Company and that is the main reason why it has had and will continue to have preferential attention in this office."[25]

Elkins had difficulty persuading Pure's Van unit partners to accept the increase. Humble vice-president John Suman informed the TRC that the increase would hurt prorationing because other Texas oil fields, in all fairness, would be entitled to similar increases. He proposed a compromise whereby the TRC would raise Pure's daily allowable from 38,000 to 42,500 barrels, in return for Pure's dropping its lawsuit.[26] Elkins countered that an increase in the Van allowable would not harm other producers because Pure had a ready market for the additional oil.[27]

On February 3, the TRC increased the Van allowable to 52,450 barrels a day. This was less than Pure had desired, but, as Dawes told Elkins, "I was never much of a hand to teach my grandmother to suck eggs, and therefore hesitate to attempt to give you any advice as to how to handle this matter." Elkins advised Pure management against dropping the lawsuit prematurely, believing that the threat of further litigation would dissuade the TRC from decreasing Van production. The longer the lawsuit hung over the TRC's head, Elkins predicted, the more likely would "the clouds . . . soon disappear and the sun . . . shine again."[28] Although Pure wanted 6,000 or 8,000 barrels more, Dawes agreed to accept less rather than risk having its allowable reduced below 52,450 barrels.[29] The injunction remained in effect and there is no evidence of the ultimate disposition of Pure's lawsuit.[30]

The legal battle over prorationing resumed before a three-judge federal court in Houston. Nichols's attorney, Rice M. Tilley, argued that the TRC's proration order was confiscatory, unreasonable, and discriminatory. A. H. Rowan testified that 5,300 of the 9,600 East Texas field oil wells had been drilled under special exception permits, and that the TRC had retained its flat per-well allocation formula in violation of the court's ruling in the *People's* case. He wanted the TRC to consider acreage, sand thickness, and other factors in determining allowables.[31]

"In order to kill the goose to get the golden egg," Tilley claimed, small operators embracing 10 to 15 percent of the East Texas field "had drilled three or four wells where one well would suffice, [trying] to get someone else's oil." He claimed to be unable to see how anyone could be "foolish enough to believe a rule could be enforced where the exceptions are more numerous than the general rule." Such tendencies were "nothing short of Socialistic," Tilley argued, pointing to his client, "with 53 acres and only four wells, [who] has had his leases drained, and earnestly endeavored to be equally protected by the law and prevent his property from being taken, without avail." The poorest operator was "no more entitled . . . to the equal protection of the laws," Tilley maintained, "than the largest and most prosperous corporation in the field, although [Rowan & Nichols] has never assumed to be in the latter class."[32]

Assistant Attorney General Maurice Cheek responded that the TRC's orders had been promulgated in good faith and carried a presumption of reasonableness. Co-counsel Robert Hardwicke argued that Rowan & Nichols were not entitled to equitable relief without first seeking relief through the TRC hearing process. The problem with that, Tilley responded, was that "as soon as one order was questioned, they [TRC] could simply pass another slightly different order."[33]

"We are trying to fix the allowable production at a point where waste will not occur," Commissioner Thompson testified, "and if the price of oil goes up as an incident, that is not our fault."[34] With the aid of a blackboard, chalk, and several prepared charts, TRC engineer E. O. Buck tried to show the court the importance of bottom-hole pressure in determining safe withdrawal rates. A befuddled and frustrated Hutcheson mused, "The oil-gas ratio was the big thing in the first case, but now it's bottom-hole pressure."[35]

Fletcher "Big Fish" Fischer, as plaintiffs' attorney, requested a temporary restraining order to keep TRC agents off his clients' properties. Known as the "legal terror of the oil patch," Fischer was a formidable country lawyer whose folksy style had endeared him to East Texas jurors. Admitted to the Oklahoma bar in 1910 after "reading" law, Fischer had migrated to Tyler in 1931 to cash in on the oil boom, and he now represented most of the "hot oilers" in the East Texas field. Fischer argued that armed TRC agents had been entering his clients' properties, replicating "the occupation of that country by military forces in 1931 which this court already has held invalid." When Hutcheson questioned whether some of his clients had been accused of violating TRC orders, Fischer admitted that "one or two" of them had. Hutcheson denied Fischer's motion and gave attorneys for both sides two weeks to file supplemental briefs before rendering a decision.[36]

"Legitimate oilmen are disgusted with present conditions," reported the *Oil and Gas Journal,* urging that "either proration . . . be enforced rigidly and 100 percent or . . . be abandoned." The problem was not simply, as in the fable, crying wolf too often. Legal devices such as injunctions effectively stymied strict, impartial, and effective enforcement of oil production controls.[37]

Mounting criticism of the TRC persuaded the Texas House to investigate the East Texas field. "We try to get the rules enforced without filing complaints, by talking with the operators," testified Homer Pierson, a supervisor for the TRC's oil and gas division, and "seven times out of ten we get it corrected this way without having to go to court." The TRC had 119 agents in East Texas and 130 employees in its oil and gas division in Austin. Agent R. L. Knight opined that the TRC needed more experienced oil men and investigators, "fewer real estate salesmen and grocery clerks." The former federal prohibition officer claimed that proration was harder to enforce than the liquor ban and added that he carried a gun when gauging wells. Knight described most TRC employees as "scared to death" of violators, who "simply change the name of their well and you have to catch them again." "We've got to put the fear of God into . . . chronic violators," insisted Agent Luther Swift, "who, by virtue of injunctions, tax the patience of law-abiding producers."[38]

On March 9, 1933, the TRC increased the East Texas field allowable from 290,000 to 400,000 barrels per day. A third of the allowable would be distributed to individual wells according to well-potential, a third by bottom-hole pressure, and a third on the basis of sand thickness. The TRC hoped the additional allowable would discourage illegal production—which averaged 125,000 to 150,000 barrels daily—and alleviate incidents of violence and sabotage. One pipeline company's lines had been dynamited three times during the first week of March, while two other pipelines and an oil well had been blown up in one week. One blast resulted in the loss of several thousand barrels of crude; damage to derricks, a bridge, and the pipelines of other companies; and a creek filled with burning oil.[39]

Holmes threatened to lower the Texas Company's posted price unless state authorities in Texas and Oklahoma curtailed production to reasonable market demand. Thompson refused to let Holmes's "most flagrant attempt at monopolistic domination and dictation go by without raising my voice as a public official . . . against such effrontery." Texas law "[did] not contemplate that the American Petroleum Institute or the president of any great oil company shall tell the State of Texas how much oil it will be permitted to produce," Thompson declared, "That is the duty of the Railroad Commission of Texas." He adamantly objected to allowing "Holmes's lawyers draft[ing] laws and writ[ing] orders." Thompson blamed cumbersome litigation for ineffective enforcement of prorationing and suggested new laws authorizing the arrest of violators on the spot.[40]

The *Dallas Morning News* blamed legal problems for chronic overproduction. It endorsed Holmes's suggestion that the TRC avail itself of the ablest lawyers to draft a legal order. Although the TRC was not a price-fixing body, the *Morning News* recognized price as an inherent feature of market demand, which statutory law now authorized the agency to consider. "The demand voiced by . . . Holmes of production so

limited as to force a rise in crude price is not that of the major companies," the *Morning News* reported, but "the cry of 95 percent of the oil
operators in Texas."[41]

Major oil company executives, independents, lawyers, and representatives of various oil associations in Texas met in Fort Worth on March
13. They condemned the TRC for increasing the East Texas field
production and called for an immediate change in existing laws to avert
a complete breakdown of the oil industry. C. A. Lester, who had succeeded Carl Estes as president of the East Texas Producers, Land, and
Royalty Owners Association, recommended revision of the Marginal
Well Act to permit greater production to flowing wells. API president
Ames implored oilmen to legally put their house in order by obeying
the law themselves and cooperating with authorities. But Gulf Coast
producers such as George Sawtelle complained of too many "Bolshe-
viks," and blamed major oil companies for not cooperating in stabilizing conditions.[42]

The TRC received more bad news on March 15, when the Texas House
Committee on Oil, Gas, and Mining filed its investigative report. It criticized the TRC for allowing "5 percent of the operators in the East Texas
field to completely demoralize the oil industry in the entire state and
the nation." The committee concluded that the TRC could have "placed
more competent and experienced men in field" and "as a result of [its]
policies . . . public confidence has been so shaken . . . that unless radical changes are resorted to," the life of the East Texas field would be
cut short. On March 21, Representative Harry M. Graves publicized a
report prepared by Griffen-Hagen and Associates indicating that the
TRC had "proved ineffective in the regulation of oil and gas production, and its authority command[ed] little respect in the oil industry."[43]

Holmes told legislators that the Texas Company refused "to plead
guilty to the humorous charge . . . that we are Octopi." Even though
the Standard companies "have been as mean as Satan," he explained,
"they usually play the game fairly," and are more desirable than some
"so-called independents and bootleg outfits whose destructive activities constantly receive unwarranted support and encouragement even
to the point of supporting organized rackets." Holmes urged Texans "to
take a neighborly view of the situation" and refrain from "the disposition . . . to frown upon cooperation and condemn all kinds of organized
business."[44]

Yet another bombshell had struck the TRC on March 17, when a three-judge federal court, in deciding *Rowan & Nichols*, struck down the TRC's proration order. In a short, unreported opinion, Hutcheson found the allowable to be lower than previous orders invalidated by the court. He also ruled that the TRC's flat per-well allocation formula arbitrarily deprived one producer to give to another. The uncontradicted testimony of TRC engineer E. O. Buck convinced Hutcheson that not all sections of the East Texas field had been accorded an equal opportunity to produce oil. He was not satisfied with the TRC's subsequent attempt to consider acreage and bottom-hole pressure in addition to well-potential. Hutcheson rejected the state's argument that aggrieved parties could not sue in court until availing themselves of the TRC hearing process. "It is generally accepted that a regulatory body may not put confiscatory orders into effect," he held, "and by a provision for a rehearing, take the property of those affected while the rehearing goes on."[45]

The decision was a serious blow to the TRC, but Hardwicke argued that it did not affect subsequent proration orders issued under the Market Demand Act, and warned that violators did so at their own peril. "Crack your whip," replied one defiant East Texas independent, "this is a free country . . . We . . . bought these leases . . . it is our property . . . bought . . . and paid for . . . and we have got the right to use it in any way we see fit."[46]

Dissatisfied oilmen complained to newly installed U.S. Secretary of the Interior Harold L. Ickes that "injunctions and counter injunctions of laws and rules, dissension in the legislature, lack of respect for orders of the state commission [i.e., the TRC], and widespread violations throughout the field" had been menacing both the oil industry's and the public's interests by allowing the "dissipation of irreplaceable natural resources and threatened disorder." They described how "armed men are protecting leases and pipelines [which] have been dynamited" and cited "the inability of state authorities to bring about effective control of production under state proration laws" as an emergency justifying "federal control of the East Texas oil field."[47] Their message echoed the cries of an increasing number of Texas oilmen, big and little, demanding what they had heretofore least desired: federal regulation to stop selfish obstruction by a handful of racketeers and politicians.[48]

Governor Miriam A. "Ma" Ferguson referred to a "reign of terror" in the East Texas field that had disturbed local inhabitants "in mind and spirit beyond comprehension." She warned that law-abiding citizens were "arming themselves with firearms and threatening to take the law into their hands" to protect their oil. Ferguson claimed that "hundreds of thousands of barrels of oil" were being illegally taken, costing the state "thousands of dollars daily" in lost tax revenues. She cautioned that the East Texas field problem had attracted too much attention outside of the state, tempting the federal government to "invade the constitutional right of our beloved state to . . . control its own affairs."[49]

On April 3, the TRC attempted to devise yet another proration order to appease the federal court. Allred did not believe that restriction of flowing wells to the same output as marginal wells would withstand judicial scrutiny. Hardwicke countered that abandonment of the per-well system would leave each of the 10,000 East Texas field wells to produce at least 40 barrels a day, or 400,000 barrels daily to start with. He doubted that 400,000 barrels could be reasonably and fairly distributed between good and bad properties as the courts required. If the TRC adopted Allred's interpretation of the Marginal Well Act, Hardwicke predicted, "It would be utter foolishness [to worry about] underground waste and pressure . . . when we are going to start off with . . . a million barrels without any question." He advised the TRC to "take a chance" in the interest of conservation and limit some flowing wells to less than 40 barrels per day.[50]

Attorney Charles L. Black argued that a well, operating without artificial stimulation and with a potential above 40 barrels a day, should not be classified as a marginal well. Humble attorney Baker believed that the TRC faced a dilemma. If it adhered to Hardwicke's advice, the courts might rule that it unreasonably discriminated in favor of flowing wells against marginal wells. By following Allred's suggestion, the TRC would have to raise the East Texas field allowable above 400,000 barrels a day, putting itself in the indefensible position of justifying an order which produced, rather than prevented, waste. Thompson proposed that the legislature amend the Marginal Well Act.[51]

Pure management worried that the TRC would have to increase East Texas field production to 700,000 barrels a day under Allred's plan. This would hurt a saturated crude oil market and pressure the TRC to compensate by reducing production in other Texas fields, such as Van. Elkins opined that Allred's opinion "may not be altogether sound," but stated his confidence that the TRC could be convinced to maintain Van's 52,400-barrel daily allowable.[52] Bearing testimony to Elkins's confidence, the TRC issued a new order on April 10 increasing statewide production from 927,645 to 941,700 barrels per day, and raising daily allowables in the East Texas and Van fields from 400,000 to 541,700 barrels and from 52,450 to 52,500 barrels, respectively.[53]

On April 15, the Texas House revised the Marginal Well Act to permit the TRC to limit production of marginal wells to fewer than 40 barrels per day. The daily allowable for each marginal well would range from 10 to 35 barrels, depending on depth. The curtailment of pumping or marginal wells would pacify East Texas producers with flowing wells, who felt that they should be allowed greater recovery. On April 23 the Texas Senate approved the bill, and Governor Ferguson signed it on April 27.[54]

But the TRC had shut down the East Texas field on April 11 to gauge the potential production of 275 key oil wells.[55] TRC engineers estimated an average hourly well potential of 517 barrels. Based on that data, the TRC prorated East Texas field production at 15 percent of 517 barrels, or 77.55 barrels per day for each of the field's 10,004 oil wells, regardless of acreage. This put total field production at 775,800 barrels a day. The April 23 order drew immediate criticism.[56]

Many operators (particularly the majors), upset over the high allowable, argued that it would prematurely dissipate reservoir energy and cause underground waste. At recent TRC hearings, engineers had testified that producing from the East Texas field in excess of 325,000 barrels a day, regardless of market demand, would create physical waste. Comparing the "absurdity" of the TRC's orders to the "emptiness" of its excuses, the *Oil and Gas Journal* asked, "Can any man with any knowledge of oil production whatever credit such nonsense? Who wants what the commission proposes?" It claimed that "ninety-five percent of the oil industry is definitely opposed to it, knowing the disastrous effect it must have." But the TRC responded that the courts would overturn a lower allowable. Judge Bryant's federal courtroom in Tyler was again flooded with lawsuits.[57]

East Texas oil producers and royalty owners soon got a foretaste of the effect of vast overproduction on market price. On April 24, the Texas Company cuts its posted price for East Texas field oil from 50 to 10 cents per barrel. The following day, Humble, Shell, Sun, Stanolind, Tide Water, and Empire committed to "dime barrel" oil. Farish claimed that low prices wrought by overproduction in the East Texas field made it "impossible for [Humble] to buy and sell oil produced in other fields on the basis of our present posted prices." Humble announced that it would restrict purchases from its East Texas field connections to 75 percent of production. Atlantic Crude Oil Purchasing Company announced that it would purchase only 60 percent of the new allowable. Shell president R. G. A. Van der Woude blamed the TRC for failing to consider "market requirements and [placing] the allowable production for Texas on an impossible basis." By lowering their postings to the "going price," the majors hoped to "break up the play house" of hot oil runners. During the 24-hour period ending at 7 A.M. on May 1, East Texas field production reached 1,100,000 barrels.[58]

Holmes vehemently excoriated oil "bootleggers" for destroying the oil industry, and blasted some of his unnamed colleagues for lacking the will to fight those responsible for "racketeering." He called for "a showdown on proration enforcement" and offered "substantial rewards" for information leading to the arrest and conviction of hot oilers. Holmes claimed that some 75 million barrels of illegal or "stolen" oil had been produced over the past fifteen months. "We are not going to be robbed and ruined by a lot of racketeers," Holmes warned, and if the state and federal governments failed to enforce the law, "we will do it."[59]

Roeser criticized the TRC's April 23 order as being "just as illegal as the others . . . struck down by the federal courts time after time." Sam Ross, president of the East Texas Oil Landowners' Association (ETOLA), said that his organization's 1,000 members would shut down their wells to protest the 10-cent barrel postings by the majors. ETOLA implored the TRC and the legislature "to attend to their respective duties and quit making a political football out of the East Texas oil field." The 200 members of the East Texas Independent Oil Operators pledged to cooperate with the ETOLA in a common course of action.

Captain E. N. Stanley, head of the TRC's field office in Kilgore, labeled the price cuts "a stab in the back." TRC chairman Smith said, "We cannot help it if there is too much oil in East Texas, we did not put it there," and stated that the TRC would not alter the allowable unless ordered to do so by a federal court. Referring to recent price declines, Smith said that the TRC "would wait and see if [majors] cut the price of gasoline and other products manufactured from crude oil in the same proportion." If they did, he believed it would indicate their sincerity in reducing prices, if not, "we will know it was done in an effort to coerce and punish the [TRC] and the people of Texas." Thompson denounced the price cuts as "the boldest, most sinister, coercive, and high-handed action the major oil companies have yet taken in their efforts to control Texas."[60]

Nothing seemed capable of stemming the flood of oil pouring out of the East Texas field. Independents and majors alike continued producing regardless of low prices. In the 24-hour period ending 7 A.M. on April 29, 698 railroad tank cars left the field. The next day, 875 tank cars rolled. Many disillusioned and discouraged proponents of market-demand prorationing now advocated unrestricted flow, come what may. They felt that the only practical way to eliminate hot oilers was to allow overproduction to force prices low enough to drive them out of business. Honest producers and land and royalty owners would suffer, but in the long run, the East Texas field would right itself, and the survivors would benefit.[61]

The legal battle over prorationing shifted back to the legislature. The Texas House passed a bill to create a new appointed natural resources commission to regulate oil and gas, but not after a long and bitter debate that had literally degenerated into fisticuffs. Roeser and two others slugged and kicked Representative Burns in a hotel lobby for opposing the bill. Burns had to be hospitalized.[62]

On April 29, the Senate State Affairs Committee voted, by 8 to 6, to recommend passage of the bill. But news of the Burns episode spread quickly, outraging the public. Many senators feared that voting for the bill would lead their constituents to look on them as frightened and driven by the oil lobby. Senator Will Pace of Tyler damned the commission bill as "conceived in inequity and hatched out for the purpose of robbing my people in East Texas." He vowed to "keep the Standard Oil Company and those allied with it from taking the birthright" of East Texans. Burns, in a wheelchair, was wheeled into the Senate chamber to witness the bill's defeat by a vote of 20 to 10.[63]

After all the figurative brawling, the Texas legislature came away with nothing more than a reputation as battered and bruised as its member from Huntsville. The major oil companies tried their hand at reversing the downward spiral. Magnolia Petroleum Company led the way on April 26 by posting a 25-cent per barrel price for East Texas field crude. Sinclair-Prairie, Tide Water, Atlantic, and the Texas Company followed. Humble soon posted a price of 25 cents per barrel and a 100 percent purchase program.[64] Nevertheless, East Texas field independents, led by H. L. Hunt, marched to the federal district courthouse in Tyler to pile injunction applications on Judge Bryant's bench. They complained that the TRC's April 23 order was a subterfuge to reestablish the old flat per-well prorationing previously struck down by the court. Bryant consolidated the individual suits into the *Hunt* case, and scheduled a hearing on May 26.[65]

In an unreported decision on that date, Hutcheson admonished Hunt and other plaintiffs to "get these cases out of this court to a higher court and get a definite decision—find out who is right and who is wrong— let's have an end to this constant running in and out of the federal courts." Meanwhile, the TRC proration order would stand as the best that could be devised under prevailing circumstances.[66]

The federal court handed the TRC another favorable decision in June against its old nemesis, Joseph Danciger. After failing in state court, Danciger tried to persuade the federal court to restrain the TRC from restricting production from his wells in the Panhandle oil field for which he had a ready market. On Danciger's behalf, former Texas Supreme Court Justice Nelson Phillips argued that the TRC's order amounted to "a complete confiscation of property." He asked, "Where does the state get this power to intercede in behalf of any industry?" and added, "It might as well step in and help the horse and wagon industry because the automobile is making them obsolete."[67]

"Whether in fact wise or unwise," Hutcheson upheld the TRC order as "a not unreasonable exercise of judgment and discretion in the discharge of the difficult and exacting administrative duties which the statutes have imposed upon the commission." The court refused to substitute its judgment for the TRC's in light of conflicting testimony regarding physical conditions in the Panhandle field. Hutcheson implied that the court would sustain administrative regulations as long as "reasonable minds reached the same conclusions." He found the TRC's proration order for the Panhandle field bore a reasonable relationship to the prevention of waste and did not arbitrarily and unfairly interfere with Danciger's private property rights. The decision signified a major breakthrough in the TRC's legal authority. Given conflicting evidence, the court would presume the TRC correct unless convinced otherwise.[68]

A local federal court handed the TRC yet another victory on August 8, when it upheld its proration order limiting each oil well in the Conroe field to 15.73 percent of its potential production, but granted exceptions depending on acreage. Hutcheson rejected Boxrolium Oil Company's complaint that the TRC had not uniformly granted exceptions resulting in inequalities in distributing the field allowable. The significance of this decision lay in stressing that the state could limit oil production as long as all producers in a given field were allowed to earn a profit.[69]

A string of favorable federal court rulings had seemingly reversed the TRC's fortunes at a time when its credibility had reached low ebb. But the TRC paid a high price for the victories. To obtain the blessing of local federal judges, it increased the East Texas field allowable to dangerous levels which had serious consequences. By the end of May, 1933, the field's reservoir pressure had dropped from 1,600 to 1,200 pounds. Engineers determined that if reservoir pressure fell below 750 pounds, the underlying oil could not be raised to the surface without artificial pumping. The TRC could maintain field pressure by reducing production, but this would invite further lawsuits and induce more hot oil production.[70]

A vicious cycle was again set into motion. The TRC attempted to avert chaos by reducing production while defiant operators produced hot oil to make up the difference. Even though both state and federal courts had finally upheld its proration orders in 1933, the TRC lacked adequate manpower to enforce them. The TRC's inability to effectively enforce the law along with declining bottom-hole pressure in the East Texas field convinced many operators, who had previously opposed any type of regulation, to turn to the federal government to save them from the destructive competition wrought by the rule of capture.[71]

The catastrophe in East Texas undermined the legal theory that every landowner had a right to drill into a common reservoir and appropriate all the oil and gas he could extract through his wells. This poorly conceived law of ownership affected a public interest that outweighed the welfare of the oil industry. It involved America's supply of gasoline and other petroleum products at a time when the world was turning to oil for motive and lubricating requirements. By the early 1930s, most American oilmen realized that the antisocial waste and destructive influences wrought by the rule of capture could be remedied only by orderly methods of production.[72]

The oil crisis was not over. The failure of voluntary and state government efforts to alleviate chronic overproduction in the East Texas field laid the basis for federal regulation.[73] Achieving and maintaining stability in the oil industry was an integral part of the "New Deal" promulgated by the recently inaugurated Franklin Roosevelt to revive the depressed national economy. The coming of the New Deal paralleled a transition period in American petroleum law; protection of the public interest from usurpation by a few gradually took precedence over protection of individual private property rights.

CHAPTER 10

New Deal for the Oil Patch

*It is a sad commentary on the pioneers of this
he-man's business when troubles—absolutely temporary
in their nature—develop a spirit of defeat and result in a
plan to practically turn over the operation of the business
to outside influences, and political influences at that.*

—Andrew M. Rowley

The failure of voluntary and state government efforts to control oil production raised the spectre of national intervention. Domestic production of 85,302,000 barrels in March, 1933, exceeded February's total by 249,000 barrels a day. Most of the additional oil came from Texas, Oklahoma, and Kansas at a time when a worldwide depression had lessened the demand for petroleum products. The oil industry reached a crossroad as crude oil prices plunged below operating costs and oilmen reluctantly turned to Uncle Sam to help them get their house in order.[1]

The new administration of Franklin D. Roosevelt was taking quick and far-reaching action to stimulate economic recovery within the framework of business-government cooperation. The National Industrial Recovery Act (NIRA), administered by the National Recovery Administration (NRA) under General Hugh S. Johnson, brought business-men into partnership with government to foster industrial self-policing with minimal regulation. The NIRA aimed to promote economic recovery by increasing employment, wages, and purchasing power to boost consumer demand, stimulate production, and raise prices so as to restore the vitality of industry. Johnson lectured oilmen who decried regulation that "Al Capone was a poor ignorant Sicilian piker next to those rugged individualists who wanted to prolong the dark ages of human relationships."[2]

After oil-industry leaders informed Interior Secretary Harold Ickes that the market structure of petroleum had gone to smash, Roosevelt instructed him to summon the governors of oil-producing states to Washington. Historian John G. Clark argues that conditions in the East Texas and Oklahoma City fields had convinced Ickes that national intervention was urgently needed, and his "concern for national security transcended all other objectives in the evaluation of oil policy." Ickes stated that the nation could ill afford to permit producers to eliminate themselves through cutthroat competition while wantonly squandering the country's "very life blood." Though he had inherited the FOCB's policy emphasizing state action in lieu of direct national control, Clark notes, "Ickes harbored no deeply embedded belief in the capacity of the states or industry, acting unilaterally or jointly, to bring production under control by means of state prorationing laws."

Events in East Texas reinforced Ickes's view. After East Texas field crude plummeted to 4 cents a barrel on May 5, Ickes was bombarded with telegrams and letters urging the appointment of a national oil czar. Texas governor "Ma" Ferguson admitted that the situation was beyond the control of state authorities and required national intervention.[3]

Ickes appealed to 200 oil industry representatives and governors of oil-producing states, meeting in Washington on March 27, to put their own house in order. He blamed widespread tax evasion, illegal production, irregular distribution of unmarketable production, and inadequate enforcement of state statutes for the breakdown in oil conservation. Ickes warned that Americans were by no means "helpless to prevent the reckless dissipation of an indispensable natural resource."[4]

Historians Linda Lear and Gerald Nash maintain that the Washington conference disabused Ickes of any notion he may have held that diverse factions within the oil industry could agree on any policy. Majors and independents continued fighting among themselves. Some rejected any production controls, while others were willing to accept national regulation as long as enforcement remained primarily in the hands of the states. Texas officials opposed any national intervention, while those from Oklahoma and Kansas wanted an interstate compact. A majority report, approved by the API and by 13 of the 18 independent oilmen's associations, proposed state production controls backed by national regulation of interstate transportation of hot oil along with import quotas and protective tariffs. A minority of independents, led by IPAT president J. R. Parten and Independent Petroleum Association of California president John B. Elliott, opposed any national intervention.[5]

Another committee, this time a Committee of Fifteen, was formed to reach a compromise. It recommended a national law banning hot oil from interstate commerce, a national production quota of two million barrels a day, an oil tariff, and appointment of an oil czar to assist the states in coordinating production control. As a temporary measure, the committee called upon the president to impose the equivalent of a banking holiday for the petroleum industry by asking the governors to shut down production in new fields for two weeks.[6]

Dissident independents organized the Independent Petroleum Association Opposed to Monopoly (IPAOM). IPAOM represented small California refiners, who lacked access to interstate pipelines and depended upon a supply of cheap crude oil to compete with major refineries, and those small East Texas producers who opposed any production controls. To ensure the survival of small independents, IPAOM demanded strict enforcement of antitrust laws and import quotas. It urged the national government to leave the oil industry to the states and to concentrate on breaking up the "big oil combinations." Listening patiently, Ickes commented, "Just how independent the independents are, God alone knows."[7]

Roosevelt informed the governors of oil-producing states that he lacked authority to declare a moratorium on crude oil production. He agreed to ask Congress to enact legislation prohibiting interstate and foreign shipments of hot oil and he approved of the strict enforcement of gasoline and pipeline taxes. Roosevelt endorsed IPOAM's request for a national law divorcing interstate oil pipelines from other branches of the petroleum industry. Pipeline divorcement had long been advocated by small producers and refiners, who protested that the majors, through ownership of the primary means of transporting crude oil, had restricted competition and controlled prices. The relatively high profits of pipeline companies galled small independents, particularly during the depression-ridden 1930s.[8]

Based on the Committee of Fifteen's recommendations, the Marland–Capper bill was introduced in Congress on May 20.[9] It gave the Secretary of the Interior broad powers to regulate domestic production and crude oil imports and to set both minimum and maximum prices for petroleum. The IPAA supported the measure realizing the inevitability of some form of national regulation and that failure to pass the bill would play into the hands of the majors who preferred controls through the general services bill. The TRC denounced the bill as a slap in the face of states' rights.[10] Roosevelt remained uncommitted. Historian Norman Nordhauser argues that Roosevelt's strategy "was probably dictated by the expectation of congressional opposition to the Marland–Capper bill and by the fear that such resistance could turn into a major fight," delaying passage of Senator Robert Wagner's measure for general recovery and public works, which eventually became the NIRA.[11] Doubts about the constitutionality of national regulation of oil production influenced the Roosevelt administration to opt for, in lieu of the Marland–Capper bill, an amendment to the NIRA restricting interstate transportation of hot oil.[12]

Two diametrically opposed views emerged within the oil industry over national regulation. Major integrated oil companies preferred state regulation reinforced by an interstate compact. API president Ames praised the NIRA's attempt "to bring the government into partnership with industry." He urged oilmen to support the NIRA because it permitted industrial self-regulation under national aegis with exemption from antitrust laws. The IPAA espoused the views of independents who preferred direct national controls, fearing that industrial self-government would give the majors too much control.[13]

Ickes believed that oil conservation and industrial stability could be achieved only through strong national action. Face-to-face contact with divided and mutually antagonistic oil factions reinforced Ickes's determination to persuade Roosevelt to push for direct national production controls, even at the risk of rejection by the courts. Ickes and the IPAA desired direct national controls for different reasons, but this marriage of convenience failed to overcome powerful opposition by majors and some independents, who wanted national aid without national control. Johnson criticized oilmen as "a discouraged and disorganized mob" incapable of agreeing on a code. Hoping to compromise, Roosevelt admitted that overproduction had a negative impact on price and conservation, but he rejected the Marland–Capper bill because it divorced the oil industry's problems from the NIRA's all-encompassing solution to the economic depression.[14]

Ickes proposed an amendment, introduced by Senator Tom Connally of Texas, that incorporated many features of the Marland–Capper bill into Title I, Section 9 of the NIRA. Section 9(c) authorized the president to "prohibit the transportation in interstate and foreign commerce of petroleum and the products thereof produced or withdrawn from storage in excess of the amount permitted to be produced or withdrawn from storage by any state law." Congress passed the NIRA on June 16, and Section 9(c) gave a majority of oilmen what they wanted: a national hot oil act with minimal national government control. Production quotas remained in the hands of the states. The national government could interdict interstate shipments of hot oil but could not impose production quotas on the states. Although the new law failed to unite the deeply divided oil industry, Congress tossed the problem back to oilmen to devise an acceptable code.[15]

On July 8, the TRC asked President Roosevelt to ban interstate and foreign shipments of hot oil, assuring him that it had the "unqualified support of the greater part of the industry." On July 11, the Texas Petroleum Council[16] petitioned Roosevelt to invoke Section 9(c). Roosevelt issued an executive order on July 12 banning interstate or foreign shipments of hot oil and delegating responsibility for enforcement to the Secretary of the Interior. Ickes immediately promulgated regulations requiring producers to file monthly affidavits with the Interior Department's Division of Investigation swearing that their oil had neither been produced nor withdrawn from storage illegally. Shippers and refiners also had to submit affidavits affirming that they had neither received nor shipped hot oil.[17]

Federal investigators were dispatched to the East Texas field, where 185,000 to 200,000 barrels of hot oil were being run each day. They examined oil refinery records, gauged oil wells, inspected tanks, and even dug up pipelines to measure the accuracy of sworn reports. After the first week of enforcement, East Texas field production dropped from 779,000 to 605,000 barrels per day. Tank car shipments of crude oil fell from 600 to 9 cars a day. "These men evidently mean business," reported the *Oil and Gas Journal,* and "the outlook is far brighter than it has been in a long time." Some resourceful East Texas field operators proved that the optimism was premature. They defied national regulations with the same impunity as they had state controls. Still, Roosevelt's executive order marked a significant advance toward effective regulation through national-state cooperation.

An atmosphere of cooperation and harmony prevailed among majors and independents at an API meeting in Chicago in June, even though Texas and California oilmen boycotted the conference. The delegates drew up the "Chicago Code," providing for a national committee of 54 oilmen, who would compute and publish periodic forecasts of domestic market demand to be allocated among the oil-producing states. Each state would then distribute its quota among individual oil fields. IPAA president Franklin demanded a price-fixing provision, arguing that production controls alone would not guarantee a profitable return. Skelly Oil's C. C. Herndon expressed the fears of most major oil company executives that price-fixing would lead to excessive government intervention and that the petroleum industry would be trading its freedom for the Biblical "mess of pottage." A price-fixing provision was adopted by a narrow margin, and Hugh Johnson persuaded the delegates to incorporate NIRA labor provisions into the code.[18]

From July 24 to August 2, more than a thousand oilmen gathered in Washington for public hearings on the code. Conflicting testimony revealed deep division and tension over price-fixing and a reduction in working hours to affect a 25 percent increase (250,000) in oil industry labor. With Roosevelt's backing, Johnson drafted his own code, which provided for a national agency to formulate production quotas based on domestic market demand to be allocated among the oil-producing states. The president would have authority to prevent interstate shipments of oil from any state that exceeded its quota. Johnson gave oilmen 24 hours to "take it or leave it."[19] He replied to TRC chairman Ernest Thompson's states' rights-based objection that "the question of whether a state shall deluge its neighbor with oil to the demoralization of the industry . . . is a federal question" and states would have "to stew in their own [excess] oil."[20]

Teagle and Pew voiced the objections of major oil company executives who believed that production controls alone would raise crude oil prices while price-fixing would encourage overproduction and break the price structure. California Standard president Oscar Sutro countered that, without price controls, "you can make codes from now to doomsday and get nowhere." IPAA president Franklin refused to endorse any code without price controls. Harry F. Sinclair warned that anyone who signed an oil code without a price regulation "might just as well sign a bankruptcy petition."[21]

Johnson submitted for the president's approval a revised code that provided for a 15-member Planning and Coordinating Committee (PCC). Twelve members would be chosen by the oil industry, three by the president. The PCC would function jointly with another national agency to be designated by the president to enforce the petroleum code. Among other things, it would issue periodic estimates of market demand and recommend production quotas to oil-producing states. Johnson incorporated a modified price-fixing provision whereby the minimum price of a barrel of crude oil (42 gallons) would be determined by multiplying the wholesale price of a gallon of regular gasoline by a fixed multiple of 18.5 (the ratio of gasoline prices to crude oil prices during the base period of 1928 to 1932).[22]

Thompson warned Roosevelt that national production controls violated state sovereignty and were unnecessary as the president's July 11 executive order had stopped hot oil shipments. He vowed to resist any attempt "to force a direct federal regime in oil control in Texas as a substitute for state authority." As an elected official with gubernatorial ambitions, Thompson was obviously playing to his native constituency. He wanted national assistance to aid the TRC in enforcing prorationing, but without national control.[23] Texas attorney general Allred echoed Thompson's demands. Major oil company officials and the IPAA supported mandatory national production quotas. "I would rather take Harold Ickes, and have state, national, international [government], or Soviet Russia control my country than a band of thieves," declared Carl Estes, a former foe of proration and government regulation, as he denounced 85 percent of the East Texas field's oilmen as "plain, unadulterated thieves." Roosevelt compromised and approved a revised code providing for voluntary national production quotas.[24]

Roosevelt appointed Secretary of Interior Ickes as petroleum administrator. Historian Gerald D. Nash argues that Ickes's appointment represented a personal triumph in his internal power struggle with Hugh Johnson for control within the administration. It more likely represented Roosevelt's attempt to continue the pattern of government-business ties that the Hoover administration had established under the aegis of the Interior Department. Ickes already had responsibility for enforcing the July 11 executive order. Since the petroleum code was designed to stabilize the oil market, it seemed logical to unify administration of the two complementary modes of regulation to maximize effectiveness and efficiency. By naming Ickes as petroleum administrator, Roosevelt avoided the interminable misunderstandings, delays, and mutual recriminations which would have surely resulted by assigning many different functions to separate and independent agencies.[25]

The PCC set up a network of regional, state, and local committees to report code violations like overproduction, price-cutting, rebates, and unfair advertising methods. Ickes established the five-member (three lawyers and two economists) Petroleum Administration Board, or PAB, to "advise and assist" him in supervising and enforcing the code. The PAB stood at the apex of what Ickes called the "new Parliament of the oil industry." There was nothing new or radical in this voluntary arrangement between national, state, and local agencies. The NRA merely formalized inter-company cooperation allowed during World War I and the trade association movement promoted by Republican administrations in the 1920s.[26]

Ickes appointed Nathan R. Margold as Solicitor of the Interior Department and PAB chairman, and J. Howard Marshall as special assistant to the attorney general. Fifteen more lawyers were designated as Special Assistants, with the authority to investigate and prosecute hot oil cases. This signified the importance of law and the role of lawyers in implementing the code.[27] The Petroleum Economics Division of the U.S. Bureau of Mines compiled statistical data to publish monthly forecasts of the market demand for crude oil. With the assistance of the Interior Department's Division of Investigations, the PAB was responsible for enforcing production quotas assigned to those states lacking petroleum administrative agencies such as the TRC. In general, the PAB acted as a mediator between warring factions within the oil industry and referred unresolvable cases to the Department of Justice for prosecution.[28]

Ickes was eager to eliminate hot oil to bring production under control and stabilize prices, but in a way that accommodated the oil industry's interests. He indicated that price controls would not be invoked unless necessary and believed that when production equalled demand and no more, producers would get a fair price. If not, then prices would fall in proportion to overproduction. Ickes insisted that the success of production controls demanded "strong nerves, clear heads, and sound hearts" and the exercise of the "best business judgment, highest technical skill, utter unselfishness, and ardent patriotism." His confidence in production controls was borne out in September, when the price of 36 gravity Mid-Continent crude rose from under 50 cents a barrel to within 22 cents of the base price of $1.11 per barrel.[29]

As Pure's chief legal advisor on oil regulations, Elkins had a profound interest in the NRA petroleum code. Although he disliked the New Deal and referred to Roosevelt as "that old crippled bastard," Elkins believed that the oil industry's crisis coupled with the general economic depression warranted national intervention.[30] "Irrespective of whether the president's policies suit us personally . . . [Roosevelt] is assuming full responsibility " Elkins said, "and I think we should help him by giving him our cooperation." Elkins believed that opposition to the NRA would "prove unpopular and unwise," because the federal courts would probably sustain the national recovery program.[31]

The relaxation of national antitrust enforcement under the NRA appealed to Elkins, as Pure and its four major oil company partners had unitized their lease-holdings in the Van field. In states (such as Texas) with strong antitrust laws, oil producers shunned unitization for fear of prosecution.[32] Pure and its Van unit partners had escaped prosecution because Texas' attorney general Allred had viewed any possible violations as "technical," believing that the Van unit operation benefitted the industry and the state.[33]

The code's production control provisions did not promise to be as beneficial to Pure's desire to increase Van production. Texas production under the code would expectedly be reduced at least 300,000 barrels a day. To be fair, Elkins surmised that the reduction would have to be evenly distributed among all Texas oil fields, meaning a 25 percent cut (13,000 barrels daily) in the Van allowable. Pure had been producing 52,459 barrels a day at Van under protection of a federal injunction. Elkins advised Pure management that it would "be embarrass[ing] to try to enforce" the injunction if the national government demanded a uniform reduction because the court would likely dismiss or modify it.[34] Dawes was amenable to some reduction at Van but suspected that since "East Texas . . . [was] the football of politics," the TRC would not cut its production in proportion to its size "unless great pressure" was brought to bear.[35]

On September 2, Ickes promulgated his first order as petroleum administrator estimating total domestic market demand for crude oil at 2,409,700 barrels per day for the month. To comply with the national quota, the TRC cut Texas production by 25 percent to 975,000 barrels a day. The East Texas field suffered the sharpest cutback—130,000 barrels daily.[36] The TRC permitted marginal wells to continue producing at 100 percent, or a maximum of 20 barrels a day, as provided by state law, and affected the 25 percent cut among the remaining wells.[37] Even though Pure's 52,500-barrel per day Van allowable was reduced to 39,375 barrels, Elkins advised Pure management that most of the lost production could be recouped by reclassifying 37 wells, which had been producing 25 barrels a day under the old order, as marginal wells. As marginal wells, they could produce 20 rather than 25 barrels a day, which was only a 20 percent cut. If the TRC affected the 25 percent reduction on a field by field basis rather than across-the-board, Elkins feared that East Texas field operators would demand a less than 25 percent cut, or maybe an increase.[38] Elkins's valuable East Texas ally, Carl Estes, backed his effort to get the TRC to impose a flat 25 percent cut throughout the state "without a lot of damn phony testimony and farcical hearings."[39]

Despite some complaints the petroleum code was not rigorously enforced. Independents and majors alike connived and dealt illicitly with impunity. With the exception of November, daily production during the last quarter of 1933 exceeded national quotas by 5 percent (118,000 barrels). Texas production exceeded the state's quota by as much as 120,000 barrels a day exclusive of hot oil runs which obviously went unreported.[40] Oklahoma and Kansas producers complained bitterly that 70 percent of all hot oil entered the stream of commerce from Texas.[41]

Still, the PAB accomplished its main task by the end of 1933. Hot oil continued to flow, but at a slower rate. Domestic production declined and crude oil prices rose and stabilized at $1 per barrel, enabling most producers to make a reasonable profit or at least recover costs. The average cost of producing a barrel of oil in 1934, including a 6 percent return on investment, was 77.5 cents. But critics warned that higher prices encouraged more hot oil.[42]

One dollar per barrel crude oil did not satisfy a majority of PCC members who argued that widespread price-cutting by retail gasoline dealers would destabilize and demoralize the market. The PCC wanted to fix the minimum price of Mid-Continent crude at $1.11 per barrel and the wholesale price of Mid-Continent gasoline at 6.5 cents a gallon, about 50 percent higher than the existing market price. Farish and Pew warned that government price-fixing would inevitably lead to government control of the industry. Although he pledged to cooperate with the NRA, Farish was "definitely on record . . . as opposed to price-fixing." NRA Consumers' Advisory Board chairman Mary Harriman Rumsey asked Ickes to postpone price controls, pointing out that since June 1, consumers had spent an additional $500 million for petroleum products while wages had advanced not more than $125 million.[43]

Ickes adhered to his position that prices would take care of themselves if production was held in line with demand. He reminded price-fixing advocates that the NRA's primary goal was to widen employment and increase wages. "The income of the oil industry is the outgo of the consuming public," Ickes stated, "and . . . too great a burden [must] not [be] placed too suddenly upon the purchasing power of the public at this time."[44] Ickes also desired to avoid becoming mired in the oil industry's problems and feared that once he began setting prices he "couldn't even pretend to function as Administrator of Public Works and as Secretary of the Interior."[45]

Roosevelt remained uncommitted to this thorny issue. He told Ickes to investigate the matter further to determine whether price controls were absolutely necessary and feasible as well as economically and legally defensible. The possibility of a legal challenge worried Roosevelt. Critics argued that the president's price-fixing authority under the petroleum code was susceptible to constitutional objection on the ground it unduly confiscated property. Margold warned Ickes to proceed cautiously since price controls could not be defended in the courts without proper cost data which the oil industry refused to furnish voluntarily.[46]

On October 16, Ickes issued an order fixing the minimum price for 36-degree gravity Mid-Continent crude oil at $1.11 a barrel to take effect December 1, after public hearings. He cited the persistence of "unfair competitive practices in the petroleum industry leading to constant and recurring price wars and price cutting . . . creat[ing] an emergency which threaten[ed] the stability of the interstate market for petroleum." Pennzoil president Charles L. Suhr aptly expressed many oilmen's feelings saying, "We were like a bunch of wild horses running aimlessly on the prairie. We liked our freedom and when someone put a halter on us we didn't like it, although it is better for us."[47]

After all the brouhaha, the PCC dropped price-fixing, realizing the futility of proceeding without the support of major oil companies, and concentrated on production control. In late November, Ickes recommended that domestic production for December be decreased by 128,000 barrels a day to 2,210,000 barrels daily. Although he remained confident that price stability could be maintained by keeping production in line with market demand, Ickes was troubled by reports of continued hot oil production in the East Texas field running as high as 80,000

Charles E. Francis, 1930s. Courtesy Vinson & Elkins Archives

barrels a day. Texas production had regularly exceeded national recommendations. Ickes vowed to wage war against the sale of low-priced hot oil to refiners who dumped cheap gasoline on the market upsetting conditions wherever the product was sold.[48] He announced the creation of an expert legal division under Margold's supervision to prosecute hot oil runners, particularly in Texas. Among the high quality attorneys on the staff, Ickes chose UT law professor A. W. Walker, Jr. and Charles Francis of Wichita Falls, Texas, both considered leading authorities on oil matters in Texas.[49]

Chronic overproduction in Texas stemmed partly from the TRC's reluctance to ratify national quotas. The TRC championed the cause of Texas oilmen who insisted that the Lone Star State deserved a larger piece of the national pie. With dollar-a-barrel crude oil and the legal production of individual wells limited to 30 barrels a day, small East Texas refiners purchased or produced their own hot oil instead of buying it on the open market. A racket developed involving a multitude of schemes devised by those intent on playing the game without any rules. Some hot oilers evaded detection by operating at night, while others fooled TRC inspectors by tampering with tank gauges or installing false valves or by-passes to run oil around inspection points. One ingenious producer connected the control valves of his oil well to his bathroom fixtures.[50]

Hot oilers also evaded the law by reclassifying crude oil shipments as "topped crude," or partially refined petroleum. The TRC had no control over hot oil disguised as petroleum products and could not require refiners to report their activities. Without access to refinery records, the TRC could not detect violations, and, even if it did, violators faced a fine which was small compared to potential profits. To make matters worse, TRC agents were accused of accepting bribes from producers and refiners. Federal officials in East Texas complained that hot oil runners were bribing telephone and telegraph employees and tapping lines used by the Interior Department. A group of bankers with oil investments in the East Texas field organized the Petroleum Committee of the Texas Bankers Association to assist the TRC. The TRC authorized the bankers to act as public agents in East Texas to review applications or tenders for intrastate shipment of unrefined petroleum to determine which ones involved hot oil. Both the Texas Bankers Association and the Texas Petroleum Council illustrated industrial self-government on the state level.[51]

Increasing government regulation presented the oil industry with a host of legal questions necessitating lawyers' expertise and advice. Lawsuits attacking state proration orders and NRA codes made it imperative for oilmen to retain the full-time services of lawyers with profound knowledge of the varied and complex legal issues that arose. The in-house legal staffs of oil companies had not acquired knowledge of the latest problems in time and were too consumed by regular company business to give proper attention to oil-related matters. For this reason, a group of Texas oilmen formed the Robert E. Hardwicke Legal Committee in the spring of 1933. The committee retained Hardwicke to handle oil-related legal matters and disseminated information regarding legal questions and lawsuits. It was more evidence of the growing importance of law and lawyers to the petroleum problem.[52]

As 1933 came to a close, the initial success of the petroleum code waned. Domestic crude oil production took a startling jump during the second week of December to 2,390,000 barrels per day, 176,381 barrels in excess of the previous week's output. Daily production in the East Texas field for the same period increased 53,263 barrels—exclusive of hot oil, which was estimated as high as 90,000 barrels per day.[53] Federal enforcement was beefed up in Texas, the only state requiring two units of special agents from the Interior Department's Division of Investigations. Its largest single office was located in Tyler, and was staffed by 67 special agents in addition to clerks and other assistants. They collected information from various sources (including customers and competitors of violators as well as state and local planning and coordinating committees), conducted investigations, and turned over evidence to the petroleum administrator, who in turn transmitted it to the attorney general for prosecution.[54]

Added enforcement did little to deter hot oil runners, now joined by others who had watched them get off by simply paying a fine and taking the chance of getting caught and being fined again. The Department of the Interior filed more than 50 lawsuits and dispatched a special prosecutor to East Texas. All 50 defendants were released on bond and resumed their illicit activities. Some East Texas field operators filed suit in federal court to restrain national officials from inspecting their property and enforcing the petroleum code, paving the way for another round in the legal battle over prorationing.[55]

The year 1933 marked a milestone in the legal history of petroleum, as the oil industry was singled out for special national regulation to protect the public interest in petroleum. The NRA petroleum code explicitly recognized that the oil industry's peculiar needs demanded special regulations within the broad parameters of public policy. For example, subject to the president's approval, the petroleum code effectively legalized a domestic oil cartel by exempting the oil industry from national antitrust laws. But it could not immunize the oil industry from the courts. In this respect, the national government fared no better than the states or private industry. The problem of petroleum was a legal one, to be resolved by lawyers.

CHAPTER 11

Déjà Vu: The Court Strikes Back

*The producers and royalty owners of this [East Texas]
field should wake up to the fact that . . . there is no
use to be like a hog eating acorns, 'never look up to
see where they fall from, until they stop falling.'*

—*Tyler Morning Telegraph*

Oil regulation reached a turning point in 1934. "We have emerged from
a condition of chaos," Humble president Robert Lee Blaffer proclaimed,
". . . toward orderly production and termination of the wasteful and
ruinous practices of the past."[1] Combined national-state efforts had
reduced hot oil production to 33,000 barrels by late 1934, improving
the price of Mid-Continent crude oil from a low of ten cents a barrel
to a high of $1.12 per barrel by the end of the year. Gasoline prices
rose an average of three cents a gallon, and nearly every oil company
enjoyed a fair profit in the final quarter of the year.[2] IPAA president
Wirt Franklin attributed the increased earnings to national regulations, which had "largely eliminated wasteful production and sales
below cost."[3]

Texas Company board chairman C. B. Ames was optimistic—"if the
courts did not interfere by becoming 'too legalistic.'" East Texas newspaper mogul Carl Estes reported that "'hot' oil merchants . . . patterned

after the desert Arabs folded their tents and slipped quietly into obscurity . . . [as] the 'Big Bad Wolf' [i.e., federal agents] . . . [came] on the scene . . . to stamp out overproduction of oil." Pure president Dawes spoke for a growing number of oilmen who had become "rather impatient with the migratory game theory . . . that . . . the oil under a man's land had essentially the same status as a wild goose which might fly over it." Dawes criticized the rule of capture as "unsound legal sophistry" and although at "times . . . we wish we did not have it," the inadequacy of state regulation convinced him "that federal control could not be worse."[4]

Elkins disliked the New Deal and feared that once the thin line between cooperation and intervention had been crossed, national production controls would lead to national regulation of all phases of the petroleum industry. "The menace of East Texas is temporary at most and after this field has faded from existence," he predicted, "the very persons who now advocate federal control will be crying the loudest to be relieved of such control." Elkins instructed Vinson & Elkins attorney W. C. Morris to brief him on the constitutionality of national regulation of state production.[5]

Morris explained that legal rather than moral authority underlay earlier national regulation of intrastate production, such as articles produced by child labor. The war powers notwithstanding, Morris suggested that the commerce power, subject to "judicial interpretations," offered the only constitutional authority for national production controls. Accordingly, Elkins assured Dawes that he could obtain an injunction restraining governmental restriction of the oil production Pure needed to supply its market demand as long as additional output did not go to waste.[6]

East Texas field producers retained local, small-town lawyers such as "Big Fish" Fischer to keep the feds off their backs.[7] In *Panama Refining Company v. Ryan,* filed in October, 1933, Fischer sought to restrain special agents such as Archie D. Ryan of the Interior Department's investigative division from, under authority of Section 9(c), gauging tanks, digging up pipelines, and prosecuting his clients for refusing to furnish daily affidavits[8] regarding production, transportation, storage, sale, purchase, refining, or disposition of crude oil.[9]

Amazon Petroleum Corporation also filed suit in federal court to enjoin enforcement of the TRC's proration order restricting East Texas field production to 400,000 barrels a day. Its attorneys alleged that the TRC had arbitrarily limited production according to national quotas to fix prices rather than to prevent waste. They argued that national quotas unduly interfered with interstate commerce by reducing Amazon's production below a level sufficient to satisfy contractual obligations to out-of-state customers.[10]

The *Panama* and *Amazon* cases were argued in federal court in Houston on December 14, 1933. Assistant U.S. Attorney Charles I. Francis[11] represented the national government in what he called "the most important case tried in the United States in the last 100 years." He was assisted by PCC general counsel Louis Titus and Charles E. Fahy, first assistant solicitor of the Department of the Interior. The NRA was on trial, Titus declared, and the entire New Deal recovery program would stand or fall according to the result.[12]

Amazon's attorneys argued that the NRA codes unconstitutionally delegated legislative authority to the executive branch without specific guidelines to illegally dictate production quotas to the states. Fischer offered sworn statements charging that federal agents had ordered Panama's employees to fill out affidavits regarding company operations in violation of the Fifth Amendment privilege against self-incrimination. He offered additional evidence showing that the East Texas field allowable was insufficient to enable local refineries to meet existing market demand forcing them to shutdown and throwing hundreds of people out of work.[13]

Fort Worth attorney Maurice Cheek defended the TRC's proration orders as conforming to national production quotas based on market demand forecasts compiled by the U.S. Bureau of Mines. He assured the court that the TRC had restricted East Texas field production to market demand only to prevent physical waste as authorized by state law.[14]

Francis argued that overproduction in East Texas affected the national petroleum market. Since 85 percent of Texas oil was shipped out of state, and because it was impossible to segregate oil intended for intrastate consumption from that destined for interstate commerce, national authorities subjected all East Texas field crude to regulation. Francis maintained that Congress had not surrendered its lawmaking power to the executive branch by authorizing the president to carry out its intent to stop interstate transportation of hot oil.[15]

Hutcheson reminded Titus of precedents classifying oil production as intrastate activity and asked him just how far the government assumed it affected commerce. Titus replied that overproduction affected interstate commerce. "If the sovereignty of Texas is gone and we're no longer a sovereign state of the Union but a branch of the Department of Interior," Hutcheson retorted, "you may be right." He also questioned the requirement that producers, transporters, and refiners file affidavits attesting to the legality of the oil they handled. Hutcheson did not believe "the American citizen had to constitute himself as some sort of secret police," adding, "even in the prohibition era, when things got pretty strong, you [government] didn't go that far."[16]

On February 12, Hutcheson upheld the TRC's proration order, "wholly unable to see that the conclusion the Commission reached is not . . . reasonable." He found no evidence that the TRC had surrendered its authority under state law to enforce oil conservation, but had simply availed itself of national assistance which he deemed less offensive than previous instances where the agency had received information and advice from "persons and unofficial bodies bent on maintaining their own self-serving views of the conduct and control of the petroleum industry." The three-judge panel lacked jurisdiction to rule on the validity of the NRA petroleum code and severed the issue to be considered separately by Judge Randolph J. Bryant in the *Panama* case.[17]

The *Amazon* decision marked a significant reversal in the lower federal court's position regarding the nexus between oil production controls and conservation. Hutcheson had heretofore rejected scientific and technical evidence showing the relationship between market-demand prorationing and conservation. The ruling strengthened the TRC's position and must have elated the phalanx of petroleum technologists whose advice Hutcheson had previously dismissed as "mere theory and speculation." After *Amazon,* few operators complained when the TRC restricted East Texas field production to 400,000 barrels per day to conserve reservoir energy and minimize waste.[18]

After issuing a string of injunctions restraining enforcement of TRC orders, on February 13, Bryant pronounced in *Panama* "the gravest misgivings, if not the absolute certainty of conviction" that Section 9(c) of the NRA petroleum code amounted to "such an invasion of rights of the States . . . not permissible in our dual form of government." He emphasized the courts' duty "to be watchful for "stealthy encroachments" upon citizens' constitutional rights. Bryant declined to overturn Section 9(c), but enjoined its enforcement against Panama and Amazon since neither company had subscribed to the petroleum code nor were they engaged in interstate commerce.[19]

The U.S. Fifth Circuit Court of Appeals in New Orleans upheld the TRC's orders on May 22. Although the court deemed the petroleum code "a novelty in legislation," it refused to "upset laws and regulations which are generally useful and necessary in public business" and overturned Bryant's decree. The decision was appealed to the U.S. Supreme Court.[20]

National jurisdiction over oil production remained in doubt and tied the hands of PAB officials in the East Texas field pending the Supreme Court's decision. Ickes predicted that an unfavorable ruling would "raise hell" with the petroleum code and create a "very serious situation." Francis advised Elkins that the federal district court decision, if upheld, meant that the "[TRC's] jurisdiction . . . to enforce the conservation laws of the state . . . is supreme over federal agents." Still, the TRC lacked the manpower and, as some critics fairly or unfairly argued, the competence to adequately enforce state oil conservation laws. On the strength of the Fifth Circuit ruling, Ickes dispatched Louis R. Glavis as new chief of investigation in the East Texas field. Glavis's reputation as a tough administrator was borne out by his "intention that these [violators] shall feel the lash of the law which they so long and brazenly flouted." This did not deter some East Texas hot oilers, who continued selling illegal oil to local refineries at prices below the $1 per barrel average. By the spring of 1934, cheap hot gasoline threatened to upset the stability achieved under national aegis.[21]

Estes declared that Texans were "sick and tired of having eighteen or twenty men do as they please." He chartered a special train to transport a group of East Texas field operators to Austin to beseech Governor "Ma" Ferguson to sign three oil bills passed by the legislature: authorizing the TRC to inspect refineries for hot oil; increasing the production tax from a tenth to an eighth of 1 percent of the oil's value to defray TRC expenses for enforcing prorationing; and making violations of TRC orders a felony punishable by imprisonment.[22] "We can and will enforce our orders," the TRC assured U.S. senators Morris Sheppard and Tom Connally, reminding them that "this is purely a state function and we . . . deplore any federal encroachment."[23]

Ferguson signed the three bills in early March, while expressing "serious doubt" that they would improve enforcement of prorationing. "If the [TRC] is so anxious to protect state sovereignty," the *Oil and Gas Journal* declared, "let it demonstrate its ability to exercise it."[24] Domestic and Texas production exceeded national quotas by 165,000 and 75,000 barrels a day respectively during the second week of March.[25]

Ickes was so irked by the decline of wholesale gasoline prices in April, 1934, that he denounced the oil industry as "one of the most ruthless, arrogant, and haughty industries in the United States," responsible for "the most reckless and extravagant exploitation of a natural resource in the history of the world . . . a tale of wasteful methods of capture." He ridiculed "one rugged individualist [for] stealing the oil of a brother rugged individualist" and noted how "this industrial behemoth, brought to its knees, came to Washington begging for help . . . a far cry from 'less government in business.'"[26]

The federal courts remained the main obstacle to curbing hot oil. Ickes turned to Margold for advice. In collaboration with Harvard University Law School Dean Roscoe Pound and University of Michigan Law School Dean Henry M. Bates, Margold designed national oil production controls based on the war powers of the U.S. Constitution, which offered ample authority to conserve a "precious, exhaustible resource" like oil which was essential to the army, navy, and air corps in times of peace and war.[27]

Bates believed that the petroleum problem illustrated the need to "rid ourselves of our early ideas of delegation and authority . . . and consider broad general principles of government." Pound argued that recent economic and social developments had compelled Americans to turn to the executive rather than the legislative branch of government for leadership, a phenomena accompanied by an increasing centralization of authority and constitutional interpretations recognizing greater authority in the branch which bore the greatest burden of government.[28]

PCC vice-chairman Amos Beaty rejected Margold's war powers thesis as an "unusual authority" to be invoked by the president only "when the country was actually engaged in war." His point was well-taken in light of the Supreme Court's 1932 ruling in the *Constantin* case. Beaty urged Congress to enact national "quotas in commerce," which would trigger as soon as oil entered the stream of commerce in order to keep supply in line with demand. He believed that the states' rights question would be rendered moot by allowing states to retain control over production and limiting national regulation to the amount of oil transported in interstate commerce.

Beaty cited Supreme Court decisions in the *Minnesota Rate Cases* and the *Shreveport Cases* sustaining the power of the Interstate Commerce Commission (ICC) to overturn interstate rates made under state authority, and *Railroad Commission of Wisconsin v. Chicago, Burlington*

& *Quincy Railroad,* in which Chief Justice William Howard Taft deemed, "Commerce is a unit and does not regard state lines."[29]

On April 30, U.S. senator Elmer Thomas of Oklahoma introduced a bill, drafted by Margold, giving the Secretary of the Interior broad and sweeping powers to regulate oil production.[30] Referred to by opponents as the "Ickes Oil Dictatorship Bill," the Thomas bill was the Roosevelt administration's response to what Ickes described as "a very dangerous situation," stemming from the *Amazon* and *Panama* decisions, that undermined the PAB's authority to control hot oil in the East Texas field.[31] Oklahoma congressman Wesley Disney introduced a companion measure in the House of Representatives on May 17 which de-emphasized, but did not eliminate, national controls. Both bills declared a national public interest in petroleum and authorized the Secretary of the Interior to establish mandatory production quotas.[32] Ickes supported passage of any bill to "give us powers that the courts cannot interfere with." Roosevelt urged Congress to enact the Thomas–Disney bill, saying that otherwise "illegal production will continue and grow in volume and result in a . . . return to the wretched conditions which existed in the spring of 1933."[33]

Texas congressman Joe Eagle vociferously opposed the Thomas–Disney bill, reminding his constituents of "the carpetbag rule of the South which came out of Washington where soldiers undertook to make . . . white people subject to Negro people." He vowed to keep the oil industry from falling "into the hands of Secretary Ickes [who] does not know . . . the difference between an oil well and an artesian water well." Eagle's constituents would never "come . . . hat in hand and . . . have [Ickes] refer them to some oil assistant out of the Standard Oil group and affiliates in Wall Street . . . to settle arbitrarily their destiny without recourse to appeal or court."[34]

Disney discredited cries by states' rights advocates of "dictatorship" as a mere "play on words," calling attention to the "oil dictatorship" in Texas' "so-called" Railroad Commission. He blasted those who made "millions of profits on 'hot oil,'" and predicted that "honest men in East Texas [would] quit following the law . . . [and] turn their wells wide open" while the industry went "to pot." Disney denounced monopolists who depressed business and ran prices down in order to fill their storage tanks with millions of barrels of cheap oil until prices rose and then selling it for "a fabulous profit."[35]

Deep divisions forestalled immediate action in Congress. The Senate Committee on Mines and Mining approved the bill, but it was pigeonholed in the House Committee on Interstate and Foreign Commerce chaired by Texas congressman Sam Rayburn. Texas congressman Martin Dies demanded an immediate vote on the bill, saying that he had "seen oil wells [in Texas] burning by the day . . . [and] oil running down the ditches," threatening a return of nickel-a-barrel oil. He warned that a dramatic fall in crude oil prices would spell "bankruptcy to the small producing companies . . . [and] unemployment [for] the four or five thousand coal miners in the United States [whose] coal [could] not possibly compete with 5-cent oil."[36]

Indiana congressman Samuel B. Pettengill preferred to delay action pending further investigation and to at least "serve notice to the bootlegging, illegal hot-oil artists . . . that Congress will act . . . if they do not behave." Disclaiming any personal interest in oil because "there is not now nor has there ever been a drop produced in [my] district," Rayburn agreed to defer the matter since too many congressmen were "jump[ing] at each other like two mad dogs."[37]

During the congressional recess, a special five-member subcommittee, chaired by Maryland congressman William P. Cole, Jr., initiated the most extensive examination ever of the petroleum industry. The "Cole Committee" served as the primary forum for testimony and debate by all interested parties representing virtually every phase of the oil business. Hearings began in Washington on September 17. The committee paid close attention to the testimony and advice of lawyers since legal and constitutional issues posed the biggest obstacle to formulating a viable petroleum policy.[38]

Margold reiterated his argument that the commerce and war powers clauses of the Constitution gave Congress ample authority to regulate oil production since petroleum propelled both the instrumentalities of commerce and the military.[39] "But when Congress holds off from the market the property of the landowner or the lessee and prevents development under the law of capture," Pettengill asked, "is not Congress depriving that man of his property without due process of law?" Margold responded that the law of capture was "merely a rule adopted by the court under the mistake that oil was migratory, like water under the ground, and that anybody who reduced it to possession got title to it."[40]

Margold discredited the theory that petroleum production was not commerce and not amenable to national regulation. He cited Taft's ruling in *United Mine Workers v. Coronado Coal Company* that the national government could not regulate production of commodities like coal even though they ultimately entered the stream of commerce. But evidence at a subsequent hearing showing that Coronado's coal production posed a serious threat to union wages at other companies and to union organizing efforts in general convinced Taft to reverse himself. He held that union activity affected the volume of coal moving in interstate commerce and therefore brought its activities within the ambit of national regulatory power.[41] Whenever a business swept across state lines and its product affected the national market, it was no longer local, but a part of interstate commerce. By reason of its nationwide organization, its integrated structure, and its national importance, the petroleum industry affected interstate commerce and this, Margold argued, provided an adequate legal basis for national regulation.[42]

Attorney Earl Oliver cited the profound public interest in petroleum conservation as adequate legal authority for reasonable regulations. He criticized the Thomas-Disney bill for failing to tackle the root problem, the rule of capture, and doubted that industrial stability and oil conservation could be realized without some practical substitute such as unitization. Oliver presented the Cole Committee with transcripts of addresses delivered by Bates and Pound before the AIMME in New York City on February 22, 1934.[43]

Bates said he could not comprehend the "species of reasoning" by which judges and lawyers presumed that due process protected "that early . . . primitive conception of property . . . that ownership was absolute and . . . nobody could interfere with your using that property precisely as you might wish to use it as long as you did not specifically injure others." He explained that due process had been given "a constricted and distorted meaning" and "applied in an artificial way" to facilitate the development of America's vast frontier by encouraging initiative and overemphasizing acquisition of private wealth. Bates cited prior Supreme Court decisions holding that due process did not prevent the adoption of reasonable regulations "that work justice . . . among owners of a particular kind of property," like petroleum, to promote a legitimate public interest.[44]

Bates disputed the theory of absolute state sovereignty, noting that the Supreme Court had sustained treaties containing provisions contrary to state law. "As our life changes, as our occupations become more intricate, and as they become more integrated into each other," he explained, "there are produced conditions not dreamed of in 1787 which the states as such cannot handle effectively . . . which not only require but which constitutionally justify federal activity." Bates insisted that sovereignty could not be "divided into pieces as if it were pie" and suggested eliminating "certain acquired notions about the distribution of powers of government into the legislative, executive, and judicial departments" which Americans had "mistakenly adopted." He pointed to the petroleum problem as an example of how erroneous fact assumptions about separation of powers, absolute property rights, and states' rights had inflicted infinite harm to the public welfare.[45]

Bates also dismissed the rule of capture as "a naive theory confined within the straightjacket of the common law," which recent scientific and technological advances had proven to be "not only grotesquely absurd," but to have "resulted in injustice violative of the spirit of the common law of property and productive of disastrous losses to all concerned." Important national interests demanded that "no narrow or distorted interpretations of broad constitutional provisions be interposed to defeat just and scientific measures."[46]

Pound believed that individualized application of the law was impractical in an exceedingly complex and crowded twentieth-century environment where revolutionary advances in transportation and communication had spurred rapid changes. "No one ever accused the judiciary of getting things done in a hurry," he explained, "and legislative bodies, by their very nature, cannot get things done in a hurry." The need for speedy results and individualization had shifted the center of gravity from the legislative to the executive branch of government.[47]

Pound discredited constitutional interpretations based on judicial perceptions of *Kleinstadtismus*. "The Constitution doesn't . . . fortify Main Streetism," he argued, "and it is getting rid of that picture of the wholly self-sufficient community . . . that really is at the root of [our] problems." Law "is eternally telling us things may be reasonable," but, he asked, "How does . . . [the court] decide what is reasonable?" Pound preferred to discard "that highbrow word 'ideal,' derived from a Greek word that means picture," which shapes the idea. He criticized judges and lawyers for defining reasonable within the framework of a certain traditional, received, and authoritative picture of the law, their roles, and the ideal American polity. "So our trouble isn't really with the Constitution," Pound declared, it "is with the picture that forms the legal background of application of the Constitution." A picture of small, isolated, and independent "island communities" remained implanted in jurists' minds even though the nation had evolved into an economically unified land.[48]

Pound also gave numerous examples of how modern conditions had transformed traditional common law rules: Standardized insurance policies restricted absolute freedom to contract. Statutes requiring the payment of employees' wages in cash restricted employers' liberties. Administrative agencies reviewed public service company contracts for reasonableness. State laws prohibiting married men from conveying property or assigning wages acquired during marriage without spousal consent compromised absolute property rights. Changes in water law limited landowners' absolute use and enjoyment of their property to reasonable use.[49]

Pound noted the steady legal transformation from things *res nullius* to things *res publici*. Traditional common law held that certain things like wild game were owned by no one until reduced to possession. Some American state constitutions reclassified things *res nullius* to *res publici*, held in trust for the people, laying the foundation for administrative regulations to protect the public interest in certain natural resources. Conservation reflected society's desire to maximize the beneficial use of natural resources as opposed to the policy of unlimited exploitation during America's formative period. It signified a growing acceptance of the reasonable exercise of state police power to promote desirable social ends in contradistinction to the free, spontaneous initiative encouraged during an earlier frontier era.[50]

Pound considered the nineteenth-century intellect underlying the rule of capture as "too much in the abstract" and not "measured by the situation of the time and place." He harkened to the Marshall Court which resolved legal disputes in terms of "'can'—these things be done." Following "the great outbursts of constitutional legislation in the post–Civil War amendments," Pound mused, the court "looked at things in terms of can't." He advocated a return to the "can" era to "try things that are constitutionally sound or logically and constitutionally and reasonably sound, even if they are out of line with that picture that obtained in the immediate past."[51]

Attorney Norman L. Meyers maintained that the national government could regulate production and transportation of petroleum in order to protect interstate commerce and conserve oil for national defense. He attributed the failure of state regulations to each state's attempt "to determine its own imperial policy of the amount it should produce."[52] Attorney J. Howard Marshall added that Congress could regulate anything which directly contributed to recurring competitive abuses responsible for wild and violent gyrations in the oil market. He cited "the entire stream of antitrust cases" as ample legal precedents where federal courts had sustained government regulation of competitive abuses in production, marketing, and other phases of business under the Sherman Act. Marshall premised the legality of national oil production controls on the nexus between conservation and interstate commerce since waste ultimately burdened consumers with higher prices and because the mechanisms of commerce depended upon petroleum.[53]

Houston attorney Elwood Fouts, who represented a group of Texas independents, argued that prorationing had nothing to do with conservation and was a pretext to artificially balance supply with demand, eliminate competition, and fix prices to benefit larger producers. He rejected Margold's broad interpretation of the commerce clause, which would "[let] down the bars and leave the whole thing open for regulation by Congress . . . [and abandon] our form of government." Fouts cited Supreme Court decisions limiting national regulation of interstate commerce to commodities which had a harmful, criminal, or evil effect, and nothing else. Even a lawyer like himself, Fouts complained, had difficulty keeping up with the "voluminous compilation of edicts and rulings promulgated by the Secretary of the Interior and his limitless horde of inferiors." He considered "bureau or dictator law" an unacceptable price to pay "for the doubtful benefit of the regimentation of the oil business."[54]

San Antonio attorney R. J. (John) Boyle, represented a group of Southwest Texas independents who preferred to be regulated by local authorities whom they could hold accountable instead of distant national bureaucrats whom they could not recall. "What I advocate is contemptuously referred to . . . as rugged individualism; in fact, the proponents of the oil monopoly call it the 'law of the jungle,'" Boyle declared, which has enabled this nation to "produce more wealth than all of the world in all history . . . and . . . the highest standards of living and greatest comforts of life ever known." He described how "the Standard Oil monopoly . . . [or] 'major companies,' had been on the ground floor of every new domestic oil discovery except the East Texas field, which remained primarily in the hands of independents." As the East Texas field had turned out to be the largest to date, the majors had to counter competition from East Texas independents to preserve their monopoly, which was their real motive for supporting conservation. Boyle recalled when antitrust laws were wielded "to strike down monopolies and prevent suppression or interference with free competition" until "a new school of thought arose . . . whose slogan was and is 'competition produces economic waste.'" Speaking as "just a country lawyer down . . . in ranch country . . . crying in the wilderness," he asked Congress to respect the consumers who greatly outnumbered oil producers and had "the greatest political weight when the final card is played on the table."[55]

Dallas attorney Marion S. Church paid homage to his "fellow citizens, the descendants of the patriots of Goliad, the Alamo, and San Jacinto, who fought and died to establish a great commonwealth." He insisted that the Constitution did not grant Congress unfettered discretion to "regulate oil, haircuts, woodchoppers, or anything or anybody." Church assured the committee that Texans did "not want the dressing down of rugged individualism to Nazism, [their] property rights to sovietism, and [their] liberties to fascism." He decried the recent political trend toward collectivism and feared that emergencies would provide an excuse to discard the Constitution anytime it impeded the efficient and speedy disposition of the general welfare. Church praised the "legally thinly clad [and] poorly financed" TRC for assuming "the colossal job" of attempting to stabilize the chaotic situation in the East Texas oil field. "What federal dictator could have met the difficulties better?" he asked, adding, "it took . . . Ickes . . . a year to get in action." Citing personal liberty and democracy as "important treasures to preserve in a crisis or emergency as money—dollars—wealth," Church implored the committee not to "forsake political freedom for economic freedom."[56]

W. P. Z. German, general counsel for the Skelly Oil Company in Tulsa, Oklahoma, questioned the wisdom or necessity of national control. "If federal interposition was made permanent and was initially limited to an effort to cure the cancerous heart of the disease, excess oil production," he asked, "would it stop there?" German feared that "once at work on the fascinating subject with its opportunities for expansion and control of a vigorous and widely extended business," politicians, "led at times by overenthusiastic members of the industry acting on the spur of the moment's impulse," would use the oil industry as "a footstool to toy and play with."[57]

Oil industry leaders offered the Cole Committee their insights. The majors suddenly withdrew their support for national production controls. They had desired national regulation so long as independents controlled domestic production, in order to eliminate competition, balance supply with demand, and stabilize prices to ensure a profit for the refining and marketing ends of the business—which they monopolized. When Ickes and Roosevelt decided to support pipeline divorcement to stem the monopolistic control of integrated companies, the majors turned against the Thomas–Disney bill in favor of an interstate compact. The national government's role would be confined to interdicting interstate transportation of hot oil. The compact's proponents warned the Cole Committee to proceed cautiously in recommending legislation which might be overturned by the courts.[58]

Texas Company board chairman C. B. Ames preferred an interstate compact since "the federal government [could] not directly control production because of the constitutional limitation."[59] Sun Oil Company president J. Howard Pew wanted to limit national involvement to assisting the states in formulating an interstate agreement of the kind "contemplated in the Constitution" which would serve "the great public interest" by ensuring adequate police protection for production and easing the tax burden.[60] Sun vice-president J. Edgar Pew argued that state production controls backed by national regulation of interstate commerce would check the flow of hot oil if administered and enforced by competent and trained personnel instead of "barbers, wood-choppers, and others."[61]

Indiana Standard president E. G. Seubert preferred to have "the states look after their own affairs and let the national government intervene only to stop interstate shipments of petroleum produced in excess of state quotas."[62] Ohio Standard president W. T. Holliday suggested that the oil problem could "best be solved by the federal government legislating in cooperation with the states to work out some proper exercise of police power within the states" to achieve orderly and efficient production.[63] Ohio Oil Company president Otto D. Donnell and Atlantic Refining Company president W. M. Irish favored an interstate compact over direct national controls because "the American public is more susceptible to a voluntary movement than . . . the enactment of laws."[64] L. V. Nicholas, of the Warner-Quinlan Company of New York, called for the repeal of the "archaic and ludicrous" rule of capture and the adoption of unitization. He called the East Texas field "a devastating blight" that had destroyed in established wealth two dollars for every dollar it created.[65]

New Jersey Standard president Walter Teagle and board chairman William Farish favored an interstate compact over rigid national controls.[66] Farish singled out various legal challenges and injunction suits for emasculating the petroleum code. He warned that passage of the Thomas–Disney bill would invite lawsuits attacking its doubtful constitutionality resulting in more "delays through injunctions and the

breaking up of programs and orders of commissions." Humble's lawyers had long maintained that the states retained constitutional
authority for regulating production, but refrained from openly attacking national production controls because of the exigencies of economic
depression.[67]

Pure president Dawes believed that an interstate compact offered a
more legally defensible plan which was supported by a majority of oilmen. He warned against "new legislation at this time when it has not
been possible to digest that which is already on the statute books."[68]
Phillips Petroleum Company president Frank Phillips disagreed, "fully
convinced that we are wholly incompetent to solve our own problems
by voluntary agreements or under existing agencies." He complained
that "price cutting, chiseling, and unfair trade practices are more prevalent today than at any other time" and that "agreements mean nothing"
as "some of those who are most active in promoting these agreements
are violators." Just as railroads had prospered under the Interstate
Commerce Act and banks had functioned under the Federal Reserve
Act, Phillips suggested, the oil industry could do likewise under "a government commission of from five to seven practical oilmen, appointed
by the president, with power to actually enforce any rules formulated."[69]

Texas independent Joseph Danciger continued his long and vehe-
ment crusade against production controls as being "beyond the ken of
any human agency, state or federal." He testified that "without the proration menace . . . the country would control the petroleum trade of
the world." Danciger accused major integrated oil companies of using
conservation as a pretext for protecting their interests in foreign production, pipelines, and refining at the expense of American commerce,
and saw "no good reason why the American producer should not be
permitted to produce his oil to supply both domestic and export trade
without restriction."[70]

Danciger urged Congress to divorce pipeline ownership from other
phases of the oil business as it had done in prohibiting railroads from
owning coal mines and retail outlets. He criticized the majors' expen-
diture of millions of dollars to "[dot] the land with expensive, elaborate, and unnecessary service stations . . . as an enormous economic
waste." Danciger advocated strict enforcement of antitrust laws lest the
independent oilman soon become the "forgotten man"; then "there will
be complete monopoly and the public will pay the price until the people
rise up in their wrath and force the taking over by government of the
oil monopoly."[71]

Interior Secretary Ickes suggested to the committee that the intrastate and interstate characters of the oil industry were so inextricably interwoven that they could not, as an economic reality, "be separated into corporate jurisdictions of state and national sovereignty." He preferred to control oil production at the well head rather than "chasing it all over the map." Ickes forewarned, "God only knows what will happen to the industry if we don't get this bill through."[72]

Declaring "the entire State of Texas [opposed to] any form of federal control of the petroleum industry," TRC chairman Thompson alluded to Aesop's fable of the sick lion. All the animals except the fox called on the sick lion; the fox later explained his absence by noting that the tracks of visiting animals led up to the lion's den, but not away. "That's federal control," Thompson said. "All the tracks go in, but none come out."[73] Texas governor-elect James Allred reiterated his firm opposition to national regulation of any kind: "You can never get away from temporary control." He predicted that courts would overturn any national attempt to impugn state sovereignty by controlling intrastate production.[74]

Unhappy at Congress's failure to enact strong national oil controls, Ickes continued to exert authority under the petroleum code. He established the Federal Tender Board (FTB) in October while waiting for the outcome of the congressional investigation and the Supreme Court's decision in the *Panama* and *Amazon* cases. Oil producers, transporters, and refiners were required to submit affidavits detailing the amount of oil they produced, shipped, bought, or sold. The FTB reviewed every proposed oil shipment before issuing a certificate of clearance. All operators were required to keep their books open for inspection. Failure to comply with any of these regulations could result in up to six months imprisonment, a fine not to exceed a thousand dollars, or both.[75]

As complicated as it appeared, the system worked primarily because of the federal courts' acquiescence. Enforcement had heretofore been stymied by lower federal court injunctions. The FTB's success was aided by a marked change in Judge Bryant's attitude, who suddenly refused to issue anymore injunctions against enforcement of national regulations. Apparently Tom Kelliher and 12 federal investigators had arrested enough hot oil runners in East Texas to overload Bryant's docket and tax the judge's capacity and patience. According to some sources, by November, 1934, hot oil production in the East Texas field had dropped from 100,000 barrels a day to fewer than 10,000 barrels daily. Only the diehard hot oil runners continued to defy national authority.[76]

But Humble's *Weekly Digest* reported that hot oil production in the East Texas field averaged 102,000 to 145,000 barrels a day in October, while local refineries shipped 110,000 barrels of petroleum products. The FTB's certificates of clearance were characterized as "a joke," many signed with spurious signatures such as those of comedians Ed Wynn and Will Rogers, Mrs. Franklin D. Roosevelt, and Julius Caesar. Federal agents caught one violator with 172 affidavits signed by various names, which he was selling for $4 each. Even though the FTB reduced hot oil production in the East Texas field to about 33,000 barrels a day by November, opposition to broad national authority gathered momentum.[77]

Testimony before the Cole Committee revealed that, by the fall of 1934, opposition to national production controls was snowballing while national production regularly exceeded legal limits. Although most majors and large independents welcomed national assistance to interdict the interstate movement of hot oil, small independents from Texas and Oklahoma opposed any national controls. Governors of oil-producing states, such as James Allred, feared that once the thin line of cooperation had been crossed, the national government would trample upon state sovereignty. They preferred an interstate compact to coordinate production controls backed by national regulation of interstate commerce in hot oil. The IPAA endorsed this position.[78]

Congress had ratified interstate agreements dealing with boundary lines, rivers, fishing rights, construction and operation of bridges, water rights to rivers traversing several states, and other concerns in which two or more states shared a common interest. At its fifteenth annual convention, held in Dallas on November 12–15, the API withdrew its support of national oil legislation and endorsed the interstate compact idea. The plan received a big boost after Ickes rattled the API delegates by threatening that, unless the oil industry put its own house in order, it would either be nationalized or declared a public utility. "Well, old Ickes and federal control are through," Thompson retorted, "that speech killed them." Ickes's remarks also undermined passage of the Thomas–Disney bill, already in dire straits under Sam Rayburn's unfriendly hand. The API chided Ickes for encouraging oilmen to solve their own problems while threatening them with antitrust and criminal prosecutions if they formulated plans to achieve stability and profits.[79]

Oklahoma congressman (and governor-elect) Marland invited the governors of the oil-producing states to meet at his home in Ponca City on December 3 to explore an interstate compact. Representatives from Texas, Oklahoma, New Mexico, Kansas, California, Wyoming, Louisiana, and Arkansas and four members of the Cole Committee, who had been conducting hearings in Oklahoma City, discussed the matter. There was unanimous opposition to any national production controls except for Kansas governor Alf M. Landon, who favored some form of national regulation pending implementation of an interstate compact. Allred was "very skeptical about the interests behind this interstate compact," such as the API, and refused to support any proposal that permitted outside agencies to control state production. To appease Allred, a compromise proposal called for the establishment of a joint national-state fact finding agency to determine market demand for domestic production and exports to allocate to the states. Allred remained unalterably opposed to any plan that fixed prices or perpetuated monopoly.[80] The delegates agreed to ask Congress to pass enabling legislation and to reconvene in February, 1935, for further negotiation.[81]

Based upon advice from attorney Northcut Ely, the Cole Committee urged the states to adopt an interstate compact as an ideal legal solution to overproduction. Ely found no constitutional bar to an interstate compact since "the regulation of production to be exercised by each state is derived solely from the police power defined in its own laws and now created by this agreement." Whether the president or an interstate fact-finding agency determined and enforced production quotas within any particular state "depend[ed] upon the constitution and statutes of that state," Ely argued, "and not upon any federal constitutional question." He also noted that antitrust laws did not apply to agreements between states.[82]

While the debate over national oil legislation and an interstate oil compact raged, the Supreme Court heard arguments in the *Panama* and *Amazon* cases on December 10 and 11. Fischer observed what he hoped to be a good omen when Justice Louis Brandeis compared the scant, 12-page brief of "Big Fish" to the government's thick two-volume brief.[83]

Assistant Attorney General Harold M. Stephens defended the government's position, citing prior Supreme Court decisions sustaining congressional power to regulate local production which substantially affected interstate and foreign commerce. The futility of voluntary and state efforts to control competitive conditions, he argued, demonstrated the interstate unity of oil production and the need for national regulation. Brandeis noted that the petroleum code failed to provide the president with specific guidelines. The "magnitude of the subject regulated and the need for speed and flexibility in carrying out the statutory purpose, and the emergency confronting Congress," Stephens replied, prohibited Congress from prescribing detailed regulations. Chief Justice Hughes pointed out that an official publication of the codes had not been distributed to the public to serve notice of the regulations. Stephens responded that bound volumes of the code had been delivered systematically "to members and groups of particular industries involved," and "it is the flimsiest kind of specious excuse for anyone to say he did not have access to orders under the oil code."[84]

Excusing himself for being just a country lawyer, Fischer elicited laughter from the justices when he claimed that the only copy of the petroleum code he ever saw was retrieved from "the hip pocket of a federal enforcer who wandered around where he wasn't supposed to be." He reached into his coat pocket and pulled out a tattered, grimy copy. "This heah Section 9(c) is inside some kind of pamphlet. Nobody really had any notice of it. I had trouble finding this. This is the only place it is!" bellowed Fischer. "That's the law, Your Honors! It's carried around in the pocket of a deputy administrator. And nobody else knows what it is!" The justices bellowed with laughter as "Big Fish" hammered away at the constitutionality of Section 9(c) and the confusing bulletins and executive orders that no East Texas field operator understood.[85]

Fischer harkened back to ancient Rome, when "a dictator rose up before the Roman Senate . . . and asked the Senators to give him two years of unrestricted power." Two years later, "the dictator returned and asked for two more years since his program was not yet completed," he added, "and when the two years was up, he went back and demanded ten years of unrestricted power, and when that was up he told the Senate he didn't need the Senate anymore." Comparing the proposal before Congress to extend the NRA after it expired in two years, Fischer said, "After ten years of NRA, a dictatorial president could very well tell Congress he didn't need it any more, and send it home."[86]

Fischer attacked the legality of the NIRA on three grounds. First, he argued, Section 9(c) unconstitutionally delegated legislative authority to the executive branch by authorizing the president to prohibit the interstate and foreign transportation of petroleum at his discretion. Second, even if Section 9(c) were valid, Fischer insisted, it was unenforceable against his clients because they were not engaged in inter-

state commerce. Third, Fischer contended, Congress could not authorize the president to create and define crimes or offenses against the
United States.[87]

Fellow Texan James N. Saye argued briefly and less dramatically on
behalf of Amazon that the economic depression did not "create such
power in the federal government that Congress and the president may
set aside the limitations of the Constitution, and thereby dictate to the
citizens of a state" how much oil to produce and to criminally prosecute
them for violating executive orders. Saye reminded the court that it
had repeatedly held, most recently in *Constantin,* that an emergency,
even a state of war, did not empower Congress or the president to disregard constitutional limitations and deprive citizens of their legal
rights.[88]

The movement away from national regulation gained momentum from
two significant developments in January, 1935. First, the Cole Committee issued its recommendations based on the testimony of 136 witnesses recorded in a 2,887-page transcript. It recommended in part:
(1) no national oil legislation pending the Supreme Court's decision in
the *Panama* and *Amazon* cases; (2) adoption of an interstate oil compact; (3) although there was "present excessive crude production to meet
current demand there was no excessive supply to meet future demand";
and (4) establishment of a national agency to study petroleum reserves,
supply and demand, production methods, and pipelines, and to represent the national government in any cooperative interstate compact.[89]

Second, Chief Justice Hughes announced the Supreme Court's long-
awaited decision in the "Hot Oil" cases on January 7. The court struck
down Section 9(c) of the NIRA. Sidestepping the validity of the petroleum code, the court found no evidence to warrant the petroleum
administrator's right to prohibit hot oil in interstate commerce. "In every
case in which the question has been raised," the chief justice ruled, "the
Court has recognized that there are limits of delegation which there is
no constitutional authority to transcend." Hughes held that Congress
had impermissibly given the president unlimited authority to determine policy and invoke Section 9(c) as he saw fit, without specific guidelines, and punish violators for criminal conduct.[90] "If the citizen is to
be punished for the crime of violating a legislative order of an executive officer, or of a board or commission," Hughes declared, "due process of law requires that it shall appear that the order is within the
authority of the officer, board or commission, and, if that authority de-

pends on determination of fact, those determinations must be shown."
The president was not immune from the application of these constitutional principles regardless of his motives.[91]

The lone dissenter, Justice Benjamin Nathan Cardozo, viewed the
judge's task as adapting past experience to best serve society's changing needs. Cardozo argued that a reasonably clear standard, conform-
able to interpretations and requirements of earlier delegatory statutes,
should be derived from the act as a whole. He did not "fear that the
nation will drift from its ancient moorings as the result of the narrow
delegation of power" permitted under Section 9(c). Cardozo stated his
belief that Section 9(c) had been framed "in the shadow of a national
disaster," in which "a host of unforeseen contingents would have to be
faced from day to day and faced with a fullness of understanding unat-
tainable by anyone except the man upon the scene." He noted that the
court "for a hundred years and more" had presumed that executive
actions pursuant to a statutory grant of authority were based upon due
inquiry and sufficient grounds.[92]

The Supreme Court had never before invalidated a congressional
statute for delegating legislative authority, satisfied that Congress had
pronounced legislative policy with sufficient definiteness.[93] Expediency
largely guided the court in sustaining grants of legislative power to
facilitate the efficient operation of government. The court apparently
realized that some situations required the legislature to delegate broad
enforcement powers to executive officials in order to carry out its goals.
Contemporary legal commentators attributed the court's departure
from precedents, in *Panama,* to the justices' fear of dictatorship. The
predominantly conservative justices feared the accelerating effect of
the NIRA on recent trends toward centralization of power, which might
allow a zealous executive to undermine separation of powers as a constitutional safeguard. In *Panama,* the court's conservative core applied
its laissez-faire philosophy and strict constructionist interpretation of
the Constitution to erect a judicial barrier to the exercise of legislative
power to cope with the exigent needs of twentieth-century society.[94]

The weakness of the *Panama* decision lay in the court's consideration
of Section 9(c) apart from the rest of the NIRA, especially Title I, which
declared the policy of the entire act. Cardozo argued in his dissenting
opinion that the purposes declared in Title I—to conserve natural resources, eliminate unfair competitive practices, and remove obstructions to the free flow of interstate commerce—provided adequate
legislative standards to keep Section 9(c) "canalized within banks that

keep it from overflowing." In this context, Section 9(c), which specifically authorized the president to prohibit hot oil from interstate commerce, seemed less objectionable than other broadly worded statutes upheld by the court. Cardozo suggested that the court had previously stretched its judgment and resorted to implications and inferences in sustaining standards that appeared to be nothing more than declarations by Congress as to why it had delegated certain powers rather than rules for guiding grantees of the powers.[95]

The *Panama* decision blazed across the East Texas thicket. From town to town and lease to lease, the cry rang out, "Big Fish has kicked the hell out of the government, so cock back your valves and let 'er rip!"[96] Fischer's victory was another illustration of the significant role Texas lawyers played in the legal battle over oil. Ickes and other administration nabobs who had looked down upon Texans such as Elkins now had to take notice. The government's Ivy League barristers, confident of victory, had been routed in the nation's highest court by a supposed backwoods lawyer from East Texas. This catastrophe came in the midst of a breakdown in code enforcement, a wave of injunction suits challenging national regulation, and a growing number of lower federal court decisions striking down New Deal statutes. Elimination of the statutory basis for national regulation precipitated a crisis like none before, as hot oilers swarmed out of hiding in the East Texas piney woods. Malcolm McCorquodale, FTB chief at Tyler, reported that 21 refineries had reopened, and that authorities were now "in exactly the same position to stop hot oil" as two years ago. In the face of this serious setback, Ickes called upon Congress to enact specific legislation to meet the court's objections.[97] Most oilmen surely experienced a sense of *déjà vu.*

EPILOGUE

The Icing of Hot Oil

While we sympathize deeply with anyone unemployed
in this era of economic unrest . . . we cannot countenance
the sanctioning of a racket in lieu of honorable employ-
ment, merely because there are mouths to be fed . . .
Right is right, and . . . the innocent must suffer for the
crimes of the guilty few . . . if they have not taken
the precaution to inquire into the legality of the
enterprise in which they engage.

—Carl Estes

In the aftermath of *Panama,* Texas senator Tom Connally asked U.S. Interior Department attorney J. Howard Marshall, "Young fellow, can you write a law that's constitutional, that'll stop this racket?"

"I think so, Senator," Marshall replied. "How long have I got?" Connally gave him 48 hours.

Marshall and PAB chairman Norman Meyers worked around the clock, and two days later they handed Connally an "airtight" bill that defined "illegal petroleum" as crude oil produced or withdrawn from storage in violation of state allowables, and flatly prohibited its shipment in interstate and foreign commerce. The bill omitted federal production controls, but specifically authorized the president to enforce its provisions. The Senate approved the Connally Hot Oil Act on January 22, 1935.[1]

In the House, however, Samuel Pettengill suggested that before Congress "embark[ed] on another effort to corral 'hot oil,' it may be worthwhile . . . to examine a little more critically the assumption upon which the proposed legislation rests." He reminded his colleagues that they were "dealing with constitutional power, rather than the question of the desirability of conserving" petroleum or stabilizing the oil industry, and that "the Supreme Court will continue as an ex post facto partner in petroleum legislation."

"Can Congress delegate its exclusive power to regulate interstate commerce to a state?" Pettengill asked. He pointed out that state agencies, concerned with local interests, regulated petroleum production and determined how much oil entered interstate commerce. "Perhaps no state would ever yield to that temptation, [but] however ingenious we may be in our efforts to permit the states . . . to regulate interstate commerce in petroleum," Pettengill warned, "we still have a Supreme Court, as we were reminded the other day."[2]

Pettengill noted that the court had never permitted Congress to ban from interstate commerce articles that were inherently harmless and incapable of injuring people in the recipient states. He argued that petroleum did not inflict the same kind of harm as intoxicating liquor, diseased cattle, adulterated products, and lottery tickets. "We may, and do, freely grant the desirability of conserving a great natural resource," Pettengill maintained, but "we . . . [also] recognize the temptation to use conservation as an excuse for stabilization, for building up profits in one state at the cost of other states." He sensed danger "in Congress tying itself too tightly to a solution . . . that is apt to be too greatly influenced by local and selfish considerations."[3]

Martin Dies, however, cited those same prior Supreme Court decisions sustaining congressional authority to exclude inherently noxious commodities or products of criminal transactions which polluted the stream of commerce. In the *Lottery* cases, the court had upheld congressional power to exclude from interstate commerce commodities deemed to be economically, socially, or morally detrimental to the public. Dies stated his belief that Congress could ban interstate shipments of hot oil as "the fruit of a law violation . . . a stolen product that we undertake to say shall not have the facilities of interstate commerce in order to effect an illegal purpose." If Congress lacked constitutional authority to pass the Connally bill, Dies concluded, then it "certainly [had no] . . . authority to conserve any other resource."[4]

Representative Cole asked how Congress could "aid or support . . . a state law, which seeks to conserve a valuable and indispensable resource, if the power of the federal government under the interstate clause cannot be used?" He suggested that a broad interpretation of the commerce clause would support the constitutionality of federal hot oil legislation as it had holding-company and stock-exchange regulations. He urged Congress to pass the Connally Hot Oil Act and not "give the State of Texas a blank check as to how much oil it can send to the consuming portion of this country."[5]

On February 19, the House unanimously approved an amended version of the Connally bill, authorizing the president to lift the ban on hot oil whenever demand exceeded supply. Some attorneys warned that the Supreme Court might construe the bill as an unconstitutional delegation of legislative authority to the executive. Cole and Pettengill assured others that the measure satisfied the court's objections. A compromise version of the Connally Hot Oil Act passed both houses of Congress and was signed by the president on February 22. On March 1, Roosevelt issued an executive order reopening the FTB's headquarters in Kilgore, Texas.[6]

Hoping to forestall additional federal legislation, representatives from nine oil-producing states had gathered in Dallas on February 18 to consider some form of interstate compact. The spectre of more federal regulations helped the compact gain favor among opponents, such as Allred and Thompson, who had previously discarded it as unfeasible. Because no compact would work without Texas, Allred's ideas prevailed. The compact, adopted unanimously by the conference, acceded to Allred's demands by omitting federal participation and providing for voluntary state participation. Texans accepted the creation of a permanent Compact Board to oversee execution of future agreements. Participating states ratified the Interstate Oil Compact (IOC) on August 9, 1935.[7]

In contemplation of congressional ratification of the IOC, the Cole Committee produced a watered-down version of the Thomas–Disney bill, providing for oil import restrictions and a new and permanent PAB to administer the Connally Hot Oil Act and recommend state production quotas. Ickes was less than enthusiastic about the bill on the grounds that "no state can regulate interstate commerce nor can one state protect its own citizens from laws or activities of the people of another state." He argued that "regulation or methodizing of crude petroleum production and control of the development of new pools of this natural resource, so necessary to the national security . . . is peculiarly a matter for the federal government."[8]

House Interstate and Foreign Commerce Committee chairman Sam Rayburn supported Cole's proposal to give the IOC a chance before considering stricter federal regulation. Some congressmen opposed strict federal production controls, doubting that "young men just out of college, posing as expert advisors in the matter of petroleum, could succeed in commanding the respect of experienced oilmen." Experience, Thompson told Congress, had proven that "injustices and grievances . . . flowed . . . from the autocratic and arbitrary exercises of . . . sweeping powers . . . in a new bureaucracy," which would exhibit "a lust for power . . . [and] an utter disregard for the sovereignty of the states."[9]

Strong opposition to stringent federal regulation of the oil industry was also voiced in the Senate. Senators William E. Borah and Gerald P. Nye bitterly denounced the entire NIRA as oppressing small businessmen. The Nye–Borah coalition pushed for a recovery program based on strict enforcement of antitrust laws. The general mood in Congress was that the Roosevelt administration should compromise with conservatives. Roosevelt treaded lightly on oil to avoid antagonizing important Democratic National Committee members from Texas and thereby jeopardize passage of his reform package. To him, the Thomas–Disney oil control bill was matched in importance by the Wagner labor relations bill, the Wagner–Rayburn utility holding company bill, a banking bill, and the social security measure. To alienate the fewest interests, Roosevelt supported the IOC and the Connally Hot Oil Act. Undercut by Roosevelt, Ickes reluctantly accepted an eviscerated Thomas–Disney bill.[10]

But opposition to the bill was mounting, and again lawyers played a crucial role. A group of Texas independent oilmen raised a war chest to hire lawyers to battle the proposed legislation.[11] On May 4, API president Axtell J. Byles vowed that a united oil industry would defeat any proposals to place it under the virtual dictatorship of some government bureau. The API asked Congress to ratify the IOC and limit federal regulation to interdicting interstate and foreign shipments of hot oil, promising that "the oil industry is prepared to do its part . . . if it can but know clearly that its efforts are not to be checkmated by constant change, bureaucratic dictation, or usurpation of power." The Texas Senate passed a resolution condemning the Thomas–Disney bill. The IPAA endorsed the principles embodied in the measure.[12]

As Congress struggled to devise a national petroleum-conservation program that would both appease various oil factions and survive judicial review, on May 31, the Supreme Court delivered the *coup de grace* to the NRA codes in the *Schechter* case. *Schechter* conformed to the strict constructionist views that had dominated American jurisprudence for the previous half-century. The *Oil and Gas Journal* praised the court for "clear[ing] the air [so] industry and business can again breathe freely." The "Constitution . . . stands like a rock," it declared, and "[all] the sophistry about emergency legislation is brushed aside into the dustbin."[13]

The NRA's demise provided additional impetus for congressional ratification of the IOC. As the Supreme Court had struck down only the NRA codes, but not the NIRA, Roosevelt suggested that new regulations could be enacted. He feared that the IOC would be difficult to enforce in non-compact states that needed federal assistance to protect their interests. Roosevelt did not reveal the kind of regulation he contemplated, but the *Schechter* decision ruled out federal production controls.[14]

To satisfy the Supreme Court's objections, Thomas revised his bill to enforce state production allowables as quotas in commerce if the states exceeded their limits and to include provisions of the Connally Hot Oil Act. Disney agreed to secure passage of a similar measure in the House, but opposed quotas in commerce as unconstitutional in light of the *Schechter* ruling.[15]

API executive vice-president W. R. Boyd told members of the Mineral Section of the American Bar Association that most oilmen recognized that conservation and good business practice entailed the application of scientific production methods. He argued that state legislatures had a duty to the public and industry to promote oil conservation, but not by controlling production. "If it were not for the devastating severity of . . . antitrust laws . . . self-regulation for an industry like ours would not be so difficult," Boyd explained. "If federal and state governments are to exercise power to negative business agreements detrimental to the public interest," he advised, "they should likewise affirmatively permit . . . agreements that are clearly in the public interest." Boyd emphasized that "business success founded upon honor, integrity, and courage should be commended and encouraged, not despised and destroyed."[16]

Attorney J. Howard Marshall recommended the creation of a new administrative agency with authority to approve trade agreements designed to correct competitive abuses. "The manner of relationship between the practice complained of and the stream of commerce as a whole, could be more clearly perceived," he argued, "if the courts had before them the disinterested findings of a board experienced in matters of trade and conscious of the actual relationship between an incident and the industry as a whole." Marshall contended that congressional power to prohibit unreasonable and unfair trade practices provided legal precedent for administrative regulation of abuses in the oil industry.[17]

As Congress neared the end of a tumultuous term, final action on an oil bill appeared bleak. With time running short, Congress scrapped proposed oil legislation, but the House ratified the IOC on August 22, and the Senate followed on August 24.[18] Congress finally acquiesced to an agreement permitting each state to control its own oil production. The IOC represented a substantial retreat even from the relatively moderate oil controls reflected in the NIRA and the NRA petroleum code.[19] It merely obligated each state to enact and enforce its own regulations. Article V specifically prohibited limitation of production to influence price. To conform to Texas' demands, the IOC provided for voluntary state production controls. Except for the prohibition on interstate transportation of hot oil, each state exercised complete freedom of action. Some IOC members, such as Illinois, did not even have prorationing laws. The Interstate Oil Compact Commission was established in September to act as a fact-finding and informational agency, and a legal committee was set up to advise it on legal issues affecting petroleum conservation.[20]

Meanwhile, on June 17, 1935, the Texas Supreme Court had, for the first time, applied the doctrine of correlative rights to ownership of oil and gas in place. "It is now . . . recognized that when an oil field has been fairly tested and developed," Justice John H. Sharp ruled, "experts can determine approximately the amount of oil and gas in place in a common pool, and can also equitably determine the amount of oil and gas recoverable by the owner of each tract of land." The decision recognized that the rule of capture was subject to state regulation to protect each landowner from unfair drainage by his neighbors. It was the most important decision ever rendered by a Texas court relating to conservation of oil and gas, affirming the TRC's authority to administer state conservation laws to not only prevent waste but also protect the correlative rights of producers.[21]

Most oilmen accepted minimal and temporary federal intervention under the Connally Hot Oil Act, which helped stabilize crude oil prices at a dollar per barrel throughout 1935.[22] The IOC and the Connally Hot Oil Act survived judicial review and became the framework for present-day oil regulation in which the federal government plays a minimal role. After 1935, state-based controls under the aegis of the IOC, and then the demands of World War II, proved sufficient to check serious instability in the oil industry. With the exception of federal regulation of offshore production and environmental legislation, no significant changes have occurred in petroleum conservation laws since 1935.

"It now seems that we have won the fight, and I just feel like telling you, as a friend, about the victory," Thompson told Elkins in summing up the long, hard-fought battle to preserve state control over oil production from bureaucratic power in Washington. "Bitter vituperation was used against our efforts by those who wanted to continue their lawlessness," he continued, "but we faced it with confidence because the people had confidence in us." Thompson credited the victory "to the glory of Texas," but warned that the fruits had to be "defended by eternal vigilance." Illegal oil was being confiscated and sold, violators were being sent to jail, and Texas had benefitted by over $100 million annually thanks to an increased oil market. Texans had "fought for" this and thereby kept the state's "independence secure."[23]

Between 1919 and 1936, oilmen and lawmakers had experienced stupendous difficulties—legal, economic, political, and administrative—in dealing with shifting voluntary, state, and federal regulation of a highly complex industry. Only after voluntary and state controls had proven ineffective in stabilizing chronic overproduction did the majority of oilmen embrace federal regulation. Even then, they accepted it on their own terms. Like the Freedmen's Bureau in the post-bellum South,[24] the FTB, despite its noble intentions and partial success, lacked manpower and resources to police the flow of hot oil adequately and enforce laws unpopular among a hostile populace. By ratifying the IOC, the national government acquiesced to an agreement that permitted each state to act as it wished. Even though the issues of private versus public interests and federal versus state authority persisted, the IOC and Connally Hot Oil Act were state-based, and were therefore hailed as a victory by states' rights advocates.[25]

The legal battle over petroleum conservation was ultimately fought and determined by lawyers in the courtroom. It illustrated the diverse domains within which lawyers operate, domains in which legal, economic, and political concerns merge. Texas lawyers played a leading and multifaceted role in shaping judges' decisions, devising new laws in accord with judicial preferences, and influencing their clients to promote both private and public interests. Humble lawyers—such as William Farish, Edgar Townes, and Hines Baker—pioneered unitization. Robert Hardwicke, Maurice Cheek, and D. Edward Greer proposed and helped to write the petroleum conservation statutes of many oil-producing states, including Texas. James Elkins, of Vinson & Elkins, used his diplomatic talents and powerful connections to influence politicians and TRC policy-making. Fletcher "Big Fish" Fischer successfully defended states' rights against national government intervention by persuading the nation's highest legal tribunal to overturn the NRA petroleum code. Texas attorney general James Allred got an IOC, which left production controls in the hands of the states. In the final analysis—to Ickes's dismay—Texans got their way: the right to control their private oil property, with federal intervention limited to regulating interstate commerce in hot oil. To the sons of the Confederacy, victory in the battle over oil was poetic justice. Southerners had again fought to protect their property and states' rights from outside interference; this time, they had defeated national forces within the parameters of a federal forum, using, ironically, the Fourteenth Amendment they had been forced to accept after the bitter military defeat of 1865.

Notes

Introduction

1. Erich W. Zimmermann, *Conservation in the Production of Petroleum: A Study in Industrial Control* (New Haven: Yale University Press, 1957); Harold F. Williamson, Ralph L. Andreano, Arnold R. Daum, and Gilbert C. Klose, *The American Petroleum Industry*, vol. 2, *The Age of Energy, 1899–1959* (Evanston, Ill.: Northwestern University Press, 1963).
2. Myron W. Watkins, *Oil: Stabilization or Conservation?: A Case Study in the Organization of Industrial Control* (New York: Harper & Row, 1937); Eugene V. Rostow, *A National Policy for the Oil Industry* (New Haven: Yale University Press, 1948); Norman E. Nordhauser, *The Quest for Stability: Domestic Oil Regulation, 1917–1935* (New York: Garland Publishing, 1979). On the other hand, Gerald D. Nash, *United States Oil Policy, 1890–1964: Business and Government in Twentieth Century America* (Pittsburgh: University of Pittsburgh Press, 1968), argues that cooperation between government and various elements in the oil industry produced a consensus on conservation that frequently overrode political considerations.
3. David F. Prindle, *Petroleum Politics and the Texas Railroad Commission* (Austin: University of Texas Press, 1981); Robert Engler, *The Politics of Oil: A Study of Private Power and Democratic Directions* (Chicago: University of Chicago Press, 1961); Daniel Yergin, *The Prize: The Epic Quest for Oil, Money, and Power* (New York: Simon & Schuster, 1991).
4. Morton Keller, *Affairs of State: Public Life in Late Nineteenth Century America* (Cambridge, Mass.: Harvard University Press, 1977); Keller, *Regulating a New Economy: Public Policy and Economic Change in America, 1900–1933* (Cambridge, Mass.: Harvard University Press, 1990); Harold M. Hyman and William M. Wiecek, *Equal Justice Under*

Law: Constitutional Development, 1835–1875 (New York: Harper & Row, 1982), pp. 20–54, maintains that private property rights were vigorously defended against state regulation whenever public policy threatened to abridge "vested" rights that the law protected from unreasonable and unwarranted governmental interference; Harry N. Scheiber, "Public Rights and the Rule of Law in American History," *California Law Review* 72 (Mar., 1984): 217–51, contends [219] that "American judges and legal commentators have given sustained, explicit, and systematic attention to the notion that the public, and not only private parties, have 'rights' that must be recognized and honored if there is to be true rule of law."

5. James Willard Hurst, *Law and Conditions of Freedom in the Nineteenth-Century United States* (Madison: University of Wisconsin Press, 1967); Stanley I. Kutler, *Privilege and Creative Destruction: The Charles River Bridge Case* (Philadelphia: J. B. Lippincott, 1971); Morton J. Horwitz, *The Transformation of American Law, 1780–1860* (Cambridge, Mass.: Harvard University Press, 1977); Horowitz, *The Transformation of American Law, 1870–1960: The Crisis of Legal Orthodoxy* [New York: Oxford University Press, 1992).

6. Arnold M. Paul, *Conservative Crisis and the Rule of Law: Attitudes of Bar and Bench, 1887–1895* (Ithaca, N.Y.: Cornell University Press, 1960); Herbert Hovenkamp, *Enterprise and American Law, 1836–1937* (Cambridge, Mass.: Harvard University Press, 1991).

7. Harry N. Scheiber, "The Road to *Munn:* Eminent Domain and the Concept of Public Purpose in State Courts," *Perspectives in American History* (Cambridge, Mass.: Harvard University Press, 1971), pp. 392–402; Thomas M. Cooley, *Constitutional Limitations Which Rest Upon the Legislative Powers of the States of the American Union* (Boston: Little, Brown, 1883); Christopher G. Tiedeman, *A Treatise on the Limitations of Police Power in the United States* (Saint Louis: F. H. Thomas, 1886).

8. Kenneth J. Lipartito and Joseph A Pratt, *Baker & Botts in the Development of Modern Houston* (Austin: University of Texas Press, 1991), is a recently published law firm history. Professor Harold M. Hyman of Rice University is currently writing the history of Vinson & Elkins; Raymond L. Wise, *Legal Ethics* (New York: Matthew Bender, 1970); Wise, *Legal Ethics: 1979 Supplement* (New York: Matthew Bender, 1979), pp. 269–75; Richard H. Underwood and William H. Fortune, *Trial Ethics* (Boston: Little, Brown, 1988), pp. 590–91, 624–27, citing American Bar Association Model Code of Professional Responsibility (Aug., 1983), Disciplinary Rule 4–101 and American Bar Association Model Rules of Professional Conduct (Aug., 1983), Rule 1.6; See Henry S. Drinker, *Legal Ethics* (New York: Columbia University Press, 1953), pp. 131–39; David Luban, *Lawyers and Justice: An Ethical Study* (Princeton, N.J.: Princeton University Press, 1988), pp. 185–89.

9. See *Restatement of the Law Third: The Law Governing Lawyers* (1983), sec. 111; Bonnie Hobbs, "Lawyers' Papers: Confidentiality Versus the Claims of History," *Washington and Lee Law Review* 49 (1992): 179, suggests a three-tiered process for opening clients' files. The first tier contains records sealed temporarily by prior agreement between lawyer and client and available only to the donor, his assignees, and the attorney. The second tier consists of partially closed files with third-party access to unrestricted portions. The third tier limits access to files to only a certain categories of researchers. Archivists would monitor the process.

10. Kermit Hall, *The Magic Mirror: Law in American History* (New York: Oxford University Press, 1989), p. 3, quotes Justice Oliver Wendell Holmes, Jr.: "This abstraction called the Law is a magic mirror, wherein we see reflected, not only our own lives, but the lives of all men that have been!"

11. David Sugarman, "Simple Images and Complex Realities: English Lawyers and Their Relationship to Business and Politics, 1750–1950," *Law and History Review* 11 (Fall, 1993): 257–301, argues that the "history of lawyers in business undermines the tenet of legal formalism that only those distinctly 'legal' tasks, separate from 'society,' 'business,' and 'politics' are what lawyering is all about." Recent analyses which illuminate the interrelationship between law, economics, and politics include: R. W. Gordon, "Legal Thought and Legal Practice in the Age of the American Enterprise, 1870–1920," in G. Geison, ed., *Professions and Professional Ideologies in America* (Chapel Hill: University of North Carolina Press, 1983); R. L. Nelson, D. M. Trubek, and R. L. Solomon, eds., *Lawyers' Ideals and Lawyers' Practices: Transformations in the American Legal Profession* (Ithaca, N.Y.: Cornell University Press, 1992); Stuart M. Speiser, *Lawyers and the American Dream* (New York: M. Evans and Company, 1993), explains how lawyers are "equalizers" who breathe life into the right to *equal justice under law* and achieve that American dream for their clients and themselves.

Chapter 1

1. Yergin, *The Prize*, pp. 86–87; James A. Clark and Michel T. Halbouty, *Spindletop* (New York: Random House, 1952), pp. 100–101; Williamson, et al., *The American Petroleum Industry*, pp. 16, 23; Joseph A. Pratt, *The Growth of a Refining Region* (Greenwich, Conn.: Jai Press, 1980), pp. 34–36, states that on the eve of Spindletop, New Jersey Standard controlled 85 to 88 percent of crude oil supplies, 82 percent of refining, 85 percent of the kerosene market, and most of the American tanker carrying capacity. Pratt argues that Spindletop's size, its proximity to

the sea, and Texas laws banning the open entry of Standard into the state, allowed "other [oil] companies . . . a chance to grow without directly competing with the dominant firm in the industry."; Prindle, *Petroleum Politics*, pp. 12–14, distinguishes between major integrated oil companies and independent operators. A major oil company integrates all four basic activities of the petroleum industry—producing, transporting, refining, and marketing. Of the four main activities, independents perform no more than two or three. However, independents vary in shape and size. Some produce, transport, and refine and are large enough to share the majors' economic perspective. Since most independents are risk takers who concentrate on production, they do not generally value stability or corporate order. In contrast, majors with vast industrial agglomerations, a bureaucratized structure, and substantial capital investments seek order and stability in lieu of risk. See James W. McKie, "Market Structure and Uncertainty in Oil and Gas Exploration," *Quarterly Journal of Economics* 74 (Nov., 1960): 547.

2. Williamson, et al., *American Petroleum Industry*, pp. 444–57, notes that gasoline production quadrupled from 88.7 million to over 382 million barrels between 1919 and 1929 in conjunction with a staggering increase in the number of registered motor vehicles in the United States from 7.6 million to over 26.5 million during the same decade. Growing gasoline consumption triggered a dramatic rise in domestic crude oil production from 1.03 million to 2.58 million barrels a day between 1919 and 1929; J. Stanley Clark, *The Oil Century: From the Drake Well to the Conservation Era* (Norman: University of Oklahoma Press, 1958), pp. 124–25, notes that in 1919 there were 6,751,000 registered automobiles and 974,000 trucks in use in the United States. By 1930, registrations totaled 23,164,000 and 4,653,000 respectively and by 1940, 27,519,000 and 6,849,000 respectively; Sam H. Schurr, Bruce Netschert, Vera Eliasberg, Joseph Lerner, and Hans H. Landsberg, *Energy in the American Economy, 1850–1975: An Economic Study of Its History and Prospects* (Baltimore: Johns Hopkins University Press, 1960), pp. 35–36, states that energy consumption in the United States increased two-and-one-half times between 1900 and 1930; Nash, *United States Oil Policy*, pp. 5–6; "Motor Registrations Gain 13.7 Per Cent," *Oil and Gas Journal* 24 (July 23, 1925): 24, 152; American Petroleum Institute [API], *Petroleum Facts and Figures* (New York: API, 1930), p. 110, (1939), p. 26; Kendall Beaton, *Enterprise in Oil: A History of Shell in the United States* (New York: Appleton–Century–Crofts, 1957), p. 403.

3. Williamson, et al., *American Petroleum Industry*, pp. 449–54; Clark, *Oil Century*, pp. 127, 139; Nash, *United States Oil Policy*, p. 5; API, *Petroleum Facts and Figures* (1931), p. 173; Stephen T. Powers, "The Develop-

ment of United States Naval Fuel-Oil Policy, 1866–1923" (M.A. Thesis, Rice University, 1960), pp. 1–5.

4. Lipartito and Pratt, *Baker & Botts,* p. 88.

5. Lipartito and Pratt, *Baker & Botts,* p. 88; For discussion of the lawyer's title work pertaining to oil and gas leases see, Lewis G. Mossburg, Jr., *Handbook on Petroleum Land Titles* (Oklahoma City: The Institute for Energy Development, 1976); Max W. Ball, *This Fascinating Oil Business* (New York: Bobbs–Merrill, 1940), pp. 85–97.

6. Lipartito and Pratt, *Baker & Botts,* pp. 99–101, 108; Robert Ashland Shepherd, Sr., "A Short History of the Firm of Vinson, Elkins, Weems & Searls," p. 9, located in the Vinson & Elkins Archives (hereafter VEA), Houston, Texas, Project Identification (hereafter PID): 052615–275.

7. Shepherd, "A Short History of the Firm," p. 9; Robert Ashland Shepherd, Sr., Feb. 13, 1980, Vinson & Elkins Oral History Interview 1 (hereafter VEOH), p. 2, VEA, PID: 052615–391; James Griffith Lawhon, May 17, 1980, VEOH Interview 2, p. 7, VEA, PID: 052615–141; William S. Elkins, Nov. 15, 1982, VEOH Interview 10, pp. 14–15, VEA, PID: 052615–407; Raybourne Thompson, Sept. 20, 1982, VEOH Interview 5, p. 19, VEA, PID: 052615–138; History of the Organization of the Humphreys–Mexia Company, Humphreys–Mexia File, VEA, Closed File 6031 (hereafter C.F.); Original Retainer Contract between Vinson & Elkins and Humphreys–Mexia Oil Company, Jan. 1, 1922, James A. Elkins Personal Correspondence–Mexia, 1918–1926, Folder 1, File H, VEA, C.F. 8001, stipulated that Humphreys–Mexia Oil Company had retained Vinson & Elkins for one year for a fee of $35,000. It was the largest retainer Vinson & Elkins had received to date. By the 1930s, oil and gas law comprised 80 percent of Vinson & Elkins's business; for history and background of Mexia oil field and Colonel Albert E. Humphreys see, Ruth Sheldon Knowles, *The Greatest Gamblers: The Epic of American Oil Exploration* (Norman: University of Oklahoma Press, 1959), pp. 180–83, 210–15; Prentiss T. Moore, "Mexia Well Making Slow But Steady Progress," *Oil Trade Journal* 12 (Jan., 1921): 20; "Texas Brazos Trail," *Texas Monthly* 19 (May, 1991): 73–83; *Mexia Evening News,* Nov. 20, 1920, 1:3, Nov. 26, 1920, 1:3, Dec. 3, 1920, 1:3, May 9, 1921, 1:2; *Fort Worth Star–Telegram,* May 9, 1921, 13:5; See Maxwell Bloomfield, "The Texas Bar in the Nineteenth Century," *Vanderbilt Law Review* 32 (1979): 261–79; Daffan Gilmer, "Early Courts and Lawyers of Texas," *Texas Law Review* 12 (1934): 435–52.

8. Shepherd, "A Short History of the Firm," pp. 10–11; Shepherd Interview, p. 3; William S. Elkins Interview, pp. 6, 15; Ardell Williams, Mar. 30, 1983, VEOH Interview 18, p. 13, VEA, PID: 052615–307; William T. Fleming, Aug. 26, 1983, VEOH Interview 33, p. 6, VEA, PID: 052615–

045; Florris Plowman, Aug. 5, 1982, VEOH Interview 14, pp. 2–4, VEA, PID: 052615–310; Ben H. Rice, Oct. 11, 1983, VEOH Interview 35, p. 12, VEA, PID: 052615–047; Thomas B. Weatherly, June 29, 1982, VEOH Interview 9, p. 32, VEA, OID: 052615–143.

9. Shepherd Interview, pp. 3–4; for background and history on slave marriages and family life see, John W. Blassingame, *The Slave Community: Plantation Life in the Antebellum South* (Oxford: Oxford University Press, 1972).

10. Shepherd Interview, pp. 3–4; Plaintiffs' Petition, May 1, 1924, Mattie Dancy File, VEA, C.F. 7588; Second Amended Answer filed by John Lindley, VEA, C.F. 7588; Cross-Action filed by Marvin Johnson, VEA, C.F. 7588; Transcript, Statement of Facts, VEA, C.F. 7588.

11. Shepherd Interview, p. 4; Leon Lusk to Sweeton, Dec. 5, 1924, VEA, C.F. 7588; Elkins to B. G. Dawes, Mar. 10, 1924, VEA, C.F. 5238.

12. Depositions of Queen Maynard, Willis Medlock, Sam Medlock, Ben Thomas, Kissi Casteele, and Ramon Casteele and Ella Baker taken by Clyde Sweeton, Dec. 5, 1924, Limestone County, Texas, VEA, C.F. 7588; Lusk to Sweeton, Dec. 6, 1924, Mar. 18, 1925, VEA, C.F. 7588; K. C. Barkley to Vinson & Elkins, Aug. 14, 1925, Oct. 8, 1925, VEA, C.F. 7588.

13. *Texas Rules of Civil Procedure* (1992), Rule 200, states in part, "A general verdict is one whereby the jury pronounces generally in favor of one or more parties to the suit upon all or any of the issues submitted to it. A special verdict is one wherein the jury finds the facts only on issues made up and submitted to them under the direction of the court."

14. Jury Instructions, Cause No. 4586–A, *Mattie Dancy, et al. v. F. L. Peyton, et al.*, VEA, C.F. 7588; Judgement of the Court, Cause No. 4586–A, VEA, C.F. 7588; verdict upheld on appeal in *Mattie Dancy, et al. v. F. L. Peyton, et al.*, 282 S.W. 819 (Tex. Civ. App.—Waco [10th Dist.] 1926).

15. The out-of-court settlements are evidenced by the following correspondence: A. C. Scurlock to Sweeton, Dec. 22, 1924, VEA, C.F. 7588; Sweeton to Scurlock, Dec. 31, 1924, VEA, C.F. 7588; M. B. Harrell to Sweeton, Jan. 16, 1925, VEA, C.F. 7588; Lusk to Elkins and Sweeton, Mar. 20, 1925, VEA, C.F. 7588.

16. Clark, *Century*, pp. 129–33, notes that Texas and Oklahoma production accounted for 74.4 percent of the nation's proven reserves and accounted for 70 percent of all oil production in the United States from 1859 to 1955. Domestic production increased by 294 percent between 1918 and 1941, from 355,928,000 barrels a year to 1,402,228,000 barrels per year; Williamson, et al., *American Petroleum Industry*, pp. 302–304, notes that "on average, for each barrel of crude produced during the 1920–29 period there were 1.8 barrels of newly discovered reserves, a replacement ratio roughly an eighth barrel smaller than in the previous ten-year period"; Teagle quoted in, George Sweet Gibb and Evelyn H.

Knowlton, *History of Standard Oil Company (New Jersey)*, vol. 2, *The Resurgent Years 1911–1917* (New York: Harper & Brothers, 1956), p. 485; John Ise, *United States Oil Policy* (New Haven: Yale University Press, 1926), traced the history of domestic oil production up until the early 1920s.

17. Flush development or production is a technique whereby oil wells are operated at capacity or wide open. Under such uncontrolled operation, an oil reservoir yields the major part of its ultimate recovery in a relatively short period of "flush production." This is usually followed by a prolonged interval of low rates of production from individual "stripper" or "marginal" wells as they are called during this latter stage of low productivity. See Stuart E. Buckley, ed., *Petroleum Conservation* (New York: American Institute of Mining and Metallurgical Engineers, 1951), p. 182.

18. Joseph E. Pogue, *The Economics of Petroleum* (New York: John Wiley & Sons, 1921), pp. 19, 249, 289–90; Charles E. Kern, "James E. O'Neal Gives Testimony," *Oil and Gas Journal* 21 (Dec. 28, 1922): 70, 72.

19. Ise, *United States Oil Policy,* pp. 111–21; Robert E. Hardwicke, Jr., "Texas, 1938–1948," Blakely M. Murphy, ed., *Conservation of Oil and Gas: A Legal History, 1948* (Chicago: American Bar Association, 1949), pp. 467–69; Prindle, *Petroleum Politics,* pp. 22–24; Economists do not completely agree on whether the petroleum industry is self-adjusting to free-market forces. Paul H. Frankel, *Essentials of Petroleum* (London: Chapman and Hall, 1946), p. 67, argues that it is not self-adjusting; Morris A. Adelman, *The World Petroleum Market* (Baltimore: Johns Hopkins University Press, 1972), pp. 13–44, argues that it is not; For additional analysis and discussion of petroleum and the free market see Edith Penrose, *The International Petroleum Industry* (Cambridge, Mass.: M.I.T. Press, 1968), pp. 165–71; Also see J. A. O'Conner, Jr., "The Role of Market Demand in the Domestic Oil Industry," *Arkansas Law Review* 12 (Fall, 1958): 345.

20. Melvin I. Urofsky, *A March of Liberty: A Constitutional History of the United States* (New York: Alfred A. Knopf, 1988), p. 157; Hurst, *Law and the Conditions of Freedom in the Nineteenth-Century United States,* pp. 5–10; Kutler, *Privilege and Creative Destruction,* pp. 15–17, 61–67, 117–22. Both Hurst and Kutler argue that American courts transformed traditional common law rules to encourage economic growth and expansion, but unlike Horwitz, they viewed the changes as benefitting the greater community rather than a small commercial elite. Kutler maintains that the "destruction of vested interests in favor of beneficial change reflected a creative process vital to ongoing development and progress" and favoring an entrepreneurial rather than a rentier spirit; Horwitz, *The Transformation of American Law, 1780–1860,* pp. 1–40,

argues that the developmental necessities of American economic life required the abrogation or modification of the essentially static and anti-developmental doctrines of the traditional English common law in a way that favored the rentier class. Horwitz's thesis has been modified by William E. Nelson, *The Americanization of the Common Law: The Impact of Legal Change on Massachusetts Society, 1760–1830* (Cambridge, Mass.: Harvard University Press, 1975). Nelson agreed with Horwitz on the changes that took place in America but pointed to different causes and suggested that the transformation occurred much earlier.

21. Urofsky, *March of Liberty,* p. 158; Horowitz, *Transformation of American Law, 1780–1860,* pp. 30–36; See Herbert Thorndike Tiffany, *The Law of Real Property,* 2nd. ed., (Chicago: Callaghan, 1920) 1, pp. 864–74; George Chase, ed., *Blackstone's Commentaries on the Laws of England,* 3rd ed. (New York: Banks & Brothers, 1977) 2, pp. 511–21.

22. Urofsky, *A March of Liberty,* pp. 158–59; Horwitz, *Transformation of American Law, 1780–1860,* pp. 30–36; Samuel C. Wiel, "Running Water," *Harvard Law Review* 22 (Jan., 1909): 190–92; Joseph Angell, "The Law of Water Privileges," *The American Jurist and Law Magazine* 2 (July–Oct., 1829): 25–38; Frank J. Trelease, *Cases and Materials on Water Law: Resource Use and Environmental Protection,* 2nd ed. (St. Paul, Minn.: West Publishing Company, 1974), pp. 1–27; Tiffany, *The Law of Real Property,* 1, pp. 1132–39; see Arthur Maas and Hiller B. Zobel, "Anglo-American Water Law: Who Appropriated the Riparian Doctrine?" *Public Policy* 10 (1960): 109; T. E. Lauer, "The Common Law Background of the Riparian Doctrine," *Missouri Law Review* 28 (1963): 60; Samuel C. Wiel, "Origin and Comparative Development of the Law of Watercourses in the Common Law and in the Civil Law," *California Law Review* 6 (1918): 245; Department of Economic and Social Affairs, *Abstraction and Use of Water: A Comparison of Legal Regimes* (New York: United Nations Publications, 1922), pp. 8–14; The leading cases deciding nineteenth-century English water law are: *Acton v. Blundell,* 12 Meeson and Welsby's Exchequer Reports 324 (1843); *Chasemore v. Richards,* 7 House of Lords 349 (1859); *Grand Junction Canal Company v. Shugar,* 6 L.R. Ch. App. 481 (1871); See Bernard Rudden, *The New River: A Legal History* (Oxford: Clarendon Press, 1985).

23. Urofsky, *March of Liberty,* pp. 159–60; Horwitz, *Transformation of American Law, 1780–1860,* p. 37; Harry M. Schieber, "Property Law, Expropriation, and Resource Allocation by Government," in Lawrence M. Friedman and Harry M. Schieber, eds., *American Law and the Constitutional Order: Historical Perspectives* (Cambridge, Mass.: Harvard University Press, 1977), p. 34; *Shorey v. Gorrell* (unreported, Mass. 1783); *Palmer v. Mulligan,* 3 Cai.R. 307 (N.Y. 1805); *Platt v. Johnson,* 15 Johns. 213 (N.Y. 1818).

24. Urofsky, *March of Liberty*, 160; Horwitz, *Transformation of American Law, 1780–1860*, pp. 38–39; *Tyler v. Wilkinson*, Fed. Case No. 14,312 (1827); Angell, "The Law of Water Privileges," 25–38, republished excerpts from his treatise on *Watercourses*; J. H. Beuscher, "Appropriation Water Law Elements in Riparian Doctrine," *Buffalo Law Review* 10 (1960–61): 450–52; T. E. Lauer, "Reflections on Riparianism," *Missouri Law Review* 35 (1970): 5–6; John K. Bennet, "Some Fundamentals of Legal Interests in Water Supplies," *Southern California Law Review* 22 (Dec., 1948): 1–5; See R. Kent Newmyer, *Supreme Court Justice Joseph Story: Statesman of the Old Republic* (Chapel Hill: University of North Carolina Press, 1985), pp. 144–46; James McClellan, *Joseph Story and the American Constitution* (Norman: University of Oklahoma Press, 1971), pp. 160–64, 194–96; Gerald T. Dunne, *Justice Joseph Story and the Rise of the Supreme Court* (New York: Simon & Schuster, 1970), p. 266.

25. Walter Lee Summers, "Property in Oil and Gas," *Yale Law Journal* 29 (1919): 174; John Stokes Adams, "The Right of A Landowner to Oil and Gas in His Land," *Pennsylvania Law Review* 63 (Apr., 1915): 471.

26. Tiffany, *Law of Real Property* 1, pp. 864–67; William Wheeler Thornton, *The Law of Oil and Gas*, 5th ed. (Cincinnati: W. H. Anderson, 1932) 1, pp. 61–65; Walter Lee Summers, "Legal Interests in Oil and Gas," *Illinois Law Quarterly* 4 (1922): 15–18; James W. Simonton, "Has A Landowner Any Property in Oil and Gas in Place?," *West Virginia Law Quarterly* 27 (June, 1921): 281–300; Melvin G. de Chazeau and Alfred E. Kahn, *Integration and Competition in the Petroleum Industry* (New Haven: Yale University Press, 1959), p. 62; Northcutt Ely, "The Conservation of Oil," *Harvard Law Review* 51 (1938): 1220–21.

27. Summers, "Legal Interests in Oil and Gas," 15–18; D. Edward Greer, "The Ownership of Petroleum Oil and Natural Gas in Place," *Texas Law Review* 1 (1923): 162–87; Robert E. Hardwicke, Jr., "The Rule of Capture and its Implications as Applied to Oil and Gas," *Texas Law Review* 13 (June, 1935): 391–422.

28. *Res communes* are those things, such as air and water, that cannot be exclusively appropriated by an individual because they are necessary for human existence and must be shared by all. Unlike fixed and inanimate objects, they have the power to move on their own volition. This principle passed from Roman law into the English common law. See Wier, "Running Water," 190–92; Angell, "Law of Water Privileges," 25–38.

29. Summers, "Legal Interests in Oil and Gas," 15–18; see Horwitz, *Transformation of American Law, 1780–1860*, pp. 253–66, which discussed how American law promoted economic growth; Hurst, *Law and Conditions of Freedom*, pp. 71–107, described how American law attempted to

balance various competing interests in the nineteenth century; Kutler, *Privilege and Creative Destruction,* pp. 146–49, noted the changes in the American legal system's approach to resolving conflicting interests.

30. *Brown v. Vandergrift, et al.,* 80 Penn. St. Reports 142 (1875).

31. Ibid., 147–48.

32. Ibid., 147–48, citing *Funk v. Haldeman,* 53 Pa. St. Reports 229, 241–42; James A. Veasey, "The Law of Oil and Gas," *Michigan Law Review* 18 (Apr., 1920): 451.

33. *Westmoreland Natural Gas Company v. DeWitt, et al.,* 130 Pa. St. 235, 18 Atl. 724 (1889); Simonton, "Has A Landowner Any Property in Oil and Gas in Place?," 292.

34. Ibid., 249; A. W. Walker, Jr., "Property Rights in Oil and Gas and Their Effect Upon Police Regulation of Production," *Texas Law Review* 16 (1938): 371, n. 6.

35. *Barnard v. Monongahela Gas Company,* 216 Pa. St. 362, 65 Atl. 801 (1907); J. Howard Marshall and Norman L. Meyers, "Legal Planning of Petroleum Production," *Yale Law Journal* 41 (Nov., 1931): 40–42; Summers, "Property in Oil and Gas," 175–78; Robert E. Hardwicke, Jr., "The Rule of Capture and its Implications as Applied to Oil and Gas," 396–97; Veasey, "The Law of Oil and Gas," 450–52; Summers, "Legal Interests in Oil and Gas," 17–18; See *Kelly v. Ohio Oil Company,* 57 Ohio St. 317, 49 N.E. 399 (1897), where the Ohio Supreme Court denied relief to a landowner seeking to recover damages from a neighbor for draining the oil and gas underlying his property and to enjoin future production to prevent further injury. The court held, "Whatever gets into the well belongs to the owner of the well no matter where it came from . . . no one can tell to a certainty from whence the oil, gas, or water which enters the well came, and no legal right as to the same can be established or enforced by an adjoining landowner."

36. Richard A. Posner, *The Problems of Jurisprudence* (Cambridge, Mass.: Harvard University Press, 1990). Quotation cited from p. 362. Posner, a judge of the United States Court of Appeals for the Seventh Circuit, discussed "legal reasoning as practical reasoning" including judicial use of analogies as authority. He stated, "The use of analogy . . . an hence 'precedent' in the nonauthoritative sense is inevitable in fields where theory is weak . . . I merely question whether [it] . . . deserves—the hoopla and reverence that members of the legal profession have bestowed on it . . . . Analogy may . . . have persuasive force in a psychological sense (89–92). Posner cited Howard R. Williams and Charles J. Meyers, *Oil and Gas Law,* 1, Sections 203.1 and 204.4 (1988), that the rule of capture made sense when applied to things that were not scarce, like rabbits and foxes, but not to resources like oil and gas. The capture theory created an incentive to exploit petroleum resources as quickly as

possible, which was too quickly. See Richard J. Pierce, Jr., "State Regulation of Natural Gas In A Federally Deregulated Market: The Tragedy of the Commons Revisited," *Cornell Law Review* 73 (1987): 15, 20–23.

37. See Peter Charles Hoffer, *The Law's Conscience: Equitable Constitutionalism in America* (Chapel Hill: University of North Carolina Press, 1990), pp. 7–12. Equity is a concept in Anglo-American jurisprudence that comprehends legal issues left remediless by the common law and guides judges in fashioning fair remedies.

38. Henry Berenger, *Le Petrole at al France* (Paris: Flammarion, 1920), pp. 175–80, cited in Yergin, *The Prize*, p. 183.

Chapter 2

1. John G. McLean and Robert W. Haigh, *The Growth of Integrated Oil Companies* (Boston: Harvard Business School, 1954), pp. 85–87, notes the impact of the discoveries of the following oil fields: Yates, Hendrick McElroy, Glasscock, and Van in Texas; Seminole, Bowlegs, and Oklahoma City in Oklahoma; Kettleman North Dome in California; and Hobbs and Eunice–Monument in New Mexico; Stanley Gill, *The Petroleum Industry of the United States,* Report to the Subcommittee on Petroleum Investigation of the Committee on Interstate and Foreign Commerce, House of Representatives, 73rd Congress (Houston: Gulf Publishing, 1934), p. 313.

2. Robert E. Hardwicke, Jr., *Antitrust Laws et al. v. Unit Operation of Oil or Gas Pools* (New York: American Institute of Mining and Metallurgical Engineers, 1948), pp. 3–8, footnotes cite publications reflecting contemporary scientific and technological advances in understanding petroleum reservoir behavior; Williamson, et al., *American Petroleum Industry,* p. 313–15, lists three basic methods of geophysical prospecting that had been developed in the 1920s: (1) gravimetric; (2) seismic; and (3) magnetic. Gravimetrics measures the density of subsurface rocks by use of torsion balance. Seismic prospecting depends on the elasticity of subsurface rocks as recorded on a seismograph. The magnetic method utilizes a magnetometer to measure differences in the intensity of the earth's magnetic field; Paul Williams, "Dynamometer Gives Important Data," *Oil and Gas Journal* 28 (May 30, 1929): 33, 154–55; Zimmermann, *Conservation in the Production of Petroleum,* p. 114; James O. Lewis, "Methods for Increasing the Recovery from Oil Sands," United States Bureau of Mines, *Bulletin 148, Petroleum Technology* (Washington, D.C.: Government Printing Office, 1917), p. 37; A. W. Ambrose, "Only 20 Percent of Oil Is Recovered," *Oil and Gas Journal* 18 (Oct. 10, 1919): 62, 66.

3. Williamson, et al., *American Petroleum Industry,* p. 316; Gibb and Knowlton, *History of Standard Oil Company (New Jersey),* vol. 2, *The*

Resurgent Years 1911–1917, pp. 428–32; Andrew M. Rowley, "Engineers Attack Oil Field Problems," *Oil and Gas Journal* 26 (June 21, 1928): 31, 164.

4. Engler, *The Politics of Oil,* pp. 59–60, states the purposes of the API were: (1) "To afford a means of cooperation with the government in all matters of national concern"; (2) "To foster foreign and domestic trade in American petroleum products"; (3) "To promote in general the interests of the petroleum industry in all its branches"; and (4) "To promote the mutual improvements of its members and the study of the arts and sciences connected with the petroleum industry." The API served as a forum for the petroleum industry. It had separate divisions for production, transportation, refining, and marketing, finance and accounting, and governmental and public relations. Engler contended that the API's policies, financial contributions, and leadership have been dominated by the major integrated oil companies and that its position generally reflects their interests; Clark, *Oil Century,* p. 190, states that the API "became the greatest single agency sponsoring the interests of the oil industry."

5. Zimmermann, *Conservation in Production of Petroleum,* p. 122; Yergin, *The Prize,* p. 220; Knowles, *The Greatest Gamblers,* pp. 147–52, describes Doherty as a self-educated "engineering genius" who dropped out of school at age twelve. He subsequently obtained 140 patents covering his inventions and processes in the oil, gas, cement, chemical, coke, smelting, and home-heating industries. Doherty built an industrial empire of electric and gas utilities known as the Cities Service Company. See Thomas M. Smiley, "Henry L. Doherty Owes His Rise to Grit," *Oil and Gas Journal* 29 (Dec. 25, 1930): 31, 98, portrayed Doherty as a tough, resourceful businessman who cherished his reputation as the "intellectual gadfly" of the petroleum industry. Doherty's ambition and tenacity elevated him to the directorship of some 150 companies including his own Cities Service Company. He became involved in the oil business when one of his companies struck oil while drilling for gas in Kansas.

6. Unitization is the joint, coordinated development of oil fields by individual owners and operators. Optimal recovery of oil and gas and efficient, low-cost operations can be realized through such cooperative agreements and efforts by individual owners and operators. Compulsory unitization statutes were advocated as a means of avoiding the often difficult problem of obtaining unanimous approval of voluntary unitization by all landowners and producers in a field. Jacqueline Lang Weaver, *Unitization of Oil and Gas Fields in Texas: A Study of Legislative, Administrative, and Judicial Policies* (Washington: Resources for the Future, 1986), pp. 1–2; See Leonard M. Logan, Jr., *Stabilization of*

the Petroleum Industry (Norman: University of Oklahoma Press, 1930), pp. 171–72 for detailed definition of unitization; Hardwicke, *Antitrust Laws,* p. 13, pointed out that Doherty was not the first to recognize and advocate unitization. As early as 1916, William F. McMurray and James O. Lewis of the United States Bureau of Mines had recommended unitization in a technical paper entitled, "Underground Wastes in Oil and Gas Fields and Methods of Prevention." Chester Gilbert and Joseph E. Pogue later suggested the same solution in their book, *America's Power Resources: The Economic Significance of Coal, Oil, and Water Power* (New York: Century, 1921), as did Max W. Ball in, "Adequate Acreage and Oil Conservation," Address delivered at the Nineteenth Annual Convention of the American Mining Congress, Nov. 16, 1916.

7. Henry L. Doherty, "The Petroleum Problem As I See It," Federal Oil Conservation Board, *Complete Record of Public Hearings,* Feb. 10–11, 1926 (Washington, D.C.: Government Printing Office, 1926), pp. 25–33 [hereafter FOCB, *Public Hearings*].

8. Nordhauser, *Quest for Stability,* pp. 14–16.

9. Zimmermann, *Conservation in the Production of Petroleum,* p. 123; Hardwicke, *Antitrust Laws,* pp. 179–90; Joseph Pratt, *The Growth of a Refining Region* (Greenwich, Conn.: Jai Press, 1980), p. 202; Yergin, *The Prize,* pp. 221–22.

10. Zimmermann, *Conservation in the Production of Petroleum,* pp. 125–26; Hardwicke, *Antitrust Laws,* pp. 18–19; James John Hayden, *Federal Regulation of the Production of Oil* (Washington: Callaghan and Company, 1929), p. 2, states that President Calvin Coolidge appointed a Federal Oil Conservation Board consisting of the Secretaries of War, Navy, Interior, and Commerce. Known as Coolidge's "Four Wise Men," the FOCB's primary purpose was to study the federal government's responsibilities and to enlist the oil industry's cooperation in investigating oil reserves, the technical conditions of production, and the economic disruption wrought by flush production; Rostow, *A National Policy for the Oil Industry,* pp. 18–19; Nash, *United States Oil Policy,* pp. 84–85; Norman S. Nordhauser, "Origins of Federal Oil Regulation in the 1920s," *Business History Review* 47 (Spring, 1973): 64–65; George Ward Stocking, *The Oil Industry and the Competitive System: A Study in Waste* (Boston: Houghton Mifflin, 1925), pp. 134–35, 177–79; Northcutt Ely, "The Use of Federal Powers to Supplement Those of the States," in Murphy, ed., *Conservation of Oil and Gas: A Legal History, 1948,* p. 681–91.

11. Zimmermann, *Conservation in the Production of Petroleum,* p. 126; Nordhauser, *Quest for Stability,* p. 22; John G. Clark, *Energy and the Federal Government: Fossil Fuel Policies, 1900–1946* (Urbana: University of Illinois Press, 1987), p. 149; Nash, *United States Oil Policy,* p. 88;

API, *American Petroleum: Supply and Demand, A Report to the Board of Directors of the American Petroleum Institute by a Committee of Eleven Members of the Board* (New York: McGraw–Hill, 1925), pp. 3–5.

12. Williamson, et al., *American Petroleum Industry*, pp. 310–19; Clark, *Oil Century*, pp. 190–91; FOCB, *Public Hearings*, p. 23 quoted Teagle; Ibid., p. 20, recorded address by Charles Evans Hughes, Counsel for the American Petroleum Institute.

13. Nash, *United States Oil Policy*, pp. 88–89; Nordhauser, *Quest for Stability*, p. 24.

14. Hayden, *Federal Regulation of the Production of Oil*, pp. 8–10; FOCB, *Report of the Federal Oil Conservation Board to the President of the United States* (Washington, D.C., 1926), pt. 1, pp. 14–15; Rostow, *A National Policy for the Oil Industry*, p. 19. For the trade association movement see, Edgar L. Heermance, "Self-Regulation and the Law," *Harvard Business Review* 10 (July, 1932): 420–29; Henry I. Harriman, "The Stabilization of Business and Employment," *American Economic Review* 22 (Mar., 1932): 63–74.

15. Engler, *Politics of Oil*, p. 137; Clark, *Energy and the Federal Government*, p. 209; Hayden, *Federal Regulation of the Production of Oil*, pp. 10–13; Wok's address before the American Bar Association published in the *Oil and Gas Journal* 26 (Sept. 1, 1927): 57, 64; Nordhauser, *Quest for Stability*, p. 35, states: "The Committee of Nine was staffed by men with a material interest in the oil industry; only one of the ABA representatives, Henry Bates, Dean of the University of Michigan Law School, was not associated with a major oil firm. The other two ABA appointees were Warren Olney, a lawyer for Shell Oil, and James A. Veasey, an attorney for an affiliate of Standard Oil (New Jersey)."

16. James A. Veasey, "Constitutional Obstacles to Oil Law," *Oil and Gas Journal* 26 (Sept. 1, 1927): 32, 91, citing *Hammer v. Dagenhart*, 247 U.S. 251 (1918) and *Bailey v. Drexel Furniture Company*, 259 U.S. 20 (1922). Veasey was general counsel of the Carter Oil Company in Tulsa, Oklahoma, and nonresident lecturer on oil and gas law at the University of Michigan Law School; See Donald H. Ford, "Controlling the Production of Oil," *Michigan Law Review* 30 (June, 1932): 1179–80.

17. Ibid.

18. Ibid.

19. Ibid.; *Ohio Oil Company v. Indiana*, 177 U.S. 190, 210 (1900); see Leon Friedman and Fred Israel, eds., *The Justices of the United States Supreme Court, 1789–1869: Their Lives and Major Opinions* (New York: Chelsea House Publishers, 1969), 3, pp. 1633–57, noted that President Grover Cleveland appointed White to the Supreme Court in 1894. President William Howard Taft promoted White to Chief Justice in 1911. White served on the Supreme Court until his death in 1921.

20. *Ohio Oil Company v. Indiana,* 208–12.
21. Maurice H. Merrill, "Stabilization of the Oil Industry and Due Process of Law," *Southern California Law Review* 3 (June, 1930): 403, in 1920, the United States Supreme Court upheld a Wyoming statute restricting the use of natural gas for domestic and industrial fuel and prohibiting its use for producing carbon black as a valid exercise of state police power. See *Walls v. Midland Carbon Company,* 254 U.S. 300 (1920). The Supreme Court of Montana, however, refused to follow the United States Supreme Court's decision in *Walls* and struck down an identical Montana statute as violative of the due process clause of the state constitution; Ford, "Controlling Oil Production," 1181–85, citing *Lindsley v. Natural Carbonic Gas Company,* 220 U.S. 61 (1911), involving a New York statute which forbade the wasteful or unreasonable pumping of mineral water, having an excess of carbonic acid gas, for the purpose of extracting or selling the gas as a commodity separate from the water. The statute was challenged by a landowner as depriving him of his private property without due process of law. On appeal, the United States Supreme Court ruled that the mineral water and carbonic gas existed in a commingled state in the underlying rock and neither could be extracted without the other. Influenced by the greater demand for gas, some landowners pumped out the water to collect and sell the gas, allowing the water to run to waste. The court found that these pumping operations resulted in an unreasonable and wasteful depletion of the common water supply and in a corresponding injury to others equally entitled to use it and upheld the New York regulatory statute as consistent with due process of law. See *Gas Products Company v. Rankin,* 63 Mont. 372, 207 Pac. 993 (1922); Veasey, "Constitutional Obstacles to Oil Legislation," 103–104, notes that, between 1868 and 1912, the United States Supreme Court struck down 6 percent of the cases it heard involving the constitutionality, under Fourteenth Amendment due process clause, of state legislation of a social or economic character. From 1913 to 1920, 7 percent were declared unconstitutional; and between 1921 and 1927, 28 percent were held unconstitutional.
22. Veasey, "Constitutional Obstacles to Oil Legislation," 159–61.
23. Ibid.
24. FOCB, *Report of the Federal Oil Conservation Board to the President of the United States* (Washington, 1928), Pt. 3, pp. 9–15.
25. William Stamps Farish received a law degree from the University of Mississippi in 1901 and moved to Beaumont, Texas, where he supervised wells for Texas Oil Fields Limited, an English syndicate. Farish organized the Brown–Farish Oil Company in 1902. In 1904, he and Robert Lee Blaffer formed a partnership to engage in drilling and lease

trading. Farish and Blaffer were among the founders and original
directors of Humble Oil & Refining Company. Cited from Henrietta M.
Larson and Kenneth Wiggins Porter, *History of Humble Oil and Refin-
ing Company: A Study in Industrial Growth* (New York: Harper &
Brothers, 1959), pp. 23–29; Hines H. Baker, Dec. 10, 1982, VEOH
Interview 20, p. 9, VEA, Houston, Texas, PID: 052615–304.

26. Yergin, *The Prize,* pp. 222–23; Larson and Porter, *History of Humble Oil,*
pp. 257–63; Henrietta M. Larson, Evelyn H. Knowlton, and Charles S.
Popple, *History of Standard Oil Company (New Jersey),* vol. 3, *New
Horizons, 1927–1950* (New York: Harper & Row, 1971), pp. 63–64, 88;
August W. Giebelhaus, *Business and Government in the Oil Industry: A
Case Study of Sun Oil, 1876–1945* (Greenwich, Conn.: Jai Press, 1980),
p. 118; Carl Coke Rister, *Oil!: Titan of the Southwest* (Norman: Univer-
sity of Oklahoma Press, 1949), pp. 244–46, 293–97.

27. Yergin, *The Prize,* pp. 223–24; Larson and Porter, *History of Humble Oil,*
pp. 253–55, 307–309.

28. For a discussion of the effect of the rule of capture on the petroleum
industry see Hardwicke, "The Rule of Capture and Its Implications as
Applied to Oil and Gas," 391–422; Larson and Porter, *History of Humble
Oil,* p. 302 quoted Farish; Weaver, *Unitization of Oil and Gas Fields in
Texas,* p. 53; Clark, *Energy and the Federal Government,* pp. 163–64.

29. Edgar E. Townes was the son of John C. Townes, a district judge and dean
of the University of Texas Law School. He headed the law firm of Townes,
Foster, and Hardwicke in Beaumont, Texas, in 1917 when, at the age of
twenty-eight, he drew up the original charter of Humble Oil Company
and became its first general counsel. Townes served on Humble's board of
directors and as vice-president from 1933 to 1943. He retired from
Humble in 1943 and entered private law practice. Townes founded South
Texas College of Law and served as its dean for twenty-six years. Cited
from *Houston Chronicle,* Dec. 9, 1991, 11:1; Herman Paul Pressler, III,
Dec. 3, 1982, VEOH Interview 40, p. 2, VEA, PID: 052615–050.

30. Larson and Porter, *History of Humble Oil,* pp. 302–303, citing Townes's
memoranda of Apr. 26 and July 6, 1927, located in the Humble Oil &
Refining Company records in Houston, Texas. Larson and Porter
pointed out that Humble's legal staff relied upon the work of other oil
and gas lawyers such as private practitioners Robert E. Hardwicke, Jr.,
and John Kilgore, and corporate counsel Lewis Foster of Sun Oil Company, W. O. Crane of the Texas Company, W. P. Z. German of Skelly Oil
Company, and James A. Veasey of Carter Oil Company. Attorney Hines
H. Baker joined Humble's legal department in 1919 and, after serving
an apprenticeship doing title work, was assigned responsibility for
studying and rendering advice on the legal aspects of petroleum conservation; Weaver, *Unitization of Oil and Gas Fields in Texas,* pp. 53–54.

31. Ibid.
32. Hines H. Baker, Dec. 10, 1982, VEOH Interview 21, p. 11, VEA, PID: 052615–304; Larson and Porter, *History of Humble Oil,* pp. 303–05; Rex Gavin Baker, Dec. 3, 1982, VEOH Interview 20, p. 5, VEA, PID: 052615–305, notes importance of lawyers' title work; For a chronological history of compulsory unitization statutes see J. Frederick Lawson, "Recent Developments in Pooling and Unitization," *Institute on Oil and Gas Law and Taxation* (Albany, N.Y.: Matthew Bender, 1972), p. 213; Twenty-seven states eventually adopted antitrust exemptions for voluntary unitization agreements. See Howard R. Williams and Charles J. Meyers, *Oil and Gas Law* 6 (Albany, N.Y.: Matthew Bender, 1980), sec. 911.
33. Larson and Porter, *History of Humble Oil,* pp. 305–306.
34. Ibid.
35. Knowles, *The Greatest Gamblers,* pp. 191–203, 324; Ernest W. Marland attended the University of Michigan where he distinguished himself as a poker player. His gambling instinct led him into oil wildcatting in Pennsylvania where he made and lost a fortune. Marland came to Oklahoma from Pittsburgh in 1908 and was living on borrowed money. He established the Marland Oil Company and eventually became governor of Oklahoma; F. C. Proctor quoted in Hardwicke, *Antitrust Laws,* p. 39; Hughes offered a somewhat contradictory view to the one he had expressed in the public hearing before the FOCB on May 27, 1926, when he stated: "The Government of the United States is one of enumerated powers and is not at liberty to control the internal affairs of the states, respectively, such as production within the states, through assertions by Congress of a desire either to provide for the common defense or to promote the general welfare." Quoted in Clark, *Oil Century,* p. 191; Larson and Porter, *History of Humble Oil,* pp. 307–308, note that Hughes reconciled the apparent inconsistency in his views by insisting that federal regulations be limited to prohibiting interstate shipments of oil produced under circumstances involving waste.
36. Larson and Porter, *History of Humble Oil,* pp. 309–10; Weaver, *Unitization of Oil and Gas Fields in Texas,* pp. 25–27, explained that unitization improves each operator's cost efficiency by eliminating the need to drill unnecessary wells thereby lowering production costs and minimizing loss of reservoir pressure allowing more oil to be recovered. On pp. 45–46, Weaver cites Farish's belief that unitization would allow 50 percent more oil to be produced at a fourth the cost of competitive drilling. For analysis of the economic efficiency derived from unitization, see Stephen L. McDonald, *Petroleum Conservation in the United States: An Economic Analysis* (Baltimore: Johns Hopkins University Press, 1971), pp. 59–110.
37. Weaver, *Unitization of Oil and Gas Fields in Texas,* pp. 29–33, cites the

following obstacles to voluntary unitization: joint decision making by a
committee under unitization did not appeal to rugged individuals who
valued pride of ownership and complete control over their own affairs;
mistrust among small independent producers who feared that major oil
company partners would not treat them fairly; multiple parties reduced
the likelihood of agreement; fear of antitrust prosecution; and fear of
other problems like the uncertainties of maintaining leases and the tax
status of profits. See Mid Continent Oil and Gas Association, *Handbook
on Unitization of Oil Pools* (Saint Louis: Blackwell Wielandy, 1930), pp.
44–55; Alan E. Friedman, "The Economics of the Common Pool: Property Rights in Exhaustible Resources," *U.C.L.A. Law Review* 18 (1975):
855–87; Garrett Hardin, "The Tragedy of the Commons," *Science* 162
(1968): 1243–48; Lawrence Berger, "The Public Use Requirement in
Eminent Domain," *Oregon Law Review* 57 (1978): 203–46.

38. Larson and Porter, *History of Humble Oil,* pp. 310–12; Hardwicke,
    Antitrust Laws, pp. 41–46.
39. Farish and Proctor quoted in Larson and Porter, *History of Humble Oil,*
    p. 315.

Chapter 3

1. Founded in 1917 by William A. Vinson and James A. Elkins, the Houston
   law firm of Vinson & Elkins (VE) initially represented local lumber and
   insurance businesses. The firm had no major oil company clients. In
   1921, Colonel Albert E. Humphreys, an independent oil producer, with
   considerable lease-holdings in the Mexia oil field near Mexia, Texas, was
   looking to retain the services of a respectable law firm. His oil operations
   had outgrown the capacity of a local small-town, solo practitioner. By
   chance, Humphreys met Elkins in Houston. Elkins persuaded the Texas
   Company to pay Humphreys some money it had owed him for recent
   crude oil purchases. Humphreys was impressed with Elkins and, on
   January 1, 1922, retained VE to represent the Humphreys Oil Company
   for a fee of $35,600 per year. In 1924, Pure Oil Company bought out
   Humphreys's producing interests in the Mexia field and retained VE to
   handle its legal business in Texas. By the 1930s, oil and gas law comprised about 80 percent of VE's legal business. VE represented many of
   Texas' independent oil producers, a group of rugged individuals appro-
   priately called "wildcatters." See Shepherd, *A Short History of the Firm,*
   p. 9; Shepherd Interview, p. 2, VEA, PID: 052615–391; William S. Elkins,
   Nov. 15, 1982, VEOH Interview 10, pp. 14–15, VEA, PID: 052615–407;
   Raybourne Thompson, Sept. 20, 1982, VEOH Interview 5, p. 19, VEA,
   PID: 052615–138; Original Retainer Contract between Vinson & Elkins
   and Humphreys–Mexia Oil Company, Jan. 1, 1922, James A. Elkins

Personal Correspondence File—Mexia, 1918–1926, Folder 1, File H, VEA, C.F. 8001. For history and background of Mexia oil field and Albert E. Humphreys see Knowles, *The Greatest Gamblers,* pp. 180–183, 210–215; Moore, "Mexia Well Making Slow But Steady Progress," 20; "Texas Brazos Trail," *Texas Monthly* 19 (May, 1991): 73–83; *Mexia Evening News,* Nov. 20, 1920, 1:3, Nov. 26, 1920, 1:3, Dec. 3, 1920, 1:3, May 9, 1921, 1:2; *Fort Worth Star–Telegram,* May 9, 1921, 13:5.

2. Minutes of General Firm Meeting, Nov. 9, 1927, VEA; Minutes of Committee Representatives of Oil Companies Operating in the Yates Pool [hereafter Minutes of Yates Committee], Sept. 2, 1927, VEA, C.F. 29159–D.

3. James Presley, *A Saga of Wealth: The Rise of the Texas Oilmen* (Austin: Texas Monthly Press, 1983), pp. 106–109, 10 years after the discovery of the Yates oil field, the Texas public school fund had earned $6.5 million in royalties. Oil income enabled the University of Texas to become one of the nation's leading universities. In 1973–74, the University of Texas library ranked tenth among the nation's university libraries; "University Royalties," *Oil Weekly* 42 (Aug. 6, 1926): 88; "Texas University Royalties," *Oil Weekly* 44 (Dec. 31, 1926): 26; Roger M. Olien and Diana Davids Olien, *Wildcatters: Texas Independent Oilmen* (Austin: Texas Monthly Press, 1984), pp. 35–41; "West Texas Producing Area Crosses Pecos," *Oil Weekly* 43 (Nov. 5, 1926): 40; "Robert R. Penn." *Oil and Gas Journal* 30 (Dec. 24, 1931): 14; Robert R. Penn Obituary, *Oil and Gas Journal* 30 (Dec. 24, 1931): 14.

4. Minutes of Yates Committee, Sept. 2, 1927, p. 1–2, VEA, C.F. 29159–D; Minutes of General Firm Meeting, Nov. 9, 1927, p. 1, Mar. 16, 1928, pp. 1–2, VEA [no PID].

5. Memorandum of Joint Operating Agreement for the Yates Oil Field [hereafter Yates Operators' Agreement], Sept. 8, 1927, p. 1–4, VEA, C.F. 29159–D, defined potential production (pp) as the amount of oil which the completed wells on a given lease, regardless of number, produce on any given date. The potential production of the entire field (ppf) is the sum of the potential production of individual leases. The field's outlet (ol) is the total amount of oil that the operators agree to produce each day. A production fraction or percentage (pf) is determined by dividing the total outlet (ol) by the total field production (ppf). The production of an individual lease is determined by multiplying potential production (pp) by the production fraction (pf). The resulting amount is the quota assigned to each operator.

6. Ibid.

7. Ibid.

8. Larson and Porter, *History of Humble Oil,* p. 317; Rister, *Oil!: Titan of the Southwest,* pp. 298–99.

9. SoRelle to McIlvain, Sept. 12, 1927, VEA, C.F. 10974; SoRelle to Elkins, Sept. 12, 1927, VEA, C.F. 10974; Elkins to SoRelle, Sept. 19, 1927, VEA, C.F. 10974; SoRelle to Elkins, Sept. 22, 1927, VEA, C.F. 10974.

10. Allwyn Barr, *Reconstruction to Reform: Texas Politics, 1876–1906* (Dallas: Southern Methodist University Press, 1955; Reprint, Austin: University of Texas Press, 1971), pp. 9, 93–99, 113–17; John S. Spratt, *The Road to Spindletop: Economic Change in Texas* (Austin: University of Texas Press, 1983), pp. 212–15; M. M. Crane, "Recollections of the Establishment of the Texas Railroad Commission," *Southwestern Historical Quarterly* 50 (1947): 478–79; H. N. G. Gammel, comp., *The Laws of Texas, 1827–1897,* 10 (Austin: Gammel Book Company, 1898), pp. 55–65; Prindle, *Petroleum Politics,* p. 19; TRC members were originally appointed by the governor to avoid the railroads' undue financial influence on elected public officials. But farmers, angry at Governor Hogg for not appointing one of their own to the TRC, pressured the legislature into changing the law to provide for election of TRC members to six-year terms, one being elected every two years. In 1891, John H. Reagan became the TRC's first chairman; see Pamela McDougald Fowler, "The Origins of the Texas Railroad Commission," (M.A. Thesis, Rice University, 1982), pp. 67–68; Robert C. Cotner, *James Stephen Hogg* (Austin: University of Texas Press, 1959).

11. *Farmers' Loan and Trust Company v. International Great Northern Railroad Company,* 51 F. Supp. 529, 535–36 (1892); Barr, *Reconstruction to Reform,* p. 122; Ben H. Proctor, *Not Without Honor: The Life of John H. Reagan* (Austin: University of Texas Press, 1962), p. 285.

12. *Reagan v. Farmers' Loan and Trust Company,* 154 U.S. 367, 394–412 (1894).

13. Spratt, *Road to Spindletop,* p. 222.

14. James P. Hart, "Oil, the Courts, and the Railroad Commission," *Southwestern Historical Quarterly* 44 (Jan., 1941): 307–17; Robert E. Hardwicke, Jr., "Legal History of Conservation of Oil in Texas," *Legal History of Conservation of Oil and Gas* (Chicago: American Bar Association, 1938), p. 215; *General and Special Laws Passed by the Twenty-sixth Legislature of the State of Texas at Regular Session* (1899), ch. 49, p. 68; *Revised Civil Statutes of Texas* (1925), Articles 6004, 6005, 6006, and 6008.

15. Rister, *Oil!: Titan of the Southwest,* p. 412.

16. *General and Special Laws Passed by the Twenty-ninth Legislature of the State of Texas at Regular Session* (1905), ch. 119, p. 228; *Thirty-third Leg., Reg. Sess.* (1913), ch. 111, p. 212; *Thirty-fifth Leg., Reg. Sess.* (1917), ch. 30, p. 48.

17. Hardwicke, "Legal History," p. 217–18; *Texas Constitution,* Article XVI, Section 59(a); available evidence does not indicate precisely why

the Texas legislature delegated authority to an existing agency, the TRC, rather than creating a new and separate commission for enforcing state petroleum conservation statutes. The legislature probably desired to save tax dollars to gain the favor of Texas voters who had ritually opposed government spending and taxation. Familiarity with its members and their track record might have been another reason why the legislature chose the TRC to enforce oil conservation. Most likely, the legislature desired to have petroleum conservation administered by an agency "which at least had the opportunity by continuous and extensive experience and study to become experts and specialists with the needs and demands of the industry. For the purpose of efficiency . . . it was advisable to have the Legislature only indicate the broad outlines of the [TRC's] policies . . . leaving all matters of detail to those who make a specialty of the study of the problems involved. Not only does the [TRC] have the advantage of specialization, but it also has the advantage of a continuity of action." Hart, "Oil, the Courts, and the Railroad Commission," pp. 307–309; see Elton M. Hyder, Jr., "Some Difficulties in the Application of the Exceptions to the Spacing Rule in Texas," *Texas Law Review* 27 (1949): 482–83, for speculation on reasons why the Texas legislature assigned the TRC responsibility for enforcing state petroleum conservation laws.

18. *Herman v. Thomas,* 143 S.W. 195, 196–97 (Tex. Civ. App. 1911).
19. *Bender v. Brooks,* 103 Tex. 329 (Tex. S. Ct. 1910); see Greer, "The Ownership of Petroleum Oil and Natural Gas in Place," 178–79.
20. *Ohio Oil Company v. Indiana,* 177 U.S. 190 (1900).
21. In *Murphy Oil Company v. Burnet,* 287 U.S. 299 (1932), the United States Supreme Court approved the Commissioner of Internal Revenue's valuation of the amount of oil and gas under a given land tract for purposes of assessing income taxes. The court held that the Commissioner's finding was based upon engineering reports and amounted to more than "mere theory and speculation." In *Utah Power and Light Company v. Post,* 286 U.S. 299 (1932), the court noted that there were many questions arising in daily business affairs which could not be answered with mathematical precision. The law, the court held, did not require impossibilities, but only fair and reasonable approximations.
22. *Texas Company v. Daugherty,* 176 S.W. 717, 718 (Tex. S. Ct. 1915).
23. Ibid., 719–22.
24. Walker, "Property Rights in Oil and Gas and Their Effect Upon Police Regulation of Production," 370–81; Greer, "The Ownership of Petroleum," 182–83; *Texas Company v. Daugherty,* 720, cited *Ohio Oil v. Indiana.*
25. C. A. Warner, *Texas Oil and Gas Since 1543* (Houston: Gulf Publishing

Company, 1939), p. 60; James E. Nugent, "The History, Purpose, and Organization of the Railroad Commission," *Oil and Gas: Texas Railroad Commission Rules and Regulations* (Austin: State Bar of Texas, 1982), p. A–18; William R. Childs, "The Transformation of the Railroad Commission of Texas, 1917–1940: Business-Government Relations and the Importance of Personality, Agency Culture, and Regional Differences," *Business History Review* 65 (Summer, 1991): 285–344, 304–307.

26. "Oil and Gas Conservation Law and Rules and Regulations for the Conservation of Crude Oil and Natural Gas," *Oil and Gas Circular No. 13* (Austin: Railroad Commission of Texas, 1923), p. 19, copy in Pure Oil Company—Proration Matters File, VEA, C.F. 11726, Rule 37 states: "No well for oil and gas shall hereafter be drilled nearer than three hundred (300) feet to any other completed or drilling well on the same or adjoining tract or farm; and no well shall be drilled nearer than one hundred and fifty (150) feet to any property line; provided, that the Commission, in order to prevent waste or to protect vested property rights, will grant exceptions permitting drilling within shorter distances than as above prescribed, upon application filed fully stating the facts, notice thereof having first been given to all adjacent lessees affected thereby. Rule 37 shall not for the present be enforced within the proven fields of the Gulf Coast"; Hart, "Oil, the Courts, and the Railroad Commission," pp. 309–10; Hardwicke, "Legal History," pp. 218–19, cited the following leading Texas cases upholding the validity of Rule 37: *Humble Oil & Refining Company v. Strauss,* 243 S.W. 528 (Tex. Civ. App.—Amarillo [7th Dist.] 1922, no application for writ of error); *Oxford Oil Company v. Atlantic Oil Producing Company,* 16 F.2d 639 (5th Cir. 1927, petition for writ of certiorari denied, 277 U.S. 585, 48 S.Ct. 433, 72 L.Ed. 1000); *Railroad Commission of Texas v. Bass,* 10 S.W.2d 586 (Tex. Civ. App.—Austin [3rd Dist.] 1928, writ of error granted, then dismissed, 51 S.W.2d 1113); *Gilmore v. Straughan,* 10 S.W.2d 589 (Tex. Civ. App.—Austin [3rd Dist.] 1928, no application for writ of error); *State v. Jarmon,* 25 S.W.2d 936 (Tex. Civ. App.—San Antonio [4th Dist.] 1930, application for writ of error dismissed).

27. H. H. King, "Hendrick Extension Starts Big Offset Campaign," *Oil Weekly* 48 (Mar. 9, 1928): 40; King, "Peculiar Water Trouble Develops in Hendrick Field," *Oil Weekly* 48 (Jan. 13, 1928): 23; E. N. Van Duzee, "Effects of Choking Wells in Winkler County," *Oil Weekly* 53 (Apr. 12, 1929): 43; Larson and Porter, *History of Humble Oil,* pp. 318–19, Humble had invested $25 million in pipeline facilities in West Texas and was purchasing half the oil produced there, paying the highest posted prices. Humble could not continue paying a higher price than competitors for West Texas crude and then incur additional expenses for storage, which added 75 cents a barrel to costs. Humble offered to share its

pipeline with other producers if they agreed to limit production so that everyone received a fair share of the market without flooding it and driving down prices.

28. Wallace F. Lovejoy, "Conservation Regulation: The Economic and Legal Setting," in Lovejoy and I. James Pikl, Jr., eds., *Essays on Petroleum Conservation Regulation* (Dallas: Southern Methodist University, 1960), p. 20, define prorationing as the limitation of petroleum production below capacity output. Production quotas are allocated to each oil field in a state, which are then distributed among individual producers and wells within a given oil field.

29. Childs, "Transformation of Railroad Commission," 288, states that Parker, who joined the TRC in 1908, continued the agency's progressive legacy; Larson and Porter, *History of Humble Oil,* pp. 318–19; Rister, *Oil!: Titan of the Southwest,* p. 299; H. H. King, "Hendrick Field Operators Appoint Conservation Commission," *Oil Weekly* 48 (Feb. 10, 1928): 23, Farish and Nazro represented major company interests on the committee while C. F. Kelsey and Ed Landreth represented the large independents. Tom Cranfill was the only small independent on the committee, and the sixth member, W. B. Hamilton, headed the oil and gas bureau of the West Texas Chamber of Commerce; A. R. McTee, "Winkler Conservation Move Follows Commission Conference," *Oil Weekly* 49 (Mar. 16, 1928): 25–27; McTee, "Commission Promises to Select Plan for Hendrick Situation," *Oil Weekly* 49 (Apr. 20, 1928): 27–28; "Commission Orders Proration for Hendrick Field," *Oil Weekly* 49 (Apr. 27, 1928): 27.

30. Olien and Olien, *Wildcatters,* p. 51; H. H. King, "Hendrick 'Umpire' Arranging Details of Proration Order," *Oil Weekly* 49 (May 4, 1928): 28; H. J. Struth, "Extended Proration or Future Reduction Is Ultimatum," *Oil Weekly* 52 (Feb. 15, 1929): 39; Struth, "Feasibility of Nationwide Control Exemplified by Winkler Plan," *Oil Weekly* 53 (Apr. 5, 1929): 21; King, "Winkler County Proration Has Increased Recovery," *Oil Weekly* 54 (July 2, 1929): 35.

31. Olien and Olien, *Wildcatters,* p. 51; H. H. King, "Plan to Curtail Winkler Output Dropped," *Oil Weekly* 52 (Mar. 8, 1929): 34; King, "Committee Seeks Permit to Increase Hendrick Runs," *Oil Weekly* 54 (June 8, 1929): 34; "Power of Texas Commission to Prorate Gets Court Test," *Oil Weekly* 59 (Dec. 28, 1929): 27; Childs, "Transformation of Railroad Commission," 307.

32. Rister, *Oil!: Titan of the Southwest,* pp. 318–19; Olien and Olien, *Wildcatters,* pp. 46–47; J. Elmer Thomas, "Production Curtailment in Texas," *Oil Weekly* 51 (Dec. 7, 1928): 54–55.

33. Larson and Porter, *History of Humble Oil,* pp. 317–20; Weaver, *Unitization of Oil and Gas Fields in Texas,* p. 46.

34. Williamson, et. al., *American Petroleum Industry,* pp. 336–37; API

Report, "World Production and Consumption of Petroleum," *Oil and Gas Journal* 27 (Apr. 4, 1929): 47; Wallace Davis, "Limitation of Crude Output Up To Regional Committees," *Oil Weekly* 53 (Mar. 22, 1929): 19; Clarence L. Linz, "Washington Withholds Approval of Institute's Conservation Plan," *Oil and Gas Weekly* 53 (Apr. 12, 1929): 37; Hardwicke, *Antitrust Laws,* p. 36; Clark, *Oil Century,* pp. 191–92; Nash, *United States Oil Policy,* pp. 137–40; George L. Sweet, *Gentlemen in Oil* (Los Angeles: Science Press, 1966), p. 50.

35. *Houston Post–Dispatch,* June 10, 1929, 1:1, June 11, 1929, 1:5; Slick quoted in Yergin, *The Prize,* p. 224.

36. Prindle, *Petroleum Politics,* pp. 30–31; Humble's position toward the 1929 Act published in the *Oil and Gas Journal* 27 (Jan. 21, 1929): 34, (Feb. 14, 1929): 102; Weaver, *Unitization of Oil and Gas Fields in Texas,* p. 54; Hardwicke, "Legal History," 220, fn. 9; text of the 1929 Act published in *General and Special Laws of the State of Texas Passed by the Forty-First Legislature at the Regular Session* (1929), ch. 313, pp. 694–96; *Houston Post–Dispatch,* Mar. 27, 1929, 1:1, Apr. 1, 1919, 1:1, reported that the act passed the House by a vote of 101 to 16, and the Senate by a vote of 26 to 2.

37. Weaver, *Unitization of Oil and Gas Fields in Texas,* p. 55; Larson and Porter, *History of Humble Oil,* p. 325, cites part of Farish's "Memorandum Concerning Conservation and Production Policy." Farish summarized Humble's policy toward oil conservation stating, "We are interested in conservation, . . . proration, [and] other forms of cooperative development and production whether voluntary or compulsory; we are interested in unit operation, . . . in producing our oil at the lowest cost under the best engineering practices [to get] the maximum amount of oil per acre."

38. Larson and Porter, *History of Humble Oil,* p. 315; Weaver, *Unitization of Oil and Gas Fields in Texas,* p. 54.

39. Warner, *Texas Oil and Gas Since 1543,* p. 191; Edgar Wesley Owen, *Trek of the Oil Finders: A History of Exploration for Petroleum* (Tulsa: American Association of Petroleum Geologists, 1975), pp. 856–57; Rister, *Oil!: Titan of the Southwest,* pp. 221–22; Presley, *Saga of Wealth,* pp. 114–16, 184; after the discovery of the Van oil field, a young man accosted Bracken on a Van street and challenged him to a fistfight. Bracken told his young adversary, "Son, you can look at my old gray white hair and tell that my fighting days are long since gone, and there ain't no way I can keep you from hitting me, but I'll tell you one thing, young feller"—he pulled a well-honed stock knife out of his pocket—"If you do, I'm gonna lay your shitbag right out there on that sidewalk!"

40. Larson and Porter, *History of Humble Oil,* p. 316; Rister, *Oil!: Titan of the Southwest,* p. 222; Weaver, *Unitization of Oil and Gas Fields in*

Texas, p. 54; Van Oil Field Operating Agreement, Nov. 1, 1929, pp. 1–6, Pure Oil Company—Van Field File, VEA, C.F. 29159–D, used the following language to avoid antitrust problems: "Whereas it is desirable that a program of exploration be conducted . . . to locate the structures favorable to the accumulation of oil and gas and to determine the areas that may be underlaid with such minerals in productive quantities . . . it will be to the mutual interest of all parties hereto and will result in material savings to all if such exploration be conducted jointly by the parties hereto; and in the event the joint efforts at exploration result in the location of any considerable quantity of oil and gas, material savings can be made and much waste of oil and gas underground prevented and the recovery of both oil and gas largely increased by a joint development and operation of said area for the production of said products."

41. Van Oil Field Operating Agreement, pp. 1–6, VEA, C.F. 29159–D; Office Memorandum from Robert A. Shepherd to James A. Elkins, Nov., 1929, VEA, C.F. 29159–D.

42. James A. Elkins, "Anti-Trust Opinion," Oct. 28, 1929, pp. 1–2, VEA, C.F. 29159–D.

43. Ibid., pp. 3–4.

44. Hardwicke, "Legal History," pp. 222–23, discussed the TRC's first statewide proration order issued on August 27, 1930; Warner, *Texas Oil and Gas Since 1543,* p. 71; SoRelle to Parker, Nov. 25, 1929, VEA, C.F. 29159–D.

45. SoRelle to Parker, Nov. 25, 1929, VEA, C.F. 29159–D.

46. Olien and Olien, *Wildcatters,* p. 53; Hardwicke, "Legal History," p. 220; H. H. King, "Big Companies Pool Interests in Van Field," *Oil Weekly* 55 (Nov. 8, 1929): 30.

Chapter 4

1. Giebelhaus, *Business and Government in the Oil Industry,* pp. 198–200; See Rex G. Tugwell, "Principle of Planning and the Institution of Laissez Faire," *American Economic Review* 22 (Mar., 1932): 75–92.

2. Larson and Porter, *History of Humble Oil,* p. 320; Rister, *Oil!: Titan of the Southwest,* p. 299.

3. Rister, *Oil!: Titan of the Southwest,* p. 262, n. 32. The Mid-Continent Oil and Gas Association was formed "on October 13, 1917 in Tulsa, Oklahoma, primarily to cooperate with the federal government in supplying the armed forces with adequate petroleum products." After World War I, "it sponsored the interests of all oilmen, local, state, and national, seeking 'the advancement and protection of the petroleum industry in Kansas, Oklahoma, Texas, Arkansas, Louisiana, Mississippi, Alabama, and other mid-continent oil states.'"

4. Larson and Porter, *History of Humble Oil,* pp. 322–23; Weaver, *Unitization of Oil and Gas Fields in Texas,* p. 55.

5. Olien and Olien, *Wildcatters,* pp. 54–55; "Texas Independent Oil Operators Organizing," *Oil Weekly* 56 (Feb. 21, 1930): 75; "Oil Tariff Beaten in Senate Vote," *Oil Weekly* 56 (Mar. 7, 1930): 45; H. H. King, "Mid-Continent Association Favors Oil Tariff," *Oil Weekly* 59 (Dec. 12, 1930): 26; *The Texas Independent,* Bulletin No. 8, copy in Pure Oil Company-Proration, Newspaper Clippings and Magazines File, VEA, C.F. 14963–4.

6. Larson and Porter, *History of Humble Oil,* pp. 322–24; Weaver, *Unitization of Oil and Gas Fields in Texas,* pp. 55–56; Olien and Olien, *Wildcatters,* p. 55; Hardwicke, "Legal History," pp. 221–22; "Drastic Change in Pipe Line Laws Before Texas Legislature," *Oil Weekly* 56 (Mar. 7, 1930): 21; The vote in the senate was 22 to 4; in the House by viva voce; *General and Special Laws of the State of Texas Passed by the Forty-first Legislature,* Fifth Session, 1930, ch. 36, pp. 171–75.

7. Section 8 of the Common Purchaser Act defined a common purchaser as "every person, association of persons or corporation who purchases crude oil or petroleum in this State, which is affiliated through stock-ownership, common control, contract, or otherwise, with a common carrier by pipeline, as defined by law, or is itself such a common carrier." The act was amended in 1931 to include gas. Cited in *Vernon's Texas Statutes* (Kansas City, Mo.: Vernon Book Company, 1948), pp. 1655–56; Hardwicke, "Legal History," p. 221; Larson and Porter, *History of Humble Oil,* pp. 323–24; Weaver, *Unitization of Oil and Gas Fields in Texas,* pp. 55–56.

8. W. E. Long to Vinson, Mar. 20, 1930, Texas Legislature, 1928–1932 File, VEA, PID: 052615–117; Vinson to Flannery, June 23, 1930, VEA, PID: 052615–117; Vinson to Powell, June 23, 1930, VEA, PID: 052615–117; Powell to Vinson, June 24, 1930, VEA, PID: 052615–117; Vinson to Flannery, June 26, 1930, VEA, PID: 052615–117.

9. Larson and Porter, *History of Humble Oil,* p. 324; Weaver, *Unitization of Oil and Gas Fields in Texas,* p. 56; L. E. Bredberg, "To Buy Panhandle–Wichita Falls Oil," *Oil and Gas Journal* 29 (June 26, 1930): 58.

10. L. E. Bredberg, "Texans Approve Further Curtailment," *Oil and Gas Journal* 29 (July 17, 1930): 31, 153; for effects of prorationing in Oklahoma see W. A. Spinney, "Proration Effective in Oklahoma," *Oil and Gas Journal* 29 (July 31, 1930): 68.

11. Childs, "Transformation of Railroad Commission," 307, Powell to Elkins, July 11, 1930, Proration Matters–Correspondence, 1929–30 File, VEA, C.F. 10605. On the success of unitization in the Van oil field see, L. E. Bredberg, "Unit Plan Wrought Big Change in Van, Texas," *Oil and Gas Journal* 29 (Aug. 14, 1930): 39, 111.

12. Petition to the Railroad Commission of Texas (unsigned), July 30, 1930, Humphreys-Proration Matters File, VEA, C.F. 11726.

13. Hardwicke, "Legal History," p. 222; L. E. Bredberg, "Texas Prorationing Seems A Step Nearer," *Oil and Gas Journal* 29 (Aug. 7, 1930): 29, 110; *Houston Post–Dispatch,* Aug. 9, 1930, 10:1.

14. Ibid.

15. Ibid.

16. D. A. Stevenson, "Difficulties Over Texas Proration Plan," *Oil and Gas Journal* 29 (Aug. 14, 1930): 37, 149–50; *Houston Post–Dispatch,* Aug. 8, 1930, 3; Aug. 9, 1930, 10.

17. Minutes of the Meeting of Pettus Oil Field Operators, Aug. 13, 1930, pp. 1–2, VEA, C.F. 11726; Petition of the Gulf Coast Operators' Committee to the Railroad Commission of Texas," Aug. 14, 1930, VEA, C.F. 11726; Murphy to Railroad Commission of Texas, Nov. 22, 1930, VEA, C.F. 10605; *Houston Post–Dispatch,* Aug. 14, 1930, 7:1.

18. Petition of the Harrison Oil Company and J. S. Abercombie to the Texas Railroad Commission (undated), VEA, C.F. 11726; B. D. Stevenson, "Some Difficulties Over Texas Proration Plan," *Oil and Gas Journal* 29 (Aug. 14, 1930); *Houston Post–Dispatch,* Aug. 26, 1930, 1:1.

19. *Houston Post–Dispatch,* Aug. 12, 1930, 2, reported that the TRC planned to issue a statewide proration order by August 25; Powell to Elkins, Dec. 10, 1930, VEA, C.F. 10605.

20. Shepherd to Elkins, Aug. 9, 1930, VEA, C.F. 10605; Shepherd, "Methods of Proration in Texas Oil Fields," pp. 1–2, VEA, C.F. 11726; Minutes of Firm General Partners' Meeting, Aug. 14, 1930.

21. Shepherd, "Methods of Proration," pp. 2–8, distinguished between physical and economic waste. Physical waste is loss of stored oil by evaporation, leakage, or from premature dissipation of reservoir pressure and rapid water encroachment which lessens recovery of underground oil. Economic waste is loss of profit due to excessive production costs and low crude oil prices; See "Texas Maximum Set at 750,000 Barrels," *Oil and Gas Journal* 29 (Aug. 21, 1930): 37, 73, which discusses waste in petroleum production as defined by Texas law.

22. Ibid.

23. Ibid.

24. Neil Williams, "Oil Running Through Pure-Van Line," *Oil and Gas Journal* 29 (July 31, 1930): 56, 213; L. E. Bredberg, "Unitization Wrought Change in Van," 39, 111; *Houston Post–Dispatch,* Aug. 24, 1930, 1:1; Powell to Elkins, Aug. 11, 1930, VEA, C.F. 10605.

25. Shepherd to Powell (undated), VEA, C.F. 10605; Powell to Elkins, Aug. 11, 1930, VEA, C.F. 10605; Elkins to McIlvain, Sept. 1, 1930, VEA, C.F. 10605; McIlvain to Elkins, Sept. 1, 1930, VEA, C.F. 10605; SoRelle to Parker, Sept. 2, 1930, VEA, C.F. 10605; Elkins to Powell, Sept. 2, 1930, VEA, C.F. 10605; Powell to Elkins, Sept. 2, 1930, VEA, C.F. 10605; J. A. Rauhut to Elkins, Sept. 3, 1930, VEA, C.F. 10605;

Unidentified newspaper clipping, Sept. 2, 1930, VEA, C.F. 10605.

26. Order of the Railroad Commission of Texas, Oil and Gas Division, "Conservation and Prevention of Waste of Crude Petroleum and Natural Gas in the Various Fields in the State of Texas, and the Prevention of Discrimination by Common Purchasers in the Purchase of Oil Therefrom," Oil and Gas Docket No. 112, Aug. 14, 1930. Copy in the Humphreys-Proration Matters File, VEA, C.F. 11726. The TRC's order also gave each producer a pipeline connection and a fair share of the market; "Texas Maximum Set at 750,000 Barrels," 37, 73; *Houston Post–Dispatch,* Aug. 15, 1930, 1:1, Aug. 26, 1930, 1:1; See Kai Bird, *John J. McCloy, The Chairman: The Making of the American Establishment* (New York: Simon & Schuster, 1992), p. 626: "For decades, the global price for oil generally mirrored the production quotas set by the Texas Railroad Commission, which was run as an unofficial industry association"; Edward W. Constant II, "Cause or Consequence: Science, Technology, and Regulatory Change in the Oil Business in Texas, 1930–1975," *Technology and Culture* 30 (Apr., 1989): 426–55, argues that, although prorationing was justified as a conservation measure, it was primarily aimed at price stabilization.

27. "Texas Commission Revises Proration," Oil and Gas Journal 29 (Aug. 28, 1930): 37, 148; *Houston Post–Dispatch,* Aug. 26, 1930, 1;1.

28. Andrade to Parker, Aug. 22, 1930, VEA, C.F. 10605.

29. Broderick and Calvert to TRC, Aug. 30, 1930, VEA, C.F. 10605; Powell to Elkins, Sept. 3, 1930, Sept. 6, 1930, VEA, C.F. 10605; Elkins to Powell, Sept. 8, 1930, VEA, C.F. 10605; Elkins to Smith, Sept. 8, 1930, VEA, C.F. 10605; Elkins to SoRelle, Sept. 8, 1930, VEA, C.F. 10605.

30. Powell to Elkins, Nov. 22, 1930, Nov. 29, 1930, Dec. 10, 1930, VEA, C.F. 10605; Holmes to Dawes, Dec. 8, 1930, VEA, C.F. 10605; Elkins to Dawes, Dec. 11, 1930, VEA, C.F. 10605.

31. Hardwicke, "Legal History," pp. 222–23.

32. Presley, *Saga of Wealth,* p. 136; Roster, *Oil!: Titan of the Southwest,* pp. 306–10; Clark, *Oil Century,* p. 134; James A. Clark, *Three Stars for the Colonel* (New York: Random House, 1954), pp. 3–15; Joe L. White, "Columbus Marion 'Dad' Joiner and the East Texas Oil Boom," *East Texas Historical Journal* 6 (1968): 20–21; *Dallas Morning News,* Oct. 5, 1930, 13:3, Oct. 6, 1930, I, 8:2, Feb. 4, 1931, 4:4; *New York Times,* July 5, 1931, VIII, 11.

33. Rister, *Oil!: Titan of the Southwest,* pp. 312–14; Clark, *Three Stars for the Colonel,* pp. 7–9; *New York Times,* July 5, 1931, VIII, 11; I. E. Bredberg, "All Roads Seem to Lead to East Texas," *Oil and Gas Journal* 29 (Feb. 5, 1931): 22–23, 111.

34. James A. Clark and Michel T. Halbouty, *The Last Boom* (New York: Random House, 1972). p. 124; Rister, *Oil!: Titan of the Southwest,* pp. 221–22, 317–18; Presley, *Saga of Wealth,* p. 147; Clark, *Three Stars for*

the Colonel, p. 5. For background and discussion of economic problems of small Texas farmers in the late nineteenth century, see Robert C. McMath, Jr., *Populist Vanguard: A History of the Southern Farmers' Alliance* (Chapel Hill: University of North Carolina Press, 1975), pp. 151–57; Spratt, *The Road to Spindletop,* pp. 111–12.

35. L. E. Bredberg, "East Central Texas Proration Meeting," *Oil and Gas Journal* 29 (Jan. 22, 1931): 21; Barbara Thompson Day, "The Oil and Gas Industry in Texas Politics, 1930–1935," (Ph.D. Dissertation, Rice University, 1973), pp. 88–90; S. A. Gray to James V. Allred, July 25, 1931, James V. Allred Papers, University of Houston, Cont. No. 233, noted that 188 East Texas oil wells lacked pipeline connections.

36. Larson and Porter, *History of Humble Oil,* pp. 449–50; Baker Interview, pp. 17–18.

37. Baker Interview, pp. 17–18; *Tyler Courier–Times,* Feb. 9, 1931, 1, copy in VEA, C.F. 14963–4; Larson and Porter, *History of Humble Oil,* p. 450.

38. Baker Interview, pp. 20–24.

39. Ibid.

40. Ibid.

41. Keller, *Affairs of State,* p. vii; Keller, *Regulating a New Economy.*

42. Hovenkamp, *Enterprise and American Law, 1836–1937;* Alfred D. Chandler, Jr., *The Visible Hand: The Managerial Revolution in American Business* (Cambridge, Mass.: Harvard University Press, 1977), *passim,* argues that modern business enterprise replaced market mechanisms in coordinating the activities of the economy and allocating resources. In many sectors of the American economy, Chandler maintains, the "visible hand" of management replaced what Adam Smith called the "invisible hand" of market forces; Constant, "Cause or Consequence," 432, argues that "historically, prorationing was not adopted because it was scientifically rational," but to stabilize the price of crude oil.

43. For the sectional crisis of the 1850s, see David M. Potter, *The Impending Crisis, 1848–1861* (New York: Harper & Row, 1976).

Chapter 5

1. Danciger to the presidents, banks of Texas, July 8, 1931, Proration Matters-Correspondence, 1931 File, VEA, C.F. 10605; *Houston Post–Dispatch,* Feb. 14, 1931, 7; Hardwicke, "Legal History," p. 228; Larson and Porter, *History of Humble Oil,* pp. 324–25.

2. "Texas Proration Test Begun Before Court," *Oil and Gas Journal* 29 (Feb. 5, 1931): 119; *New York Times,* Feb. 13, 1931, 10:7; *Houston Post–Dispatch,* Feb. 14, 1931, 7.

3. Ibid.

4. Ibid.

5. *New York Times,* Feb. 14, 1931, 10:4; *Houston Post–Dispatch,* Feb. 14, 1931, 7:1; Wheeler's ruling followed decisions by the supreme courts of Oklahoma and California upholding the constitutionality of oil prorationing in those states. See *C. C. Julian Oil and Royalties Company v. Capshaw, et al.,* 145 Okla. 237, 292 Pac. 811 (Oct. 14, 1930); *People v. Associated Oil Company, et al.,* 211 Calif. 93; 294 Pac. 717 (Dec. 3, 1930). Danciger appealed to the Court of Civil Appeals in Austin; Memorandum on Proration Laws of Texas (undated), p. 7, VEA, C.F. 10923.

6. Zimmermann, *Conservation in the Production of Petroleum,* p. 151; Hardwicke, "Legal History," p. 229; "Greed Versus Proration in Texas," *Oil and Gas Journal* 30 (July 2, 1931): 14, 115; Larson and Porter, *History of Humble Oil,* p. 452.

7. Charles E. Kern, "Second Day's Oil Conference Session," *Oil and Gas Journal* 29 (Jan. 22, 1931): 23, 117, quoted Texas independent oilman Tom Cranfill.

8. *Thirty-Ninth Annual Report of the Railroad Commission of Texas, Covering Railroad and Express Transportation, for the Year 1930* (Austin: Von Boeckmann–Jones Company, 1931), p. 7; Larson and Porter, *History of Humble Oil,* p. 153; *Houston Post–Dispatch,* Jan. 23, 1931, 4; for the effects of politics on the TRC members, see Prindle, *Petroleum Politics,* pp. 145–81.

9. Joe R. Feagin, *Free Enterprise City: Houston in Political-Economic Perspective* (New Brunswick, N.J.: Rutgers University Press, 1988), p. 124; Marguerite Johnson, *Houston: The Unknown City, 1836–1946* (College Station: Texas A&M University Press, 1991), pp. 198–99, 288, 385–87; Thompson Interview, p. 26, states, "Elkins wanted good government, he wanted conservative government, and he was unselfish with the firm's money as he was with his in trying to get good people elected . . . was sort of the ex-officio chairman of the group that got behind the various candidates for public office"; Gertrude Peddy Cornwall, July 26, 1982, VEOH Interview 6, p. 10, VEA. PID: 052615–176, states Elkins was a close friend of Texas governor William P. Hobby and other public officials like the Texas Railroad Commissioners. "He had all of them in his pocket," Cornwall claimed, "Coke Stevenson and Jimmy Allred, and all of them (Texas governors from Hobby through Preston Smith)"; Lois O'Brien, June 10, 1982, VEOH Interview 4, p. 21, VEA, PID: 052615–179, recalled, "All these political figures came in to see Judge . . . Lyndon Johnson, Senator (John) Tower, and Jimmy Allred"; Dana Blankenhorn, "James A. Elkins, Sr.: For Half a Century, 'The Judge' Held Reigns of Houston Power," *Houston Business Journal* (Mar. 12, 1979): 1–2, notes that Elkins held a succession of public offices in Huntsville, Texas, between 1901 and 1905, culminating in a brief

stint as Walker County Judge (from late 1904 until early 1905). From that time on, Elkins was respectfully and affectionately referred to as "Judge." The practice of assigning titles (e.g., Colonel, Major, Captain, Judge, Senator, etc.), was rooted in the antebellum South. It was not necessary for the titleholder actually to have served in the military or have held public office. Titles were ascribed as a gesture of respect and affection. See John Hope Franklin, *The Militant South, 1800–1861* (Cambridge, Mass.: Harvard University Press, 1956), pp. 190–92.

10. Powell to Elkins, Nov. 26, 1930, Nov. 29, 1930, Dec. 10, 1930, VEA, C.F. 10605; Elkins to Powell, Nov. 29, 1930, VEA, C.F. 10605; Holmes to Dawes, Dec. 8, 1930, VEA, C.F. 10605; Dawes to Holmes, Dec. 12, 1930, VEA, C.F. 10605.

11. Pew to McIlvain, Dec. 10, 1930, VEA, C.F. 10605.

12. Dawes to Elkins, Dec. 11, 1930, VEA, C.F. 10605; Elkins to Dawes, Dec. 11, 1930, VEA, C.F. 10605; Dawes to Elkins, Dec. 12, 1930, VEA, C.F. 10605; Dawes to Elkins, Dec. 27, 1930, VEA, C.F. 10605; Dawes to Pew, Dec. 27, 1930, VEA, C.F. 10605.

13. Elkins to Dawes, Jan. 3, 1931, VEA, C.F. 10605.

14. Sadler to Dawes, Dec. 30, 1930, VEA, C.F. 10605; Elkins to McIlvain, Jan. 2, 1931, VEA, C.F. 10605.

15. Daly to Dawes, Jan. 2, 1931, VEA, C.F. 10605.

16. Sadler to Dawes, Dec. 30, 1930, VEA, C.F. 10605; Larson and Porter, *History of Humble Oil,* p. 153.

17. Ratable share means that each operator in a field produces only a stipulated proportion of the oil which his wells are capable of producing. In some cases, individual wells are allowed to produce a straight percentage of their full productive potential. In other instances, production rates are determined by the amount of acreage drained by each well. A third method takes into consideration acreage, reservoir pressure, and other factors in addition to well potential. As applied to pipeline operators, ratable taking refers to the percentage of total oil production purchased from each producer in a given field. See Ball, *This Fascinating Oil Business,* p. 147.

18. Elkins to A. C. Harvey, Jan. 5, 1931, VEA, C.F. 10605.

19. Olien and Olien, *Wildcatters,* p. 218, define a marginal producer as one with "marginal" or "stripper" wells that each produce less than 10 barrels of oil a day or whose output is less than in paying quantities.

20. Powell to Elkins, Jan. 6, 1931, VEA, C.F. 10605.

21. Dawes to Elkins, Jan. 7, 1931, VEA, C.F. 10605.

22. Elkins to Dawes, Jan. 8, 1931, VEA, C.F. 10605.

23. Ibid.

24. Dawes to Pew, Jan. 15, 1931, VEA, C.F. 10605; Dawes to Elkins, Jan. 20, 1931, VEA, C.F. 10605.

25. Peddy to Elkins, Jan. 21, 1931, VEA, C.F. 10605.

26. See Blankenhorn, 1–2, for brief profile of Elkins's background and personality.

27. Elkins to McIlvain, Jan. 22, 1931, VEA, C.F. 10605; Thompson Interview, p. 15, recalls that during the 1930s, at least 80 percent of Vinson & Elkins's law practice was oil and gas related and, p. 20, that Pure Oil Company was one of the firm's major oil and gas clients.

28. "Allowable Production in Texas Reduced by New State Order," *Oil and Gas Journal* 29 (Jan. 29, 1931): 169–70; *Houston Post–Dispatch,* Jan. 23, 1931, 4:1.

29. Ibid.; Tyler Morning–Telegraph, Jan. 23, 1931, 1:1, copy in Pure Oil—Proration, Newspaper Clippings and Magazines File, VEA, C.F. 14963–4.

30. Ibid.; Elkins to McIlvain, Jan. 22, 1931, VEA, C.F. 10605.

31. McIlvain to Elkins, Jan. 22, 1931, 23 Jan. 1931, VEA, C.F. 10605.

32. Dawes to Elkins, Jan. 23, 1931, VEA, C.F. 10605.

33. *Tyler Morning—Telegraph,* Jan. 23, 1931, 1:1, copy in VEA, C.F. 14963–4.

34. Day, "The Oil and Gas Industry and Texas Politics, 1930–1935," pp. 92–93; Ruel McDaniel, *Some Ran Hot* (Dallas: Regional Press, 1939), pp. 90–92.

35. Pettengill, *Hot Oil!,* p. 199; Clark, *Oil Century,* p. 192–93; Rister, *Oil!: Titan of the Southwest,* p. 375; *New York Times,* Apr. 12, 1931, II, 9:5, Apr. 21, 1931, 38:7.

36. McDaniel, *Some Ran Hot,* pp. 94–96; Olien and Olien, *Wildcatters,* pp. 58–59; *New York Times,* Apr. 4, 1931, 31:2, Apr. 5, 1931, III, 5:3, Apr. 21, 1931, 42:8, Apr. 22, 1931, 38:7; June 7, 1931, III, 5:6; Raymond Brooks, "Lucey Has New Plan for East Texas," *Oil and Gas Journal* 30 (July 2, 1931): 13; Larson and Porter, *History of Humble Oil,* pp. 452–53; *Houston Post–Dispatch,* June 22, 1931, 1:7, July 25, 1931, 6:1, reports that 625 East Texas operators had drilled 1140 wells.

37. *New York Times,* Apr. 26, 1931, 20:6.

38. A similar wave of hysteria struck the Seminole oil field in Oklahoma. Seminole police chief Jake Sims dismissed it as a rumor, and attributed oil field vandalism and thefts to "common thieves." *Houston Post–Dispatch,* June 15, 1931, 1:3; *New York Times,* Apr. 5, 1931, III, 5:1.

39. Cornwall Interview, pp. 10–11, recalls that Elkins told her that Texas governors never made an important political appointment, such as that of a railroad commissioner or judge, without first checking with him. Cornwall, then Ms. Erwin, had been a secretary in Governor William Hobby's office while she attended the University of Texas from 1916 to 1921. In 1921, she married George Peddy, a future Vinson & Elkins attorney, who unsuccessfully campaigned for the United States Senate in 1922 and 1948. Following Peddy's death in 1951, she married Barry

Cornwall. Ms.Cornwall came to Vinson & Elkins in 1924, when William A. Vinson hired her, and soon became Elkins's personal secretary; Thompson Interview, p. 8, attributed the firm's success to Elkins and the acquisition of Pure Oil Company as a client and, p. 13, recalls how Elkins devoted all his time to handling oil regulation matters for Pure. On pp. 26–27, Thompson states that Elkins "was very instrumental in providing Mr. [Oscar] Holcombe [then Houston's mayor] with an awful lot of financial help in his elections . . . [and] Judge and Jesse Jones were very close . . . along with Governor Hobby. Judge was Governor Hobby's campaign manager."

Chapter 6

1. de Chazeau and Kahn, *Integration and Competition in the Petroleum Industry,* pp. 140–41; Neil Williams, "East Texas Crude Prices Cut 30 Cents," *Oil and Gas Journal* 30 (May 26, 1931): 24; James B. McIntyre, "East Texans' Policy Brings Price Cut," *Oil and Gas Journal* 30 (May 28, 1931): 11; Prindle, *Petroleum Politics,* p. 34; Bobby H. Johnson, "Oil in the Pea Patch," *East Texas Historical Journal* 13 (Spring, 1975): 34–42; *New York Times,* June 7, 1931, 6:1.
2. Johnson, "Oil in the Pea Patch," 38–39; Clark and Halbouty, *The Last Boom,* pp. 135–37, describe Texas Ranger Sergeant Manuel T. Gonzaulles as the most feared and respected man in Texas. He bore the scars of gun battles fought in other Texas oil boomtowns and along cattle trails near the Mexican border. Gonzaulles played judge, jury, and jailer to thieves, robbers, and con men. Because Kilgore lacked a jail, Gonzaulles secured some 300 arrestees to a chain and marched them to a local Baptist church that had been vandalized. There, he fastened the chain-bound prisoners in front of the church to be displayed, identified, and fingerprinted. "Lone Wolf's Trotline" was dreaded by local misfits. A common joke related: "Lone Wolf gave the misfits four hours to get out of town and they gave three hours and fifty minutes of it back to Lone Wolf."
3. Clark and Halbouty, *The Last Boom,* pp. 123–43; Johnson, "Oil in the Pea Patch," 34–37; *New York Times,* July 5, 1931, XIII, 11:1.
4. Ibid.
5. Larson and Porter, *History of Humble Oil,* pp. 454–55; Andrew M. Rowley, "Suppose We Lift the Lid on Proration," *Oil and Gas Journal* 30 (June 4, 1931): 17; *New York Times,* June 18, 1931, 47:2; William S. Farish, "A Rational Plan for the Oil Industry," *Oil and Gas Journal* 31 (Oct. 6, 1931): 12–14; Robert E. Hardwicke, Jr., "Limitation of Oil Production to Market Demand," *Oil and Gas Journal* 31 (Oct. 6, 1931): 54–55.

6. Yergin, *The Prize,* pp. 249–50.

7. C. V. Terrell, Lon A. Smith, and R. D. Parker to Governor Ross S. Sterling, May 19, 1931, VEA, C.F. 10605.

8. Hardwicke, "Legal History," p. 232; Olien and Olien, *Wildcatters,* p. 59; Prindle, *Petroleum Politics,* pp. 31–32, describes the three Railroad Commissioners in 1931: 69-year-old Charles V. Terrel had served as a judge, state treasurer and legislator; 61-year-old Lon A. Smith was a former state legislator and comptroller; and 58-year-old Pat Neff had been governor of Texas; Ibid., pp. 145–81, analyzes and discusses the political aspects of the TRC; Childs, "Transformation of Railroad Commission," 288, maintains that "the TRC held a prominent position built both on the character of its commissioners and their staff people, all of whom were dedicated to progressive-style policy-making."

9. Prindle, *Petroleum Politics,* pp. 32–34, discusses the political dilemma facing the TRC; according to Clark and Halbouty, *The Last Boom,* p. 217, respect for the TRC was undermined by incidents such as that involving Commissioner Lon A. Smith's attorney son, who was allowed to represent certain East Texas field operators before TRC hearings even after the son had been indicted for attempting to bribe a TRC employee; For a scholarly and colorful account of antebellum southern patriarchalism, see Drew Gilpin Faust, *James Henry Hammond and the Old South: A Design for Mastery* (Baton Rouge: Louisiana State University Press, 1982); Eugene D. Genovese, *Roll, Jordan, Roll: The World the Slaves Made* (New York: Random House, 1974).

10. *New York Times,* May 27, 1931, 44:2; *Houston Post–Dispatch,* May 7, 1931, 1:2, 16 May 1931, 1:1, May 27, 1931, 1:1.

11. *Houston Post–Dispatch,* May 7, 1931, 1:2, 14:1, May 15, 1931, 5:5, 8:1; Danciger to "My dear oppressed brother oil operator," J. R. Parten Papers, cited in Day, "The Oil and Gas Industry and Texas Politics, 1930–1935," p. 15.

12. Clark, *Three Stars for the Colonel,* p. 65, Ross S. Sterling was elected governor of Texas in 1930 and took office in January, 1931. Sterling and his brother Frank had helped to organize the Humble Oil & Refining Company in 1911. Sterling resigned as company director in 1925, after Standard Oil Company of New Jersey purchased a majority of Humble's stock. He purchased the *Houston Post* and the *Houston Dispatch* and merged the two into the *Houston Post–Dispatch.* Sterling sold the newspaper when he became chairman of the Texas Highway Commission. He served on the Highway Commission until being elected governor.

13. *New York Times,* May 27, 1931, 44:2, June 18, 1931, 47:2; *Houston Post–Dispatch,* May 27, 1931, 1:1, June 2, 1931, 1:5, June 4, 1931, 1:2, June 16, 1931, 1:6, reported that the East Texas Arbitration Committee

would be composed of three representatives of the independent operators, two representatives of the East Texas Land, Royalty & Producers'
Association, and two representatives of the major oil companies to be
chosen by the other five committeemen; *Houston Chronicle,* June 11,
1931, 1:1; *Oil and Gas Journal* 30 (May 28, 1931): 11, 24.

14. C. P. Burton to the East Texas Arbitration Committee, June 18, 1931;
    Roeser to Parten, June 18, 1931, J. R. Parten Papers, cited in Day, "The
    Oil and Gas Industry and Texas Politics, 1930–1935" p. 100; *Houston
    Post–Dispatch,* June 16, 1931, 1:6, June 18, 1931, 1:2, June 22, 1931,
    7:1.
15. *New York Times,* June 7, 1931, III, 5:6
16. Ibid.
17. *New York Times,* July 4, 1931, 21:1; *Houston Post–Dispatch,* July 4,
    1931, 1:8, July 5, 1931, 1:5.
18. Powell to Elkins, Mar. 9, 1931, Mar. 31, 1931, Apr. 13, 1931, VEA, C.F.
    10605; SoRelle to Elkins, Mar. 10, 1931, Mar. 14, 1931, VEA, C.F. 10605.
19. Rister, *Oil!: Titan of the Southwest,* pp. 318–19, United States District
    Judge Duval West of the Western District for Texas (Austin) called upon
    Fifth Circuit Judge Joseph C. Hutcheson, Jr., and District Judge
    Randolph Bryant of the Eastern District of Texas (Tyler) to make up the
    three-judge panel.
20. *MacMillan, et al. v. Railroad Commission of Texas, et al.,* 51 F.2d 400,
    400–01 (W.D. Tex. 1931); *New York Times,* July 25, 1931, 20:1; *Houston
    Post–Dispatch,* July 25, 1931, 6:3; "Court Decides Proration Order of
    Commission Are 'Usurpations,'" *Oil and Gas Journal* 30 (July 30, 1931):
    155.
21. *New York Times,* July 4, 1931, 22:1, July 10, 1931, 26:5; *Houston Post–
    Dispatch,* June 2, 1931, 1:5, July 4, 1931, 2:5; Hardwicke, "Legal His-
    tory," p. 230; Rister, *Oil!: Titan of the Southwest,* p. 318; Lovejoy, "Con-
    servation Regulation," p. 26; Giebelhaus, *Business and Government in
    the Oil Industry,* p. 200.
22. *Houston Post–Dispatch,* June 6, 1931, 1:5.
23. Larson and Porter, *History of Humble Oil,* pp. 455–56; *New York Times,*
    July 19, 1931, III, 5:3; Farish, "A Rational Program for the Oil Industry,"
    pp. 12–14; Prindle, *Petroleum Politics,* pp. 32–39, discusses the political
    dilemma of regulating petroleum production.
24. Hardwicke, "Legal History," pp. 230–31; *New York Times,* July 19, 1931,
    III, 5:3, 30:5; *Houston Post–Dispatch,* July 17, 1931, 1:1; "Texas Legisla-
    ture for Conservation," *Oil and Gas Journal* 30 (July 16, 1931): 17,
    reported that a proposed bill prepared by the Texas Oil Emergency
    Committee retained the TRC as the state agency responsible for oil
    conservation, but redefined waste as "every kind of physical waste in
    excess of reasonable market demand." Another bill prepared by Al

Guiberson, Dan Moody, Carl Estes, and other members of the "East Texas Bloc" provided for a new six-member conservation commission with each commissioner representing a separate district of the state. The governor would appoint the six commissioners from a list of candidates submitted by oil producers and royalty owners from each district. Sterling opposed this proposal because he believed it was unconstitutional and impractical. Neither bill provided for conservation of any natural resources except petroleum.

25. Office Memorandum from Shepherd to Elkins, July 13, 1931, VEA, C.F. 10605.

26. Ibid.

27. Richards to Elkins, July 16, 1931, VEA, C.F. 10605; Elkins to Richards, July 16, 1931, VEA, C.F. 10605; Elkins to McIlvain and SoRelle, July 21, 1931, VEA, C.F. 10605.

28. *Houston Post–Dispatch,* July 25, 1931, 1:5; *Oil and Gas Journal* 30 (July 30, 1931): 21 .

29. *MacMillan v. TRC,* 404–05; *New York Times,* July 25, 1931, 20:1; *Houston Post–Dispatch,* July 25, 1931, 6:3; *Oil and Gas Journal* 30 (July 30, 1931): 155.

30. Ibid.

31. Charles Zeldin, "Regional Growth and the Federal District Courts: The Impact of Judge Joseph C. Hutcheson, Jr. on Southeast Texas, 1918–1931," *Houston Review* 10 (1989): 71–75; Paul, *Conservative Crisis and the Rule of Law,* pp. 2, 229, 235–37.

32. Zeldin, citing *Swift v. Tyson,* 16 Pet. 1 (1842).

33. Ibid.; See Joseph C. Hutcheson, Jr., "The Judgment Intuitive: The Function of the 'Hunch' in Judicial Decision," *Cornell Law Quarterly* 14 (Feb., 1929): 274–88.

34. *Oil and Gas Journal* 30 (July 30, 1931): 155; *Houston Post–Dispatch,* Aug. 4, 1931, 1:2, 7:3; Clark and Halbouty, *The Last Boom,* pp. 168–69, state that Wolters served as a first lieutenant in a Texas cavalry unit he helped organize during the Spanish–American War, but never went overseas. In June, 1919, he and his troops were dispatched to Longview to quell racial violence between whites and blacks. Later that year, Wolters commanded a militia force in hurricane-ravaged Corpus Christi. When martial law was declared in Galveston in 1920 following a violent shipping strike, Wolters commanded a militia force sent there to restore peace and order. He commanded other militia units sent to Mexia in 1922 and Borger in 1926, to assist local law enforcement officers in dealing with disorder in those oil boomtowns. In 1931, Wolters became general counsel for the Texas Oil Company as well as a brigadier general in the Texas National Guard.

35. Prindle, *Petroleum Politics,* p. 31; Hardwicke, "Legal History," p. 231;

Rister, *Oil!: Titan of the Southwest,* pp. 318–19; Larson and Porter, *History of Humble Oil,* p. 458; Giebelhaus, *Business and Government in the Oil Industry,* pp. 200–201; *Houston Post–Dispatch,* July 25, 1931, 1:5, July 29, 1931, 1:8; unsigned Correspondence to "T" given to Allred by an aide, Allred Papers, Cont. 233.

36. *Houston Post–Dispatch,* Aug. 4, 1931, 1:2, 7:3, Aug. 5, 1931, 1:5; "Texas Legislature Fails to Take Action: Deadlock on Measures Between Houses Brings Veto Threat from Governor Sterling to Use Militia as Last Resort," *Oil and Gas Journal* 30 (Aug. 13, 1931): 13, 134; James V. Allred to M. E. Foster, editor, *Houston Press,* Aug. 28, 1931, Allred Papers, Cont. 66.

37. *New York Times,* Aug. 11, 1931, 23:4, Aug. 12, 1931, 27:5, reported that total domestic oil production for the first week in August averaged 2,555,550 barrels a day, compared to 2,500,650 barrels per day during the preceding week. East Texas field production rose by 56,650 barrels, to a record high of 654,200 barrels, during the same period; "Texas Legislature Fails to Take Action," 13, 134; Presley, *Saga of Wealth,* p. 140; Olien and Olien, *Wildcatters,* p. 59, note that some 1,500 East Texas field producers petitioned Sterling to declare martial law in the East Texas field to control overproduction.

38. *New York Times,* Aug. 7, 1931, 2:5, Aug. 11, 1931, 23:4, Aug. 12, 1931, 27:5; "Texas Legislature Fails to Take Action," 13, 134; American Petroleum Institute, *Birth and Development of Oil Proration* (New York: American Petroleum Institute, 1931), p. 15, copy in Pure Oil Company, Van Field Proration Matters File, VEA, C.F. 10923, Oklahoma governor William H. Murray imposed martial law in the Oklahoma City and Seminole oil fields on August 4, 1931; see Garret Logan, "The Use of Martial Law to Regulate the Economic Welfare of the State and Its Citizens: A Recent Instance," *Iowa Law Review* 17 (Nov., 1931): 40–49.

39. "Texas Legislature Fails to Take Action," 13, 134.

40. Clark and Halbouty, *The Last Boom,* pp. 123–43.

41. Richards to Elkins, July 22, 1931, VEA, C.F. 10605.

42. Elkins to Allred, Aug. 3, 1931, VEA, C.F. 10605; Allred to Elkins, Aug. 5, 1931, VEA, C.F. 10605; Van Field Unitization Agreement, located in Pure Oil Company, Van Field Operating Agreement & Assignment File, VEA, C.F. 29159–D; SoRelle to Elkins, Aug. 3, 1931, VEA, C.F. 10605; Elkins to SoRelle, Aug. 8, 1931, VEA, C.F. 10605.

43. *New York Times,* Nov. 13, 1931, 4:2, named the 15 defendant corporations as Standard Oil Company of New Jersey, Standard Oil Company of New York, Standard Oil Company of California, Shell Union Oil Corporation, Humble Oil & Refining Company, the Texas Company, Gulf Refining Company, Paso-Tex Petroleum Company, Continental Oil Company, Sinclair Refining Company, Magnolia Petroleum Company,

Simms Oil Company, Shell Petroleum Corporation, Cities Service Oil
Company, and the Texas Pacific Coal and Oil Company; also included
were the Texas Petroleum Marketers Association and the American
Petroleum Institute; *Houston Post–Dispatch,* Nov. 13, 1931, 1:8; Allred's
Second Amended Petition, Apr. 15, 1932, copy in Allred Papers, Cont.
No. 233.

44. *New York Times,* Nov. 13, 1931, 4:2, Nov. 14, 1931, 20:4, Nov. 22,
1931, III, 5:3; Some of the letters of support Allred received included
J. Emmor Harston to Allred, Sept. 12, 1932; Will L. Barbee to Allred,
early 1932, Allred Papers, Cont. No. 233–37.

45. *New York Times,* Mar. 8, 1932, 25:8, Mar. 29, 1932, 32:1; Larson and
Porter, *History of Humble Oil,* p. 465.

46. Clark, *Three Stars for the Colonel,* pp. 7–10, described conditions in the
East Texas oil field during the summer of 1931.

47. *New York Times,* Aug. 13, 1931, 34:2; *Houston Post–Dispatch,* Aug. 13,
1931, 1:8, 10:4; Hardwicke, "Legal History," p. 232; Rister, *Oil!: Titan of
the Southwest,* p. 319; Prindle, *Petroleum Politics,* p. 31; Olien and
Olien, *Wildcatters,* p. 59; *General and Special Laws of the State of Texas
Passed by the Forty-second Legislature, First-called Session, 1931,* p. 46;
Memorandum on Proration Laws of Texas, p. 10, VEA, C.F. 10923.

48. *Houston Post–Dispatch,* Aug. 13, 1931, 1:8, 10:4; Elkins to McIlvain and
SoRelle, Aug. 12, 1931, VEA, C.F. 10605.

49. Memorandum on Proration Laws of Texas, pp. 9–10, VEA, C.F. 10923;
New York Times, Aug. 16, 1931, II, 7:3; Giebelhaus, *Business and Government in the Oil Industry,* pp. 200–201; Constant, "Cause or Consequence," 431–32; Hardwicke, "Legal History," pp. 231–32, states, "Beyond
doubt, the opinion in the *MacMillan* case had a great deal to do with the
character of legislation which was passed at the Special Session of the
Legislature of 1931. Governor Sterling . . . adopted the viewpoint of the
judges in the *MacMillan* case, and declared that he would veto a bill
which authorized limitation of production to reasonable market demand,
since he was interested only in preventing physical waste, and he could
not see how limitation of production to reasonable market demand had
the effect of preventing such waste"; see Hardwicke, "Limitation of Oil
Production to Market Demand: Review of Legislation Shows Confusion,"
Oil and Gas Journal 31 (Oct. 6, 1931): 54–55; in *Julian Oil and Royalties Company v. Capshaw,* 145 Okla. 237, 229 Pac. 811 (1930), the
Oklahoma Supreme Court upheld market-demand prorationing as a
reasonable and effective means of preventing physical waste in petroleum production. The court further held that any effect on price or other
economic considerations was merely incidental to elimination of physical
waste and promotion of conservation. A state district court in Austin,
Texas, rendered the same decision in the *Danciger* case.

50. Memorandum on Proration Laws of Texas, p. 10, VEA, C.F. 10923; Larson and Porter, *History of Humble Oil,* pp. 458–59; Rister, *Oil!: Titan of the Southwest,* p. 319; Prindle, *Petroleum Politics,* p. 31.

51. SoRelle to Elkins, Aug. 17, 1931, VEA, C.F. 10605; Parker to All Proration Advisory Committees, Aug. 14, 1931, VEA, C.F. 10605; Parker to All Umpires, Aug. 14, 1931, VEA, C.F. 10605.

52. Knowles, *The Greatest Gamblers,* pp. 264–65; Rister, *Oil!: Titan of the Southwest,* p. 319; Hardwicke, "Legal History," pp. 232–33; Larson and Porter, *History of Humble Oil,* pp. 458–59; *New York Times,* Aug. 15, 1931, 20:6.

53. Hardwicke, "Legal History," pp. 232–33; Olien and Olien, *Wildcatters,* p. 59; Andrew M. Rowley, "Oklahoma Shutdown Has Little Effect," *Oil and Gas Journal* 30 (Aug. 13, 1931): 13, 132; "Murrayism: A Dramatization of Popular Unrest," *National Petroleum News* 23 (Aug. 19, 1931): 19–20, 22.

54. L. E. Bredberg, "East Texas Meeting Asks Martial Law," *Oil and Gas Journal* 30 (Aug. 20, 1931): 20, 103–104; *New York Times,* Aug. 15, 1931, 20:6.

55. Ibid.

56. Hardwicke, "Legal History," p. 233; Lovejoy, "Conservation Regulation," p. 26; Rister, *Oil!: Titan of the Southwest,* p. 320; Olien and Olien, *Wildcatters,* pp. 59–61; "Meeting Postponed," *Oil and Gas Journal* 30 (Aug. 20, 1931): 104; "Martial Law in Four Counties Declared by Governor Sterling: Wells Closed Without Disorder, None Expected," *Oil and Gas Journal* 30 (Aug. 20, 1931): 15, 104; *New York Times,* Aug. 16, 1931, 1:4, 24:17, Aug. 17, 1931, 6:3, Aug. 18, 1931, 1:5; *Houston Post–Dispatch,* Aug. 19, 1931, 1:1; Memorandum on Proration Laws of Texas, pp. 10–11, VEA, C.F. 10923; Lawrence E. Smith, "Scramble for Crude as East Texas Output is Shut Off Under Martial Law," *National Petroleum News* 23 (Aug. 19, 1931): 19–20, 22.

57. Warren E. Mills, Jr., *Martial Law in East Texas* (Indianapolis: Bobbs–Merrill, 1960), pp. 23–28; Hardwicke, "Legal History," p. 233; Prindle, *Petroleum Politics,* p. 31; Clark and Halbouty, *The Last Boom,* pp. 167–69; *New York Times,* Aug. 16, 1931, 1:4, Aug. 17, 1931, 6:3, Aug. 18, 1931, 1:5; Olien and Olien, *Wildcatters,* pp. 59–60, note that attempts to enforce prorationing in East Texas in the early 1930s instigated "howling confrontations," dynamiting of oil wells, and vigilantism; "Troops Shut Down East Texas Field," *Oil and Gas Journal* 30 (Aug. 20, 1931): 15, 104.

58. L. E. Bredberg, "East Texas Fields Under Military Rule," *Oil and Gas Journal* 30 (Aug. 27, 1931): 13, 106, 109, "Troops Shut Down East Texas Field," 104; Lawrence E. Smith, "Troops Occupation of East Texas Fields Marked by Order and Efficiency," *National Petroleum News* 23

(Aug. 26, 1931): 32–33; Clark and Halbouty, *The Last Boom,* pp. 168–69; *New York Times,* Aug. 18, 1931, 1:5, Aug. 23, 1931, 17:2, reported that national guardsmen and Texas Rangers were placed on guard in Kilgore following an outburst of incendiary fires and threats of more. A Presbyterian and a Methodist church were both destroyed by "mysterious" fires within a two-hour span. Later that day, gasoline-soaked rags were used to start fires at a seed house, a gin, and a wholesale grocery store; Ibid., Aug. 31, 1931, 2:4, reported that Wolters ordered the militia to "shoot at the waist line" following the burning of a combination rooming house–morgue and a grain warehouse in Kilgore. Wolters blamed "Reds" for the arson.

59. Clark and Halbouty, *The Last Boom,* pp. 170–71.
60. Larson and Porter, *History of Humble Oil,* p. 459; Rister, *Oil!: Titan of the Southwest,* p. 320; "Troops Shut Down East Texas Field," 104; Elkins to Sterling, Aug. 17, 1931, VEA, C.F. 10605.
61. *New York Times,* Aug. 20, 1931, 3:2.
62. "Hearing on Texas Proration Rules," *Oil and Gas Journal* 30 (Sept. 3, 1931): 77–79, 99; *New York Times,* Sept. 1, 1931, 37:5, Sept. 2, 1931, 11:1, Sept. 3, 1931, 35:1, Sept. 5, 1931, 19:1, Sept. 6, 1931, II, 10:2; Memorandum on Proration Laws of Texas, pp. 10–11, VEA, C.F. 10923; Lovejoy, "Conservation Regulation," pp. 26–27; Prindle, *Petroleum Politics,* p. 31; Hardwicke, "Legal History," p. 233.
63. "East Texas Cut to 165 Barrels Per Well in Revised Order," *Oil and Gas Journal* 30 (Oct. 15, 1931): 13; *New York Times,* Sept. 24, 1931, 36:1; Prindle, *Petroleum Politics,* p. 31; Hardwicke, "Legal History," p. 233; McLean and Haigh, *The Growth of Integrated Oil Companies,* p. 590; McDaniel, *Some Run Hot,* pp. 206–207.
64. Ibid.
65. Hardwicke, "Legal History," p. 234.
66. Memorandum on Proration Laws of Texas, p. 11, VEA, C.F. 10923; anonymous independent quoted from Clark and Halbouty, *The Last Boom,* pp. 171–72.

Chapter 7

1. Earl Oliver, "Lawyers Hear of Industry's Problems," *Oil and Gas Journal* 30 (Sept. 24, 1931): 22, 122. Oliver, a lawyer, served as chairman of the AIMME in 1931. This article was a republication of Oliver's address to the Mineral Section of the American Bar Association at Atlantic City, New Jersey, Sept. 16, 1931.
2. Ibid.
3. A. E. Mockler, "Oil Industry Getting Its House In Order," *Oil and Gas Journal* 30 (Jan. 8, 1932): 23, 116–17.

4. Oliver, "Lawyers Hear of Industry's Problems," 122; Oliver, "Why Adequate Oil Legislation Failed," *Oil and Gas Journal* 30 (Sept. 17, 1931): 15, 100.

5. Mockler, "Oil Industry Getting Its House In Order," 23, 116–17; J. Edgar Pew, "Time Is Ripe for Unitization," *Oil and Gas Journal* 30 (Nov. 12, 1931): 38, 89.

6. William S. Farish, "A Rational Program for the Oil Industry," address before the Petroleum Division of the AIMME, Oct. 3, 1931, Ponca City, Oklahoma, copy in VEA, C.F. 10923; see Farish, "Problems of Preventing Waste of Oil and Gas and Stabilizing the Petroleum Industry," *Oil and Gas Journal* 31 (June 30, 1932): 10–12.

7. Pew, "Time Is Ripe for Unitization," 38, 89; Giebelhaus, *Business and Government in the Oil Industry,* pp. 202–205.

8. Ibid.

9. Day, "The Oil and Gas Industry and Texas Politics, 1930–1935," pp. 137–40, notes that Parten entered the oil business in Louisiana upon his return from World War I. In 1922, he helped to organize the Woodley Petroleum Company and served as its president and general manager from 1927 until 1960. In the 1930s, Woodley moved its headquarters to Texas where it held oil properties throughout the state, including the East Texas field. Parten became a leading spokesman for independents.

10. L. E. Bredberg, "Five East Texas Associations Affiliate In One Organization," *Oil and Gas Journal* 30 (Sept. 17, 1931): 13, 32, the Texas Oil and Gas Conservation Association was organized by merging five associations of Texas independent oilmen: the Texas Oil Emergency Committee, the East Texas Steering Committee, the North Texas Oil and Gas Association, the San Antonio Petroleum Club, and the East Texas Home and Land Owners Association; Bredberg, "Texans Organize to Conserve Oil and Gas," *Oil and Gas Journal* 30 (Nov. 12, 1931): 156; Larson and Porter, *History of Humble Oil,* p. 465, TOGCA's membership reached 5,000 in June, 1932, but the association broke up in 1933, apparently over disagreements among members regarding state versus federal regulation of petroleum production; "IPA of Texas Opposes Present Proration Rules," *Oil and Gas Journal* 31 (Dec. 15, 1932): 31.

11. Earl Oliver, "Changes Needed In Oil Ownership Law," *Oil and Gas Journal* 30 (July 23, 1931): 15, 181, cited quotation from Mills. See Robert Penn's address to the Production Division of the American Petroleum Institute meeting in Dallas in June, 1931, published in Pettengill, *Hot Oil!,* pp. 97–98.

12. Ibid.

13. Henry M. Gray, "Need Extension of Conservation Laws: Concrete Statutes Must Replace Court-Made Law," *Oil and Gas Journal* 30 (July 23, 1931): 24, 98.

14. Ibid., citing the U.S. Supreme Court decisions *Block v. Hirsch,* 256 U.S. 135 (1921); and *Levy Leasing Company v. Siegel,* 258 U.S. 242 (1921).
15. Ibid., citing *Ohio Oil Company v. Indiana,* 177 U.S. 190 (1900); *Munn v. Illinois,* 94 U.S. 113 (1876); *Marrs v. City of Oxford,* 24 F.2d 541 (D.C.-Kansas 1928), affirmed in 32 F.2d 134 (8th Cir. 1929).
16. Oliver, "Changes Needed In Oil Ownership Law," 15, 81.
17. Robert E. Hardwicke, Jr., "Ratable Taking API Meeting Keynote," *Oil and Gas Journal* 30 (June 11, 1931): 15, 104; Hardwicke, "Legal Aspects of Gas Conservation," *Oil and Gas Journal* 30 (June 25, 1931): 17, 125.
18. Hardwicke, "Limitation of Oil Production to Market Demand," citing *Walls v. Midland Carbon Company,* 254 U.S. 300 (1920); "Review of Legislation Shows Confusion," *Oil and Gas Journal* 31 (Oct. 6, 1932): 54; Ford, "Controlling Oil Production," 1170–82.
19. Ibid.
20. Oliver, "Why Adequate Oil Legislation Failed," 15, 100; William E. Forbath, *Law and the Shaping of the American Labor Movement* (Cambridge, Mass.: Harvard University Press, 1991), p. 94, states that by the mid-1890s, "both federal and state high courts had made plain that the law was implacably opposed to broad unionism and the kinds of aggressive, industry-, community-, and class-based tactics it often entailed."
21. Ibid.
22. Richard O'Connor, *The Oil Barons: Men of Greed and Grandeur* (Boston: Little, Brown, 1971), p. 309, compares violence in East Texas to Chicago gang wars; effect of martial law in restoring stability in the East Texas field reported in *Oil and Gas Journal* 30 (Sept. 24, 1931): 17, (Oct. 1, 1931): 11, (Oct. 8, 1931): 11, 30 (Oct. 15, 1931): 13; *New York Times,* Sept. 6, 1931, II, 10:2, Sept. 12, 1931, 23:6, Sept. 22, 1931, 46:1, Sept. 24, 1931, 36:1; see Hardwicke, "Legal History," p. 233; Lovejoy, "Conservation Regulation," pp. 26–27.
23. Sterling quoted in, *Oil and Gas Journal* 30 (Oct. 15, 1931): 13; Clark and Halbouty, *The Last Boom,* pp. 172–79; Presley, *Saga of Wealth,* pp. 141–42.
24. Harry Harter, *East Texas Oil Parade* (San Antonio: Naylor Company, 1934), pp. 110–14; Clark and Halbouty, *The Last Boom,* pp. 173–79, 182–83; Presley, *Saga of Wealth,* p. 142; Petition for Injunction filed by E. Constantin and J. D. Wrather, In the District Court of the United States for the Eastern District of Texas, Tyler Division (hereafter Plaintiff's Petition), Oct. 29, 1931, Pure Oil Company—Legal Committee, Legal Opinions, Etc. File, VEA, C.F. 14963–6; Sterling quoted in *New York Times,* Oct. 15, 1931, 2:4.
25. Rister, *Oil!: Titan of the Southwest,* p. 321; Olien and Olien, *Wildcatters,* p. 60; *Oil and Gas Journal* 30 (Oct. 15, 1931): 13; "Martial Law Needed in East Texas," *Oil and Gas Journal* 30 (Oct. 22, 1931): 14, 96; *New York*

Times, Oct. 15, 1931, 2:4; Presley, *Saga of Wealth,* pp. 142–43; Clark and Halbouty, *Last Boom,* pp. 173–79, 182–83; Harter, *East Texas Oil Parade,* pp. 110–14.

26. A three-judge court, consisting of two district court judges and one circuit court judge, was impanelled to decide the constitutionality of a state law. Its decision could be appealed directly to the U.S. Supreme Court. See Joseph C. Hutcheson, Jr., "A Case for Three Judges," *Harvard Law Review* 47 (Mar., 1934): 795–826. In the *Constantin* case, the three-judge court consisted of Fifth Circuit Chief Judge Joseph C. Hutcheson, Jr. (Houston), and District Court Judges Randolph C. Bryant (Sherman, Texas) and William I. Grubb (Birmingham, Alabama).

27. "Martial Law Needed in East Texas," 14.

28. Ibid., 99, Under Special Order 48, Major C. E. Parker was named president of the special military court. Other members were captains C. K. Davis and McCord McIntyre. Representative of the provost marshal, Colonel L. S. Davidson and A. B. Capers, deputy supervisor in charge of proration in East Texas, were empowered by the order to sit with the board and interrogate witnesses. The provost marshal was directed to issue a summons or attachment, or *summons duces tecum,* requiring any designated person to appear or produce before the board at a time fixed by it, or forthwith, any books, records, or papers for examination by the board; *New York Times,* Oct. 15, 1931, 2:4.

29. Argument for Defendants Ross S. Sterling, W. W. Sterling, and Jacob F. Wolters by Paul D. Page, Jr., In the District Court of the United States for the Eastern District of Texas, Tyler Division (hereafter Defendants' Argument by Page), *E. Constantin, et al. v. Lon Smith, et al.,* Oct. 29, 1931, located in the Pure Oil Company—Briefs, Legal Opinions, Etc. File, VEA, C.F. 17771, pp. 4–12, citing Article 4, Sections 7 and 10 of the Texas Constitution, Article 5778 of the Revised Civil Statutes of the State of Texas and the United States Supreme Court's decision in *Ex Parte Milligan,* 4 Wallace 2 (1866).

30. Argument for Defendants Ross S. Sterling, W. W. Sterling, and Jacob F. Wolters by Dan Moody and E. F. Smith, In the District Court of the United States for the Eastern District of Texas, Tyler Division (hereafter Defendants' Argument by Moody and Smith), *E. Constantin, et al. v. Lon Smith, et al.,* Oct. 29, 1931, Pure Oil Company—Briefs, Legal Opinions, Etc. File, VEA, C.F. 17771.

31. Ibid., pp. 13–16, citing *Martin v. Mott,* 12 Wheaton 19 (1827).

32. Ibid., pp. 24–50, citing *Luther v. Borden,* 7 Howard 1 (1849) at pp. 39–42 and Michigan Supreme Court Justice Thomas M. Cooley's opinion in *Weimer v. Bunbury,* 30 Mich. 201 (1874) at p. 49; see Harold M. Hyman, *A More Perfect Union: The Impact of the Civil War and Reconstruction on the Constitution* (New York: Alfred E. Knopf, 1973), Chapter 10, "A Chaos

of Doctrines: Military Occupation and Martial Law," which discusses the legal and constitutional aspects of military occupation and martial law up to and during the American Civil War and Reconstruction.

33. *Constantin, et al. v. Smith, et al.,* 57 F.2d 227, 229–40 (E.D. Texas—Tyler, 1932), citing 28 U.S.C.A., Section 380; "No Injunction Issued in East Texas," *Oil and Gas Journal* 30 (Feb. 25, 1932): 13, 93–95; see Tony Freyer, *Harmony and Dissonance: The Swift and Erie Cases in American Federalism* (New York: New York University Press, 1981), *passim,* maintains that since the United States Supreme Court's decision in *Swift v. Tyson,* 16 Pet. 1 (1842), federal district court judges could base their decisions on a national common law which existed independently of state court decisions. Federal judges could apply their own conceptions of the common law to decide cases even if the result was in opposition to precedents established by state court decisions on similar issues. This power effectively made federal district courts as an alternative forum to state courts. Federal judges had the power to interpret the law as they saw fit. For example, federal judges employed the *Swift* doctrine to protect large corporations from local discriminatory regulations. The result fostered economic growth and domination of large corporations in the twentieth century. The Swift doctrine was overturned by the Supreme Court in *Erie Railroad Company v. Tompkins,* 304 U.S. 64 (1938). See Freyer, *Forums of Order: The Federal Courts and Business in American History* (Greenwich, Conn.: Jai Press, 1979); Zelden, "Regional Growth and the Federal District Courts: The Impact of Judge Joseph C. Hutcheson," pp. 89–90, states that "the power of the federal district courts at this time were broad, and Hutcheson never hesitated to use them. He also used the considerable force of his personality to underscore his ideas of justice. He did not like disrespect for the law at any time, and when his own decisions were not heeded he was swift to act. A contemporary described him as 'an old-time Southern hot-head, and a real overstepping of his ideas of right and wrong, and particularly his ideas of fairness and justice, was like monkeying with a naked bolt of lightning.' Hutcheson's opposition to those who ignored the law shows up at its extreme in the 1932 case of *Constantin v. Smith.*"

34. Ibid., citing *Luther v. Borden,* 7 How. 1 (1849), Taney held that whichever of two factions constitute the legitimate government of Rhode Island was a political question. He did not hold that the necessity for martial law was a political question. Taney's opinion in *Luther v. Borden* was generally interpreted to mean that the Supreme Court would tolerate martial law rule in times of emergency. Taney took precisely the opposite view in his opinion as Circuit Justice in *Ex Parte Merryman,* 17 Fed. Cas. No. 9,487 (1861). See Hyman, *A More Perfect Union,* pp. 81–98; *United States v. Wolters,* 268 Fed. 69 (S.D. Tex. 1920), involved a petition

for writ of habeas corpus for release from imprisonment in default of payment of a fine imposed by a military court set up in Galveston after martial law had been proclaimed. Some of the civil magistrates had been removed from office and a military court set up in their stead. The relator conceded the governor's power to declare martial law. Judge Rufus Foster, however, carried the point further and held that the governor could do anything necessary to make his proclamation effective; Charles Fairman, "Martial Rule, In Light of *Sterling v. Constantin*," *Cornell Law Quarterly* 19 (Dec., 1933): 29, noted that martial law had been invoked in Texas seven times between 1919 and 1932.

35. *Constantin v. Smith*, 240–42; "No Injunction Issued in East Texas," 94–95; *New York Times*, Feb. 19, 1932, 26:2.

36. Ibid.

37. "Railroad Commission Ready to Issue New Proration Rules," *Oil and Gas Journal* 30 (Feb. 25, 1932): 13; *New York Times*, Feb. 21, 1932, 5:2.

38. "Commission Rule Back in Texas," *Oil and Gas Journal* 31 (Mar. 3, 1932): 13, 87; *New York Times*, Feb. 26, 1932, 11:5, Feb. 27, 1932, 26:6.

39. Hardwicke, "Legal History," pp. 235–36; Rister, *Oil!: Titan of the Southwest*, p. 321; "Commission Rule Back in Texas," 13, 87.

40. W. F. Bryan to the Pure Oil Company, Feb. 15, 1932, Pure Oil Company—Proration Matters, Correspondence, 1932, VEA, C.F. 10605; Elkins to Pure Oil Company, Feb. 16, 1932, VEA, C.F. 10605.

41. Elkins to McIlvain, Feb. 16, 1932, VEA, C.F. 10605.

42. McIlvain to Elkins, Feb. 17, 1932, VEA, C.F. 10605.

43. McIlvain to SoRelle, Jan. 5, 1934, Pure Oil Company—Proration Matters, Correspondence, 1934 File, VEA, C.F. 10963; SoRelle to Elkins, Jan. 9, 1934, VEA, C.F. 10963.

44. Hardwicke, "Legal History," p. 236; Prindle, *Petroleum Politics*, pp. 32–33; Clark and Halbouty, *The Last Boom*, p. 217.

45. William S. Farish, "What the Oil Industry Needs," address delivered to the Twentieth Annual Meeting of the Chamber of Commerce of the United States of America, May 19, 1932, San Francisco, copy in Pure Oil Company—Proration Matters, Legal Briefs, Memoranda, Etc. File, VEA, C.F. 17771.

46. *Champlin Refining Company v. Corporation Commission of Oklahoma, et al.*, 286 U.S. 210 (1932); *Danciger Oil & Refining Company v. Railroad Commission of Texas*, 49 S. W.2d 837 (Tex. App.—Austin [3rd Dist.] 1932).

Chapter 8

1. Larson and Porter, *History of Humble Oil*, p. 460; Olien and Olien, *Wildcatters*, p. 60; Nordhauser, *Quest for Stability*, p. 91; J. Howard Marshall and Norman L. Meyers, "Legal Planning of Petroleum Produc-

tion: Two Years of Proration," *Yale Law Journal* 42 (1933): 720–21; Hardwicke, "Legal History," p. 236.

2. Hardwicke, "Legal History," p. 236; *Champlin Refining Company v. Oklahoma Corporation Commission,* 286 U.S. 210 (1932); *Danciger Oil & Refining Company v. Railroad Commission of Texas,* 49 S. W.2d 837 (Tex. App.—Austin [3rd Dist.] 1932).

3. *Danciger v. Railroad Commission,* 839–45; Hardwicke, "Legal History," p. 236; *Houston Post–Dispatch,* Mar. 24, 1932, 13; "Decision of Federal Bench Challenged by Texas Court," *Oil and Gas Journal* 30 (Mar. 31, 1932): 155.

4. Ibid.

5. *Danciger Oil & Refining Company v. Railroad Commission of Texas,* 122 Tex. 243, 56 S.W.2d 1075 (1933). The Third Court of Civil Appeals at Austin continued to sustain the TRC's broad authority to regulate petroleum production to prevent waste. See *Corzelius v. Railroad Commission of Texas,* 161 S.W.2d 412, 416 (Tex. App.—Austin [3rd Dist.] 1944); Weaver, *Unitization of Oil and Gas Fields in Texas,* pp. 262–63; Hardwicke, "Legal History," p. 236.

6. Clark, *Oil Century,* pp. 182–83, states that the Oklahoma Oil Conservation Act of 1915 had been upheld by the Oklahoma Supreme Court in *Julian Oil and Royalties Company v. Capshaw, et al.,* 145 Okla. 237 (1930); W. P. Z. German, "Legal History of Conservation of Oil and Gas in Oklahoma," *Legal History of Conservation of Oil and Gas* (Chicago: American Bar Association Symposium, 1938): 110–213; Rister, *Oil!: Titan of the Southwest,* p. 263; *Champlin Refining Company v. Corporation Commission of Oklahoma, et al.,* 286 U.S. 210 (1932); Hardwicke, "Legal History," 237, speculated, "If the Champlin . . . and the Danciger case[s] had been decided prior to . . . MacMillan, would the court in . . . MacMillan . . . have reached a different conclusion, and, if so, would the legislature have written into the 1931 Act the prohibition against limitation of production to reasonable market demand on the theory that such limitation had no relation to physical waste but to economic waste and price fixing? This much is certain: if the Act of 1931 had specifically authorized limitation of production to reasonable market demand, a year of turmoil would likely have been averted. It is also certain that a year later the Legislature of Texas did authorize such a limitation, and the governor signed the bill, both changing viewpoints to conform with that of the state courts in . . . Danciger . . . and the United States Supreme Court in the *Champlin* case"; Larson and Porter, *History of Humble Oil,* pp. 470–71, quoted Hardwicke, "If the Supreme Court of the United States affirms the judgment in the *Champlin* case, I take it that the next legislature in Texas will be asked to re-write the conservation statutes. The bug-a-boo of market demand will be overthrown."

7. Weaver, *Unitization of Oil and Gas Fields in Texas,* ch. 5, n. 63, describes two types of TRC hearings: The TRC could conduct either a "trial balloon" hearing, to give interested parties an opportunity to testify about possible regulatory changes, or a "show cause" hearing, requiring operators to appear and explain why the TRC should not issue a particular order. See Jim C. Langdon, "Rules of Regulatory Bodies: Texas," *National Institute for Petroleum Landmen,* vol. 7 (Albany, N. Y.: Matthew Bender, 1966), pp. 159, 173–74; Hardwicke, "Legal History," p. 240, notes that under a similar statute, a Texas appellate court had held, as a rule, that TRC records were inadmissible in a trial court except for purposes of impeachment. Should an order be attacked as being the result of arbitrary action (such as no evidence to support it) then the record of the TRC hearing would be admissible to show upon what evidence, if any, the TRC based its order. See *State v. Saint Louis, etc. Railway Company,* 165 S. W. 491 (Tex. App.—Austin [3rd Dist.] 1913). TRC orders are usually attacked as being unreasonable or confiscatory in effect. In such a case, there is a trial *de novo* in the court and the validity of the order is tested in light of evidence introduced therein.

8. Broderick and Calvert to SoRelle, Mar. 5, 1932, VEA, C.F. 10605.

9. Estes to Elkins, Apr. 7, 1932, VEA, C.F. 10605; Broderick and Calvert to Estes, Apr. 6, 1932, VEA, C.F. 10605.

10. McKinney to Elkins, Mar. 14, 1932, VEA, C.F. 10605.

11. Powell to Elkins, Mar. 15, 1932, Mar. 18, 1932, VEA, C.F. 10605; Elkins to Powell, Mar. 31, 1932, VEA, C.F. 10605. The TRC employed the 10 percent "readjustment" to correct past withdrawals made under inequitable proration orders. It reduced existing allowables by 10 percent to compensate for production under a prior order which had been subsequently revised. Many operators, such as Broderick and Calvert, complained that the retroactiveness of the rule was unfair because it presumed the unfairness of prior proration orders.

12. Elkins to Estes, June 28, 1932, VEA, C.F. 10605; Estes to C. V. Terrell, Apr. 5, 1932, VEA, C.F. 10605.

13. Transcript of Van Pool Proration Hearing (hereafter TRVH) on Apr. 5, 1932, pp. 1–3, copy in Pure Oil Company—Changing Method of Proration at Van, 1932–1936 File, VEA, C.F. 14963–8.

14. Testimony before the TRC hearing in Apr., 1932, as reported by Elkins to McIlvain, Apr. 7, 1932, VEA, C.F. 10605.

15. TRVH, Apr. 5, 1932, pp. 1–3, VEA, C.F. 14963–8.

16. TRVH, Apr. 5, 1932, pp. 3–4, VEA, C.F. 14963–8; Elkins to McIlvain, Apr. 7, 1932, VEA, C.F. 10605.

17. Ibid.

18. Ibid.

19. Powell to Elkins, Apr. 9. 1932, VEA, C.F. 10605; McIlvain to Elkins, Apr.

9, 1932, VEA, C.F. 10605; Elkins to Estes, Apr. 9, 1932, VEA, C.F. 10605.

20. Neil Williams, "Federal Judges Hear Suit on East Texas Production," *Oil and Gas Journal* 31 (June 2, 1932): 13, lists the plaintiffs as Atlas Pipe Line Company, E. Constantin, People's Petroleum Products, Inc., Whittle Kavanaugh Corporation, T. W. Murray, Imperator Oil Corporation, Bill & Dave Oil Corporation, A. S. Palmer, Arthur F. Graf, and Alfred E. MacMillan. These lawsuits were consolidated by agreement into the People's Petroleum case; *People's Petroleum Producers v. Sterling,* 60 F.2d 1041 (E. D. Tex., 1932). The three-judge federal panel included Joseph C. Hutcheson, Randolph Bryant, and William I. Grubb.

21. Elkins to Adjutant General W. W. Sterling, June 28, 1932, VEA, C.F. 10605.

22. Rister, *Oil!: Titan of the Southwest,* pp. 321–22; "Commission Withholds Order on East Texas Awaiting Protests from Producers," *Oil and Gas Journal* 31 (June 30, 1932): 8.

23. Sterling appointed Colonel Ernest O. Thompson to the TRC on June 4, 1932, following the resignation of Pat Neff. Thompson was born in 1892 in the small North-Central Texas town of Alvord. He attended the Virginia Military Institute and received a law degree from the University of Texas in 1917. Thompson was a highly decorated machine-gun battalion commander in World War I, and later became mayor of Amarillo. See Eldon Stephen Branda, ed., *The Handbook of Texas: A Supplement,* vol. 3 (Austin: Texas State Historical Association, 1976), p. 1004; Clark, *Three Stars for the Colonel,* pp. 41–43, 47–64; As past TOGCA vice-president, many East Texas field operators suspected Thompson of being a front for major oil companies. They were wrong, according to Prindle, *Petroleum Politics,* p. 35, who maintains that Thompson "was not a spokesman for any particular viewpoint or set of interests . . . [but] a great politician— finely tuned to the social forces that would somehow have to be reconciled if peace were to come to the Texas petroleum industry. To the colonel would belong much of the credit for solving the political dilemma facing the Commission and thus preventing the Texas petroleum industry from destroying itself . . . Thompson grasped the problem facing the Commission: to stabilize the industry and promote conservation . . . prorationing was a necessity, but it must be done in a manner that reassured the independents and royalty owners that they would not be exploited by the major companies"; Childs, "Transformation of Railroad Commission," 288–89, states, "Ernest O. Thompson, a commissioner appointed in 1932, adopted the political strategies shunned by Parker. The enormous size of the East Texas field made Thompson a major player in the national industry, but it was Thompson's personality-based regulatory politics that helped the enormous interest groups come to terms with the immense changes brought about by the huge oil field."

24. Prindle, *Petroleum Politics,* pp. 35–36, quotes Thompson from the *Kilgore Daily News,* Sept. 23, 1932.
25. "Commission Withholds Order," 8.
26. Elkins to Estes, June 28, 1932, June 29, 1932, VEA, C.F. 10605.
27. Estes to Elkins, June 30, 1932, VEA, C.F. 10605; Estes to C. V. Terrell, Ernest O. Thompson, and Lon A. Smith, Texas Railroad Commission, June 30, 1932, VEA, C.F. 10605.
28. Elkins to Dawes and McIlvain, July 5, 1932, VEA, C.F. 10605; Elkins to Dawes, July 7, 1932, VEA, C.F. 10605.
29. Dawes to Elkins, July 6, 1932, July 7, 1932, VEA, C.F. 10605; Elkins to Powell, July 7, 1932, VEA, C.F. 10605; Powell to Elkins, July 8, 1932, VEA, C.F. 10605; W. E. McKinney to Elkins, July 7, 1932, VEA, C.F. 10605.
30. "East Texas Claim for Cuts in Other Districts Heard by State Railroad Commission," *Oil and Gas Journal* 31 (July 14, 1932): 8; Neil Williams, "Texas Commission to Make Own Survey Naming Engineers to Get Data," *Oil and Gas Journal* 31 (July 21, 1932): 53, reported that the TRC retained J. S. Hudnall, a consulting geologist, petroleum engineer, and partner in the firm of Hudnall & Pirtle of Tyler, Texas, and E. V. Foran, a consulting engineer from Fort Worth. They were expected to complete their investigations of the Gulf Coast, Southwest Texas, Yates, and Van fields by September 1; *Houston Post–Dispatch,* July 11, 1932, 2:1, July 13, 1932, 2:1; McIlvain to Elkins, July 14, 1932, Pure Oil Company—Van Proration Hearing File, Aug., 1932, VEA, C.F. 14963–7; Moody to Elkins, July 9, 1932, VEA, C.F. 10605; Elkins to Dawes, July 13, 1932, VEA, C.F. 10605; Powell to Elkins, July 15, 1932. Powell told Elkins that Hudnall had testified that the East Texas field could produce more oil without unusual or excessive waste. He also informed Elkins that the TRC had been disgusted with the miserable showing made by the witnesses and, for that reason, decided to conduct its own investigation.
31. Powell to Elkins, July 15, 1932, VEA, C.F. 14963–7; Elkins to McIlvain, July 11, 1932, VEA, C.F. 10605.
32. Elkins to McIlvain, July 12, 1932, VEA, C.F. 10605; Elkins to Dawes, Aug. 18, 1932, VEA, C.F. 14963–7; Elkins to Dawes and McIlvain, July 11, 1932, July 12, 1932, VEA, C.F. 10605; Elkins to McIlvain, July 12, 1932, VEA, C.F. 10605; Powell to Elkins, July 15, 1932, VEA, C.F. 14963–7.
33. Tilley to Elkins, July 16, 1932, VEA, C.F. 14963–7.
34. Elkins to Tilley, July 19, 1932, VEA, C.F. 14963–7.
35. *People's Petroleum Producers v. Sterling, et al.,* 60 F.2d 1041, 1048 (E. D. Tex., 1932); Hardwicke, "Legal History," 238.
36. Elkins to McIlvain, Aug. 29, 1932, Aug. 30, 1932, VEA, C.F. 14963–7.

37. Notes for Van Field Hearing Before the Railroad Commission of Texas at Austin Texas, Aug. 29, 1932, pp. 11–14, VEA, C.F. 14963–7, on Aug. 24, 1932, the Pure Oil Company had an interest in 41 producing oil wells and held about 1,000 producing acres in the East Texas field.

38. Elkins to McIlvain, Aug. 30, 1932, Aug. 31, 1932, VEA, C.F. 14963–7; Powell to Elkins, Sept. 9, 1932, VEA, C.F. 14963–8, Powell informed Elkins that Parker had prepared a proration order cutting the Van allowable to 45,000 barrels per day, but that it had not been signed by all three members of the TRC and therefore had not become effective; Elkins to Dawes and McIlvain, Sept. 14, 1932, Sept. 15, 1932, VEA, C.F. 14963–7, Elkins said that the Mid-Kansas Oil Company had secured a federal court injunction against enforcement of the TRC's order, which cut production in the Yates field by 10 percent. Elkins also noted that the TRC had ordered a 10 percent reduction in the Gulf Coast field, limiting each well to 240 barrels per day; Elkins to R. van der Woude, Oct. 4, 1932, VEA, C.F. 14963–7; McIlvain to Elkins, Sept. 1, 1932, VEA, C.F. 14963–7; C. B. Watson to Elkins, Oct. 6, 1932, VEA, C.F. 14963–7.

39. Cranfill to Elkins, July 19, 1932, VEA, C.F. 14963–7, Cranfill thanked Elkins for allowing royalty gaugers employed by his group to conduct an investigation of the Van field. Cranfill informed Elkins that they "found no irregularities," adding, "My motto is 'Peace and Plenty,' and if at any time I can be of assistance it certainly will be a pleasure to me." Elkins replied, "I have always known that your motto was 'Peace and Plenty'— in which I join you most heartily as I possess the 'Peace' and you possess the 'Plenty.'" Elkins to Cranfill, July 20, 1932, VEA, C.F. 14963–7; McIlvain to Elkins, Sept. 7, 1932, Sept. 14, 1932, VEA, C.F. 14963–7.

40. Elkins to Parker, Sept. 1, 1932, VEA, C.F. 14963–8.

41. Simon to Elkins, Sept. 1, 1932, VEA, C.F. 14963–8; TRVH, Sept. 24, 1932, pp. 1–17, 39, VEA, C.F. 14963–8.

42. J. A. Rauhut (associate attorney of Ben Powell) to Elkins, Oct. 10, 1932, VEA, C.F. 14963–7; Elkins to McIlvain, Oct. 10, 1932, VEA, C.F. 14963–7.

43. Elkins to R. van der Woude, Oct. 4, 1932, VEA, C.F. 14963–7.

44. "Texas Proration Is Attacked in Hearing in Federal Court at Houston, Texas," *Oil and Gas Journal* 31 (Sept. 22, 1932): 14, listed the plaintiffs as People's Production, Inc., Bill & Dave Oil Corporation, A. S. Palmer, Arthur F. Graf, Alfred MacMillan, C.F. Smith, and I. V. Holifield; Neil Williams, "Three-Judge Federal Court in Session at Houston Hears Proration Assailed and Defended," *Oil and Gas Journal* 31 (Sept. 29, 1932): 14–15, listed the seven plaintiffs consolidated for trail as People's Production, Inc., Bill & Dave Oil Company, A. S. Palmer, Arthur F. Graf, Alfred MacMillan, C.F. Smith, and I. V. Holifield. The three-judge panel consisted of Circuit Judge Joseph C. Hutcheson, Jr., and District Judges Randolph Bryant and William I. Grubb.

45. Williams, "Federal Court . . . Hears Proration Assailed and Defended,"
    14–15, listed the plaintiffs' witnesses as J. S. Hudnall, consulting
    geologist from Tyler; LaVerne Decker, geologist from Marshall;
    Herbert Aid and H. H. Yoakum, geologists from Tyler; Stanley Gill,
    consulting engineer from Houston; Joseph W. Bartlett, consulting
    engineer from Dallas; Walter Reid, vice-president and general man-
    ager of the Southern Union Gas Company in Dallas; David Donoghue
    of Fort Worth, federal receiver of certain oil properties in East Texas;
    H. J. Struth, petroleum economist from Houston; and R. D. Parker,
    supervisor of the Oil and Gas Division of the TRC. State witnesses
    included E. O. Buck, TRC engineer from Henderson; C. V. Millikan,
    petroleum engineer from Tulsa; F. E. Heath of Dallas, representing
    Sun Oil Company; W. F. Fulton of Houston, chemical engineer for
    United Gas Public Service Corporation; J. A. Clark, executive assistant
    to the president and vice-president of the Stanolind Oil & Gas Com-
    pany of Fort Worth; E. V. Foran, petroleum engineer; K. B. Nowels,
    engineer for Forrest Petroleum Company in Bradford, Pennsylvania;
    and E. R. Radcliffe, engineer for the Atlas Pipe Line Company; "Texas
    Proration is Attacked," 14.
46. *People's Petroleum Producers v. Smith,* 365; "Texas Commission Calls
    New Hearing," 8; "Full Text of Decision on Proration," 10–11, 32;
    Houston Post–Dispatch, Oct. 25, 1932, 1:2, 3:7.
47. Hardwicke, "Legal History," 239.
48. *Houston Post–Dispatch,* Sept. 25, 1932, 3:1; Estes to Elkins, Sept. 25,
    1932, VEA, C.F. 10605; Elkins to Estes, Sept. 26, 1932, VEA, C.F. 10605;
    Larson and Porter, *History of Humble Oil,* p. 463; "Texas Commission
    Calls New Hearing," 8; "East Texans Declare Field Shall Not be Opened
    to Ruinous Overproduction," *Oil and Gas Journal* 31 (Nov. 3, 1932): 32;
    Houston Post–Dispatch, Sept. 28, 1932, 3:1; Ibid., Oct. 25, 1932, 3:6.
49. *Houston Post–Dispatch,* Oct. 26, 1932, 1:8, 5:4; L. E. Bredberg, "Engi-
    neers Studying Plans for Equitable System of Proration in East Texas,"
    Oil and Gas Journal 31 (Nov. 3, 1932): 11.
50. *Houston Post–Dispatch,* Oct. 27, 1932, 2:3.
51. "Texas Will Ask a Stay of Execution in Case Against Railroad Commis-
    sion," *Oil and Gas Journal* 31 (Nov. 3, 1932): 10; *Houston Post–Dispatch,*
    Oct. 26, 1932, 1:8, 5:4; Ibid., Oct. 28, 1932, 1:7.
52. "Texas Commission Calls New Hearing," 8, reported that Sterling
    ordered out 25 additional soldiers to join the 38 soldiers already sta-
    tioned in the East Texas field under the command of Colonel Louis S.
    Davidson. Twenty-five Texas Rangers were also assigned to the field;
    New York Times, 18 Oct. 1932, 14:5, Oct. 26, 1932, 2:4; *Houston Post–
    Dispatch,* Oct. 26, 1932, 1:7, 5:5, reported that Sterling was besieged
    with requests for additional Texas Rangers and to call a special session

of the legislature to enact legislation to preserve the East Texas field; Ibid., Oct. 27, 1932, 1:7, 2:2.

53. Senate Journal, *Forty-second Legislature—Fourth Called Session,* Nov. 4, 1932, pp. 4–7, copy in VEA, C.F. 14963–9; *Houston Post–Dispatch,* Nov. 1, 1932, 1:1; Nov. 3, 1932, 1:8, 3:1, Nov. 5, 1932, 1:4, 2:1; Elkins to Dawes, Oct. 31, 1932, VEA, C.F. 14963–9. Elkins said, "In view of [the] recent decision of [a] three-judge federal court which in effect held that proration orders affecting [the] East Texas [field] were illegal, in that they were based on economic instead of physical waste, the Governor has been urged to call [a] special session of the legislature. He is extremely reluctant to do this, but has indicated that he will do so provided that members of both house and senate will agree to pass a law similar to that of Oklahoma which permits economic waste to be taken into consideration in promulgating proration orders. It seems that these commitments can be had and probabilities are that a special session will be called." Elkins warned Dawes that without market-demand prorationing it would be impossible to hold oil production down to its present level in light of the *People's* decision.

54. *Houston Post–Dispatch,* Nov. 5, 1932, 1:4, 2:2; "Bill Reported Favorably by House Committee; May be Approved Before End of Week," *Oil and Gas Journal* 31 (Nov. 10, 1932): 8, 31.

55. Ibid.

56. Ibid.

57. *Houston Post–Dispatch,* Nov. 6, 1932, 1:1, 6:2; Joseph C. Danciger, "Market Demand and Proration: A Scheme for Monopoly," p. 9, copy in VEA, C.F. 14963–9.

58. *Houston Post–Dispatch,* Nov. 8, 1932, 2:1; "Bill Reported Favorably by House Committee; May be Approved Before End of Week," *Oil and Gas Journal* 31 (Nov. 10, 1932): 8, 31.

59. *Houston Post–Dispatch,* Nov. 5, 1932, 2:2.

60. Ibid., Nov. 4, 1932, 5:1, Nov. 5, 1932, 2:3, Nov. 6, 1932, 1:1, 6:2.

61. *Houston Post–Dispatch,* Nov. 5, 1932, 2:3, Nov. 6, 1932, 1:1; Danciger, "Market Demand and Proration: A Scheme for Monopoly," VEA, C.F. 14963–9, p. 11.

62. Ibid.

63. Ibid.

64. *Houston Post–Dispatch,* Nov. 8, 1932, 2:3.

65. Ibid., Nov. 10, 1932, 2:4.

66. Elkins had a list of all the senators and representatives in the Texas legislature, including their Austin addresses and telephone numbers. He obtained the list from the Southwestern Bell Telephone Company. Some of the listed names had either a checkmark or the letters A, C, or D pencilled next to them, indicating a system that Elkins may have

utilized to keep track of individual legislators' attendance and votes on issues such as the oil conservation bill. The fact that he obtained their Austin addresses and telephone numbers suggests that Elkins contacted individual lawmakers to solicit their views or press his own. List located in VEA, C.F. 14963–9; Elkins to Dawes and McIlvain, Nov. 7, 1932, Nov. 9, 1932, VEA, C.F. 14963–9.

67. Hardwicke, "Legal History," p. 239; "Market Demand Is Feature of Texas Measure; Full Text of Proposed Conservation Bill," *Oil and Gas Journal* 31 (Nov. 10, 1932): 8, 32; *Houston Post–Dispatch,* Nov. 13, 1932, 1:7, 8:2; *New York Times,* Nov. 14, 1932, 32:1; Market Demand Act, Text of Oil and Conservation Bill (S. B. No. 1) passed and sent to the governor on Nov. 12, 1932, copy in VEA, C.F. 14963–9; Larson and Porter, *History of Humble Oil,* p. 471; Weaver, *Unitization of Oil and Gas Fields in Texas,* pp. 60–61; Nordhauser, *Quest for Stability,* p. 91.

68. *Houston Post–Dispatch,* Nov. 5, 1932, 1:2, Nov. 13, 1932, 8:2; Amos L. Beaty, "Texas Law Declared Outstanding Achievement in President Beaty's Address to Institute," *Oil and Gas Journal* 31 (Nov. 7, 1932): 24, 46; Dawes to Elkins, Nov. 11, 1932, VEA, C.F. 14963–9; address by J. R. Parten to the Annual Convention of the Independent Petroleum Association of Texas, Dec. 9, 1932, J. R. Parten Papers, cited in Day, "The Oil and Gas Industry and Texas Politics, 1930–1935," p. 157.

69. *Houston Post–Dispatch,* Nov. 15, 1932, 1:8.

70. Appellants Brief, *Sterling, et al. v. Constantin, et al.,* In the Supreme Court of the United States, Oct. Term, 1932, filed by E. F. Smith, Paul D. Page, and Dan Moody, Attorneys for Appellants, copy in Pure Oil Company—Briefs, Memoranda, Etc. File, VEA, C.F. 17771; *Houston Post–Dispatch,* Nov. 16, 1932, 6:6, Nov. 17, 1932, 1:1, 7:3; *New York Times,* Dec. 7, 1932, 35:4, reported that the Supreme Court had refused to hear arguments in the MacMillan case because the issues had been mooted by passage of the Market Demand Act.

71. Bottom-hole pressure is the natural gas pressure at the bottom of an oil well, as opposed to "tubing-head" or "casing-head" pressure at the surface of the well. Water movement in a petroleum reservoir affects bottom-hole pressure. If the rate of oil and gas production exceeds the rate of water encroachment, bottom-hole pressure drops. If oil and gas production and water intrusion are equalized, bottom-hole pressure remains fairly constant. As defined by L. G. E. Bignell, "Texas Railroad Commission Has the Authority to Prevent Imminent Waste of Oil and Gas," *Oil and Gas Journal* 31 (Aug. 4, 1932): 10–11.

72. *Houston Post–Dispatch,* Nov. 29, 1932, 1:2, 2:6; "Commission Holds East Texas to 325,000 Barrels on Bottom Hole Pressure—Acreage Basis," *Oil and Gas Journal* 31 (Dec. 1, 1932): 9, reported over 9,000 oil wells in the 114,000-acre East Texas field. Buck contemplated zoning the field,

starting with a bottom-hole pressure of 1,000 pounds and increasing to 100 pounds per zone. The highest pressure in the field at the time was 1,490 pounds. Oil wells with higher bottom-hole pressures had higher production potentials. Under Buck's plan, well allowables would vary from 26 to 44 barrels depending upon acreage and bottom-hole pressure. The plan was predicated upon data secured from a survey of bottom-hole pressures from all sections of the field. Buck's formula worked as follows: "Two-thirds of the daily allowable would be divided by the number of producing wells. The other one-third would be divided by the acreage in the field. This second factor would be multiplied by zone bottom-hole pressure divided by the average pressure for the field. This third factor would then be multiplied by the number of acres assigned to each well to arrive at the barrels per day allowable based upon acreage and bottom-hole pressure. As an example, of the 325,000-barrel daily allowable for the East Texas field, two-thirds would be 216,667 barrels divided by the total number of 9,000 wells to give 24 barrels per well. One-third of the daily allowable would be 108,333 barrels divided by the total 114,000 acres to give .9502 barrels per well. The field's average bottom-hole pressure was 1,390 pounds. A well pressure of 1,000 pounds would be divided by 1,390 to give .72; .95 times .72 gives .684 which is multiplied by the number of acres surrounding a well. If it is 20 acres, the allowable would be 13.68 barrels added to 24 barrels to make the total well allowable 37.68 barrels per day." Buck explained the formula thus: "A well or a tract of 12.7 acres with 1,500 pounds of bottom-hole pressure would be permitted to produce 38 barrels of oil daily; a single well on a 20-acre tract with 1,000 pounds pressure would be allotted 38 barrels; a well of 1,500 pounds pressure on 20 acres would be permitted to take out 45.6 barrels; and nine wells on a 200-acre tract with 1,380 pounds of pressure would have a combined production allowable of 340.2 barrels daily, or 37.8 barrels per well."

73. *Houston Post–Dispatch,* Nov. 29, 1932, 1:2, 2:6, Nov. 30, 1932, 1:5, 2:4, Dec. 1, 1932, 1:4; *New York Times,* Nov. 30, 1932, 32:2; "Texas' Allowable Set at 845,625 Barrels Daily," *Oil and Gas Journal* 31 (Dec. 1, 1932): 9, also listed the daily allowables for the following Texas oil fields: Panhandle, 45,000 barrels; North Texas, 56,000 barrels; West-Central Texas, 31,500 barrels; West Texas, 157,000 barrels; Southwest Texas, 48,950 barrels; East-Central Texas, 51,700 barrels; East Texas, 325,000 barrels; and Gulf Coast, 129,575 barrels. The Van field allowable was set at 45,000 barrels; L. G. E. Bignell, "New Method of Prorating East Texas Forward Step; May Extend Plan to Cover all Fields," *Oil and Gas Journal* 31 (Dec. 8, 1932): 8–9; "Railroad Commission Issues Orders for Allowable Output in East Texas," *Oil and Gas Journal* 31 (Dec. 8, 1932): 8.

74. *Sterling, et al. v. Constantin, et al.,* 287 U.S. 378, 393–98 (1932); "Su-

preme Court of the United States Sets Aside the Orders of Governor Sterling of Texas," *Oil and Gas Journal* 31 (Dec. 15, 1932): 10, 30; "Historic Decision on Martial Law in East Texas Defines the Power of Governor and Courts," *Oil and Gas Journal* 31 (Dec. 15, 1932): 13–14, 30–32; *New York Times,* Dec. 8, 1932, 29:8, 35:2, Dec. 13, 1932, 29:8, 35:2, Dec. 14, 1932, 20:1, Dec. 18, 1932, II, 14:1; Fairman, "Martial Rule, In The Light of Sterling v. Constantin," 32–34.

75. Ibid.
76. Ibid., citing, *Moyer v. Peabody,* 148 Fed. 870 (C.C.D. Colo. 1906); *Moyer v. Peabody,* 212 U.S. 78, 84–85 (1909); Fairman, "Martial Rule, In the Light of *Sterling v. Constantin,*" 20–34, citing cases in which state and lower federal courts denied *habeas corpus* relief to persons held in military custody under martial law. In Texas, martial law had been invoked seven times between 1919 and 1933; for relevant state court decisions, see Henry Winthrop Ballantine, "Unconstitutional Claims of Military Authority," *Yale Law Journal* 24 (1915): 189–216; Ballantine, "Military Dictatorship in California and West Virginia," *California Law Review* 1 (July, 1913): 413–26.
77. "Sterling Considering Position," *Oil and Gas Journal* 31 (Dec. 15, 1932): 30; *New York Times,* Dec. 13, 1932, 35:2; "Ames Holds State Power Is Unimpaired by Decision of the Supreme Court," *Oil and Gas Journal* 31 (Dec. 22, 1932): 13.
78. "Texas Allowable Revised by Railroad Commission," *Oil and Gas Journal* 31 (Dec. 15, 1932): 32, reported that the Van allowable had been increased from 42,500 to 45,000 barrels a day.
79. Larson and Porter, *History of Humble Oil,* pp. 474–75.
80. *New York Times,* Dec. 18, 1932, II, 14:1, Dec. 22, 1932, 26:1.

Chapter 9

1. "President W. S. Farish Hopes New Year Will See Supply Balancing Demand," *Oil and Gas Journal* 31 (Jan. 5, 1933): 34.
2. Editorial, "Is Proration Doomed?" *Oil and Gas Journal* 31 (Jan. 5, 1933): 18; Andrew M. Rowley, "Crude Oil Price Cutters Are Largely Responsible for Present Uncertainty in the Oil Business," *Oil and Gas Journal* 31 (Jan. 12, 1933): 7; Rowley, "Unless Price Cutting and Unethical Practices Are Discontinued Another Reduction Is Probable," *Oil and Gas Journal* 31 (Jan. 19, 1933): 5, reported that "with sales of . . . gasoline showing a decline of only 9.2 percent from last year and domestic demand only off 7.8 percent from the peak figure in history, the industry certainly cannot attribute price cutting to the decrease in business. And with crude oil production in 1932 approximately 45,000,000 barrels less than during 1931 . . . there certainly is no justification for cutting crude oil prices."

3. J. Edgar Pew to Charles F. Roeser, January 2, 1933, Pure Oil Company—Proration Matters, Correspondence, 1933 File, VEA, C.F. 10605.

4. "Is Proration Doomed?" 18.

5. "Commission Opens Case by Statement Criticizing Tactics of Obstruction," *Oil and Gas Journal* 31 (Jan. 5, 1933): 8; *Houston Post–Dispatch,* Jan. 6, 1933, 11:1.

6. "New Allowable Orders for Texas Fields Issued After Operators Express Ideas at Austin," *Oil and Gas Journal* 31 (Jan. 5, 1933): 8; "New Texas Railroad Commission Order Correcting Allowable for East Texas," *Oil and Gas Journal* 31 (Jan. 12, 1933): 12, reported that the TRC amended its January 1 order reducing the East Texas field to 290,000 barrels per day and limiting each producing well to 26 barrels a day. Well allowables were computed as follows: At the beginning of each monthly period, TRC agents divided the field allowable by the number of producing wells to determine the well allowable. Individual wells were permitted to produce more depending upon bottom-hole pressure. Dissatisfied operators could appeal to the TRC for reconsideration; James McIntyre, "With East Texas Shut In Crude Oil Production in U.S. Falls to Lowest Figure in 10 Years," *Oil and Gas Journal* 31 (Jan. 5, 1933): 7, reported that total domestic crude oil production averaged 2,201,111 barrels a day during the week ending January 2, 1932 and 1,760,335 barrels per day during the week ending December 24, 1932. In 1922, domestic production had averaged 1,500,000 barrels a day. The high point was reached in 1929, when domestic production averaged 2,750,000 barrels a day.

7. Powell to Elkins, Jan. 4, 1933, *Pure Oil Company vs. Texas Railroad Commission File,* VEA, C.F. 14963–13; Dawes to Elkins, Jan. 13, 1933, VEA, C.F. 10605.

8. Dawes to Elkins, Jan. 12, 1933, VEA, C.F. 14963–13, Dawes told Elkins; Elkins to Dawes, Jan. 14, 1933, Jan. 20, 1933, Elkins to McIlvain, Jan. 20, 1933, VEA, C.F. 10605.

9. L. E. Bredberg, "First Annual Meeting of the Texas Oil and Gas Association Is Held at Fort Worth, Texas," *Oil and Gas Journal* 31 (Jan. 12, 1933): 9, 32; C. B. Ames, "East Texas Situation as Seen by President Ames Put Before Texas Oil and Gas Association," *Oil and Gas Journal* 31 (Jan. 12, 1933): 9, 30.

10. Bredberg, "First Annual Meeting," 9, 32; Pew to Roeser, Jan. 2, 1933, VEA, C.F. 10605.

11. Transcript of the Texas Railroad Commission Hearing in Tyler, Texas (hereafter TRCH), Jan. 12, 1933, pp. 6–41, Pure Oil Company, Transcripts—Van Proration Hearing File, VEA, C.F. 14963–7–A; *Houston Post–Dispatch,* Jan. 13, 1933, 1:7, reported that Cosby testified that one of P & G's wells had run 465 barrels of oil in one night when the legal

per well allowable was 37 barrels; Bredberg, "Commission Opens East Texas Hearing at Tyler," 7, 23.

12. TRCH, Jan. 12–13, 1933, pp. 73–113; *Houston Post–Dispatch,* Jan. 13, 1933, 1:7, 3:3, Jan. 14, 1933, 1:8, 2:1, reported that individual contracts read into the record disclosed that, in addition to purchasing oil from Golding & Murchison, Atlantic had acquired crude oil from a number of other East Texas producers, including Byrd–Frost, Inc., who gave Atlantic a full interest in 24 wells which yielded $500,000 worth of oil at 70 percent of the market price; Bredberg, "Commission Opens East Texas Hearing at Tyler," 7, 23.

13. Ibid.

14. L. E. Bredberg, "Railroad Commission Adjourns Its Probe Into Proration Observance in East Texas Area," *Oil and Gas Journal* 31 (Jan. 26, 1933): 13.

15. While Pure and Liberty officials denied allegations of shipping or receiving illegally produced oil, they were being sued by the East Texas Refining Company for not running enough oil. Elkins to Dawes, March 14, 1933, VEA, C.F. 10605, Elkins said that the East Texas Refining Company had procured an injunction from the district court in Fort Worth compelling the Liberty Pipe Line and the Pure Van Pipe Line to transport 185,000 barrels of East Texas oil; Elkins to Lon A. Smith, Chairman Railroad Commission, Mar. 14, 1933, VEA, C.F. 10605; Elkins to Dawes, Mar. 15, 1933, VEA, C.F. 10605, Elkins said that he had filed a motion to dissolve the injunction and was "doing everything possible to avoid being compelled to accept oil for transportation"; Hamilton & Hamilton to J. Hart Willis, Mar. 31, 1933, VEA, C.F. 14963–13, attorneys representing the East Texas Refining Company informed Vinson & Elkins attorney, J. Hart Willis, that Pure Van Pipe Line and Liberty Pipe Line had not been taking oil in reasonable quantities as required by the injunction and, although they regretted having to file contempt proceedings, they insisted that the injunction be obeyed; J. Hart Willis to Hamilton & Hamilton, Mar. 31, 1933, VEA, C.F. 14963–13, Willis responded that Pure Van Pipe Line had been running all the oil possible from East Texas, but would not be able to take as much in the future.

16. TRCH, Jan. 19, 1933, pp. 367–422, VEA, C.F. 14963–7–A; Bredberg, "Railroad Commission Adjourns," 13; *Houston Post–Dispatch,* January 22, 1933, 1:7.

17. *Houston Post–Dispatch,* Jan. 20, 1933, 1:2, 2:3, Jan. 21, 1933, 1:2, 2:1; Pew to Roeser, Jan. 2, 1933, VEA, C.F. 10605.

18. *Houston Post–Dispatch,* Jan. 21, 1933, 2:2, Jan. 22, 1933, 1:3; Elkins to Dawes and McIlvain, Jan. 26, 1933, VEA, C.F. 10605.

19. Ibid., Jan. 21, 1933, 2:4, reported that the three-judge court consisted of Joseph C. Hutcheson, Jr.; James C. Wilson; and William I. Grubb.

20. Hardwicke, "Legal History," pp. 240–41.
21. The Marginal Well Act, enacted April 16, 1931, defined marginal wells as pumping oil wells that produced only a stated number of barrels of oil daily from a particular depth. The act prohibited restriction of production of wells that produced such small amounts of oil that curtailment would damage them, cause their premature abandonment, or result in the loss of recoverable oil. See *General Laws of the Regular Session of the Texas Legislature,* 1931, ch. 58, p. 92, now appearing in *Vernon's Texas Natural Resources Code Annotated,* sections 85.121–85.125 (1978); Weaver, *Unitization of Oil and Gas Fields in Texas,* pp. 64–65, argued that the TRC was in a predicament after its per-well allocation formula had been invalidated by the *People's* decision. The 1931 Marginal Well Act exempted marginal wells from regulation. A prorationing formula based upon well potentials, according to Weaver, offered the least disruptive replacement for the outlawed, flat per-well formula, but it would require the restriction of free flowing wells to less than the 40-barrel daily limit allowed to pumping wells. Weaver maintains that "surely the federal court would not consider as reasonable this perverse situation that good wells should receive *less* than bad wells." The TRC asked the Texas attorney general for advice. Allred replied that "certainly no order is valid . . . which does not, upon some reasonable basis, substantially give to each operator the same proportion of production to which he would be entitled if there were not proration." (Texas Attorney General Opinion No. 2916 [1933]). Weaver claims that Allred's opinion essentially recognized producers' vested rights in the rule of capture, which applied in the absence of prorationing. Allred believed that prorationing based solely on well potential closely approximated the rule of capture and was therefore valid.
22. Clark, *Three Stars for the Colonel,* pp. 93–94.
23. Plaintiff's Original Bill of Complaint and Petition for Temporary Restraining Order, *Pure Oil Company v. Railroad Commission of Texas, et al.,* filed in the U.S. District Court for the Eastern District of Texas, Tyler Division, Complaint in Equity No. 506, Jan. 24, 1933, VEA, C.F. 14963–13; TRCH, Feb. 2, 1933, Oil and Gas Docket No. 123, pp. 16–17, VEA, C.F. 14963–13.
24. Temporary Restraining Order signed by Judge Randolph J. Bryant, Jan. 24, 1933, VEA, C.F. 14963–13; *Houston Post–Dispatch,* Jan. 26, 1933, 1:5; L. E. Bredberg, "Commission Is Tightening Control of East Texas; Legislature Discusses Appointive Body," *Oil and Gas Journal* 31 (Feb. 2, 1933): 30; Clyde Sweeton to Lon A. Smith, Chairman, Texas Railroad Commission, Jan. 24, 1933, VEA, C.F. 14963–13; Elkins to Parker, Jan. 25, 1933, VEA, C.F. 14963–13; Elkins to Dawes, McIlvain, and SoRelle, Jan. 25, 1933, VEA, C.F. 14963–13.

25. Dawes to Sweeton, Jan. 25, 1933, VEA, C.F. 10605; Elkins to McIlvain, Jan. 31, 1933, VEA, C.F. 10605.

26. Special Order Again Amending Rule 1 of Rules and Regulations Adopted to Govern Said (Van) Field, Railroad Commission of Texas, Oil and Gas Division, Oil and Gas Docket No. 123, December 31, 1932, VEA, C.F. 14963–13, the TRC set the Van field allowable at 41,500 barrels a day, effective January 10 to April 1, 1933, of which Pure's daily allowable was 38,000 barrels; Elkins to Dawes, Jan. 25, 1933, VEA, C.F. 14963–13; Elkins said, "I have stated to the Railroad Commission that we are going to maintain our rights from now on and assert them vigorously"; Suman to the Railroad Commission of Texas, Feb. 2, 1933, VEA, C.F. 14963–13; Baker to Elkins, Feb. 2, 1933, VEA, C.F. 14963–13.

27. TRCH, Feb. 2, 1933, pp. 16–17, VEA, C.F. 14963–13.

28. Powell to Elkins, Feb. 3, 1933, Feb. 8, 1933, VEA, C.F. 10605; Kelly to Elkins, Feb. 3, 1933, VEA, C.F. 14963–13; Dawes to Elkins, Mar. 1, 1933, VEA, C.F. 10605; Elkins to Dawes, Mar. 8, 1933, VEA, C.F. 10605.

29. Dawes to Elkins, Mar. 10, 1933, VEA, C.F. 10605.

30. Elkins to SoRelle, Mar. 1, 1933, VEA, C.F. 14963–13; Willis to Elkins, Apr. 3, 1933, VEA, C.F. 14963–13, Willis informed Elkins that the court had left the injunction in effect; Elkins to Adams, May 6, 1933, VEA, C.F. 14963–13, Elkins informed R. W. Adams of Pure Oil Company's Texas Producing Division office in Fort Worth that Judge Bryant had not vacated or modified the injunction; Elkins to Harvey, Dec. 27, 1933, VEA, C.F. 14963–13, Elkins reported to Arlington C. Harvey at Pure's Chicago headquarters that the injunction bond would be continued; Sweeton to Adams, Apr. 23, 1935, VEA, C.F. 14963–13, Sweeton informed Adams that the injunction would remain in effect until the court heard Pure's application for a permanent injunction. As of April 23, 1935, the court had issued no further orders.

31. Complainant's Original and Supplemental Brief on Application for Temporary Injunction (hereafter Complainant's Brief), *Rowan & Nichols Oil Company v. C. V. Terrell, et al.,* filed in the U.S. District Court for the Eastern District of Texas, Tyler Division, by Rice M. Tilley, Attorney for Complainant, pp. 41–42, 78–80, copy in the Pure Oil Company, Briefs, Memoranda, and Legal Opinions File, VEA, C.F. 17771; Neil Williams, "East Texas Hearing Before Federal Court Ends, Three Judges Withholding Their Decision," *Oil and Gas Journal* 31 (Feb. 2, 1933): 6, 29; *Houston Post–Dispatch,* Jan. 28, 1933, 1:2, 2:3, Jan. 29, 1933, 1:4, 4:3.

32. Complainant's Brief, pp. 65–67, VEA, C.F. 17771.

33. Williams, "East Texas Hearing Before Federal Court," 29; *Houston Post–Dispatch,* Jan. 28, 1933, 1:2, 2:3, Jan. 29, 1933, 1:4, 4:3.

34. Ibid.

35. Buck's testimony cited in Complainant's Brief, pp. 45–47, VEA, C.F. 17771; Williams, "East Texas Hearing Before Federal Court," 29; *Houston Post–Dispatch,* Jan. 31, 1933, 1:5, 2:6.

36. Presley, *Saga of Wealth,* pp. 161–65, notes that after losing a race for governor of Texas in 1936 against incumbent James V. Allred, Fisher explained, "There wasn't many folks in the state who knew I was running, that was the only trouble"; *Houston Post–Dispatch,* Feb. 1, 1933, 1:3, 2:3.

37. Andrew M. Rowley, "Question of Continuing Proration Now Agitating Many Oil Men Dissatisfied With Conditions," *Oil and Gas Journal* 31 (Feb. 2, 1933): 7; Editorial, "Politics and Proration," *Oil and Gas Journal* 31 (Feb. 2, 1933): 16.

38. *Houston Post–Dispatch,* Feb. 7, 1933, 1:3, Feb. 9, 1933, 1:2, 2:4; "Allred Protests Entertaining Hearsay Testimony Before the Texas Legislative Investigation," *Oil and Gas Journal* 31 (Feb. 16, 1933): 10, 16.

39. *Houston Post–Dispatch,* Mar. 10, 1933, 1:1; *Dallas Morning News,* Mar. 11, 1933 (no page cited), clipping in VEA, C.F. 10605; *New York Times,* Mar. 11, 1933, 28:4; L. E. Bredberg, "East Texas Crisis Is Rapidly Approaching Climax; Must Either Cut Production or Price of Oil," *Oil and Gas Journal* 31 (Mar. 1, 1933): 9, 25.

40. Notice by Holmes to Producers and State Authorities, March 4, 1933, copy in, VEA, C.F. 10605; *Dallas Morning News,* Mar. 12, 1933, clipping in VEA, C.F. 10605; Thompson to Wolters, Mar. 10, 1933, J. R. Parten Papers, cited in Day, "The Oil and Gas Industry and Texas Politics, 1930–1935," p. 191.

41. *Dallas Morning News,* Mar. 12, 1933, clipping in VEA, C.F. 10605.

42. Bredberg, "East Texas Crisis Is Rapidly Approaching Climax," 9, 25.

43. *Houston Post–Dispatch,* Mar. 15, 1933, 5:4; "Legislative Committee Criticizes Commission," *Oil and Gas Journal* 31 (Mar. 23, 1933): 29.

44. Address by Ralph C. Holmes, president of the Texas Company, before the House of Representatives, Austin, Texas, Mar. 16, 1933, pp. 9–12, copy in VEA, C.F. 10605.

45. *Houston Post–Dispatch,* Mar. 18, 1933, 1:1, 2:3; "Federal Court Upsets Old Rules of East Texas; approves Oklahoma System as Model," *Oil and Gas Journal* 31 (Mar. 23, 1933): 8, 28.

46. "Federal Court Upsets Old Rules of East Texas," 8, 28; Anonymous independent quoted in Presley, *Saga of Wealth,* p. 158.

47. *Houston Post–Dispatch,* Mar. 26, 1933, 1:2.

48. *New York Times,* Mar. 28, 1933, 34:3, Captain E. N. Stanley, in charge of the TRC headquarters in the East Texas field, reported an average of 60 to 70 violations a day; *ibid,* Apr. 2, 1933, IV, 6:4; Andrew M. Rowley, "Immediate Strengthening of Crude and Refined Oil Markets Expected as Result of Meeting," *Oil and Gas Journal* 31 (Mar. 30, 1933): 7;

Editorial, "The People Are Not Helpless," *Oil and Gas Journal* 31 (Mar. 30, 1933): 18.

49. *Houston Post–Dispatch,* Apr. 4, 1933, 1:5, 2:3.

50. Allred's opinion reported in "New Texas Bill Proposes to Cut Marginal Wells," *Oil and Gas Journal* 31 (Apr. 13, 1933): 31; Hardwicke cited from, TRCH, Apr. 3, 1933, pp. 1–2, copy in, Pure Oil Company—Changing the Method of Prorationing at Van, 1932–1936 File, VEA, C.F. 14963–8; *Houston Post–Dispatch,* Apr. 3, 1933, 1:4, 2:4, April 4, 1933, 1:6, 2:6.

51. TRCH, pp. 5–9, VEA, C.F. 10605; *Houston Post–Dispatch,* Apr. 4, 1933, 1:6, 2:6.

52. Elkins to Dawes and McIlvain, Apr. 3, 1933, VEA, C.F. 10605; Elkins to McIlvain, Apr. 4, 1933, VEA, C.F. 10605.

53. "New Allowables in Texas as Ordered by Commission," *Oil and Gas Journal* 31 (Apr. 13, 1933): 31; Elkins to Dawes and McIlvain, Apr. 10, 1933, VEA, C.F. 10605.

54. L. E. Bredberg, "East Texas Tests Completed; New Order Friday; Many Violations During the Shut In Period," *Oil and Gas Journal* 31 (Apr. 20, 1933): 43; *Houston Post–Dispatch,* Apr. 15, 1933, 1:3, Apr. 19, 1933, 1:8, Apr. 23, 1933, 1:4; Elkins to Dawes, Apr. 28, 1933, VEA, C.F. 10605.

55. L. E. Bredberg, "Renewed Hope for Proration in East Texas Area; Field Shut Down Awaiting Test of Key Wells," *Oil and Gas Journal* 31 (Apr. 13, 1933): 45; *Houston Post–Dispatch,* Apr. 1, 1933, 1:1, Apr. 6, 1933, 1:7; *New York Times,* Apr. 6, 1933, 33:3.

56. L. G. E. Bignell, "High Allowable in East Texas Field Will Result in Early Reduction to Pumping Conditions," *Oil and Gas Journal* 31 (Apr. 27, 1933): 11, 16; *Houston Post–Dispatch,* Apr. 23, 1933, 3:3, Apr. 24, 1933, 1:8, 3:6; *New York Times,* Apr. 24, 1933, 25:1.

57. Editorial, "Cannot Last Long," *Oil and Gas Journal* 31 (Apr. 27, 1933): 20; Hardwicke, "Legal History," pp. 242–43; Bignell, "High Allowable in East Texas," 11.

58. "East Texas Crude Price Cut to 10 Cents Barrel," *Oil and Gas Journal* 31 (Apr. 27, 1933): 26; L. E. Bredberg, "New Order and Cut Hits East Texas Violators; Test in Federal Court to Follow Immediately," *Oil and Gas Journal* 31 (Apr. 27, 1933): 42; Andrew M. Rowley, "Wild Orgy in East Texas Brings Inevitable Cut; Voluntary Curtailment Elsewhere Suggested," *Oil and Gas Journal* 31 (May 4, 1933): 7; "Humble Cuts Crude Prices as Result of Flood of Oil From East Texas Fields," *Oil and Gas Journal* 31 (May 4, 1933): 9; Larson and Porter, *History of Humble Oil,* pp. 475–76; *Houston Post–Dispatch,* Apr. 26, 1933, 1:2, 2:3; *New York Times,* Apr. 25, 1933, 23:2, May 3, 1933, 30:1, cited an API report for the week ending April 30, showing average domestic crude oil production to be 2,383,100 barrels, compared to 1,795,500 barrels

during the preceding week. The 550,000-barrel increase was attributed almost entirely to production in the East Texas field.

59. A. E. Mockler, "Industry Is Prepared for Showdown on Proration Enforcement Measures, Says R. C. Holmes," *Oil and Gas Journal* 31 (Apr. 27, 1933): 13, 16; *New York Times,* Apr. 25, 1933, 23:2; *Houston Post–Dispatch,* Apr. 26, 1933, 1:2.

60. *Houston Post–Dispatch,* Apr. 24, 1933, 1:7, Apr. 25, 1933, 7:1, Apr. 26, 1933, 2:3; *New York Times,* Apr. 25, 1933, 23:2, Apr. 26, 1933, 21:2.

61. L. E. Bredberg, "Flood of Oil Is Pouring From East Texas Area; Watching Effect on Bottom Hole Pressure," *Oil and Gas Journal* 31 (May 4, 1933): 14.

62. "Texas House for New Oil Commission; Marginal Well Bill to Governor," *Oil and Gas Journal* 31 (Apr. 27, 1933): 11; *Houston Post–Dispatch,* Apr. 27, 1933, 1:6, 5:5, Apr. 28, 1933, 1:1, 2:1, Apr. 29, 1933, 1:4, 2:3, reported that the legislature cited the three assailants for contempt. Roeser apologized, stating that the fight had been "without thought or intention of offending or being disrespectful to any member." Burns asked House Speaker Coke Stevenson not to punish Roeser. Representative John M. Mathis of Houston argued that contempt proceedings would prolong the legislative session by ten days, costing the taxpayers some $30,000. "The most that we can do if we find the accused guilty," he claimed, "is to send him to jail for 48 hours." The House never tried Roeser on the contempt charges.

63. *Houston Post–Dispatch,* Apr. 29, 1933, 1:4, 2:3, May 2, 1933, 1:2; May 3, 1933, 1:1, May 4, 1933, 1:7; Prindle, *Petroleum Politics,* p. 37; Pace quoted in Presley, *Saga of Wealth,* p. 157.

64. *Houston Post–Dispatch,* Apr. 27, 1933, 2:5; "Magnolia Posts 25 Cents for East Texas Oil, But 10-Cent Market Prevails," *Oil and Gas Journal* 31 (May 4, 1933): 10; *New York Times,* May 6, 1933, 21:3, May 10, 1933, 30:1; Larson and Porter, *History of Humble Oil,* p. 477.

65. "Application for New Injunction," *Oil and Gas Journal* 32 (May 18, 1933): 16.

66. *Hunt Production Company v. Lon A. Smith, et al.,* Unpublished Opinion, (N.D. Tex. 1933), copy in Pure Oil Company—Legal Committee, Legal Opinions, Etc. File, VEA, C.F. 14963–6; "Federal Court in Texas Asks Producers to Stop Wrangling and Go to U.S. Supreme Court," *Oil and Gas Journal* 32 (June 1, 1933): 9, 18, reported that the plaintiffs accused the TRC of misusing data in calculating well potentials and allocating production. Hunt and Rowan & Nichols argued that the allowable was too high and that acreage should be considered. Plaintiffs represented by attorney F. W. Fisher argued that the allowable was too low and that acreage should not be considered. Fisher maintained that the daily per-well allowable was only two-thirds of 1 percent of the daily capacity of the

wells in the East Texas field. Hunt testified that the TRC's proration order permitted a 16.5-acre tract with 21 wells to produce more than twice as much oil as a 108-acre tract with 8 wells that he owned. Judge Hutcheson held that even though there might be inequalities in the TRC's orders, producers should first seek redress from the TRC before coming to court; Hardwicke, "Legal History," p. 243, notes that the Hunt ruling was subsequently cited to support the validity of per-well-potential prorationing regardless of acreage or density of wells drilled. See *Boxrollium v. Smith,* 4 F.Supp. 624 (S.D. Tex., 1933), where a three-judge federal court refused to restrain enforcement of a TRC proration order for the Conroe oil field which gave acreage a 50 percent value. Hardwicke maintains that the courts had simply balanced conveniences, denying injunctions without decisions on the merits in either case. He believed that the courts would sustain a proration order as long as it gave each operator a fair share of production, regardless of the allocation formula.

67. Hardwicke, "Legal History," pp. 243–44; *Danciger Oil and Refining Company of Texas v. Smith,* 4 F. Supp. 236, 236–37 (N.D. Tex., 1933), *cert. denied,* 290 U.S. 599 (1933); *Houston Post–Dispatch,* Mar. 11, 1933, 2:1, Mar. 12, 1933, 7:1.

68. "Panhandle Proration Held Not To Be Unreasonable," *Oil and Gas Journal* 32 (July 6, 1933): 16; *Danciger v. Smith,* 238–39, decided by Judges Hutcheson, West, and Wilson.

69. *Boxrollium Oil Company v. Smith, et al.,* 4 F. Supp. 624 (S.D. Tex., 1933); Charles L. Zelden, *Justice Lies in the District: The U.S. District Court, Southern District of Texas, 1902–1960* (College Station: Texas A&M University Press, 1993), pp. 102–104.

70. L. G. E. Bignell, "Recent Orgy of Drilling in East Texas Field Has Definitely Shortened the Flowing Life," *Oil and Gas Journal* 31 (May 18, 1933): 10–11, 17–18.

71. Editorial, "Out of the Depths," *Oil and Gas Journal* 31 (May 18, 1933): 22; Andrew M. Rowley, "No Hope for Any Effective Curtailment in Texas Under the Present Political Set-up," *Oil and Gas Journal* 32 (May 25, 1933): 5.

72. Earl Oliver, "The Problems of the Petroleum Industry," *Oil and Gas Journal* 31 (May 11, 1933): 10–11.

73. Nordhauser, *Quest for Stability,* pp. 106–107; "Bill Being Prepared at Washington for Federal Dictator of the Oil Industry," *Oil and Gas Journal* 31 (May 4, 1933): 32, reported the Marland–Capper bill proposed to vest the secretary of interior, rather than the states, with the authority to: (1) fix the estimated market demand for oil, (2) recommend quotas to be produced in the oil states with the estimates of consumption, (3) recommend to the states uniform laws to prevent overproduction, and (4) issue regulations to aid in the enforcement of the law. The

states would be allowed to allocate their respective quotas among individual oil fields and producers. The bill was sponsored by Rep. Ernest W. Marland, an Oklahoma oilman and former API director, and Senator Arthur Capper, an advocate for Kansas oilmen. They introduced the bill in Congress in May, 1933.

Chapter 10

1. Statistics compiled by the U.S. Bureau of Mines, Department of Commerce, published in the *Oil and Gas Journal* 31 (May 11, 1933): 12, reported that production in the East Texas field had increased from 450,000 barrels a day to a million barrels per day in March; Andrew M. Rowley, "Temporary Troubles Should Not Blind Business to Dangers Incident to Government Control," *Oil and Gas Journal* 31 (May 11, 1933): 9.

2. Arthur M. Schlesinger, Jr., *The Age of Roosevelt,* vol. 2: *The Politics of Upheaval* (Boston: Houghton Mifflin Company, 1958), pp. 87, 108–10, 120, states, "From the viewpoint of the national planners, NRA . . . provided the mechanism for straight-out government direction of the economy." On p. 110, Schlesinger notes that Hugh Johnson was interested in industrial self-government, and viewed NRA's function as "not to impose codes, but to accept them"; Nordhauser, *Quest for Stability,* pp. 116–17.

3. Harold L. Ickes, *The Secret Diary of Harold L. Ickes,* vol. 1: *The First Thousand Days, 1933–1936* (New York: Simon & Schuster, 1954), p. 6, 29, 31–32; Charles E. Kern, "Governors of Oil-Producing States Are Invited to Attend Business Restoration Conference," *Oil and Gas Journal* 31 (Mar. 23, 1933): 8; *New York Times,* Mar. 16, 1933, 25:2, Mar. 19, 1933, II, 5:6, Mar. 23, 1933, 29:3; Clark, *Energy and the Federal Government,* pp. 221–22; Schlesinger, *Age of Roosevelt,* 2, p. 89, states that as voluntary and state controls on oil production broke down, "industry leaders by early 1933, seeing anarchy ahead, began to plead for a federal oil dictator."

4. Clark, *Energy and the Federal Government,* p. 222; *New York Times,* Mar. 27, 1933, 23:1, Mar. 28, 1933, 27:6, 34:2.

5. Linda J. Lear, "Harold L. Ickes and the Oil Crisis of the First Hundred Days," *Mid-America* 63 (Jan., 1981): 5–8; Nash, *United States Oil Policy,* pp. 131–32; Clark, *Energy and the Federal Government,* p. 222; Nordhauser, *Quest for Stability,* pp. 101–103; *New York Times,* Mar. 28, 1933, 27:6; Charles E. Kern, "Roosevelt Is Asked to Appoint Oil Supervisor and to Shut In Flush Wells Until April 15," *Oil and Gas Journal* 31 (Mar. 30, 1933): 11, 30, reported that three committees—representing, respectively, the governors of the oil-producing states, the oil and gas

associations representing independent producers, and the major oil and gas producing and importing companies—after conferring together, unanimously recommended that President Roosevelt: (1) call upon the governors of oil-producing states to close down oil fields in their respective states until April 15, (2) ask those states, without adequate conservation statutes, to adopt laws to facilitate scientific and orderly development of oil and gas resources, (3) recommend to Congress the adoption of a law prohibiting the transportation in interstate and foreign commerce of any oil or petroleum products produced or manufactured in violation of state laws, and (4) request Congress to enact emergency legislation authorizing the president to appoint a personal representative to cooperate with the duly constituted authorities of the oil-producing states to enforce the foregoing program.

6. Kern, "Roosevelt Is Asked to Appoint Oil Supervisor," 11, 30, the Committee of Fifteen consisted of representatives of the governors of the four major oil-producing states (Texas, Oklahoma, Kansas, and California) and the API, the majors, and independents. Executives including Walter Teagle of New Jersey Standard, API president C. B. Ames, and Texas Company president R. C. Holmes represented the majors. IPAA president Wirt Franklin and TOGCA president Charles Roeser represented the independents. With the exception of Kansas governor Alf Landon, the governors were represented by local oilmen; Ickes, *Secret Diary,* 1, pp. 9–10.

7. *New York Times,* Mar. 29, 1933, 21:1, 27:2; Nordhauser, *Quest for Stability,* pp. 102–104; Ickes, *Secret Diary,* 1, pp. 10–11.

8. Charles E. Kern, "Roosevelt Hopes States Will Aid Oil Industry; Favors Divorcement of Interstate Pipe Lines," *Oil and Gas Journal* 31 (Apr. 6, 1933): 9; *New York Times,* Apr. 4, 1933, 25:7; Ickes, *Secret Diary,* 1, pp. 12–16; Nordhauser, *Quest for Stability,* pp. 104–105, notes that although the Hepburn Act of 1906 had classified interstate pipelines as common carriers, small producers and refiners had not obtained open access to their use. See Arthur M. Johnson, *Petroleum Pipelines and Public Policy, 1906–1959* (Cambridge, Mass.: Harvard University Press, 1967), pp. 24–33, 188–206. Johnson concluded that between 1914 and 1931, federal regulation "remained largely a formality, and the pipeline companies found the ICC willing and even anxious to consult with them on how the formalities should be handled." For the revenues, expenses, and income of the oil pipelines see API, *Petroleum Facts and Figures, Centennial Edition* (New York: American Petroleum Institute, 1959), p. 415.

9. The Marland–Capper bill was sponsored by Rep. E. W. Marland and Senator Arthur Capper, both of Oklahoma. See Watkins, *Oil: Stabilization or Conservation?,* pp. 53–54; Nash, *United States Oil Policy,* p. 132.

10. *Congressional Record,* 77, 73rd Congress, 1st sess. (Washington, D.C.: Government Printing Office, 1933), pp. 3805, 3810, recorded the attitudes of Texas officials; *New York Times,* May 7, 1933, II, 7:3, 15:7, May 9, 1933, 25:6, May 12, 1933, 28:1, reported the attitudes of major oil company officials.

11. Nordhauser, *Quest for Stability,* pp. 108–109.

12. Watkins, *Oil: Stabilization or Conservation?,* p. 54; U.S. Congress, House of Representatives, Committee on Ways and Means, *Hearings on Conservation of Petroleum, Pursuant to H.R. 5720,* 73rd Congress, 1st sess. (Washington, D.C.: Government Printing Office, 1933), pp. 5–15.

13. Ickes, *Secret Diary,* 1, p. 39; "Oil May Be Included in Industry Agreement Bill; Single Dictatorship Out of the Picture?" *Oil and Gas Journal* 31 (May 18, 1933): 13, 20; *Conservation Hearings,* pp. 16, 30; Clark, *Energy and the Federal Government,* p. 223; Rene de Visme Williamson, *The Politics of Planning in the Oil Industry Under the Code* (New York: Harper & Brothers, 1936), pp. 49–57; Charles E. Kern, "Senate Finance Committee Holds Oil Hearing on Industry Recovery and Marland–Ickes Bills," *Oil and Gas Journal* 32 (June 1, 1933): 9, 18, reported that Russell B. Brown, IPAA legal counsel, supported the Marland–Capper bill because "the industry has a code of practices but that meant nothing in preventing the evils that existed when that code was formulated," adding, "What the industry needs is not a code but a dictator." TOGCA president Roeser favored the Marland–Capper measure because the failure of the oil industry and the state regulative agencies made federal intervention imperative.

14. Clark, *Energy and the Federal Government,* p. 223; Nordhauser, *Quest for Stability,* pp. 109–10; Ickes, *Secret Diary,* 1, p. 39; Johnson quoted in Schlesinger, *Age of Roosevelt,* 2, p. 116.

15. Clark, *Energy and the Federal Government,* p. 224; Nordhauser, *Quest for Stability,* pp. 110–12, notes that, on May 8, 1933, the Texas House of Representatives informed President Roosevelt of its opposition to any measure giving the secretary of the interior control over oil; *Conservation Hearings,* pp. 5–6, 61, 65; *New York Times,* June 4, 1933, 1:6, June 6, 1933, 1:1. Section 9(a) authorized the president to initiate ICC proceedings to regulate the operation of oil pipelines and to establish reasonable rates. Section 9(b) authorized the president to institute divorcement proceedings whenever a pipeline, through unfair practices or unreasonable rates, tended to create a monopoly. Section 3(e) gave the president regulatory power over imports, and Section 4(a) provided for presidential approval of agreements between companies. In addition, the NIRA permitted the president to establish an agency separate from the National Recovery Administration to supervise the operation of the oil code; *Conservation Hearings,* p. 16, 165; Ickes, *Secret Diary,* 1, pp. 10,

49–50; Kern, "Senate Finance Committee Holds Oil Hearing," 9, 18.

16. Nordhauser, *Quest for Stability,* pp. 113–14; L. E. Bredberg, "Texas Commission Asks President Roosevelt to Ban Interstate Transportation of Hot Oil," *Oil and Gas Journal* 32 (July 13, 1933): 45; Neil Williams, "Texas Petroleum Council Organized at Houston to Support Enforcement of Proration Orders," *Oil and Gas Journal* 32 (July 13, 1933): 12, 31, reported that the Texas Petroleum Council was organized in Houston in July, 1933, to "promote harmony and cooperate with the TRC and other regulatory bodies" to achieve more effective enforcement of prorationing. Members included leaders from all branches of the petroleum industry, and its central office was located in Austin, Texas. Robert W. Slayton, head of the University of Texas law department, became the council's first president. The legal committee included lawyers Robert E. Hardwicke, Jr. of Fort Worth, Edgar E. Townes of Houston, and William A. Vinson of Houston; Elkins to Dawes, October 1, 1934, VEA, C.F. 14963–3, Elkins noted that the Texas Petroleum Council had been organized through the efforts of Houston Oil Company president George A. Hill; Receipt for Contribution to Texas Petroleum Council, Feb. 24, 1934, VEA, C.F. 14963–3, stated the association's aims: "The Texas Petroleum Council will confine its activities strictly to the purposes for which it was organized . . . to assist all federal and state officials and agencies in the enforcement of all federal and state laws, orders and/or regulations relating to the oil industry; and to investigate, collect and disseminate authentic data with respect to salt water pollution, with respect to the illegal production of oil or gas and the disposition made thereof, with respect to physical waste in the production, storage and transportation of oil or gas and with respect to the refining of crude oil and gasoline and the evasion of tax payments due by reason thereof. The Texas Petroleum Council agrees that it will not engage in any character of political activity; that it will not collect, disburse or expend any sum of money whatsoever for any political purpose, directly or indirectly; that it will not lobby, directly or indirectly, for or against any proposed legislation, state or federal; and that it will not sort or oppose any candidate for political office. The Texas Petroleum Council further agrees that it will not, directly or indirectly, in any violate the letter or spirit of the Anti-Trust Laws of the State of Texas or of any other laws of the State of Texas."

17. U.S. Congress, House of Representatives, Subcommittee of the House Committee on Interstate and Foreign Commerce, *Hearings on H.R. 441, Petroleum Investigation, Parts 1–5,* 73rd Cong., recess. (Washington, D.C., 1934), 3, p. 814; Nordhauser, *Quest for Stability,* p. 114; Watkins, *Oil: Stabilization or Conservation?,* p. 57; "Federal Regulations Banning Transportation of Hot Oil Put Into Effect Promptly in East Texas," *Oil and Gas Journal* 32 (July 20, 1933): 7, 30.

18. Clark, *Energy and the Federal Government,* pp. 224–25; Robert C. Conine, "Independents and Majors Unanimously Approve Code of Fair Competition for Oil Industry," *Oil and Gas Journal* 32 (June 22, 1933): 6–7, 26; text of "Code of Fair Competition," adopted by the Chicago conference published in *Oil and Gas Journal* 32 (June 22, 1933): 6–7, 26; Nordhauser, *Quest for Stability,* pp. 118–19, noted that, significantly, 95 percent of the delegates agreed upon a code after frank discussion. The API's board of directors endorsed it on June 26.

19. Charles E. Kern, "Oil Code Hearing Set at Washington Monday; Statement by the Recovery Administration," *Oil and Gas Journal* 32 (July 20, 1933): 6, 30; Kern, "Labor Provisions Prove Troublesome at Hearings on Oil Industry's Code for Fair Competition," *Oil and Gas Journal* 32 (July 27, 1933): 7; Kern, "Federal Allocation of Production Stipulated in Government's Code for Petroleum Industry," *Oil and Gas Journal* 32 (Aug. 3, 1933): 6–8.

20. Text of Johnson's code published in *Oil and Gas Journal* 32 (Aug. 3, 1933): 6–9; Charles E. Kern, "General Johnson at Work on Revised Oil Code Following Stormy Hearings at Washington," *Oil and Gas Journal* 32 (Aug. 10, 1933): 9–10, 32.

21. Nordhauser, *Quest for Stability,* pp. 123–24; Kern, "General Johnson at Work on Revised Oil Code," 9–10, 32.

22. Charles E. Kern, "Oil Code Signed by President to Be Revised Before It Is Put Into Effect September 2," *Oil and Gas Journal* 32 (Aug. 24, 1933): 8, 31; Kern, "Ickes Named Oil Code Administration Head; Secretary Will Supervise Oil Price Fixing," *Oil and Gas Journal* 32 (Aug. 31, 1933): 9, 14. The president was authorized to fix the minimum wholesale price for gasoline. By invoking this power, in conjunction with the 18.5 ratio, the president could fix minimum crude oil prices; Watkins, *Oil: Stabilization or Conservation?,* pp. 68–69, notes that the NRA petroleum code provided for eight subcommittees on statistics, production, refineries, marketing, accounting, labor, adjustments, and transportation. The PCC was empowered to collect necessary statistical data from the oil industry or other sources such as the U.S. Bureau of Mines.

23. *Petroleum Investigations,* 3, p. 818; Nordhauser, *Quest for Stability,* pp. 134–35; Kern, "No Oil Price Fixing by the Government," 9, 30; Clark, *Energy and the Federal Government,* p. 232.

24. Nordhauser, *Quest for Stability,* pp. 127–31, Roosevelt appointed Michael L. Benedum, James A. Moffett, and Donald Richberg as government members of the PCC. Benedum had substantial investments in the oil industry and was a large contributor to the Democratic party. Moffett had resigned as vice-president of Jersey Standard to join the PCC. Richberg, the only committee member without oil connections, was considered a friend of organized labor. According to Nordhauser, the

PCC generally ignored Richberg, who attended only one meeting in 1933 and resigned in 1934. The president received 3 lists of nominees from which to select the 12 industry members. Eleven of the 12 industry PCC members were price-control advocates. Eight members were independents, including Wirt Franklin, who was designated as chairman. Four members came from major oil companies. The PCC's membership made it appear heavily tilted toward federal price-fixing and hostile to states' rights, thereby incurring the wrath of price-control opponents; Kern, "Oil Code Signed by President," 8, 31, reported that 7 articles and 2 appendices made up the entire petroleum code. The major oil companies and the IPAA agreed to abide by the new rules and regulations, but the IPAOM refused to sign; the names of the PCC nominees and their respective position on price controls were published in the *Oil and Gas Journal* 32 (Aug. 24, 1933): 31; Clark, *Energy and the Federal Government,* p. 226; Williamson, *Planning in Oil Under the Code,* pp. 58–60, states that Ickes subsequently enlarged the PCC by 11 members, mostly from among unrepresented independents and the marketing branch of the petroleum industry; complete text of Petroleum Code published in, *Oil and Gas Journal* 32 (Aug. 24, 1933): 9–12, 32; Estes quoted in Olien and Olien, *Wildcatters,* p. 63; *Code of Fair Competition for the Petroleum Industry* (Washington, D.C.: Planning and Coordinating Committee, 1933), copy in Pure Oil Company—Amazon Petroleum Company v. Railroad Commission of Texas File, VEA, C.F. 10921.

25. Nash, *United States Oil Policy,* pp. 139–40; Watkins, *Oil: Stabilization or Conservation?,* p. 72; Kern, "Ickes Named Oil Code Administration Head," 9, 14.

26. Watkins, *Oil: Stabilization or Conservation?,* p. 75; Nash, *United States Oil Policy,* ch. 7, emphasizes the links between the NRA and the trade association movement fostered by World War I.

27. Peter H. Irons, *The New Deal Lawyers* (Princeton, N.J.: Princeton University Press, 1982), pp. 60–62; Nathan Margold was born in Romania and migrated with his parents to New York City. After graduation from the City College of New York, Margold studied law at Harvard University, where he became a protégé of Felix Frankfurter. He served as an assistant U.S. attorney in New York City before returning to Harvard to teach law from 1927 to 1928. Margold then spent three years as special counsel to the National Association for Advancement of Colored People (NAACP). In 1933, on Frankfurter's recommendation, Ickes appointed Margold, then 34 years old, to serve as solicitor of the interior department as well as PAB chairman. J. Howard Marshal was graduated in 1931 from Yale University Law School, where he became an assistant dean and instructor of law. He

was appointed to the PAB in 1933 to investigate and prosecute hot oil cases in Texas.

28. Watkins, *Oil: Stabilization or Conservation?*, p. 75; C. O. Wilson, "Price Fixing by Government Is Again Postponed; Meanwhile Prices Are Expected to Improve," *Oil and Gas Journal* 32 (Sept. 21, 1933): 9–10. In addition to Margold, PAB members included Charles Fahy, ranking assistant solicitor of the interior department; Norman L. Meyers, assistant solicitor of the interior department; J. Howard Marshall, assistant solicitor of the interior department; J. Elmer Thomas, petroleum analyst from Fort Worth; Edward B. Swanson, chief of the petroleum economics division of the U.S. Bureau of Mines; and Dr. John W. Frey, petroleum specialist with the U.S. Commerce Department; see "Legal Background of Nathan R. Margold, Now Chairman of Petroleum Administrative Board," *Oil and Gas Journal* 33 (Mar. 29, 1934): 11, 118.

29. Charles E. Kern, "No Oil Price Fixing by the Government Now; Section Remains in Code, but Inoperative," *Oil and Gas Journal* 32 (Sept. 14, 1933): 9, 30; Editorial, "The White House Conference," *Oil and Gas Journal* 32 (Sept. 14, 1933): 20; Wilson, "Price Fixing by Government Is Again Postponed," 9–10; Ickes reminded oilmen that the primary purpose of the NIRA was to put people back to work and raise wages in order to enlarge the purchasing power of industry; Andrew M. Rowley, "Further Price Increases Expected as Production of Crude Is Curtailed Near to Quota Limits," *Oil and Gas Journal* 32 (Sept. 21, 1933): 7.

30. John C. Snodgrass, Feb. 22, 1984, VEOH Interview 42, p. 11, PID: 052615–051, "Pure was Judge Elkins's client, and he always looked at it very jealously"; Thompson Interview, p. 26; William S. Elkins Interview, p. 48; Cornwall Interview, p. 22, states that Elkins called Roosevelt "that old crippled bastard"; Irons, *New Deal Lawyers,* p. 61.

31. Elkins to Terrell, Aug. 2, 1933, VEA, Aug. 9, 1933, C.F. 10605; Terrell to Elkins, Aug. 8, 1933, VEA, C.F. 10605; Terrell told Elkins, "It is my intention to cooperate with the federal government in every way possible."

32. Weaver, *Unitization of Oil and Gas Fields in Texas,* p. 32; Hardwicke, *Antitrust Laws,* p. 43.

33. Elkins to Dillard Estes, July 5, 1933, VEA, C.F. 10605, Elkins told Fort Worth attorney Dillard Estes that, at Allred's request, Pure had sent him copies of its Van unitization agreement. Elkins said that Allred assured him that "if the agreement did violate the antitrust law, the violations were technical and that in his opinion the purposes of the agreement were beneficial to the industry and to the state." Elkins added, "To say the least of it, he [Allred] has never attempted to give us any trouble in regard thereto." Estes was interested in drawing up a unitization agreement for the development of a new oil field and asked

Elkins for a copy of the Van unit agreement. Estes to Elkins, July 4, 1933, VEA, C.F. 10605; cooperative development of oil and gas fields was not legalized in Texas until passage of the Voluntary Unitization Act in 1949 Tex. Gen. Laws, Reg. Sess., ch. 259, pp. 477–83, now codified at Texas Natural Resources Code Ann., secs. 101.011–101.052; twenty-seven states have antitrust exemptions for voluntary unitization agreements. See Williams and Meyers, *Oil and Gas Law,* vol. 6, sec. 911.

34. Elkins to Dawes, Aug. 10, 1933, VEA, C.F. 10605.
35. Dawes to Elkins, Aug. 11, 1933, VEA, C.F. 10605; R. B. Kelly to Elkins, Aug. 17, 1933, VEA, C.F. 10605, cited a report by petroleum engineer Harold Vance of Kilgore, titled "Petroleum in East Texas During 1932, Except the Gulf Coast Area," in the AIMME, *Petroleum Development and Technology During the Year 1933,* which noted that at the end of 1932, the Van field produced 40,550,000 barrels whereas the East Texas field had produced 230,000,000 barrels. Comparing the original reserves of both the Van (579,300,000 barrels) and East Texas fields (2 billion barrels), Van was only 7 percent depleted, as compared to 12 percent depletion in East Texas. Vance estimated productive area for the Van and East Texas oil fields at 4,350 and 100,000 acres respectively. Copy of report in VEA, C.F. 10605; Foran to Kelly, August 18, 1933, VEA, C.F. 10605, TRC petroleum engineer E. V. Foran reported that the Van field had a reserve equal to 20.3 percent of the East Texas field and had produced only 15.6 percent of the amount produced from the East Texas field, approximately 5 percent less than should have been produced had the fields been depleted to the same degree. Van's reservoir pressure had declined only 10.4 percent, compared to a 24.5 percent decline in the East Texas field. Foran concluded that although Van production had been restricted to 10 percent of East Texas' output, it could produce twice the amount and still maintain the most approved conservation standards. Kelly forwarded Foran's report to Elkins, Kelly to Elkins, Aug. 19, 1933, VEA, C.F. 10605.
36. Watkins, *Oil: Stabilization or Conservation?,* p. 90; Kern, "No Oil Price Fixing by the Government Now," 9, 30; Rowley, "Further Price Increases Expected," 7; Clark, *Energy and the Federal Government,* pp. 230–31, noted the following state quotas: Texas, 975,000 barrels (40 percent); Oklahoma, 540,000 barrels (22 percent); California, 480,000 barrels (20 percent); and Kansas, 111,000 barrels (5 percent). National oil production quotas varied after September's order from a high of 2,530,000 barrels per day in July, 1934, to a low of 2,183,000 barrels per day in January, 1934; L. E. Bredberg, "Law Making Proration Violation Felony Helping to Tighten Enforcement in East Texas Field," *Oil and Gas Journal* 32 (Sept. 7, 1933): 41, reported that a new Texas law making violations of TRC proration orders a felony punishable by a fine and

imprisonment went into effect September 1, 1933; L. E. Bredberg,
"Reduction in East Texas Allowable Now Causes Feverish Search for
Pipe Line Connections," *Oil and Gas Journal* 32 (September 14, 1933):
42, reported that the TRC ordered a 25 percent reduction in the existing
618,000-barrel a day allowable for the East Texas field; Elkins to Dawes
and McIlvain, Sept. 6, 1933, VEA, C.F. 10605, Elkins advised Pure
management that under the TRC's 975,000-barrel a day statewide
proration order, Van would probably be allocated 40,000 barrels daily.

37. Elkins to Dawes and McIlvain, Sept. 6, 1933, Elkins to McIlvain and
SoRelle, Sept. 7, 1933, VEA, C.F. 10605.

38. Kelly to Elkins, Sept. 7, 1933, VEA, C.F. 10605; Elkins to McIlvain,
Sept., 1933, Elkins to Kelly, Sept. 7, 1933, Elkins to R. D. Parker, Sept.
7, 1933, VEA, C.F. 10605; Elkins to McIlvain, Sept. 13, 1933, Elkins to
SoRelle, Sept. 13, 1933, VEA, C.F. 10605.

39. Estes to Elkins, Sept. 7, 1933, VEA, C.F. 10605.

40. Gertrude Peddy to McIlvain, Nov. 10, 1933, VEA C.F. 10605, informed
Pure management that the TRC had reduced the statewide allowable to
875,000 barrels a day; McIlvain to Elkins, Nov. 15, 1933, VEA, C.F.
10605, Pure management congratulated Elkins on maintaining the Van
allowable in the face of statewide production cuts.

41. Watkins, *Oil: Stabilization or Conservation?*, pp. 90–91, 99, 141; Clark,
Energy and the Federal Government, pp. 231–32.

42. Nordhauser, *Quest for Stability*, p. 135; Editorial, "Making It Stick," *Oil
and Gas Journal* 32 (Oct. 5, 1933): 18.

43. Nordhauser, *Quest for Stability*, p. 136; Kern, "No Oil Price Fixing by
the Government Now," 9, 30; Kern, "Constitutional Questions and Lack
of Facts Delay Decision on Government Price Fixing Policy," *Oil and Gas
Journal* 32 (Oct. 12, 1933): 9, 54.

44. Wilson, "Price Fixing by Government Is Again Postponed," 9–10.

45. Ickes, *Secret Diary*, 1, pp. 85–86.

46. Ickes, *Secret Diary*, 1, pp. 95–99, 102; Kern, "Constitutional Questions . . . Delay Price Fixing," 9, 54.

47. Ickes, *Secret Diary*, I, pp. 107–108; Charles E. Kern, "Government Fixes
Crude and Refined Oil Prices Throughout United States, Effective Dec.
1," *Oil and Gas Journal* 32 (Oct. 19, 1933): 8–9; Andrew M. Rowley, "API
Takes Action to Strengthen Oil Code; Proposes Tightening of Commerce
Rules," *Oil and Gas Journal* 32 (Oct. 26, 1933): 21–22.

48. Nordhauser, *Quest for Stability*, pp. 140–41; James McIntyre, "Decem-
ber Allowable Production of Crude Oil Is Reduced to 2,210,000 Barrels
Per Day," *Oil and Gas Journal* 32 (Nov. 23, 1933): 7; McIntyre, "Reduced
Allowable Production Goes Into Effect With Industry Prepared to
Conform to It," *Oil and Gas Journal* 32 (Dec. 7, 1933): 9.

49. Andrew M. Rowley, "Oil Industry Should Use the Code to Establish Solid Foundation for Future Operations," *Oil and Gas Journal* 32 (Nov. 30, 1933): 9, 32; Powell to Elkins, Nov. 29, 1933, VEA, C.F. 10605, informed Elkins that Van production would not be cut under the TRC's new proration order for December; Elkins to McIlvain and SoRelle, Dec. 28, 1933, VEA, C.F. 10605, reported to Pure management, "Van will remain undisturbed."

50. U.S. Congress, House of Representatives, Committee on Interstate and Foreign Commerce, 73rd Cong., 2nd Sess., *Hearings on H. R. 9676 and H. R. 8572, Oil and Gas Pipelines* (Washington, D.C.: Government Printing Office, 1934), p. 55.

51. *Petroleum Investigations,* 4, pp. 1995–2000; Nordhauser, *Quest for Stability,* pp. 142–43.

52. T. L. Foster to Members of Legal Committee, Nov. 10, 1933, VEA, C.F. 10605, listed the legal committee members as Shell Petroleum Corporation, Humble Oil & Refining Company, the Texas Company, Pure Oil Company, Magnolia Oil Company, Sun Oil Company, Stanolind Oil Company, Atlantic Production Company, Tidewater Oil Company, Sinclair Prairie Oil Company, Continental Oil Company, Phillips Petroleum Company, Arkansas Fuel Oil Company, Empire Gas & Fuel Company, Vinson & Elkins, Sweeton & Weems, and Turner, Rogers, and Winn.

53. James McIntyre, "Texas, Oklahoma and California on Production Rampage in the Past Week; Hot Oil Stories," *Oil and Gas Journal* 32 (Dec. 14, 1933): 5, reported the following daily production increases for the second week in December: Oklahoma, 79,775 barrels; Texas, 63,244 barrels; California, 39,000 barrels. The total increase of the three states named, 182,019 barrels per day, was more than the total increase for the entire country, indicating that other oil-producing states were not to blame for the excess production; L. E. Bredberg, "Hot Oil Production in East Texas Now Estimated at 27,000 Barrels Daily," *Oil and Gas Journal* 32 (Dec. 21, 1933): 7, reported that hot oil production in the East Texas field varied from 20,000 to 90,000 barrels daily. During November, the East Texas field overproduced some 1,094,000 barrels of crude oil.

54. "Investigation Division Ready to Enforce Code," *Oil and Gas Journal* 32 (Dec. 14, 1933): 32.

55. L. E. Bredberg, "Hot Oil Situation in East Texas Will Not Get Better Until the Violators Can Be Jailed," *Oil and Gas Journal* 32 (Dec. 14, 1933): 10.

Chapter 11

1. Larson and Porter, *History of Humble Oil,* p. 480. Blaffer succeeded Farish as Humble president on June 7, 1933. Farish had resigned on June 6 to become board chairman of Standard Oil Company of New Jersey.
2. *New York Times,* January 3, 1934, 35:3.
3. Ickes, *Secret Diary* 1, p. 142; Williamson, et al., *The American Petroleum Industry,* p. 694; *New York Times,* January 22, 1934, 25:1. 4. *New York Times,* Feb. 8, 1934, 27:2; *Tyler Morning Telegraph,* Jan. 9, 1934, 1:1, copy in VEA, C.F. 14963–4; Dawes to James A. Elkins, Oct. 26, 1934, Nov. 2, 1934, Pure Oil Company—Proration Matters, Correspondence, 1934 File, VEA, C.F. 10923.
5. Elkins to Dawes, Oct. 31, 1934, VEA, C.F. 10923.
6. Morris to Elkins, Oct. 31, 1934, VEA, C.F. 10923; Elkins to Dawes, Jan. 7, 1935, VEA, C.F. 10923; Elkins to Senator J. D. Parnell, Jan. 11, 1935, VEA, C.F. 10923.
7. James B. McIntyre, "East Texas Producers Say Demand Now Exceeds Allowable and They Seek An Increase," *Oil and Gas Journal* 32 (Jan. 11, 1934): 7; Clark, *Three Stars for the Colonel,* pp. 98–99.
8. Section 9(c) was enforced through a complicated system of affidavits certifying the legality of oil being shipped. Pursuant to an executive order issued by President Roosevelt on July 12, 1933, invoking Section 9(c) of the NIRA and designating Secretary of the Interior Harold L. Ickes as the president's agent to enforce the order, oil produced or withdrawn from storage in excess of state proration orders was prohibited from moving in interstate commerce. The Interior Department promulgated regulations requiring every well owner to file monthly reports with the department's Division of Investigation regarding production and sales. Operators had to declare under oath that they had neither produced nor removed from storage any hot oil. Oil transporters and refiners also had to submit sworn affidavits. Penalties for violations included a fine not to exceed $1,000 and/or up to six months imprisonment. See Nordhauser, *Quest for Stability,* pp. 113–14; "Federal Regulations . . . Put Into Effect Promptly in East Texas," 7, 30.
9. Clark and Halbouty, *The Last Boom,* pp. 224–25; Presley, *Saga of Wealth,* pp. 176–77; "Briefs to Be Filed by Opposing Sides in East Texas Case," *Oil and Gas Journal* 32 (Oct. 12, 1933): 28; Notes, "Hot Oil Cases," *The George Washington Law Review* 3 (Mar., 1935): 391–94.
10. Hardwicke, "Legal History," pp. 246–47; *Houston Post–Dispatch,* Dec. 15, 1933, 1:1, 2:2; Olien and Olien, *Wildcatters,* p. 62.
11. Thompson Interview, pp. 16–18, Charles I. "Charlie" Francis, a native of Denton who practiced law in Wichita Falls, defended the API against

antitrust charges. The API recommended Francis's appointment as
assistant U.S. attorney and special prosecutor of hot oil cases in East
Texas and paid his salary. Elkins hired Francis in 1934, hoping to
utilize his assets as a competent lawyer with intimate ties to powerful
oil and gas executives. Francis became a Vinson & Elkins partner in
1936; "Mr. Francis Complimented," *Pure Oil News* (Dec., 1936): 16, copy
in Biographical Data of Lawyers File, VEA, C.F. 17785.

12. Neil Williams, "Houston Three Judge Court Will Not Decide Proration
    NRA Test Case Until After January 4," *Oil and Gas Journal* 32 (Dec. 21,
    1933): 13–14; *Houston Post–Dispatch,* Dec. 15, 1933, 1:1, 2:2, Dec. 16,
    1933, 1:3, 3:2.

13. Ibid.

14. Ibid.; Notes, "Delegation of Power by Congress," *Harvard Law Review*
    48 (Mar., 1935): 798–806, 798, Article III of the petroleum code, as
    originally approved by Executive Order No. 6256 on August 19, 1933,
    prohibited the hot oil production. This provision was inadvertently
    eliminated on September 13, 1933 by Executive Order No. 6284–A
    which intended to modify other code provisions. The *Panama* and
    Amazon cases were subsequently instituted in October, 1933. Plaintiffs'
    attorneys sought to enjoin enforcement of regulations issued pursuant
    to Section 9(c) of the NIRA and the impending prosecution under
    Section 3(f) for violation of a code provision which did not exist at the
    time of the lawsuit.

15. Ibid.

16. Ibid.

17. Ibid., Under Section 266 of the Judicial Code (28 U.S.C. 380), a three-
    judge court could determine the constitutional validity of orders of a
    state commission, but actions of federal officials involving federal
    constitutional law had to be considered by a federal district court.

18. *Amazon Petroleum Corporation v. Railroad Commission of Texas, et al.,*
    5 F.Supp. 633, 634–637 (E.D. Tex. 1934); Ibid., copy of original decision
    in Pure Oil Company—*Amazon Petroleum Corporation v. Railroad
    Commission of Texas* File, VEA, C.F. 10921; Bredberg, "Federal Court
    Upholds State Regulation in Texas," 13, 32; *Houston Post–Dispatch,* Feb.
    13, 1934, 1:3; *New York Times,* Feb. 13, 1934, 9:1.

19. *Panama Refining Company, et al. v. Ryan, et al.,* 5 F.Supp. 639, 645–49
    (E.D. Tex. 1934); Ibid., copy of original decision in Pure Oil Company—
    Panama Refining Company, et al. v. Ryan, et al. File, VEA, C.F. 10921;
    L. E. Bredberg, "Federal Court Upholds State Regulation in Texas;
    Bryant Would Restrict Federal Intervention," *Oil and Gas Journal* 32
    (Feb. 15, 1934): 13, 32; Albert C. Johnston, "Governmental Limitations
    on Oil Production," *The George Washington Law Review* 2 (May, 1934):
    474–86; Clark and Halbouty, *The Last Boom,* pp. 225–26; Robert L.

Stern, "The Commerce Clause and the National Economy, 1933–1946," *Harvard Law Review* 57 (1946): 644–55.

20. *Ryan, et al. v. Amazon Petroleum Corporation, et al.,* 71 F.2d 1, 7–8; *Ryan, et al. v. Panama Refining Company, et al.,* 71 F.2d 8; Harvey C. Couch, *A History of the Fifth Circuit, 1891–1981* (Washington, D.C.: Bicentennial Committee of the Judicial Conference of the United States, 1983), p. 64; Irons, *New Deal Lawyers,* p. 69; Allen V. Peden, "Memorandum to the Directors [Texas Petroleum Council]," May 23, 1934, copy in Pure Oil Company—Proration Matters, Correspondence, 1934 File, VEA, C.F. 14963–4; *New York Times,* May 23, 1934, 33:5; Clark and Halbouty, *The Last Boom,* p. 226.

21. *New York Times,* Feb. 14, 1934, 8:3; Nordhauser, *Quest for Stability,* p. 145; Charlie Francis, Untitled Memorandum of Law, p. 3, VEA, C.F. 10921; *Fort Worth Star–Telegram,* Feb. 21, 1934, 7:1, copy in VEA, C.F. 14963–4, cited API statistics showing a 4,950-barrel increase in domestic production during the week ending February 17. Texas production averaged 915,450 barrels—31,450 barrels in excess of the federal allowable; *Tyler Morning Telegraph,* Jan. 11, 1934, 1:1, 3:2, copy in VEA, C.F. 14963–4, reported 56 refineries operating in the East Texas oil field, exclusive of 71 reclaiming plants. Fifty-five of the 56 refineries were owned by independents. They were divided into two general types, cracking and skimming plants. There were only five cracking plants in the field. Cracking plants were the most modern refineries, securing a much higher percentage of gasoline recovery than the skimmers.

22. *The Dallas Journal,* Mar. 30, 1934, 1:7, copy in VEA, C.F. 14963–4.

23. L. E. Bredberg, "Hearing on Oil Bills in Progress at Austin, Texas; Hot Oil Situation Is Forcing State Action," *Oil and Gas Journal* 33 (Mar. 8, 1934): 8, reported that 400 oilmen petitioned Governor Ferguson to sign the bills.

24. Editorial, "No Illusions," *Oil and Gas Journal* 32 (Mar. 15, 1934): 20; "New Law for Supervision of Refineries Is Upheld by Texas District Judge," *Oil and Gas Journal* 32 (Mar. 29, 1934): 9, reported that the state won its first legal battle with East Texas refiners over the validity of the new law authorizing TRC supervision of refineries. On March 26, 1934, State District Judge J. D. Moore denied George L. Culver's application for a permanent injunction in a suit challenging the constitutionality of the statute. A native of Gladewater, Culver owned two refineries in Upshur County and alleged that the act was unconstitutional because it violated the search and seizure provisions of the state and federal constitutions, was an unwarranted delegation of legislative power to the TRC, placed unreasonable burdens on refineries, and invaded private property rights by permitting disclosure of trade secrets. Attorney General Allred urged Moore "to interpret this law in the spirit and light

of the new day . . . [and] not to consider lightly the recent five-to-four liberal decisions of the U.S. Supreme Court." On October 9, 1933, Judge Moore had held that the NIRA and the NRA codes superseded Texas antitrust laws in a suit by the state against Standard Oil and other major oil companies. "Should we find it difficult to determine exactly as to whether intrastate transactions burden interstate commerce," Moore ruled, "we might look to the human side, on account of the emergency, and on the human side remark that the father has a right to go into the homes of his children to do those things which are for the public good." Reported in the *Oil and Gas Journal* 32 (Oct. 12, 1933): 28.

25. Andrew M. Rowley, "Overproduction, Weak Refined Market, Show Need of Quick Action on Corrective Plans," *Oil and Gas Journal* 32 (Mar. 22, 1934): 7.

26. "Ickes Declares Oil Industry Perfect Example of Unchecked and Ruthless Exploitation," *Oil and Gas Journal* 32 (Mar. 1, 1934): 16.

27. C. O. Wilson, "Government May Use Its War Powers to Control the Operations of the Petroleum Industry," *Oil and Gas Journal* 32 (Mar. 1, 1934): 12, 42; *New York Times,* Feb. 23, 1934, 14:4.

28. Ibid.

29. Amos L. Beaty, "Federal Control of Petroleum Production," *American Bar Association Journal* 20 (June, 1934): 349–52, citing *Minnesota Rate Cases,* 230 U.S. 352 (1913); *Shreveport Rate Cases,* 234 U.S. 342 (1914); *Railroad Commission of Wisconsin v. Chicago, Burlington & Quincy Railroad,* 257 U.S. 563 (1922).

30. *New York Times,* May 1, 1934, 19:1; see Hugh D. Mallon, "Ickes' Bill to Provide Permanent Control Crude Production and to Extend Life of Oil Code," *Oil and Gas Journal* 32 (Apr. 26, 1934): 9, 42; Mallon, "Administration Bill to Control Crude Oil Production Introduced in Senate; Time for Passage Short," *Oil and Gas Journal* 33 (May 3, 1934): 9, 16, reported that the Thomas Bill authorized the secretary of the interior to periodically determine the consumptive and export demand for petroleum and its products in the United States. The interior secretary would then determine the reasonable market demand for petroleum and its products from each state, oil field, lease, or property. Based on those findings, the secretary would establish quotas of petroleum for movement in interstate commerce. In setting "quotas in commerce," a plan would be devised for the scientific development of new petroleum reservoirs and the orderly entry of oil into the stream of commerce. Certificates of clearance would be required to clear the movement of crude oil or petroleum products in interstate or foreign commerce.

31. *New York Times,* May 1, 1934, 19:1; "Complete Revised Text of Federal Petroleum Act Sent to Congress by Administrator Ickes," *Oil and Gas Journal* 33 (May 3, 1934): 10, 17–18.

32. Nordhauser, *Quest for Stability,* p. 157; Text of Thomas–Disney Bill published in Pettengill, *Hot Oil!,* pp. 270–82.

33. Ickes, *Secret Diary,* 1, p. 164; *Congressional Record,* 73rd Cong., 2nd Sess. (June 7, 1934) 78, p. 11,740; "President Roosevelt Urging the Oil Bill Quotes the Oil and Gas Journal," *Oil and Gas Journal* 33 (May 31, 1934): 91.

34. *Congressional Record,* 73rd Cong., 2nd Sess. 78 (June 15, 1934), p. 11,795; Eagle to Summerfield B. Roberts, March 4, 1935, copy in Pure Oil Company—Proration Matters, Correspondence,1934–1935 File, VEA, C.F. 14963–4; Sam Jackson to Carl Estes, May 3, 1934, VEA, C.F. 14963–4, Jackson, a Vinson & Elkins attorney, expressed VE's dissatisfaction with the "Ickes bill."

35. Ibid., p. 11,799.

36. Ibid., p. 11,800.

37. Ibid., pp. 11,799–801; "Congressional Investigating Committee Named; Representative Dies, Texas, Chosen Counsel," *Oil and Gas Journal* 33 (June 21, 1934): 9, 26.

38. Williamson, et al., *The American Petroleum Industry,* pp. 549–50; Giebelhaus, *Business and Government in the Oil Industry,* p. 217; Mallon, "Congressional Investigating Committee Named," 9, 26; the other four congressmen on the "Cole Committee" were Samuel B. Pettengill of Indiana, Edward A. Kelly of Illinois, Carl E. Mapes of Michigan, and Charles A. Wolverton of New Jersey. Texas Congressman Martin Dies acted as counsel for the committee; transcripts of the Cole Committee hearings published in U.S. Congress, House of Representatives, *Petroleum Investigations,* vols. 1–5, 73rd Cong., recess, 1934 (Washington, D.C.: Government Printing Office, 1934).

39. *Petroleum Investigations,* 1, pp. 431–35; Pettengill, *Hot Oil!,* pp. 120–21.

40. Ibid.

41. Ibid., pp. 447–48, citing *United Mine Workers v. Coronado Coal Company,* 259 U.S. 344 (1922), 268 U.S. 295 (1925). In *Hammer v. Dagenhart,* 247 U.S. 251 (1918), the U.S. Supreme Court held that mining was not interstate commerce, but like manufacturing, a local business subject to local regulation and taxation.

42. Ibid., pp. 450–56; Pettengill, *Hot Oil!,* pp. 127–28; Robert E. Stern, "That Commerce Which Concerns More States Than One," *Harvard Law Review* 47 (1934): 1335, suggests that the history of the commerce clause indicates that it was intended to give the federal government power to regulate commercial transactions which the states could not separately control.

43. *Petroleum Investigations,* 3, pp. 1580–90. According to his testimony on pp. 1574–75, Oliver grew up working in Pennsylvania oil fields and eventually owned and operated his own wells. He worked for the

Marland and Shell Oil companies and served as chairman of the AIMME.

44. Ibid., pp. 1556–68; Pettengill, *Hot Oil!*, pp. 229–38.
45. Ibid.
46. Ibid.
47. Ibid.
48. Ibid.
49. Ibid., p. 1568–73; See N. E. H. Hull, "Some Realism About the Llewellyn–Pound Exchange Over Realism: The Newly Uncovered Private Correspondence, 1927–1931," *Wisconsin Law Review* (1987): 921–69. "While the Realists reacted to Pound's criticism," Hull argued, "they overlooked the fact that the Dean understood the origins and methodology of legal Realism perhaps even better than they did themselves (966)."
50. Ibid.
51. Ibid.
52. Ibid., 3, pp. 1972–94. Meyers earned a Ph.D. in economics from the Brookings School of Economics and Government in 1930, and was graduated from Yale Law School in 1931. In 1930 he published two articles in the *Yale Law Journal* on the legal phases of proration and production control. In the summer of 1931, Meyers came to Texas and Oklahoma in connection with the Champlin case, which made its way up to the U.S. Supreme Court. While employed with the Federal Power Commission in March 1933, Meyers was loaned to the Department of the Interior as an executive secretary of the PAB. He later served as chairman of the Federal Tender Board; Andrew M. Rowley, "Government Official Favors Nationalizing Crude Oil Production," *Oil and Gas Journal* 33 (Nov. 22, 1934): 6–7.
53. Ibid., pp. 2599–621, citing *Chicago Board of Trade v. Olsen*, 262 U.S. 1 (1923). While attending Yale Law School, Marshall collaborated with Norman L. Meyers in publishing two articles on the legal aspects of prorationing. He was a case and comment editor for the *Yale Law Journal* and after graduation worked for the AIMME. In addition to his service on the PAB, Marshall served as special assistant to the U.S. attorney general, special agent of the Division of Investigation of the Department of the Interior, and as a member of the Federal Tender Board.
54. *Petroleum Investigations,* 4, p. 2070–82, citing *Northern Securities v. United States,* 193 U.S. 197 (1904); *Hammer v. Dagenhart,* 247 U.S. 251 (1918); *Champlin Refining Company v. Oklahoma Corporation Commission,* 286 U.S. 210 (1932). Fouts represented the following Texas independent oil operators: J. M. West, West Production Company; Hugh Roy Cullen, Cullen & West, Quintana Oil Company; James S. Abercombie; D. J. Harrison, Harrison Oil Company; Mills Bennet, Liberty Pipe Line

Company, Mills Bennet Producing Company; Woodleigh Petroleum Company; J. R. Parten; George W. Strake, Strake Oil Corporation; Gulf Coast Producing Company; Harry Hanzen; McAlbert Oil Company; Brown & Wheeler; Adrian Moore; D. B. McDaniel; Albert Plumer; and Mike Hogg; Pettengill, *Hot Oil!,* pp. 146–48; Irons, *New Deal Lawyers,* p. 61.

55. Ibid., pp. 2353–61.

56. Ibid., pp. 2477–84.

57. W. P. Z. German, "Federal Regulation of the Oil Industry Carried to Extremes," *Oil and Gas Journal* 33 (Oct. 18, 1934): 45, 50.

58. *Petroleum Investigations,* 4, p. 2108; Johnson, *Petroleum Pipelines and Public Policy,* pp. 222–23; Prindle, *Petroleum Politics,* p. 36; Hugh D. Mallon, "Leaders in Industry Outspoken Before Washington Committee in Opposing Government Control," *Oil and Gas Journal* 33 (Sept. 27, 1934): 8–10, 58.

59. *Petroleum Investigations,* 1, pp. 345–49. Ames practiced law in Oklahoma and moved to New York City in 1923, where he served as general counsel to the Texas Company. After returning to Oklahoma in 1925, Ames went back to New York in 1928 to become vice president of the Texas Company. He resigned in 1932 to serve as API president. In 1933, Ames became chairman of the board of the Texas Company; Mallon, "Leaders in Industry Outspoken . . . in Opposing Government Control," 8–10, 58.

60. Ibid., pp. 375–78. J. Howard Pew, cousin of J. Edgar Pew, joined the Sun Oil Company in 1901, became vice president in 1906, and president in 1912.

61. Ibid., 4, pp. 2027–70; Rowley, "Government Official Favors Nationalizing Crude Oil Production," 6–7.

62. Ibid., 1, pp. 482–92; Mallon, "Leaders in Industry Outspoken . . . in Opposing Government Control," 8–10, 58.

63. Ibid., pp. 232, 247.

64. Ibid., p. 507.

65. Ibid., pp. 514–35.

66. Ibid., pp. 750–56.

67. Ibid., pp. 671–86. Farish testified that an average of 5 million barrels of oil a month had been produced in excess of legal allowables set by the petroleum administrator; Mallon, "Leaders in Industry Outspoken . . . in Opposing Government Control," 8–10, 58; Larson and Porter, *History of Humble Oil,* pp. 483–84.

68. Henry M. Dawes, Untitled Legislative Statement on Petroleum Overproduction Problem, October 25, 1934, copy in VEA, C.F. 14963–4; Dawes to Elkins, October 26, 1934, VEA, C.F. 14963–4; *Petroleum Investigations,* 3, pp. 1728–54; Rowley, "Government Official Favors Nationalizing Crude Oil Production," 6–7.

69. *Petroleum Investigations,* 3, pp. 1602–24; "Divergent Views Developed at Oklahoma City Hearing of Cole Oil Committee," *Oil and Gas Journal* 33 (November 22, 1934): 7.

70. Ibid., 4, pp. 2196–99.

71. Ibid., pp. 2202–2203. Danciger estimated that a few integrated oil companies owned or controlled 95 percent of the transportation facilities, 80 percent of the refining capacity, and 80 percent of the service stations.

72. Ibid., 1, pp. 167–97; Mallon, "Leaders in Industry Outspoken . . . in Opposing Government Control," 8–10, 58.

73. Ibid., 3, pp. 1765–815; Rowley, "Government Official Favors Nationalizing Crude Oil Production," 6–7; *Lockwood's Texas Oil Report,* May 10, 1934 (Confidential Reports on Texas and Southeastern New Mexico Oil Developments published daily at Houston, Texas), copy in VEA, C.F. 14963–4; *Houston Chronicle,* May 9, 1934, 1:1.

74. Ibid., pp. 1727–28; Andrew M. Rowley, "Allred Strongly Opposes Federal Control, Even Temporary; Making Careful Study of Compact Proposal," *Oil and Gas Journal* 33 (Oct. 4, 1934): 8, reported that Allred was elected governor of Texas in 1934 and would assume office in January, 1935; Rowley, "Government Official Favors Nationalizing Crude Oil Production," 6–7.

75. Clark and Halbouty, *The Last Boom,* pp. 219–20; Presley, *Saga of Wealth,* pp. 165–68; Clark, Halbouty, note that the FTB was the brain child of J. Howard Marshall, who took charge of the federal legal effort in East Texas in late 1933. His initial efforts at enforcing the law had been frustrated by wily and unprincipled lawyers schooled in the "real world" practice of law. Marshall learned fast. He traced a hot-oil shipment from East Texas to the Eastern States Refining Company on the Houston Ship Channel, where gasoline processed from the hot oil was shipped by tanker via the Panama Canal to Portland and Seattle and sold to the Fletcher Oil Company in Boise. Marshall went to Boise to obtain an injunction restraining Fletcher from selling the gasoline. During the hearing, Marshall realized that he would have to trace the gasoline back to its origin in the East Texas field to determine who had shipped the hot oil to the Eastern States refinery. The idea occurred to him to devise a system of requiring shippers to provide proof of the oil's origin before it left a field. Marshall returned to East Texas, and the Federal Tender Board was established on October 18, 1934, with its headquarters in Kilgore; *New York Times,* Aug. 24, 1934, 2:5, Aug. 27, 1934, 33:2; Nordhauser, *Quest for Stability,* pp. 149–50; Watkins, *Oil: Conservation or Stabilization?,* pp. 100–101; Order Establishing the Federal Tender Board, copy in VEA, C.F. 10921; U.S. Department of the Interior, Federal Tender Committee, Tender Form, copy in VEA, C.F. 10921.

76. Nordhauser, *Quest for Stability,* p. 150; Presley, *Saga of Wealth,* pp. 168–70; Clark and Halbouty, *The Last Boom,* pp. 222–23; note that Kelliher, a graduate of Boston College and Georgetown Law School, was a former FBI agent who had worked on the Lindbergh kidnapping case and been involved in the manhunts for John Dillinger, "Pretty Boy" Floyd, and "Machine Gun" Kelly. FBI Director J. Edgar Hoover was reportedly so enraged at Ickes for hiring Kelliher that he forbade FBI agents to aid Kelliher in any way. Kelliher met with four independent oilmen who were conservative supporters: H. L. Hunt, Wirt Franklin, Craig Cullinan, and George Heyer. They financed a company of Texas Rangers to aid Kelliher and his 12 investigators in the East Texas oil field.

77. Larson and Porter, *History of Humble Oil,* pp. 484–85; Elkins to McIlvain, June 15, 1934, VEA, C.F. 14963–4; C. D. Lockwood, *Texas Oil Report,* Dec. 15, 1934, copy in VEA, C.F. 14963–3; Minutes of the Annual Meeting of the Texas Petroleum Council, Austin, Texas, Jan. 21, 1935, p. 2, copy in VEA, C.F. 14963–3, W. F. Weeks, the Texas Petroleum Council's East Texas; Thompson Interview, p. 18.

78. Clark, *Energy and the Federal Government,* p. 238; Williamson, et al., *The American Petroleum Industry,* pp. 549–50; Clark, *Oil Century,* p. 196.

79. Clark, *Oil Century,* p. 197; Andrew M. Rowley, "A.P.I. Directors Vote Against Federal Control of Petroleum Industry," *Oil and Gas Journal* 33 (Nov. 22, 1934): 8, 10; "Text of Speech by Harold Ickes," *Lockwood's Texas Oil Reports,* Nov. 14, 1934, copy in VEA, C.F. 14963–4.

80. Clark, *Energy and the Federal Government,* p. 240; Williamson, et al., *The American Petroleum Industry,* p. 550; Zimmermann, *Conservation in the Production Petroleum,* p. 207; Hardwicke, "Legal History," p. 252; Andrew M. Rowley, "Oklahoma Will Initiate Legislation for Interstate Compact; Marland to Call Oil Conference in December," *Oil and Gas Journal* 33 (Oct. 4, 1934): 9; Rowley, "Governors' Conference Against Federal Control," *Oil and Gas Journal* 33 (Dec. 6, 1934): 8–10, 29; Allred to Senator Ben G. Oneal, Nov. 27, 1934, Nov. 28, 1934, Allred Papers, Cont. No. 236; see Northcutt Ely, *Oil Conservation Through Interstate Agreement* (Washington, D.C.: Superintendent of Documents, 1933), p. 217, discussed the legality of an interstate compact.

81. Andrew M. Rowley, "Eight Oil States, Including Texas, Vote for an Interstate Compact," *Oil and Gas Journal* 33 (Jan. 10, 1935): 8, 37.

82. Hugh D. Mallon, "Cole Committee Report May Not Recommend Any Specific Legislation," *Oil and Gas Journal* 33 (Jan. 3, 1935): 6.

83. Clark and Halbouty, *The Last Boom,* p. 226; *New York Times,* Dec. 11, 1934, 4:3; Hugh D. Mallon, "Supreme Court May Not Rule on Code in Amazon–Panama Case," *Oil and Gas Journal* 33 (Dec. 13, 1934): 15, 32.

84. *Panama Refining Company, et al. v. Ryan, et al.,* 293 U.S. 388, 398–405

(1935); Ibid., Brief for Respondents, copy in VEA, C.F. 10921. Stephens cited the *Lottery Case,* 188 U.S. 321 (1902), sustaining a federal law prohibiting the interstate transportation of lottery tickets; *Hippolite Egg Company v. United States,* 220 U.S. 45 (1911), upholding congressional power to prohibit importation of impure food and drugs; *Hoke v. United States,* 227 U.S. 308 (1912), sustaining a federal ban on the transportation of women across state lines for immoral purposes; *Clark Distilling Company v. Western Maryland Railway Company,* 242 U.S. 311 (1916), upholding congressional power to prohibit the interstate transportation of liquor; *Field v. Clark,* 143 U.S. 649 (1892), sanctioning limited delegation of legislative power where it would be impracticable for Congress to provide detailed regulations for various and varying items of management; and *United States v. Grimaud,* 220 U.S. 506 (1911), the Court held, in authorizing the Secretary of Agriculture to meet local conditions, Congress had not delegated legislative power, but merely conferred administrative functions upon an agent; *New York Times,* Dec. 11, 1934, 4:3, Dec. 12, 1934, 27:4, Dec. 14, 1934, 26:6; Mallon, "Supreme Court May Not Rule on Code in Amazon–Panama Case," 15, 32; "Interstate Regulation of 'Hot Oil,'" *Georgetown Law Journal* 23 (Mar., 1935): 487–98.

85. *Panama Refining Company, et al. v. A. D. Ryan, et al.,* Brief for Petitioners (hereafter Petitioner's Brief), copy in VEA, C.F. 10921; Clark and Halbouty, *The Last Boom,* p. 228–29; Presley, *Saga of Wealth,* p. 177; *New York Times,* Dec. 11, 1934, 4:3.

86. Ibid.

87. Petitioner's Brief, VEA, C.F. 10921; *Panama v. Ryan*, 391–98, citing Thomas M. Cooley, *A Treatise on the Constitutional Limitations Which Rest Upon the Legislative Powers of the States of the American Union* (Boston, 1868); Clark and Halbouty, *The Last Boom,* pp. 229–30; *New York Times,* Dec. 11, 1934, 4:3; Mallon, "Supreme Court May Not Rule on Code in Amazon–Panama Case," 15, 32.

88. Clark and Halbouty, *The Last Boom,* p. 226; *New York Times,* Dec. 11, 1934, 4:3.

89. Williamson, et al., *The American Petroleum Industry,* p. 550; Pettengill, *Hot Oil!,* pp. 282–84; Mallon, "Cole Committee Report May Not Recommend Any Specific Legislation," 6; complete text of Cole Committee report on petroleum investigation published in the *Oil and Gas Journal* 33 (Jan. 10, 1935): 14, 36–37; *New York Times,* Jan. 4, 1935, 31:6.

90. *New York Times,* Jan. 8, 1935, 1:3, published full text of decision; "Full Decision of U.S. Supreme Court Invalidating Section 9(c) of Recovery Act; Code Untouched," *Oil and Gas Journal* 33 (Jan. 10, 1935): 10–11, 33–34; *Panama v. Ryan,* 412–15, noted that Article 3 of the petroleum code, which declared production in excess of assigned quotas an unfair

trade practice, had been inadvertently omitted. The government could
therefore not prosecute Panama, Amazon, and other oil producers for
violations incurred prior to September 25, 1933, when the PCC and PAB
amended the code to declare production of oil in excess of state quotas
an unfair trade practice. Hughes refused to rule on this issue since the
provision was nonexistent at the time the *Amazon* and *Panama* cases
were decided by the lower courts. The government's negligence turned
out to be a blessing in disguise, sparing the petroleum code from judicial
review. In numerous instances, the U.S. Supreme Court had reviewed
similar cases involving the issue of congressional delegation of power. It
first considered the issue in *The Cargo of the Aurora Burnsides v. United
States,* 7 Cranch 382 (1813). The cargo of the Aurora Burnsides had
been condemned for being imported from Great Britain in violation of
the Non-Intercourse Act of March 1, 1809. The act expired on May 1,
1810, when Congress passed another act that made revival of the 1809
act dependent upon a presidential proclamation that the edicts of
certain nations had been revoked or modified. The Court upheld the
1810 act. In *Field v. Clark,* 143 U.S. 649 (1892), the Court sustained
Section 3 of the Reciprocal Trade Act of October 1, 1890, which authorized the president to impose duties and exactions upon certain imports.
In *Butterfield v. Stranahan,* 192 U.S. 470 (1904), the Court upheld
Section 3 of the Act of March 2, 1897, which authorized the secretary of
the treasury, upon the recommendation of a board of experts, to establish uniform standards of purity, quality, and fitness for the consumption of imported tea. In *Union Bridge Company v. United States,* 204
U.S. 364 (1906) and *Monongahela Bridge Company v. United States,* 216
U.S. 177 (1909) the Court upheld Section 18 of the Act of March 3, 1899,
which authorized the secretary of war to determine whether bridges and
structures constituted unreasonable obstructions to navigation and to
remove them. In other decisions, the Court sustained legislation creating the Interstate Commerce Commission. In *Radio Commission v.
Nelson Brothers,* 289 U.S. 266 (1933) the Court upheld the Radio Act of
1927, which declared that everyone living in the various zones established by the act were entitled to equality of radio broadcasting service
and conferred authority upon the Federal Radio Commission to make a
fair and equitable allocation of licenses, wavelengths, time for operation, and station power to each of the states according to population.
See Sidney E. McClellan, "The Hot Oil Cases," *Illinois Law Review* 10
(Mar., 1935): 343–49.

91. *Panama v. Ryan,* 417–18, 431–33; *New York Times,* Jan. 8, 1935, 1:3;
"Full Decision of U.S. Supreme Court," 10–11, 33–34; Notes, "Delegation
of Power by Congress—Section 9(c) of Title I, NIRA," *Harvard Law
Review* 48 (Mar., 1935): 798–806, states, "Compared with standards

seeming scarcely less broad and indefinite which have been upheld in previous cases, the declaration of policies in Section 1, Title I, as applied to Section 9(c), does not appear so clearly inadequate as to require the present decision." However, the most crucial issue to the Court in the *Panama* case appeared to be the necessity for Section 9(c). The court had sustained broad executive discretionary powers in wartime legislation, tariff acts, and the Interstate Commerce Commission because it was convinced of the necessity for prompt action, the handling of complex details, and the application of expert knowledge. In contrast, the legislative history of Section 9(c) reveals no reason why its provisions were made permissive rather mandatory. Section 9(c) made no provision for obtaining expert handling, but left the creation of administrative machinery entirely to the president. "The willingness of the Court to uphold legislation intrusting wide discretion to the Interstate Commerce Commission," the article noted, "may be based in some degree on confidence engendered by fair and efficient execution of more limited powers previously granted. No such background existed to lend support to the present statute"; Notes, "Delegation of Legislative Powers—Validity of Act of Congress Conferring Discretionary Authority Upon the President," *New York University Law Quarterly Review* 12 (Mar., 1935): 520–22, notes that the majority opinion in the *Panama* case expressly held that Title I of the NIRA was not a standard but a broad discretionary outline, which left the legislative policy regarding the interstate transportation of hot oil to be declared and defined, if at all, by subsequent sections.

92. Bernard Schwartz, *A History of the Supreme Court* (New York: Oxford University Press, 1993), pp. 229–30, stated, "To [Cardozo], the law was neither an *is* nor an *ought;* it was also an endless *becoming. . . .* Cardozo showed how the common law could be freed to serve present needs— how the judge could be truly innovative while remaining true to the experience of the past"; *Panama v. Ryan,* 433–48; *New York Times,* Jan. 8, 1935, 1:3; "Full Decision of U.S. Supreme Court," 10–11, 33–34; Presley, *Saga of Wealth,* p. 178, Cardozo told his law clerk, "Bill, you tell your friends down at the Interior Department that next time they get one of those orders, to attach 1,500 pages of statistics, tie it up with blue ribbons of the department, call it a finding of fact, and send it up here and put it on Mr. Justice [James C.] McReynolds's desk with the comment, 'You asked for it; now, goddamn it, read it.'" See Emery E. Olson, "Delegation of Legislative Powers—National Industrial Recovery Act," *Southern California Law Review* 8 (Mar., 1935): 226–30, states that Cardozo held that the president must be distinguished from other executive officers who may be required to furnish findings in order to make review more intelligent; "Delegation of Legislative Power—

Section 9(c) of Title I of the National Industrial Recovery Act," *Texas Law Review* 13 (Apr., 1935): 364–66, notes that Cardozo interpreted the act as a whole to find a standard governing executive discretion.

93. *Butterfield v. Stranahan,* 192 U.S. 479 (1904), upheld a statute empowering the secretary of the treasury to establish standards of quality to determine what tea might be imported; *United States v. Grimaud,* 220 U.S. 506 (1911), sustained a statute authorizing the Secretary of the Interior to prescribe rules and regulations for the forest reservations of the nation; *Hampton Jr. v. United States,* 276 U.S. 394 (1928), upheld a statute empowering the president to vary tariff rates in order to equalize production costs; and *New York Central Securities Corporation v. United States,* 287 U.S. 12 (1932), sustained a provision of the Interstate Commerce Act giving the Interstate Commerce Commission power to authorize acquisition of one carrier by another if in the public interest.

94. "Delegation of Legislative Power—NIRA—Panama Case," *California Law Review* 23 (Mar., 1935): 435–38; Notes, "Delegation of Legislative Power to the President—Lack of 'Primary Standard'—The Hot Oil Cases," *Columbia Law Review* 35 (Feb., 1935): 280–81; McClellan, "The Hot Oil Cases," 348; Schwartz, *A History of the Supreme Court,* pp. 232–33.

95. *Panama v. Ryan,* 439–48, Cardozo held, "Plainly, section 1, with its declaration of the will of Congress, is the chart that has been furnished to the President to enable him to shape his course among the reefs and shallows of this act . . . . I am persuaded that a reference, express or implied, to the policy of Congress as declared in section 1 is a sufficient definition of a standard to make the statute valid"; Notes, "Delegation of Legislative Power—NIRA—Panama Case," *California Law Review* 23 (Mar., 1935): 435–38; Lawrence G. Williams, "Direct Federal Control of Petroleum Production," *American Bar Association Journal* 21 (May, 1935): 309–15, citing prior Supreme Court decisions regarding the constitutionality of congressional enactments. In *McCulloch v. Maryland,* 4 Wheaton 316 (1819), Chief Justice John Marshall ruled, "Let the end be legitimate, let it be within the scope of the Constitution, and all means which are appropriate, which are plainly adapted to that end, which are not prohibited, but consist with the letter and spirit of the Constitution, are constitutional." In the *Child Labor Cases,* 247 U.S. 251 (1918) and 259 U.S. 20 (1922), in determining whether a congressional act declared its intent to curtail child labor, the Court held that the means adopted for executing express powers were not necessarily related to the execution of such powers.

96. Quoted in Clark and Halbouty, *The Last Boom,* p. 231.

97. Clark, *Energy and the Federal Government,* p. 239; Irons, *New Deal Lawyers,* p. 73.

Epilogue

1. Williamson, et al., *The American Petroleum Industry,* p. 549–50, 692; Clark, *Energy and the Federal Government,* pp. 239–40; Hardwicke, "Legal History," 252–53; Nordhauser, *Quest for Stability,* pp. 154–55; "Opinions in Texas and Washington Agree That Shipment Regulation Will Continue," *Oil and Gas Journal* 33 (Jan. 10, 1935): 8, 32; Presley, *Saga of Wealth,* pp. 178–79; Clark and Halbouty, *The Last Boom,* pp. 231–32; *Congressional Record,* 74th Cong., 1st Sess. (Jan. 21, 1935) 79, pp. 693–94; Text of the Connally Act published in Pettengill, *Hot Oil!,* pp. 296–300; Zimmermann, *Conservation in the Production of Petroleum,* p. 158; Nash, *United States Oil Policy,* p. 145; Olien and Olien, *Wildcatters,* p. 63; Hugh D. Mallon, "Senate Passes Section; Pettengill Is Doubtful of Its Constitutionality," *Oil and Gas Journal* 33 (Jan. 24, 1935): 8, 32; Mallon, "Federal Tender Board, Senate Oil Investigation Interesting Washington," *Oil and Gas Journal* 33 (Mar. 7, 1935): 10; *New York Times,* Jan. 11, 1935, 27:6, Jan. 23, 1935, 25:2.
2. *Congressional Record,* 74th Cong., 1st. Sess. (Jan. 18, 1935) 79, p. 654, citing U.S. Supreme Court Chief Justice John Marshall's ruling in *Brown v. Maryland,* 12 Wheat. 419 (1827); Mallon, "Senate Passes Section; Pettengill Is Doubtful of Its Constitutionality," 8, 32.
3. *Congressional Record,* 74th Cong., 1st Sess. (Jan. 18, 1935) 79, pp. 654–56, (Feb. 18, 1935) 79, p. 2135.
4. Ibid., pp. 2124–27.
5. Ibid., pp. 2129–30.
6. Hugh D. Mallon, "Amended Connally Bill Is Passed by the House; To Authorize Compact," *Oil and Gas Journal* 33 (Feb. 21, 1935): 10; *New York Times,* Feb. 23, 1935, 6:2, Feb. 24, 1935, 27:4; Williamson, et al., *The American Petroleum Industry,* p. 549; Clark, *Energy and the Federal Government,* p. 239; Murphy, *Conservation of Oil and Gas: A Legal History,* pp. 693–94; Giebelhaus, *Business and Government in the Oil Industry,* p. 216.
7. Andrew M. Rowley, "Conference Approves Interstate Oil Compact; Quick Action Assured," *Oil and Gas Journal* 33 (Feb. 21, 1935): 8–9, 32; text of Interstate Oil Compact published in *Oil and Gas Journal* 33 (Feb. 21, 1935): 9; *New York Times,* Feb. 16, 1935, 19:8, Feb. 17, 1935, II, 9:1; Ernest Thompson, C. V. Terrell, and Lon A. Smith to James V. Allred, Feb. 21, 1935, Allred Papers, Cont. No. 236; John W. Frey, "The Interstate Oil Compact," *Energy Resources and National Policy, Report of the Energy Resources Committee to the United States National Resources Committee* (Washington, D.C.: Government Printing Office, 1939), pp. 397–401. Congress approved the compact on August 27, 1935; Clark, *Oil Century,* pp. 197–98, fn. 3, California did not ratify the

agreement. The following states ratified the measure: Texas, Oklahoma, New Mexico, Kansas, Illinois, and Colorado in 1935; Michigan in 1939; Arkansas, Louisiana, New York, and Pennsylvania in 1941; Kentucky in 1942; Ohio in 1943; Alabama, Florida, Montana, and West Virginia in 1945; Georgia in 1946; Indiana and Tennessee in 1947; Mississippi in 1948; Arizona in 1951; Nevada, Nebraska, North Dakota, Washington, and Alaska in 1953; Oregon in 1954; South Dakota and Wyoming in 1955; and Utah in 1957; see Blakely M. Murphy, "The Interstate Compact to Conserve Oil and Gas: An Experiment in Co-Operative State Production Control," *Mississippi Law Journal* 17 (Mar.–May, 1946): 314–46; Felix Frankfurter and James M. Landis, "The Compact Clause of the Constitution—A Study in Interstate Adjustments," *Yale Law Journal* 34 (May, 1925): 685–758.

8. Clark, *Energy and the Federal Government,* pp. 241–42; Nash, *United States Oil Policy,* pp. 151–52; Ickes, *Secret Diary,* 1, pp. 413–18; "Administrator Ickes Insists That Federal Control of Oil Industry Is Necessary," *Oil and Gas Journal* 33 (Apr. 18, 1935): 12, 25; William E. Leuchtenburg, *Franklin D. Roosevelt and the New Deal, 1932–1940* (New York: Harper & Row, 1963), pp. 150–51.

9. Andrew M. Rowley, "Clashing Opinions at Thomas Bill Hearings in Senate Committee," *Oil and Gas Journal* 33 (Apr. 18, 1935): 12, 25.

10. Hugh D. Mallon, "Changing Opinion in Congress May Force Compromise on NRA," *Oil and Gas Journal* 33 (Apr. 25, 1935): 10; Clark, *Energy and the Federal Government,* p. 242; Nash, *U.S. Oil Policy,* pp. 151–52; Leuchtenburg, *Franklin D. Roosevelt and the New Deal,* pp. 150–51.

11. A group of Texas independent oilmen and lawyers—including Elwood Fouts, Jack Blalock, Hugh Roy Cullen, Mike Hogg, Steve L. Pickney, George W. Strake, Messrs. Brown and Wheeler, Mills Bennett, J. S. Abercombie, D. J. Harrison, Adrian Moore, Hugh Montgomery, and William Kreck—set up a trust account with J. M. West as trustee. As of May 31, 1935, contributions totaled $57,500. The group retained Blalock & Blalock; Amerman and Moore; and Boyle, Wheeler, Gresham & Terrell. PCC Executive Secretary R. B. Brown gave Ickes a list of Texas oilmen who had contributed money to make up the deficit of the Democratic National Committee with the understanding that the Thomas–Disney bill would be defeated. Ickes said, "Here would be the makings of a nice scandal if the Cole bill should pass and it should then appear in the newspapers that it was in return for political contributions made to the Democratic committee." According to J. R. Parten to Elwood Fouts, March 1, 1935, Parten Papers, as cited in Day, "The Oil and Gas Industry and Texas Politics, 1930–1935," pp. 300–301; Ickes, *Secret Diary,* 1, pp. 414–15.

12. Andrew M. Rowley, "Institute Directors Vote Unanimously Against Any

Form of Federal Control," *Oil and Gas Journal* 33 (May 9, 1935): 9;
"IPAA Opposes Federal Control of Oil Industry," *Oil and Gas Journal* 33
(May 9, 1935): 9; Tom Connally to James Allred, 6 May 1935, Allred
Papers, Cont. No. 236.

13. *Schechter Poultry Company v. United States,* 295 U.S. 495 (1935); Ibid.,
    copy of original opinion in VEA, C.F. 10921; Schwartz, *A History of the
    Supreme Court,* pp. 232–33; Williamson, *The American Petroleum
    Industry,* p. 694; Clark, *Energy and the Federal Government,* p. 239;
    Editorial, "Out of the Fog," *Oil and Gas Journal* 33 (May 30, 1935): 24.

14. Hugh D. Mallon, "President Outlines His Views Regarding Legislation
    About Oil," *Oil and Gas Journal* 34 (June 6, 1935): 10; *New York Times,*
    June 5, 1935, 1:8, 8:2.

15. Hugh D. Mallon, "Revised Control Bill To Rivet Federal Rule On Petro-
    leum Industry," *Oil and Gas Journal* 34 (June 20, 1935): 10, 32; Mallon,
    "New Attempts to Obtain Compromise On Federal Oil Legislation," *Oil
    and Gas Journal* 34 (July 11, 1935): 10.

16. W. R. Boyd, Jr., "Government Should Permit Industrial Agreements in
    the Public Interest," *Oil and Gas Journal* 34 (July 18, 1935): 11.

17. L. P. Stockman, "Oil Problem Analyzed in Mineral Law Section, Ameri-
    can Bar Association," *Oil and Gas Journal* 34 (July 25, 1935): 27.

18. Hugh D. Mallon, "Congress Ratifies Interstate Compact; Oil Bills Off
    Until Next Session," *Oil and Gas Journal* 34 (Aug. 29, 1935): 25; *New
    York Times,* Aug. 25, 1935, 27:6.

19. Nordhauser, "Origins of Federal Oil Regulation in the 1920s," 70–71.

20. Clark, *Energy and the Federal Government,* p. 240; Williamson, et al.,
    The American Petroleum Industry, pp. 550–51; Frey, "The Interstate Oil
    Compact," pp. 397–401; Hardwicke, "Legal History," pp. 252–53; Andrew
    M. Rowley, "Oil State Governors Meet Sept. 12 to Form Interstate
    Compact Commission," *Oil and Gas Journal* 34 (Aug. 29, 1935): 25;
    Murphy, *Conservation of Oil and Gas: A Legal History, 1948,* p. 578;
    Clark, *Oil Century,* pp. 198–201, states the central office of the Inter-
    state Compact Commission was established in the State Capitol Build-
    ing in Oklahoma City, Oklahoma. The Interstate Compact Commission's
    activities were financed by voluntary contributions from member-states.
    Each state contributed whatever it deemed appropriate, and outside
    contributions were accepted. Until 1950, the Commission met quarterly
    each year, and since then has met semiannually; Mark S. Adams, "The
    Interstate Compact Act," *The Consumer* 1 (Nov. 1, 1935): 11, copy in the
    Pure Oil Company—Hearings, Legislative Bills, Etc. Through 1941 File,
    VEA, C.F. 14963–3, criticized the Interstate Compact Act for failing to
    include any provision to encourage low cost petroleum production. As
    consumers were not represented on the Interstate Oil Compact Com-
    mission, their interests were remembered only insofar as the oil re-

serves were "being conserved" for their future use—without reference to future price—and their protests were, as far as the formal hearing process went, irrelevant. The report concluded, "The device for keeping price up being what it is, the consumer is licked from the start, even if had a representative. The consumer is confronted with industrial control that, by its oblique approach to price, leaves him out in the cold while its direction is decided in the inner sanctums, that leaves him without representation, and that does not even encourage him with prospects of lower costs—the benefits of which, in any event, might or might not be passed on to him."

21. *Brown v. Humble Oil & Refining Company,* 126 Tex. 296, 83 S.W.2d 935, on rehearing 87 S.W.2d 1069 (Tex. S. Ct. 1935); Ibid., copy of original opinion in Pure Oil Company—Legal Committee, Legal Opinions, Etc. File, VEA, C.F. 14963–6; Robert E. Hardwicke, Jr. to Members of the Legal Committee, Memorandum of Law on *Brown v. Humble Oil & Refining Company,* Oct. 4, 1935, VEA, C.F. 14963–6; "Decision by Texas Supreme Court on Well Spacing Law Far Reaching," *Oil and Gas Journal* 34 (June 20, 1935): 17; L. G. E. Bignell, "Correlative Rights Are Recognized in Texas by Supreme Court Decision," *Oil and Gas Journal* 34 (June 27, 1935): 16–17; Murphy, *Conservation of Oil and Gas: A Legal History, 1948,* p. 713, noted that in *Railroad Commission v. Rowan & Nichols Oil Company,* 310 U.S. 573 (1940), the U.S. Supreme Court held that the issue of the reasonableness of a TRC proration order was a matter for administrative rather than judicial judgment.

22. Nordhauser, *Quest for Stability,* pp. 155–56; Williamson, et al., *The American Petroleum Industry,* p. 692; Hardwicke, "Legal History," pp. 248–51.

23. Thompson to Elkins, Sept. 9, 1935, VEA, C.F. 14963–4; Kelly to Elkins & McIlvain, Nov. 27, 1935, reported the TRC had increased the Van daily allowable by a thousand barrels, to 36,733 barrels per day, VEA, C.F. 14963–4.

24. See Donald G. Nieman, *To Set the Law in Motion: The Freedmen's Bureau and the Legal Rights of Blacks, 1865–1868* (Millwood, N.Y.: KTO Press, 1979), which argues that any fair assessment of the Freedmen's Bureau efforts to provide security for blacks against white violence, oppressive employers, and unequal treatment before the law must take into account the constraints under which it labored.

25. See Hyman, *A More Perfect Union,* which argues that Reconstruction did not revolutionize the federal structure of American government.

Glossary

Aboveground Waste Oil waste caused by either production in excess of storage capacity, loss through natural evaporation, or natural fire hazards due to unnecessary storage of large quantities.

Allowable Maximum quantity of oil or gas to be produced within a given field and within individual leases and wells.

Barrel Standard oil barrel holding 42 U.S., or 35 Imperial, gallons.

Bottom-Hole Pressure The natural gas pressure at the bottom of an oil well, as opposed to tubing-head or casing-head pressure, which is at the surface of the well.

Casing A large pipe inserted into an oil well bore to act as a permanent wall to prevent earth caving and seepage of water.

Casing Head The part of an oil-well casing that protrudes above the surface of the ground.

Choke A steel nipple inserted into the flow pipe to reduce its cross-sectional area in order to regulate a well's oil flow.

Common Law The body of principles and rules of action that derive their authority from usages and customs or from judgments and decrees of courts; distinguished from law created by legislative enactments.

Common Purchaser Any person, association of persons, or company that purchases crude oil and is affiliated—through ownership, control, contract, or otherwise—with a common carrier by pipeline.

Conservation Restrained and orderly production of petroleum to maximize ultimate recovery, avoid waste, and promote efficient use of an unreplenishable natural resource.

Consolidated Actions Act or process of uniting several actions into one trial and judgment, by order of the court, where all the actions are between the same parties, pending in the same court, and involving substantially the same subject matter, issues, and defenses.

Correlative Rights Doctrine applied to the rights of owners to use their land with respect to rights of adjoining or lower landowners in water or oil.

Crude Oil Unrefined petroleum.

Damnum Absque Injuria Loss, hurt, or harm without injury in the legal sense; a loss that does not give rise to an action for damages against the person causing it.

Depletion Allowance A partial federal tax exemption on income from the production and sale of oil and gas.

Dry Hole A completed well that fails to produce oil or gas.

Economic Waste Production in excess of market demand that causes the price of oil to fall below a profitable margin for most producers. Economic waste also includes excessively high costs of production resulting from drilling more wells than necessary to offset drainage by neighboring producers.

Equity Justice administered according to fairness, as contrasted with strictly formulated rules.

Ferae Naturae Of a wild nature or disposition.

Flush Production Operation of an oil well at capacity production under natural gas pressure, without artificial pumping.

Gas-Oil Ratio Proportion of gas to oil produced by a well.

Hot Oil Bootlegged or stolen oil; oil produced in violation of state or federal regulations.

Independent As used in the oil industry, the term is not easily defined. Traditionally, the word has been applied to wildcatters, producers, lease brokers, royalty owners, refiners, retailers, marginal well operators, and even large companies. According to one source, independents are those who "do as they please." Since the 1930s, *independent* has been applied generally to those oil operators and companies remaining after major companies are subtracted from industry ranks.

Injunction A prohibitive, equitable remedy issued or granted by a court at the suit of a party complainant, directed to a party defendant, forbidding the latter to do some act which is unjust and inequitable, injurious to the plaintiff, and cannot be adequately redressed by an action at law.

In Situ In an original place or location, such as oil in its natural underground state.

Integrated Company A company that engages in the four basic functions of the petroleum industry—production, transportation, refining, and marketing.

Judicial Notice Act by which a court, in conducting a trial, or framing its decision, on its own motion, and without the production of evidence, recognizes the existence and truth of certain facts which are universally regarded as established by common notoriety.

Judicial Review Resort to a superior court to review the decision of an inferior court or administrative agency.

Jurisdiction Power and authority of a court to hear and decide a judicial proceeding.

Lease A legal instrument whereby a landowner conveys all or part of the subsurface mineral rights to an operator to drill and produce oil or gas.

Major Shorthand for a major oil company, generally including the largest and most profitable in the world: Exxon, Gulf, Texaco, Mobil, Shell, and Standard Oil. Majors are usually, though not always, *integrated*.

Market Demand The popular need for crude oil at any given time.

Marginal Well Pumping well that produces less than a paying quantity of oil; a well drilled to a depth of 2,000 feet or fewer and produces fewer than 10 barrels a day, or at a depth of between 2,000 and 4,000 feet and produces fewer than 20 barrels per day, or in excess of 4,000 feet and produces fewer than 25 barrels a day.

Natural Gas Pressure Expansive power of natural gas trapped in a porous rock formation.

Offset Well A well drilled for the purpose of counteracting production from a common reservoir by a well on adjoining property.

Operator An individual or company that conducts the drilling of a well, the production of oil from a tract or field, or both of these.

Permeability The ability of a porous rock formation to yield oil.

Physical Waste Either *aboveground* or *underground* oil waste.

Pool An underground accumulation of oil in a single and separate reservoir.

Porosity Capacity of a porous rock formation to contain oil.

Potential Production The estimated oil yield of a completed well at any given time.

Proration Restriction and allocation of petroleum production from a common reservoir or source, usually by a state regulatory agency such as the Texas Railroad Commission.

Proven Acreage Land known to be capable of producing oil or gas.

Ratable Share A stipulated proportion of the full productive capacity of individual wells which operators are allowed to produce.

Res Communes Things used and enjoyed by everyone that can never be exclusively appropriated by an individual.

Reserve Unproduced oil and gas.

Reservoir Porous, permeable rock formation containing oil or gas, or both, and surrounded by less permeable rock.

Res Publicae Things belonging to the public.

Royalty Percentage or portion (usually an eighth) of oil and gas, or its cash equivalent, paid to the land or royalty owner by the leaseholder.

Stripper Well A well that has already yielded most of its oil and produces only a few barrels of oil a day by artificial pumping.

Underground Waste Oil waste occasioned by premature dissipation of reservoir natural gas pressure and by rapid water encroachment, both of which materially lessen the amount ultimately recovered.

Unitization Joint, coordinated development and operation of all leases in an oil field as a single unit to promote efficiency.

Water Drive Water pressure below or along the edges of an oil reservoir that forces oil to the well bore.

Wildcatter An operator who leases and drills for oil in unproven territory.

Bibliography

I. Archival and Manuscript Collections

Allred, James V. Personal Papers. University of Houston. Houston, Texas.

Vinson & Elkins Archives. Houston, Texas. Collection includes the following papers and documents:

Danciger, Joseph C. "Market Demand and Proration: A Scheme for Monopoly."

Dawes, Henry M. Personal Correspondence, 1927–35.

Elkins, James A. Personal Correspondence, 1918–35.

Humphreys–Mexia Oil Company File.

Lockwood's Texas Oil Report, 1934–35.

Mattie Dancy, et al. v. F. L. Peyton, et al. File.

McIlvain, R. W. Personal Correspondence, 1927–35.

Memorandum of Joint Operating Agreement for the Yates Oil Field. September 8, 1927.

Memorandum on Proration Laws of Texas.

Minutes of Committee Representatives of Oil Companies Operating in the Yates Pool. September 2, 1927.

Minutes of General Firm Meeting. November 9, 1927, March 16, 1928, August 14, 1930.

Minutes of the Meeting of Pettus Oil Field Operators, August 13, 1930.

Pure Oil Company Files.

———. *Amazon Petroleum Company v. United States.*

———. Briefs, Memoranda, Etc.

———. Changing Method of Proration at Van, 1932–1936.

———. Legal Committee, Legal Opinions, Etc.

———. Magazines, Newspaper Clippings, Etc.

———. Market Demand: New Conservation Law.

——. *Panama Refining Company v. Ryan.*

——. Proration Matters—Correspondence.

——. *Pure Oil Company vs. Texas Railroad Commission.*

——. Van Field.

——. Van Proration Hearing.

Shepherd, Robert A., Sr. "A Short History of the Firm of Vinson, Elkins, Weems & Searls."

——. "Methods of Proration in Texas Oil Fields."

SoRelle, B. S. Personal Correspondence, 1927–35.

Texas Petroleum Council File.

Texas Railroad Commission. "Oil and Gas Conservation Law and Rules and Regulations for the Conservation of Crude Oil and Natural Gas." *Oil and Gas Circular No. 13.* 1923.

——. Proration Order, August 14, 1930.

——. Special Order Again Amending Rule 1 of Rules and Regulations Adopted to Govern Said [Van] Field, Oil and Gas Docket No. 123, December 31, 1933.

——. Transcript of Investigative Hearing, January 12–14, 19–22, 1933, Tyler, Texas.

——. Transcript of Proration Hearing, Van Oil Field, April 5, 1932, Austin, Texas.

——. September 24, 1932, Fort Worth, Texas.

Van Oil Field Operating Agreement. November 1, 1929.

Van Oil Field Agreement & Assignment File.

II. Public Records

Atlantic Reporter.

California Reports.

Federal Cases.

Federal Oil Conservation Board. *Complete Record of Public Hearings.* Washington, D.C.: Government Printing Office, 1926.

——. *Report of the Federal Oil Conservation Board to the President of the United States.* Parts 1 and 3. Washington, D.C.: Government Printing Office, 1926.

Federal Reporter.

Federal Supplement.

Frey, John W. "The Interstate Oil Compact." In *Energy Resources and National Policy: Report of the Energy Resources Committee to the United States National Resources Committee.* Washington, D.C.: Government Printing Office, 1939.

General Laws of the State of Texas.

House of Lords Reports.

Lewis, James O. "Methods for Increasing the Recovery From Oil Sands." In United States Bureau of Mines. *Bulletin 148, Petroleum Technology.* Washington, D.C.: Government Printing Office, 1917.

Meeson & Welsby's Exchequer Reports.

Ohio Reports.

Oklahoma Reports.

Michigan Reports.

Montana Reports.

Northeastern Reporter.

Pacific Reporter.

Pennsylvania State Reports.

Southwestern Reporter.

Texas Reports.

United States Congress. *Congressional Record.* 73rd–74th Congresses. Washington, D.C.: Government Printing Office, 1933–34.

———. House of Representatives. Committee on Ways and Means. *Hearings on Conservation of Petroleum Pursuant to H. R. 5720,* 73rd Cong., 1st Sess. Washington, D.C.: Government Printing Office,1933.

———. House of Representatives. Committee on Interstate and Foreign Commerce. *Hearings on H. R. 9676 and H. R. 8572, Oil and Gas Pipelines.* 73rd Cong. 2nd Sess. Washington, D.C.: Government Printing Office, 1934.

———. House of Representatives. Subcommittee of the Committee on Interstate and Foreign Commerce. *Hearings on H. R. 441, Petroleum Investigations.* 73rd Cong., recess. 4 vols. Washington, D.C.: Government Printing Office, 1934.

United States Reports.

United States Statutes at Large.

Vernon's Civil Statutes of Texas.

III. Interviews

[Conducted by Irvin May. Transcribed and recorded in the Vinson & Elkins Oral History Collection, Vinson & Elkins Archives, Houston, Texas.]

Baker, Hines H. Interview 20. December 10, 1982.

Baker, Rex Gavin. Interview 20. December 3, 1982.

Cornwall, Gertrude Peddy. Interview 6. July 26, 1982.

Elkins, William S. Interview 10. November 15, 1982.

Fleming, William T. Interview 33. August 26, 1983.

Lawhon, James Griffith. Interview 2. May 17, 1980.

O'Brien, Lois. Interview 4. June 10, 1982.

Plowman, Florris. Interview 14. August 5, 1982.

Pressler, Herman Paul, III. Interview 40. December 3, 1982.

Rice, Ben H. Interview 35. October 11, 1983.
Shepherd, Robert Ashland, Sr. Interview 1. February 13, 1980.
Snodgrass, John C. Interview 42. February 22, 1984.
Thompson, Raybourne, Sr. Interview 5. September 20, 1982.
Weatherly, Thomas B. Interview 9. June 29, 1982.
Williams, Ardell. Interview 18. March 30, 1983.

IV. Selected Cases

Acton v. Blundell, 12 Meeson and Welsby's Exchequer Reports 324 (1843).
Amazon Petroleum Corporation v. Railroad Commission of Texas, et al.,
    5 F.Supp. 633 (E.D. Tex. 1934).
Bailey v. Drexel Furniture Company, 259 U.S. 20 (1922).
Bender v. Brooks, 103 Tex. 329 (Tex.S.Ct. 1910).
Bernard v. Monongahela Gas Company, 216 Penn.St.Reports 362, 65 Atl.
    801 (1907).
Block v. Hirsch, 256 U.S. 135 (1921).
Boxrollium v. Smith, 4 F. Supp. 624 (S.D. Tex. 1933).
Brown v. Humble Oil & Refining Company, 126 Tex. 296, 83 S.W.2d 935
    (Tex.S.Ct. 1935).
Brown v. Maryland, 12 Wheaton 419 (1827).
Brown v. Vandergrift, 80 Penn.St.Reports 142 (1875).
Butterfield v. Stranahan, 192 U.S. 470 (1904).
*Champlin Refining Company v. Corporation Commission of Oklahoma, et
    al.,* 286 U.S. 210 (1932).
Chasemore v. Richards, 7 House of Lords 349 (1859).
Chicago Board of Trade v. Olsen, 262 U.S. 1 (1923).
Child Labor Cases, 247 U.S. 251 (1918).
Clark Distilling Company v. Western Maryland Railway Company, 242 U.S.
    311 (1916).
Constantin, et al. v. Smith, et al., 57 F.2d 227 (E.D. Tex. 1932).
Corzelius v. Railroad Commission of Texas, 161 S.W. 2d 412 (Tex. App.—
    Austin [3rd Dist.] 1944).
Danciger Oil & Refining Company v. Railroad Commission of Texas, 49
    S.W.2d 837 (Tex. App.—Austin [3rd Dist.] 1932), reversed, 56 S.W.2d 1075
    (1933).
Danciger Oil and Refining Company of Texas v. Smith, 4 F. Supp. 236 (N.D.
    Tex. 1933), *cert. denied,* 290 U.S. 599 (1933).
Erie Railroad Company v. Tompkins, 304 U.S. 64 (1938).
Ex Parte Merryman, 17 Fed. Cas. No. 9,487 (1861).
Ex Parte Milligan, 4 Wallace 2 (1866).
*Farmers' Loan and Trust Company v. International Great Northern Railroad
    Company,* 51 F.Supp. 529 (W.D. Tex. 1892).

Field v. Clark, 143 U.S. 649 (1892).

Funk v. Haldeman, 53 Penn.St.Reports 229 (1866).

Gas Products Company v. Rankin, 63 Mont. 372, 207 Pac. 993 (1922).

Gilmore v. Straughan, 10 S.W.2d 589 (Tex.Civ.App.—Austin [3rd Dist.] 1928, no application for writ of error).

Grand Junction Canal Company v. Shugar, 6 L.R. Ch. App. 481 (1871).

Hammer v. Dagenhart, 247 U.S. 251 (1918).

Hampton, Jr. v. United States, 276 U.S. 394 (1911).

Herman v. Thomas, 143 S.W. 195 (Tex.Civ.App. 1911).

Hippolite Egg Company v. United States, 220 U.S. 45 (1911).

Hoke v. United States, 227 U.S. 308 (1912).

Humble Oil & Refining Company v. Strauss, 243 S.W. 528 (Tex.Civ.App.—Amarillo [7th Dist.] 1922, no application for writ of error).

Julian Oil and Royalties Company v. Capshaw, et al., 145 Okla. 237, 292 Pac. 811 (1930).

Kelly v. Ohio Oil Company, 57 Ohio St. 317, 49 N.E. 399 (1897).

Levy Leasing Company v. Siegel, 258 U.S. 242 (1921).

Lindsley v. Natural Carbonic Gas Company, 220 U.S. 61 (1911).

Lottery Case, 188 U.S. 321 (1902).

Luther v. Borden, 7 Howard 1 (1849).

MacMillan, et al. v. Railroad Commission of Texas, et al., 51 F.2d 400 (W.D. Tex. 1931).

Marrs v. City of Oxford, 24 F.2d 541 (D.C. Kansas 1928), affirmed, 32 F.2d 134 (8th Cir. 1929).

Martin v. Mott, 12 Wheaton 19 (1827).

Mattie Dancy, et al. v. F. L. Peyton, et al., 282 S.W. 819 (Tex.Civ.App.—Waco [10th Dist.] 1926).

McCulloch v. Maryland, 4 Wheaton 316 (1819).

Minnesota Rate Cases, 230 U.S. 352 (1913).

Monongahela Bridge Company v. United States, 216 U.S. 177 (1909).

Moyer v. Peabody, 148 Fed. 870 (C.C.D. Colo. 1906).

Moyer v. Peabody, 212 U.S. 78 (1909).

Munn v. Illinois, 94 U.S. 113 (1876).

Murphy Oil Company v. Burnet, 287 U.S. 299 (1932).

New York Central Securities Corporation v. United States, 287 U.S. 12 (1932).

Northern Securities v. United States, 193 U.S. 197 (1904).

Ohio Oil Company v. Indiana, 177 U.S. 190 (1900).

Oxford Oil Company v. Atlantic Oil Producing Company, 16 F.2d 639 (5th Cir. 1927, petition for writ of certiori denied, 277 U.S. 585).

Palmer v. Michigan, 3 Cai.R. 307 (N.Y. 1805).

Panama Refining Company, et al. v. Ryan, et al., 5 F. Supp. 639 (E.D. Tex. 1934), 293 U.S. 388 (1935).

People v. Associated Oil Company, et al., 211 Calif. 93, 294 Pac. 717 (1930).

People's Petroleum Producers v. Sterling, 60 F.2d 1041 (E.D. Tex. 1932).

Platt v. Johnson, 15 Johns. 213 (N.Y. 1818).

Radio Commission v. Nelson Brothers, 289 U.S. 266 (1933).

Railroad Commission v. Bass, 10 S.W.2d 586 (Tex.Civ.App.— Austin [3rd Dist.] 1928, writ of error granted, then dismissed, 51 S.W.2d 1113).

Railroad Commission v. Rowan & Nichols Oil Company, 310 U.S. 573 (1940).

Railroad Commission of Wisconsin v. Chicago, Burlington & Quincy Railroad, 257 U.S. 563 (1922).

Reagan v. Farmers' Loan and Trust Company, 154 U.S. 367 (1894).

Schechter Poultry Company v. United States, 295 U.S. 495 (1935).

Shorey v. Gorrell, (unreported, Mass. 1783).

Shreveport Rate Cases, 234 U.S. 342 (1914).

State v. Jarmon, 25 S.W.2d 936 (Tex.Civ.App.—San Antonio [4th Dist.] 1930, application for writ of error dismissed).

State v. Ohio Oil Company, 150 Ind. 21, 49 N.E. 809 (1898).

State v. Saint Louis, Etc. Railway Company, 165 S.W. 491 (Tex. App.— Austin [3rd Dist.] 1913).

Sterling, et al. v. Constantin, et al., 287 U.S. 378 (1932).

Swift v. Tyson, 16 Pet. 1 (1842).

Texas Company v. Daugherty, 176 S.W. 717 (Tex.S.Ct. 1915).

The Cargo of the Aurora Burnsides v. United States, 7 Cranch 382 (1813).

Tyler v. Wilkinson, Fed. Case No. 14,312 (1827).

Union Bridge Company v. United States, 204 U.S. 364 (1906).

United Mine Workers v. Coronado Coal Company, 259 U.S. 344 (1922), 268 U.S. 295 (1925).

United States v. Grimaud, 220 U.S. 506 (1911).

United States v. Wolters, 268 Fed. 69 (S.D. Tex. 1920).

Utah Power and Light Company v. Post, 286 U.S. 299 (1932).

Walls v. Midland Carbon Company, 254 U.S. 300 (1920).

Weimer v. Bunbury, 30 Mich. 201 (1874).

Westmoreland Natural Gas Company v. DeWitt, et al., 130 Penn. St. Reports 235, 18 Atl. 724 (1889).

V. Books

Adelman, Morris A. *The World Petroleum Market.* Baltimore: Johns Hopkins University Press, 1972.

American Institute of Mining and Metallurgical Engineers. *Petroleum Development and Technology During the Year 1933.* New York: American Institute of Mining and Metallurgical Engineers, 1933.

American Petroleum Institute. *American Petroleum: Supply and Demand, A Report to the Board of Directors of the American Petroleum Institute by a Committee of Eleven Members of the Board.* New York: McGraw–Hill, 1925.

———. *Petroleum Facts and Figures.* New York: American Petroleum Institute, 1930.

———. *Petroleum Facts and Figures.* New York: American Petroleum Institute, 1931.

———. *Petroleum Facts and Figures.* New York: American Petroleum Institute, 1959.

———. *Birth and Development of Oil Proration.* New York: American Petroleum Institute, 1931.

Ball, Max. W. *This Fascinating Oil Business.* New York: Bobbs–Merrill, 1940.

Barr, Allwyn. *Reconstruction to Reform: Texas Politics, 1876–1906.* Austin: University of Texas Press, 1971.

Beaton, Kendall. *Enterprise in Oil: A History of Shell in the United States.* New York: Appleton–Century–Crofts, 1957.

Berenger, Henry. *Le Petrole at al France.* Paris: Flammarion, 1920.

Bird, Kai. *John J. McCloy, The Chairman: The Making of the American Establishment.* New York: Simon & Schuster, 1992.

Blassingame, John W. *The Slave Community: Plantation Life in the Antebellum South.* Oxford: Oxford University Press, 1972.

Branda, Eldon Stephen, ed. *The Handbook of Texas: A Supplement.* Vol. 3. Austin: Texas State Historical Association, 1976.

Buckley, Stuart, ed. *Petroleum Conservation.* New York: American Institute of Mining and Metallurgical Engineers, 1951.

Chandler, Alfred D., Jr. *The Visible Hand: The Managerial Revolution in American Business.* Cambridge, Mass.: Harvard University Press, 1977.

Chase, George, ed. *Blackstone's Commentaries on the Laws of England.* 3rd ed. New York: Banks & Brothers, 1977.

Clark, James A. *Three Stars for the Colonel.* New York: Random House, 1954.

Clark, James A., and Michael T. Halbouty, *Spindletop.* New York: Random House, 1952.

———. *The Last Boom.* New York: Random House, 1972.

Clark, J. Stanley. *The Oil Century: From the Drake Well to the Conservation Era.* Norman: University of Oklahoma Press, 1958.

Clark, John G. *Energy and the Federal Government: Fossil Fuel Policies, 1900–1946.* Urbana: University of Illinois Press, 1987.

Cooley, Thomas M. *Constitutional Limitations Which Rest Upon the Legislative Powers of the States of the American Union.* Boston: Little, Brown, 1883.

Cotner, Robert C. *James Stephen Hogg.* Austin: University of Texas Press, 1959.

Couch, Harvey C. *A History of the Fifth Circuit, 1891–1981.* Washington, D.C.: Bicentennial Committee of the Judicial Conference of the United States, 1983.

deChazeau, Melvin G., and Alfred E. Kahn. *Integration and Competition in the Petroleum Industry.* New Haven: Yale University Press, 1959.

Department of Economic and Social Affairs. *Abstraction and Use of Water: A*

Comparison of Legal Regimes. New York: United Nations Publications, 1922.

Drinker, Henry S. *Legal Ethics.* New York: Columbia University Press, 1953.

Dunne, Gerald T. *Justice Joseph Story and the Rise of the Supreme Court.* New York: Simon & Schuster, 1970.

Ely, Northcutt. "The Use of Federal Powers to Supplement Those of the States." In *Conservation of Oil and Gas: A Legal History, 1948,* edited by Blakely M. Murphy. Chicago: American Bar Association, 1949.

———. *Oil Conservation Through Interstate Agreement.* Washington, D.C.: Superintendent of Documents, 1933.

Engler, Robert. *The Politics of Oil: A Study of Private Power and Democratic Directions.* Chicago: University of Chicago Press, 1961.

Faust, Drew Gilpin. *James Henry Hammond and the Old South: A Design for Mastery.* Baton Rouge: Louisiana State University Press, 1982.

Fegan, Joe R. *Free Enterprise City: Houston in Political–Economic Perspective.* New Brunswick, N.J.: Rutgers University Press, 1988.

Frankel, Paul H. *Essentials of Petroleum.* London: Chapman and Hall, 1946.

Franklin, John Hope. *The Militant South, 1800–1861.* Cambridge, Mass.: Harvard University Press, 1956.

Freyer, Tony. *Forums of Order: The Federal Courts and Business in American History.* Greenwich, Conn.: Jai Press, 1979.

———. *Harmony and Dissonance: The Swift and Erie Cases in American Federalism.* New York: New York University Press, 1981.

Friedman, Leon, and Fred Israel, eds. *The Justices of the United States Supreme Court, 1789–1869: Their Lives and Major Opinions.* New York: Chelsea House, 1969.

Forbath, William E. *Law and the Shaping of the American Labor Movement.* Cambridge, Mass.: Harvard University Press, 1991.

Gammel, H. N. G. *The Laws of Texas, 1827–1897.* Austin: Gammel Book Company, 1898.

Geison, G., ed. *Professions and Professional Ideologies in America.* Chapel Hill: University of North Carolina Press, 1983.

Genovese, Eugene D. *Roll, Jordon, Roll: The World the Slaves Made.* New York: Random House, 1974.

German, W. P. Z. "Legal History of Conservation of Oil and Gas in Oklahoma." In *Legal History of Conservation of Oil and Gas,* edited by Blakely M. Murphy. Chicago: American Bar Association, 1938.

Gibb, George Sweet, and Evelyn H. Knowlton. *History of Standard Oil Company (New Jersey).* Vol. 2: *The Resurgent Years 1911–1917.* New York: Harper & Brothers, 1956.

Gieblehaus, August W. *Business and Government in the Oil Industry: A Case Study of Sun Oil, 1876–1945.* Greenwich, Conn.: Jai Press, 1980.

Gilbert, Chester, and Joseph E. Pogue. *America's Power Resources: The Economic Significance of Coal, Oil, and Water Power.* New York: Century, 1921.

Gill, Stanley. *The Petroleum Industry of the United States.* Report to the
    Subcommittee on Petroleum Investigation of the Committee on Interstate
    and Foreign Commerce, House of Representatives, 73rd Congress.
    Houston: Gulf Publishing, 1934.
Hall, Kermit. *The Magic Mirror: Law in American History.* New York:
    Oxford University Press, 1989.
Hardwicke, Robert E., Jr. *Antitrust Laws et al. v. Unit Operation of Oil or
    Gas Pools.* New York: American Institute of Mining and Metallurgical
    Engineers, 1948.
———. "Texas, 1938–1948." In *Conservation of Oil and Gas, A Legal History,
    1948,* edited by Blakely M. Murphy. Chicago: American Bar Association, 1949.
Harter, Harry. *East Texas Oil Parade.* San Antonio: Naylor Company, 1934.
Hayden, James John. *Federal Regulation of the Production of Oil.* Washing-
    ton: Callaghan and Company, 1929.
Hoffer, Peter Charles. *The Law's Conscience: Equitable Constitutionalism in
    America.* Chapel Hill: University of North Carolina Press, 1990.
Horwitz, Morton J. *The Transformation of American Law, 1780–1860.* Cam-
    bridge, Mass.: Harvard University Press, 1977.
———. *The Transformation of American Law, 1870–1960: The Crisis of Legal
    Orthodoxy:* New York: Oxford University Press, 1992.
Hovenkamp, Herbert. *Enterprise and American Law, 1836–1937.* Cam-
    bridge, Mass.: Harvard University Press, 1991.
Hurst, James Willard. *Law and Conditions of Freedom in the Nineteenth–
    Century United States.* Madison: University of Wisconsin Press, 1967.
Hyman, Harold M. *A More Perfect Union: The Impact of the Civil War and
    Reconstruction on the Constitution.* New York: Alfred E. Knopf, 1973.
Hyman, Harold M. and William M. Wiecek. *Equal Justice Under Law:
    Constitutional Development, 1835–1875.* New York: Harper & Row, 1982.
Ickes Harold L. *The Secret Diary of Harold L. Ickes.* Vol. 1: *The First Thou-
    sand Days, 1933–1936.* New York: Simon & Schuster, 1954.
Irons, Peter H. *The New Deal Lawyers.* Princeton, N.J.: Princeton University
    Press, 1982.
Ise, John. *United States Oil Policy.* New Haven: Yale University Press, 1926.
Johnson, Arthur M. *Petroleum Pipelines and Public Policy, 1906–1959.*
    Cambridge, Mass.: Harvard University Press, 1967.
Johnson, Marguerite. *Houston: The Unknown City, 1836–1946.* College
    Station: Texas A&M University Press, 1991.
Keller, Morton. *Affairs of State: Public Life in Late Nineteenth Century
    America.* Cambridge, Mass.: Harvard University Press, 1977.
———. *Regulating A New Economy: Public Policy and Economic Change in
    America, 1900–1933.* Cambridge, Mass.: Harvard University Press, 1990.
Knowles, Ruth Sheldon. *The Greatest Gamblers: The Epic of American Oil
    Exploration.* Norman: University of Oklahoma Press, 1959.

Kutler, Stanley. *Privilege and Creative Destruction: The Charles River Bridge Case.* Philadelphia: J. B. Lippincott, 1971.

Langdon, Jim C. "Rules of Regulatory Bodies: Texas." *National Institute for Petroleum Landmen.* Vol. 7. Albany, N.Y.: Matthew Bender, 1965.

Larson, Henrietta M., and Kenneth Wiggins Porter. *History of Humble Oil and Refining Company: A Study in Industrial Growth.* New York: Harper & Brothers, 1959.

Larson, Henrietta M.; Evelyn H. Knowlton; and Charles S. Popple. *History of Standard Oil Company (New Jersey).* Vol. 3: *New Horizons, 1927–1950.* New York: Harper & Row, 1971.

Lawson, J. Frederick. "Recent Developments in Pooling and Unitization." In *Institute on Oil and Gas Law and Taxation.* Albany, N.Y.: Matthew Bender, 1972.

Leuchtenburg, William E. *Franklin D. Roosevelt and the New Deal, 1932–1940.* New York: Harper & Row, 1963.

Lipartito, Kenneth J. and Joseph A. Pratt. *Baker & Botts in the Development of Modern Houston.* Austin: University of Texas Press, 1991.

Logan, Leonard M., Jr. *Stabilization of the Petroleum Industry.* Norman: University of Oklahoma Press, 1930.

Lovejoy, Wallace M., and James I. Pikl, eds. *Essays on Petroleum Conservation Regulation.* Dallas: Southern Methodist University, 1960.

Luban, David. *Lawyers and Justice: An Ethical Study.* Princeton, N.J.: Princeton University Press, 1988.

McClellan, James. *Joseph Story and the American Constitution.* Norman: University of Oklahoma Press, 1971.

McDaniel, Ruel. *Some Ran Hot.* Dallas: Regional Press, 1939.

McDonald, Stephen L. *Petroleum Conservation in the United States: An Economic Analysis.* Baltimore: Johns Hopkins University Press, 1971.

McLean, John G. and Robert W. Haigh. *The Growth of Integrated Oil Companies.* Boston: Harvard Business School, 1954.

McMath, Robert C., Jr. *Populist Vanguard: A History of the Southern Farmers' Alliance.* Chapel Hill: University of North Carolina Press, 1975.

Mid-Continent Oil and Gas Association. *Handbook on Unitization of Oil Pools.* Saint Louis: Blackwell Wielandy, 1930.

Mills, Warren E., Jr. *Martial Law in East Texas.* Indianapolis: Bobbs–Merrill, 1960.

Mossburg, Lewis G., Jr. *Handbook on Petroleum Land Titles.* Oklahoma City: The Institute for Energy Development, 1976.

Murphy, Blakely M., ed. *Legal History of Conservation of Oil and Gas.* Chicago: American Bar Association, 1938.

Knowles, Ruth Sheldon. *The Greatest Gamblers: The Epic of American Oil Exploration.* Norman: University of Oklahoma Press, 1959.

———. *Conservation of Oil and Gas: A Legal History.* Chicago: American Bar Association, 1949.

Nash, Gerald D. *United States Oil Policy, 1890–1964: Business and Government in Twentieth Century America.* Pittsburgh: University of Pittsburgh Press, 1968.

Nelson, R. L., D. M. Trubek, and R. L. Solomon, eds. *Lawyers' Ideals and Lawyers' Practices: Transformations in the American Legal Profession.* Ithaca, N.Y.: Cornell University Press, 1992.

Nelson, William E. *The Americanization of the Common Law: The Impact of Legal Change on Massachusetts Society, 1760–1830.* Cambridge, Mass.: Harvard University Press, 1975.

Newmyer, R. Kent. *Supreme Court Justice Joseph Story: Statesman of the Old Republic.* Chapel Hill: University of North Carolina Press, 1985.

Nieman, Donald G. *To Set the Law in Motion: The Freedmen's Bureau and the Legal Rights of Blacks, 1865–1868.* Millwood, N.Y.: KTO Press, 1979.

Nordhauser, Norman E. *The Quest for Stability: Domestic Oil Regulation, 1917–1935 .* New York: Garland Publishing, 1979.

Nugent, James E. "The History, Purpose, and Organization of the Railroad Commission." In *Oil and Gas: Texas Railroad Commission Rules and Regulations.* Austin: State Bar of Texas, 1982.

O'Conner, Richard. *The Oil Barons: Men of Greed and Grandeur.* Boston: Little, Brown, 1971.

Olien, Roger M., and Diana Davids Olien. *Wildcatters: Texas Independent Oilmen.* Austin: Texas Monthly Press, 1984.

Owen, Edgar Wesley. *Trek of the Oil Finders: A History of Exploration for Petroleum.* Tulsa: American Association of Petroleum Geologists, 1975.

Paul, Arnold M. *Conservative Crisis and the Rule of Law: Attitudes of Bar and Bench, 1887–1895.* Ithaca, N.Y.: Cornell University Press, 1960.

Penrose, Edith. *The International Petroleum Industry.* Cambridge, Mass.: Massachusetts Institute of Technology Press, 1968.

Pogue, Joseph E. *The Economics of Petroleum.* New York: John Wiley & Sons, 1921.

Posner, Richard A. *The Problems of Jurisprudence.* Cambridge, Mass.: Harvard University Press, 1990.

Potter, David M. *The Impending Crisis, 1848–1861.* New York: Harper & Row, 1976.

Pratt, Joseph A. *The Growth of a Refining Region.* Greenwich, Conn.: Jai Press, 1980.

Presley, James. *A Saga of Wealth: The Rise of the Texas Oilmen.* Austin: Texas Monthly Press, 1983.

Prindle, David. *Petroleum Politics and the Texas Railroad Commission.* Austin: University of Texas Press, 1981.

Proctor, Ben H. *Not Without Honor: The Life of John H. Reagan.* Austin: University of Texas Press, 1962.

Rister, Carl Coke. *Oil!: Titan of the Southwest.* Norman: University of Oklahoma Press, 1949.

Rostow, Eugene V. *A National Policy for the Oil Industry.* New Haven: Yale University Press, 1948.

Rudden, Bernard. *The New River: A Legal History.* Oxford: Clarendon Press, 1985.

Schieber, Harry M. "Property Law, Expropriation, and Resource Allocation by Government." In *American Law and the Constitutional Order: Historical Perspectives,* edited by Lawrence M. Friedman and Harry M. Schieber. Cambridge, Mass.: Harvard University Press, 1977.

———. "The Road to *Munn*: Eminent Domain and the Concept of Public Purpose in State Courts." In *Perspectives in American History.* Cambridge, Mass.: Harvard University Press, 1971.

Schlesinger, Arthur M., Jr. *The Age of Roosevelt.* Vol. 2: *The Politics of Upheaval.* Boston: Houghton Mifflin Company, 1958.

Schurr, Sam H.; Bruce Netschert; Vera Eliasberg; Joseph Lerner; and Hans H. Landsberg. *Energy in the American Economy, 1850–1975: An Economic Study of Its History and Prospects.* Baltimore: Johns Hopkins University Press, 1960.

Schwartz, Bernard. *A History of the Supreme Court.* New York: Oxford University Press, 1993.

Speiser, Stuart M. *Lawyers and the American Dream.* New York: M. Evans and Company, 1993.

Spratt, John S. *The Road to Spindletop: Economic Change in Texas.* Dallas: Southern Methodist University Press, 1955. Reprint, Austin: University of Texas Press, 1983.

Stocking, George Ward. *The Oil Industry and the Competitive System: A Study in Waste.* Boston: Houghton Mifflin, 1925.

Sweet, George L. *Gentlemen in Oil.* Los Angeles: Science Press, 1966.

Texas Railroad Commission. *Thirty-Ninth Annual Report of the Railroad Commission of Texas, Covering Railroad and Express Transportation for the Year 1930.* Austin: Von Boeckmann–Jones Company, 1931.

Thornton, William Wheeler. *The Law of Oil and Gas.* 5th ed. Cincinnati: W. H. Anderson, 1932.

Tiedeman, Christopher G. *A Treatise on the Limitations of Police Power in the United States.* Saint Louis: F. H. Thomas, 1886.

Tiffany, Herbert Thorndike. *The Law of Real Property.* 2nd ed. Chicago: Callaghan, 1920.

Trelease, Frank J. *Cases and Materials on Water Law: Resource Use and Environmental Protection.* 2nd ed. Saint Paul, Minn.: West Publishing Company, 1974.

Underwood, Richard H., and William H. Fortune. *Trial Ethics.* Boston: Little, Brown, 1988.

Urofsky, Melvin I. *A March of Liberty: A Constitutional History of the United States.* New York: Alfred A. Knopf, 1988.

Warner, C. A. *Texas Oil and Gas Since 1543.* Houston: Gulf Publishing Company, 1939.

Watkins, Myron W. *Oil: Stabilization or Conservation?: A Case Study in the Organization of Industrial Control.* New York: Harper & Row, 1937.

Weaver, Jacqueline Lang. *Unitization of Oil and Gas Fields in Texas: A Study of Legislative, Administrative, and Judicial Policies.* Washington: Resources for the Future, 1986.

Williams, Howard R., and Charles J. Meyers. *Oil and Gas Law.* Albany, N.Y.: Matthew Bender, 1980.

Williamson, Harold F.; Ralph L. Andreano; Arnold R. Daum; and Gilbert C. Klose. *The American Petroleum Industry* . Vol. 2: *The Age of Energy, 1899–1959.* Evanston, Ill.: Northwestern University Press, 1963.

Williamson, Rene de Visme. *The Politics of Planning in the Oil Industry Under the Code.* New York: Harper & Brothers, 1936.

Wise, Raymond L. *Legal Ethics.* New York: Matthew Bender, 1970.

———. *Legal Ethics: 1979 Supplement.* New York: Matthew Bender, 1979.

Yergin, Daniel. *The Prize: The Epic Quest for Oil, Money, and Power.* New York: Simon & Schuster, 1991.

Zelden, Charles L. *Justice Lies in the District: The U.S. District Court, Southern District of Texas, 1902–1960.* College Station: Texas A&M University Press, 1993.

Zimmermann, Erich W. *Conservation in the Production of Petroleum: Study in Industrial Control.* New Haven: Yale University Press, 1957.

VI. Journal and Periodical Articles

Adams, John Stokes. "The Right of A Landowner to Oil and Gas in His Land." *Pennsylvania Law Review* 63 (April, 1915): 471–89.

Adams, Mark S. "The Interstate Compact Act." *The Consumer* 1 (November 1, 1935): 11.

"Administrator Ickes Insists That Federal Control of Oil Industry Is Necessary." *Oil and Gas Journal* 33 (April 18, 1935): 12, 25.

"Allowable Production in Texas Reduced by New State Order." *Oil and Gas Journal* 29 (January 29, 1931): 169–70.

"Allred Protests Entertaining Hearsay Testimony Before the Texas Legislative Investigation." *Oil and Gas Journal* 31 (February 16, 1933): 10, 16.

Ambrose, A. W. "Only 20 Percent of Oil Is Recovered." *Oil and Gas Journal* 18 (October 10, 1919): 62, 66.

American Petroleum Institute. "World Production and Consumption of Petroleum." *Oil and Gas Journal* 27 (April 4, 1929): 47.

Ames, C. B. "East Texas Situation as Seen by President Ames Put Before Texas Oil and Gas Association." *Oil and Gas Journal* 31 (January 12, 1933): 9, 30.

"Ames Holds State Power Is Unimpaired by Decision of the Supreme Court." *Oil and Gas Journal* 31 (December 22, 1932): 13.

Angel, Joseph. "The Law of Water Privileges." *The American Jurist and Law Magazine* 2 (July–October, 1829): 25–38.

"Application for New Injunction." *Oil and Gas Journal* 32 (May 18, 1933): 16.

Ballantine, Henry Winthrop. "Military Dictatorship in California and West Virginia," *California Law Review* 1 (July, 1913): 413–26.

———. "Unconstitutional Claims of Military Authority." *Yale Law Journal* 24 (1915): 189–216.

Beaty, Amos L. "Texas Law Declared Outstanding Achievement in President Beaty's Address to Institute." *Oil and Gas Journal* 31 (November 7, 1932): 24, 46.

———. "Federal Control of Petroleum Production." *American Bar Association Journal* 20 (June, 1934): 349–52.

Bennet, John K. "Some Fundamentals of Legal Interests in Water Supplies." *Southern California Law Review* 22 (December, 1948): 1–15.

Berger, Lawrence. "The Public Use Requirement in Eminent Domain." *Oregon Law Review* 57 (1978): 203–46.

Beuscher, J. H. "Appropriation Water Law Elements in Riparian Doctrine." *Buffalo Law Review* 10 (1960–61): 448–58.

Bignell, L. G. E. "Texas Railroad Commission Has the Authority to Prevent Imminent Waste of Oil and Gas." *Oil and Gas Journal* 31 (August 4, 1932): 10–11.

———. "New Method of Prorating East Texas Forward Step; May Extend Plan to Cover all Fields." *Oil and Gas Journal* 31 (December 8, 1932): 8–9.

———. "High Allowable in East Texas Field Will Result in Early Reduction to Pumping Conditions." *Oil and Gas Journal* 31 (April 27, 1933): 11, 16.

———. "Recent Orgy of Drilling in East Texas Field Has Definitely Shortened the Flowing Life." *Oil and Gas Journal* 31 (May 18, 1933): 10–11, 17–18.

———. "Correlative Rights Are Recognized in Texas by Supreme Court Decision." *Oil and Gas Journal* 34 (June 27, 1935): 16–17.

"Bill Being Prepared at Washington for Federal Dictator of the Oil Industry." *Oil and Gas Journal* 31 (May 4, 1933): 32.

"Bill Reported Favorably by House Committee; May be Approved Before End of Week." *Oil and Gas Journal* 31 (November 10, 1932): 8, 31.

Blankenhorn, Dana. "James A. Elkins, Sr.: For Half a Century, 'The Judge' Held Reigns of Houston Power." *Houston Business Journal* (September 24, 1984): 1, 4–6.

Bloomfield, Maxwell. "The Texas Bar in the Nineteenth Century." *Vanderbilt Law Review* 32 (1979): 261–76.

Boyd, W. R., Jr. "Government Should Permit Industrial Agreements in the Public Interest." *Oil and Gas Journal* 34 (July 18, 1935): 11.

Bredberg, L. E. "Texans Approve further Curtailment." *Oil and Gas Journal* 29 (June 26, 1930): 58.

———. "Unit Plan Wrought Big Change in Van, Texas." *Oil and Gas Journal* 29 (August 14, 1930): 39, 111.

———. "Texas Prorationing Seems A Step Nearer." *Oil and Gas Journal* 29 (August 7, 1930): 29, 110.

———. "All Roads Seem to Lead to East Texas." *Oil and Gas Journal* 29 (February 5, 1931): 22–23, 111.

———. "East Central Texas Proration Meeting." *Oil and Gas Journal* 29 (January 22, 1931): 21.

———. "East Texas Fields Under Military Rule." *Oil and Gas Journal* 30 (August 27, 1931): 13, 106, 109.

———. "Five East Texas Associations Affiliate In One Organization." *Oil and Gas Journal* 30 (September 17, 1931): 13, 32.

———. "Texans Organize to Conserve Oil and Gas." *Oil and Gas Journal* 30 (November 12, 1931): 156.

———. "Engineers Studying Plans for Equitable System of Proration in East Texas." *Oil and Gas Journal* 31 (November 3, 1932): 11.

———. "First Annual Meeting of the Texas Oil and Gas Association Is Held at Fort Worth, Texas." *Oil and Gas Journal* 31 (January 12, 1933): 9, 32.

———. "Commission Opens East Texas Hearing at Tyler by Questioning Purchasers and Pipe Lines." *Oil and Gas Journal* 31 (January 19, 1933): 7, 23.

———. "Railroad Commission Adjourns Its Probe Into Proration Observance in East Texas Area." *Oil and Gas Journal* 31 (January 26, 1933): 13.

———. "Commission Is Tightening Control of East Texas; Legislature Discusses Appointive Body." *Oil and Gas Journal* 31 (February 2, 1933): 30.

———. "East Texas Crisis Is Rapidly Approaching Climax; Must Either Cut Production or Price of Oil." *Oil and Gas Journal* 31 (March 16, 1933): 9, 25.

———. "East Texas Tests Completed; New Order Friday; Many Violations During the Shut In Period." *Oil and Gas Journal* 31 (April 20, 1933): 43.

———. "Renewed Hope for Proration in East Texas Area; Field Shut Down Awaiting Test of Key Wells." *Oil and Gas Journal* 31 (April 13, 1933): 45.

———. "New Order and Cut Hits East Texas Violators; Test in Federal Court to Follow Immediately." *Oil and Gas Journal* 31 (April 27, 1933): 42.

———. "Flood of Oil is Pouring From East Texas Area; Watching Effect on Bottom Hole Pressure." *Oil and Gas Journal* 31 (May 4,1933): 14.

———. "Texas Commission Asks President Roosevelt to Ban Interstate Transportation of Hot Oil." *Oil and Gas Journal* 32 (July 13, 1933): 45.

———. "Law Making Proration Violation Felony helping to Tighten Enforcement in East Texas Field." *Oil and Gas Journal* 32 (September 7, 1933): 41.

———. "Reduction in East Texas Allowable Now Causes Feverish Search for Pipe Line Connections." *Oil and Gas Journal* 32 (September 14, 1933): 42.

———. "Hot Oil Production in East Texas Now Estimated at 27,000 Barrels Daily." *Oil and Gas Journal* 32 (December 21, 1933): 7.

———. "Hot Oil Situation in East Texas Will Not Get Better Until the Violators Can Be Jailed." *Oil and Gas Journal* 32 (December 14, 1933): 10.

———. "Federal Court Upholds State Regulation in Texas; Bryant Would Restrict Federal Intervention." *Oil and Gas Journal* 32 (February 15, 1934): 13, 32.

———. "Hearing on Oil Bills in Progress at Austin, Texas; Hot Oil Situation Is Forcing State Action." *Oil and Gas Journal* 33 (March 8, 1934): 8.

"Briefs to be Filed by Opposing Sides in East Texas Case." *Oil and Gas Journal* 32 (October 12, 1933): 28.

Brooks, Raymond. "Lucey Has New Plan for East Texas." *Oil and Gas Journal* 30 (July 2, 1931): 13.

Bruce, Andrew A. "The Oil Cases and the Public Interest." *American Bar Association Journal* 19 (February, 1933): 82–86.

———. "The Oil Cases and the Public Interest—II." *American Bar Association Journal* 19 (March, 1933): 168–72.

"Cannot Last Long." *Oil and Gas Journal* 31 (April 27, 1933): 20.

Childs, William R. "The Transformation of the Railroad Commission of Texas, 1917–1940: Business-Government Relations and the Importance of Personality, Agency Culture, and Regional Differences." *Business History Review* 65 (Summer, 1991): 285–344.

"Commission Holds East Texas to 325,000 Barrels on Bottom Hole Pressure—Acreage Basis." *Oil and Gas Journal* 31 (December 1, 1932): 9.

"Commission Opens Case by Statement Criticizing Tactics of Obstruction." *Oil and Gas Journal* 31 (January 5, 1933): 8.

"Commission Orders Proration for Hendrick Field." *Oil Weekly* 49 (April 27, 1928): 27.

"Commission Rule Back in Texas." *Oil and Gas Journal* 31 (March 3, 1932): 13, 87.

"Commission Withholds Order on East Texas Awaiting Protests from Producers." *Oil and Gas Journal* 31 (June 30, 1932): 8.

"Complete Revised Text of Federal Petroleum Act Sent to Congress by Administrator Ickes." *Oil and Gas Journal* 33 (May 3,1934): 10, 17–18.

Conine, Robert C. "Independents and Majors Unanimously Approve Code of Fair Competition for Oil Industry." *Oil and Gas Journal* 32 (June 22, 1933): 6–7, 26.

Constant, Edward II. "Cause or Consequence: Science, Technology, and Regulatory Change in the Oil Business in Texas, 1930–1975." *Technology and Culture* 30 (April, 1989): 426–55.

Corwin, Harold B. "Hot Oil Cases." *The George Washington Law Review* 3 (March, 1935): 391–94.

Crane, M. M. "Recollections of the Establishment of the Texas Railroad Commission." *Southwestern Historical Quarterly* 50 (1947): 478–86.

"Court Decides Proration Order of Commission Are Usurpations." *Oil and Gas Journal* 30 (July 30, 1931): 155.

Davis, Wallace. "Limitation of Crude Output to Regional Committees." *Oil Weekly* 53 (March 22, 1929): 19.

"Decision by Texas Supreme Court on Well Spacing Law Far Reaching." *Oil and Journal* 34 (June 20, 1935): 17.

"Decision of Federal Bench Challenged by Texas Court." *Oil and Gas Journal* 30 (March 31, 1932): 155.

"Delegation of Legislative Power—NIRA—Panama Case." *California Law Review* 23 (March, 1935): 435–38.

"Delegation of Legislative Power—Section 9 (c) of Title I of the National Industrial Recovery Act." *Texas Law Review* 13 (April, 1935): 364–66.

"Delegation of Legislative Power to the President—Lack of 'Primary Standard'—The Hot Oil Cases." *Columbia Law Review* 35 (February, 1935): 280–82.

"Delegation of Legislative Powers—Validity of Act of Congress Conferring Discretionary Authority Upon the President." *New York University Law Quarterly Review* 12 (March, 1935): 520–22.

"Delegation of Power by Congress." *Harvard Law Review* 48 (March, 1935): 798–806.

"Divergent Views developed at Oklahoma City Hearing of Cole Committee." *Oil and Gas Journal* 33 (November 22, 1934): 7.

"Drastic Change in Pipe Line Laws Before Texas Legislature." *Oil Weekly* 56 (March 7, 1930): 21.

"East Texans Declare Field Shall Not be Opened to Ruinous Overproduction." *Oil and Gas Journal* 31 (November 3, 1932): 32.

"East Texas Claim for Cuts in Other Districts Heard by State Railroad Commission." *Oil and Gas Journal* 31 (July 14, 1932): 8.

"East Texas Crude Cut to 10 Cents Barrel." *Oil and Gas Journal* 31 (April 27, 1933): 26.

"East Texas Cut to 165 Barrels Per Well in Revised Order." *Oil and Gas Journal* 30 (October 15, 1931): 13.

Ely, Northcutt. "The Conservation of Oil." *Harvard Law Review* 51 (1938): 1209–44.

Fairman, Charles. "Martial Law, In Light of Sterling v. Constantin." *Cornell Law Quarterly* 19 (December, 1933): 20–34.

Farish, William S. "A Rational Plan for the Oil Industry." *Oil and Gas Journal* 31 (October 6, 1931): 12–14.

———. "Problems of Preventing Waste of Oil and Gas and Stabilizing the Petroleum Industry." *Oil and Gas Journal* 31 (June 30, 1932): 10–12.

"Federal Court Upsets Old Rules of East Texas; Approves Oklahoma System as Model." *Oil and Gas Journal* 31 (March 23, 1933): 8, 28.

"Federal Court in Texas Asks Producers to Stop Wrangling and Go to U.S. Supreme Court." *Oil and Gas Journal* 32 (June 1, 1933): 9, 18.

"Federal Regulations Banning Transportation of Hot Oil Put Into Effect Promptly in East Texas." *Oil and Gas Journal* 32 (July 20, 1933): 7, 30.

Ford, Donald H. "Controlling the Production of Oil." *Michigan Law Review* 30 (June, 1932): 1170–1223.

Frankfurter, Felix, and James M. Landis. "The Compact Clause of the Constitution—A Study in Interstate Adjustments." *Yale Law Journal* 34 (May, 1925): 685–758.

Friedman, Alan E. "The Economics of the Common Pool: Property Rights in Exhaustible Resources." *U.C.L.A. Law Review* 18 (1975): 855–87.

"Full Decision of U.S. Supreme Court Invalidating Section 9 (c) of Recovery Act; Code Untouched." *Oil and Gas Journal* 33 (January 10, 1935): 10–11, 33–34.

German, W. P. Z. "Federal Regulation of the Oil Industry Carried to Extremes." *Oil and Gas Journal* 33 (October 18, 1934): 45, 50.

Gilmer, Daffan. "Early Courts and Lawyers in Texas." *Texas Law Review* 12 (1934): 435–52.

Gray, Henry M. "Need Extension of Conservation Laws: Concrete Statutes Must Replace Court-Made Law." *Oil and Gas Journal* 30 (July 23, 1931): 24, 98.

"Greed Versus Proration in Texas." *Oil and Gas Journal* 30 (July 2, 1931): 14, 115.

Greer, D. Edward. "The Ownership of Petroleum Oil and Natural Gas in Place." *Texas Law Review* 1 (1923): 162–87.

Hardin, Garrett. "The Tragedy of the Commons." *Science* 162 (December 13, 1968): 1243–48.

Hardwicke, Robert E., Jr. "The Rule of Capture and its Implications as Applied to Oil and Gas." *Texas Law Review* 13 (June, 1935): 391–422.

———. "Limitation of Oil Production to Market Demand. Review of Legislation Shows Confusion" *Oil and Gas Journal* 31 (October 6, 1931): 54–55.

———. "Ratable Taking API Meeting Keynote." *Oil and Gas Journal* 30 (June 11, 1931): 15, 104.

———. "Legal Aspects of Oil Conservation." *Oil and Gas Journal* 30 (June 25, 1931): 17, 125.

Harriman, Henry I. "The Stabilization of Business and Employment." *American Economic Review* 22 (March, 1932): 63–74.

Hart, James P. "Oil, the Courts, and the Railroad Commission." *Southwestern Historical Quarterly* 44 (January, 1941): 303–20.

"Hearing on Texas Proration Rules." *Oil and Gas Journal* 30 (September 3, 1931): 77–79, 99.

Heermance, Edgar L. "Self-Regulation and the Law." *Harvard Business Review* 10 (July, 1932): 420–29.

"Historic Decision on Martial Law in East Texas Defines the Power of Governor and Courts." *Oil and Gas Journal* 31 (December 15, 1932): 13–14, 30–32.

Hobbs, Bonnie. "Lawyers' Papers: Confidentiality Versus the Claims of History." *Washington and Lee Law Review* 49 (1992): 179–211.

Hull, N. E. H. "Some Realism About the Llewellyn-Pound Exchange Over Realism: The Newly Uncovered Private Correspondence, 1927–1931." *Wisconsin Law Review* (1987): 921–69.

"Humble Cuts Crude Prices as Result of Flood of Oil From East Texas Fields." *Oil and Gas Journal* 31 (May 4, 1933): 9.

Hutcheson, Joseph C., Jr. "A Case for Three Judges." *Harvard Law Review* 47 (March, 1934): 795–826.

———. "The Judgment Intuitive: The Function of the 'Hunch' in Judicial Decision." *Cornell Law Quarterly* 14 (February, 1929): 274–88.

Hyder, Elton M., Jr. "Some Difficulties in the Application of the Exceptions to the Spacing Rule in Texas." *Texas Law Review* 27 (1949): 481–512.

"Ickes Declares Oil Industry Perfect Example of Unchecked and Ruthless Exploitation." *Oil and Gas Journal* 32 (March 1, 1934): 16.

"Interstate Regulation of Hot Oil." *Georgetown Law Journal* 23 (March, 1935): 487–98.

"Investigation Division Ready to Enforce Code." *Oil and Gas Journal* 32 (December 14, 1933): 32.

"IPA of Texas Opposes Present Proration Rules." *Oil and Gas Journal* 31 (December 15, 1931): 31.

"IPPA Opposes Federal Control of Oil Industry." *Oil and Gas Journal* 33 (May 9, 1935): 9.

"Is Proration Doomed?" *Oil and Gas Journal* 31 (January 5, 1933): 18.

Johnson, Bobby H. "Oil in the Pea Patch." *East Texas Historical Journal* 13 (Spring, 1975): 34–42.

Johnston, Albert C. "Governmental Limitations on Oil Production." *The George Washington Law Review* 2 (May, 1934): 474–86.

Kern, Charles, E. "James E. O'Neal Gives Testimony." *Oil and Gas Journal* 21 (December 28, 1922): 70, 72.

———. "Second Day's Oil Conference Session." *Oil and Gas Journal* 29 (January 22, 1931): 23, 117.

———. "Governors of Oil-Producing States Are Invited to Attend Business Restoration Conference." *Oil and Gas Journal* 31 (March 23, 1933): 8.

———. "Roosevelt Is Asked to Appoint Oil Supervisor and to Shut In Flush Wells Until April 15." *Oil and Gas Journal* 31 (March 30, 1933): 11, 30.

———. "Senate Finance Committee Holds Oil Hearing on Industry Recovery and Marland–Ickes Bills." *Oil and Gas Journal* 32 (June 1, 1933): 9, 18.

———. "Roosevelt Hopes States Will Aid Oil Industry; Favors Divorcement of Interstate Pipe Lines." *Oil and Gas Journal* 31 (April 6, 1933): 9.

———. "Oil Code Hearing Set at Washington Monday; Statement by the Recovery Administration." *Oil and Gas Journal* 32 (July 20, 1933): 6, 30.

———. "Labor Provisions Prove Troublesome at Hearings on Oil Industry's Code for Fair Competition." *Oil and Gas Journal* 32 (July 27, 1933): 7.

———. "Federal Allocation of Production Stipulated in Government's Code for Petroleum Industry." *Oil and Gas Journal* 32 (August 3, 1933): 6–8.

———. "General Johnson at Work on Revised Oil Code Following Stormy Hearings at Washington." *Oil and Gas Journal* 32 (August 10, 1933): 9–10, 32.

———. "Oil Code Signed by President to be Revised Before It Is Put Into Effect September 2." *Oil and Gas Journal* 32 (August 24, 1933): 8, 31.

———. "Ickes Named Oil Code Administration Head; Secretary Will Supervise Oil Price Fixing." *Oil and Gas Journal* 32 (August 31, 1933): 9, 14.

———. "No Oil Price Fixing by the Government Now; Section Remains in Code, But Inoperative." *Oil and Gas Journal* 32 (September 14, 1933): 9, 30.

———. "Constitutional Questions and Lack of Facts Delay Decision on Government Price Fixing Policy." *Oil and Gas Journal* 32 (October 12, 1933): 9, 54.

———. "Government Fixes Crude and Refined Oil Prices Throughout United States, Effective Dec. 1." *Oil and Gas Journal* 32 (October 26, 1933): 21–22.

King, H. H. "Hendrick Extension Starts Big Offset Campaign." *Oil Weekly* 48 (March 9, 1928): 40.

———. "Peculiar Water Trouble Develops in Hendrick Field." *Oil Weekly* 48 (January 13, 1928): 23.

———. "Hendrick Field Operators Appoint Conservation Commission." *Oil Weekly* 48 (February 10, 1928): 23.

———. "Hendrick 'Umpire' Arranging Details of Proration Order." *Oil Weekly* 49 (May 4,1928): 28.

———. "Winkler County Proration Has Increased Recovery." *Oil Weekly* 54 (July 2, 1929): 35.

———. "Plan to Curtail Winkler Output Dropped." *Oil Weekly* 52 (March 8, 1929): 34.

———. "Committee Seeks Permit to Increase Hendrick Runs." *Oil Weekly* 54 (June 8, 1929): 34.

———. "Mid-Continent Association Favors Oil Tariff." *Oil Weekly* 59 (December 12, 1930): 26.

————. "Big Companies Pool Interests in Van Field." *Oil Weekly* 55 (November 8, 1929): 30.

Lauer, T. E. "The Common Law Background of the Riparian Doctrine." *Missouri Law Review* 28 (1963): 60–107.

————. "Reflections on Riparianism." *Missouri Law Review* 35 (1970): 1–25.

Lear, Linda J. "Harold L. Ickes and the Oil Crisis of the First Hundred Days." *Mid-America* 63 (January, 1981): 5–8.

"Legal Background of Nathan R. Margold, Now Chairman of Petroleum Administrative Board." *Oil and Gas Journal* 33 (March 29, 1934): 11, 118.

"Legislative Committee Criticizes Commission." *Oil and Gas Journal* 31 (March 23,1933): 29.

Linz, Clarence L. "Washington Withholds Approval of Institute's Conservation Plan." *Oil Weekly* 53 (April 12, 1929): 37.

Logan, Garret. "The Use of Martial Law to Regulate the Economic Welfare of the State and Its Citizens: A Recent Instance." *Iowa Law Review* 17 (November, 1931): 40–49.

"Magnolia Posts 25 Cents for East Texas Oil, But 10-Cent Market Prevails." *Oil and Gas Journal* 31 (May 4, 1933): 10.

"Making It Stick." *Oil and Gas Journal* 32 (October 5, 1933): 18.

Mallon, Hugh D. "Ickes' Bill to Provide Permanent Control Crude Production and to Extend Life of Oil Code." *Oil and Gas Journal* 32 (April 26, 1934): 9, 42.

————. "Administration Bill to Control Crude Oil Production Introduced in Senate; Time for Passage Short." *Oil and Gas Journal* 32 (May 3, 1934): 9, 16.

————. "Congressional Investigating Committee Named; Representative Dies, Texas, Chosen Counsel." *Oil and Gas Journal* 33 (June 21, 1934): 9, 26.

————. "Leaders in Industry Outspoken Before Washington Committee in Opposing Government Control." *Oil and Gas Journal* 33 (September 27, 1934): 8–10, 58.

————. "Cole Committee report May Not Recommend Any Specific Legislation." *Oil and Gas Journal* 33 (January 3, 1935): 6.

————. "Supreme Court May Not Rule on Code in Amazon-Panama Case." *Oil and Gas Journal* 33 (December 13, 1934): 15, 32.

————. "Senate Passes Section; Pettengill Is Doubtful of Its Constitutionality." *Oil and Gas Journal* 33 (January 24, 1935): 8, 32.

————. "Federal Tender Board, Senate Oil Investigation Interesting Washington." *Oil and Gas Journal* 33 (March 7, 1935): 10.

————. "Amended Connally Bill Is Passed by the House; To Authorize Compact." *Oil and Gas Journal* 33 (February 21, 1935): 10.

————. "Changing Opinion in Congress May Force Compromise on NRA." *Oil and Gas Journal* 33 (April 25, 1935): 10.

————. "President Outlines His Views Regarding Legislation About Oil." *Oil and Gas Journal* 34 (June 6, 1935): 10.

————. "Revised Control Bill To Rivet Federal Rule On Petroleum Industry." *Oil and Gas Journal* 34 (June 20, 1935): 10, 32.

————. "New Attempts to Obtain Compromise on Federal Oil Legislation." *Oil and Gas Journal* 34 (July 11, 1935): 10.

————. "Congress Ratifies Interstate Compact; Oil Bills Off Until Next Session." *Oil and Gas Journal* 34 (August 29, 1935): 25.

"Market Demand Is Feature of Texas Measure; Full Text of Proposed Conservation Bill." *Oil and Gas Journal* 31 (November 10, 1932): 8, 32.

Marshall, J. Howard, and Norman L. Meyers. "Legal Planning of Petroleum Production." *Yale Law Journal* 41 (November, 1931): 33–68.

————. "Legal Planning of Petroleum Production: Two Years of Proration." *Yale Law Journal* 42 (1933): 702–46.

"Martial Law in Four Counties Declared by Governor Sterling: Wells Closed Without Disorder, None Expected." *Oil and Gas Journal* 30 (August 20, 1931): 15, 104.

"Martial Law Needed in East Texas." *Oil and Gas Journal* 30 (October 22, 1931): 14, 96.

Mass, Arthur, and Hiller B. Zobel. "Anglo-American Water Law: Who Appropriated the Riparian Doctrine?" *Public Policy* 10 (1960): 109.

McClellan, Sydney E. "The Hot Oil Cases." *Illinois Law Review* 10 (March, 1935): 343–49.

McKie, James W. "Market Structure and Uncertainty in Oil and Gas Exploration." *Quarterly Journal of Economics* 74 (November, 1960): 543–71.

McIntyre, James B. "East Texans' Policy Brings Price Cut." *Oil and Gas Journal* 30 (May 28, 1931): 11.

————. "With East Texas Shut In Crude Oil Production in U.S. Falls to Lowest Figure in 10 Years." *Oil and Gas Journal* 31 (January 5, 1933): 7.

————. "December Allowable Production of Crude Oil Is Reduced to 2,210,000 Barrels Per Day." *Oil and Gas Journal* 32 (November 23, 1933): 7.

————. "Reduced Allowable Production Goes Into Effect With Industry Prepared to Conform to It." *Oil and Gas Journal* 32 (December 7, 1933): 9.

————. "Texas, Oklahoma and California on Production Rampage in the Past Week; Hot Oil Stories." *Oil and Gas Journal* 32 (December 14, 1933): 5.

————. "East Texas Producers Say Demand Now Exceeds Allowable and They Seek An Increase." *Oil and Gas Journal* 32 (January 11, 1934): 7.

McTee, A. R. "Winkler Conservation Move Follows Commission Conference." *Oil Weekly* 49 (March 16, 1928): 25–27.

————. "Commission Promises to Select Plan for Hendrick Situation." *Oil Weekly* 49 (April 20, 1928): 27–28.

"Meeting Postponed." *Oil and Gas Journal* 30 (August 20, 1931): 104.

Merrill, Maurice H. "Stabilization of the Oil Industry and Due Process of Law." *Southern California Law Review* 3 (June, 1930): 396–410.

Mockler, A. E. "Oil Industry Getting Its House In Order." *Oil and Gas Journal* 30 (January 8, 1932): 23, 116–17.

————. "Industry Is Prepared for Showdown on Proration Enforcement Measures, Says R. C. Holmes." *Oil and Gas Journal* 31 (April 27, 1933): 13, 16.

Moore, Prentiss T. "Mexia Well Making Slow But Steady Progress." *Oil Trade Journal* 12 (January, 1921): 20.

"Motor Registrations Gain 13.7 Per Cent." *Oil and Gas Journal* 24 (July 23, 1925): 24, 152.

Murphy, Blakely M. "The Interstate Compact to Conserve Oil and Gas: An Experiment in Co-Operative State Production Control." *Mississippi Law Journal* 17 (March–May, 1946): 314–46.

"Murrayism: A Dramatization of Popular Unrest." *National Petroleum News* 23 (August 19, 1931): 19–20, 22.

"New Allowable Orders for Texas Fields Issued After Operators Express Ideas at Austin." *Oil and Gas Journal* 31 (January 12, 1933): 12.

"New Allowables in Texas as Ordered by Commission." *Oil and Gas Journal* 31 (April 13, 1933): 31.

"New Law for Supervision of Refineries Is Upheld by Texas District Judge." *Oil and Gas Journal* 32 (March 29, 1934): 9.

"New Texas Bill Proposes to Cut Marginal Wells." *Oil and Gas Journal* 31 (April 13, 1933): 31.

"No Illusions." *Oil and Gas Journal* 32 (March 15, 1934): 20.

"No Injunction Issued In East Texas." *Oil and Gas Journal* 30 (February 25, 1932): 13, 93–95.

Nordhauser, Norman E. "Origins of Federal Oil Regulation in the 1920s." *Business History Review* 47 (Spring, 1973): 53–71.

O'Conner, J. A., Jr. "The Role of Market Demand in the Domestic Oil Industry." *Arkansas Law Review* 12 (Fall, 1958): 342–52.

"Oil May Be Included in Industry Agreement Bill; Single Dictatorship Out of the Picture?" *Oil and Gas Journal* 31 (May 18, 1933): 13, 20.

"Oil Tariff Beaten in Senate Vote." *Oil Weekly* 56 (March 7, 1930): 45.

Oliver, Earl. "Lawyers Hear of Industry's Problems." *Oil and Gas Journal* 30 (September 24, 1931): 22, 122.

————. "Why Adequate Oil Legislation Failed." *Oil and Gas Journal* 30 (September 17, 1931): 15, 100–101.

————. "Change Needed In Oil Ownership Law." *Oil and Gas Journal* 30 (July 23, 1931): 15, 181.

——. "The Problems of the Petroleum Industry." *Oil and Gas Journal* 31 (May 11, 1933): 10–11.

Olson, Emery E. "Delegation of Legislative Powers—National Industrial Recovery Act." *Southern California Law Review* 8 (March, 1935): 226–30.

"Opinions in Texas and Washington Agree That Shipment Regulation Will Continue." *Oil and Gas Journal* 33 (January 10, 1935): 8, 32.

"Out of the Depths." *Oil and Gas Journal* 31 (May 18, 1933): 22.

"Out of the Fog." *Oil and Gas Journal* 33 (May 30, 1935): 24.

"Panhandle Proration Held Not To Be Unreasonable." *Oil and Gas Journal* 32 (July 6, 1933): 16.

Pierce, Richard J., Jr. "State Regulation of Natural Gas In A Federally Deregulated Market." *Cornell Law Review* 73 (1987): 15–53.

Pew, J. Edgar. "Time Is Ripe for Unitization." *Oil and Gas Journal* 30 (November 12, 1931): 38, 89.

"Politics and Proration." *Oil and Gas Journal* 31 (February 2, 1933): 16.

"Power of Texas Railroad Commission to Prorate Gets Court Test." *Oil Weekly* 59 (December 28, 1929): 27.

"President Roosevelt Urging the Oil Bill Quotes the Oil and Gas Journal." *Oil and Gas Journal* 33 (May 31, 1934): 91.

"President W. S. Farish Hopes New Year Will See Supply Balancing Demand." *Oil and Gas Journal* 31 (January 5, 1933): 34.

"Railroad Commission Issues Orders for Allowable Output in East Texas." *Oil and Gas Journal* 31 (December 8, 1932): 8.

"Railroad Commission Ready to Issue New Proration Rules." *Oil and Gas Journal* 30 (February 8, 1932): 13.

"Robert R. Penn." *Oil and Gas Journal* 30 (December 24, 1931): 14.

Rowley, Andrew M. "Engineers Attack Oil Field Problem." *Oil and Gas Journal* 26 (June 21, 1928): 31, 164.

——. "Suppose We Lift the Lid on Proration." *Oil and Gas Journal* 30 (June 4, 1931): 17.

——. "Oklahoma Shutdown Has Little Effect." *Oil and Gas Journal* 30 (August 13, 1931): 13, 132.

——. "Crude Oil Price Cutters Are Largely Responsible for Present Uncertainty in the Oil Business." *Oil and Gas Journal* 31 (January 12, 1933): 7.

——. "Question of Continuing Proration Now Agitating many Oil Men Dissatisfied With Conditions." *Oil and Gas Journal* 31 (February 2, 1933): 7.

——. "Immediate Strengthening of Crude and Refined Oil Markets Expected as Result of Meeting." *Oil and Gas Journal* 31 (March 30, 1933): 7.

——. "Wild Orgy in East Texas Brings Inevitable Cut; Voluntary Curtailment Elsewhere Suggested." *Oil and Gas Journal* 31 (May 4, 1933): 7.

——. "No Hope for Any Effective Curtailment in Texas Under the Present Political Set-up." *Oil and Gas Journal* 32 (May 25, 1933): 5.

———. "Temporary Troubles Should Not Blind Business to Dangers Incident to Government Control." *Oil and Gas Journal* 31 (May 11, 1933): 9.

———. "Ban on Hot Oil Shipments Strengthens Crude and Refined Oil Price Structures; Outlook Good." *Oil and Gas Journal* 32 (July 20, 1933): 5.

———. "Petroleum Industry, Entering New Era, Hopeful of Elimination of Hot Oil and Price Cutting." *Oil and Gas Journal* 32 (July 20, 1933): 11.

———. "Further Price Increases Expected as Production of Crude Is Curtailed Near to Quota Limits." *Oil and Gas Journal* 32 (September 21, 1933): 7.

———. "Oil Industry Should Use the Code to Establish Solid Foundation for Future Operations." *Oil and Gas Journal* 32 (November 30, 1933): 9, 32.

———. "Overproduction, Weak Refined market, Show Need of Quick Action on Corrective Plans." *Oil and Gas Journal* 32 (March 22, 1934): 7.

———. "Government Official Favors Nationalizing Crude Oil Production." *Oil and Gas Journal* 33 (November 22, 1934): 6–7.

———. "Allred Strongly Opposes Federal Control, Even Temporary; Making Careful Study of Compact Proposal." *Oil and Gas Journal* 33 (October 4, 1934): 8.

———. "A.P.I. Directors Vote Against Federal Control of Petroleum Industry." *Oil and Gas Journal* 33 (November 22, 1934): 8, 10.

———. "Oklahoma Will Initiate Legislation for Interstate Compact; Marland to Call Oil Conference in December." *Oil and Gas Journal* 33 (October 4, 1934): 9.

———. "Governors' Conference Against Federal Control." *Oil and Gas Journal* 33 (December 6, 1934): 8–10.

———. "Eight Oil States, Including Texas, Vote for an Interstate Compact." *Oil and Gas Journal* 33 (January 3, 1935): 6.

———. "Conference Approves Interstate Oil Compact; Quick Action Assured." *Oil and Gas Journal* 33 (February 21, 1935): 8–9, 32.

———. "Clashing Opinions at Thomas Bill Hearings in Senate Committee." *Oil and Gas Journal* 33 (April 18, 1935): 12, 25.

———. "Institute Directors Vote Unanimously Against Any Form of Federal Control." *Oil and Gas Journal* 33 (May 9, 1935): 9.

———. "Oil State Governors Meet Sept. 12 to Form Interstate Compact Commission." *Oil and Gas Journal* 34 (August 29, 1935): 25.

Scheiber, Harry N., "Public Rights and the Rule of Law in American History," *California Law Review* 72 (March, 1964): 217–51.

Simonton, James W. "Has A Landowner Any Property in Oil and Gas in Place?" *West Virginia Law Quarterly* 27 (June, 1921): 281–300.

Smiley, Thomas M. "Henry L. Doherty Owes His Rise to Grit." *Oil and Gas Journal* 29 (December 25, 1930): 31, 98.

Smith, Lawrence E. "Scramble for Crude as East Texas Output is Shut Off Under Martial Law." *National Petroleum News* 23 (August 19, 1931): 19–20, 22.

———. "Troops Occupation of East Texas Fields Marked by Order and Efficiency." *National Petroleum News* 23 (August 26,1931): 32–33.

Spiney, W. A. "Proration Effective in Oklahoma." *Oil and Gas Journal* 29 (July 31, 1930): 68.

"Sterling Considering Position." *Oil and Gas Journal* 31 (December 15, 1932): 30.

Stern, Robert E. "That Commerce Which Concerns More States Than One." *Harvard Law Review* 47 (1934): 1335–66.

Stevenson, D. A. "Difficulties Over Texas Proration Plan." *Oil and Gas Journal* 29 (August 14, 1930): 37, 149–50.

Stockman, L. P. "Oil Problem Analyzed in Mineral Law Section, American Bar Association." *Oil and Gas Journal* 34 (July 25, 1935): 27.

Struth, H. J. "Extended Proration or Future Reduction Is Ultimatum." *Oil Weekly* 52 (February 15, 1929): 39.

———. "Feasibility of Nationwide Control Exemplified by Winkler Plan." *Oil Weekly* 53 (April 5, 1929): 21.

Sugarman, David, "Simple Images and Complex Realities: English Lawyers and Their Relationship to Business and Politics, 1750–1950." *Law and History Review* 11 (Fall, 1993): 257–301.

Summers, Walter Lee. "Property in Oil and Gas." *Yale Law Journal* 29 (1919): 174–87.

———. "Legal Interests in Oil and Gas." *Illinois Law Quarterly* 4 (1922): 15–18.

"Supreme Court of the United States Sets Aside the Orders of Governor Sterling of Texas." *Oil and Gas Journal* 31 (December 15, 1932): 10, 30.

"Texas Allowable Revised by Railroad Commission." *Oil and Gas Journal* 31 (December 15, 1932): 32.

"Texas Allowable Set at 845,625 Barrels Daily." *Oil and Gas Journal* 31 (December 1, 1932): 9.

"Texas Brazos Trail." *Texas Monthly* 19 (May, 1991): 73–83.

"Texas Commission Revises Proration." *Oil and Gas Journal* 29 (August 28, 1930): 37, 148.

"Texas House for New Oil Commission; Marginal Well Bill to Governor." *Oil and Gas Journal* 31 (April 27, 1933): 11.

"Texas Independent Oil Operators Organizing." *Oil Weekly* 56 (February 21, 1930): 75.

"Texas Legislature Fails to Take Action: Deadlock on Measures Between Houses Brings Veto Threat From Governor Sterling to Use Militia as Last Resort." *Oil and Gas Journal* 30 (August 13, 1931): 13, 134.

"Texas Legislature for Conservation." *Oil and Gas Journal* 30 (July 16, 1931): 17.

"Texas Maximum Set at 750,000 Barrels." *Oil and Gas Journal* 29 (August 21, 1930): 37, 73.

"Texas Proration Test Begun Before Court." *Oil and Gas Journal* 29 (February 5, 1931): 119.

"Texas Proration is Attacked in Hearing in Federal Court at Houston." *Oil and Gas Journal* 31 (September 22, 1932): 14.

"Texas University Royalties." *Oil Weekly* 44 (December 31, 1926): 26.

"Texas Will Ask A Stay of Execution in Case Against Railroad Commission." *Oil and Gas Journal* 31 (November 3, 1932): 10.

"The People Are Not Helpless." *Oil and Gas Journal* 31 (March 30, 1933): 18.

"The White House Conference." *Oil and Gas Journal* 32 (September 14, 1933): 20.

Thomas, J. Elmer. "Production Curtailment in Texas." *Oil Weekly* 51 (December 7, 1928): 54–55.

"Troops Shut Down East Texas Field." *Oil and Gas Journal* 30 (August 20, 1931): 15, 104.

Tugwell, Rex G. "Principle of Planning and the Institution of Laissez Faire." *American Economic Review* 22 (March, 1932): 75–92.

"University Royalties." *Oil Weekly* 42 (August 6, 1926): 88.

Van Duzee, E. N. "Effects of Choking Wells in Winkler County." *Oil Weekly* 53 (April 12, 1929): 43.

Veasey, James A. "The Law of Oil and Gas." *Michigan Law Review* 18 (April, 1920): 445–69.

———. "Constitutional Obstacles to Oil Law." *Oil and Gas Journal* 26 (September 1, 1927): 32, 91.

Walker, A. W., Jr. "Property Rights in Oil and Gas and Their Effect Upon Police Regulation of Property." *Texas Law Review* 16 (1938): 370–81.

———. "Legal Interests in Oil and Gas." *Illinois Law Quarterly* 4 (1922): 15–18.

"West Texas Producing Area Crosses Pecos." *Oil Weekly* 43 (November 5, 1926): 40.

White, Joe L. "Columbus Marion 'Dad' Joiner and the East Texas Oil Boom." *East Texas Historical Journal* 6 (1968): 20–21.

Wiel, Samuel C. "Running Water." *Harvard Law Review* 22 (January, 1909): 190–215.

———. "Origin and Comparative Development of the Law of Watercourses in the Common Law and in the Civil Law." *California Law Review* 6 (1918): 245–67.

Williams, Lawrence G. "Direct Federal Control of Petroleum Production." *American Bar Association Journal* 21 (May, 1935): 309–15.

Williams, Neil. "Oil Running Through Pure-Van Line." *Oil and Gas Journal* 29 (July 31, 1930): 56, 213.

———. "East Texas Crude Prices Cut 30 Cents." *Oil and Gas Journal* 30 (May 26, 1931): 24.

——. "Federal Judges Hear Suit on East Texas Production." *Oil and Gas Journal* 31 (June 2, 1932): 13.

——. "Texas Commission to Make Own Survey Naming Engineers to Get Data." *Oil and Gas Journal* 31 (July 21, 1932): 53.

——. "Three-Judge Federal Court in Session at Houston Hears Proration Assailed and Defended." *Oil and Gas Journal* 31 (September 29, 1932): 14–15.

——. "East Texas Hearing Before Federal Court Ends, Three Judges Withholding Their Decision." *Oil and Gas Journal* 31 (February 2, 1933): 6, 29.

——. "Texas Petroleum Council Organized at Houston to Support Enforcement of Proration Orders." *Oil and Gas Journal* 32 (July 13, 1933): 12, 31.

——. "Houston Three Judge Court Will Not Decide Proration NRA Test Case Until After January 4." *Oil and Gas Journal* 32 (December 21, 1933): 13–14.

Williams, Paul. "Dynamometer Gives Important Data." *Oil and Gas Journal* 28 (May 30, 1929): 33, 154–55.

Wilson, C. O. "Price Fixing by Government Is Again Postponed; Meanwhile Prices Are Expected to Improve." *Oil and Gas Journal* 32 (September 21, 1933): 9–10.

——. "Government May Use Its War Powers to Control the Operations of the Petroleum Industry." *Oil and Gas Journal* 33 (March 1, 1934): 12, 42.

Zelden, Charles. "Regional Growth and the Federal District Courts: The Impact of Judge Joseph C. Hutcheson, Jr. on Southeast Texas, 1918–1931." *Houston Review* 10 (1989): 66–94.

VII. Theses and Dissertations

Day, Barbara Thompson. "The Oil and Gas Industry in Texas Politics, 1930–1935." Ph.D. Dissertation. Rice University, 1973.

Fowler, Pamela McDougald. "The Origins of the Texas Railroad Commission." M. A. Thesis. Rice University, 1982.

Powers, Stephen T. "The Development of United States Naval Fuel-Oil Policy, 1866–1923." M. A. Thesis. Rice University, 1960.

Index

Abercombie, J. S., 50
absolute ownership theory, 11–12
Allred, James V.: defense of the TRC, 63; interpretation of the Marginal Well Act, 142; on interstate compact, 179, 180; Interstate Oil Compact and, 187; investigation of Pure's Van unit, 88–89; opposition to national regulation, 178
Amazon case, 164–66, 169, 180–82
American Petroleum Institute. *See* API
Ames, C. B., 133, 151, 176
Andrade, C., 55
Andrews, R. E., 54
Angell, Joseph, 11
Anti-Market Demand Act, 90–91, 108
antitrust laws: Baker on, 27; legislative probe for violations of, 83–84; recommended relaxation of, 21–22, 24; unitization and, 25–26; Van unitization agreement and, 42–43; Yates unitization agreement and, 31, 32, 39
antitrust suits, 89
API (American Petroleum Institute), 18, 40, 188
Atlantic Oil Producing Company, 134
Austin hearing, 49–50

Baker, Hines H., 26–27, 59–60, 142
Baker & Botts, 5

Barnard v. Monongahela Gas Company, 14
Bates, Henry M., 168, 171–72
Beaty, Amos L., 19, 168
Berenger, Harry G., 16
Black, Charles L., 49–50, 63, 81
bootlegging oil, 104
Borah, William E., 188
bottom-hole pressure, 128–29
Boyd, W. R., 189
Boyle, R. J., 174–75
Bracken, J. A., 42
Brandeis, Louis, 180, 181
Brewer, David J., 33–34
bribery, 95, 160
Broderick, A. J., 113, 116, 121
Brown v. Vandergrift, 13
Bryan, W. F., 109
Bryant, Randolph J., 104–105, 130–31, 166, 178
Buck, E. O., 128, 138, 141
Burns, Gordon, 145
Burns assault, 145
Byles, Axtell J., 188

Calhoun, George, 62
Calvert, George, 113, 114, 115, 116, 121
Cardozo, Benjamin Nathan, 183–84
central prorationing committee, 48–49
Champlin case, 110, 112, 123, 127
Cheek, Maurice, 165

Chicago code, 153
Clark, E. W., 25
Clark, John G., 149
coal, 4
code of fair practices, 89
Cole, William P. Jr., 170, 187
Cole Committee: advice of lawyers to, 170–75; findings of, 179; oil industry leaders advice to, 175–78; recommendations of, 180, 182; Thomas-Disney bill and, 187
Colorado Springs conference, 40
Committee of Eleven, 20
Committee of Fifteen, 150, 151
Committee of Nine, 21–22, 24
common law, 10–11, 15, 173
Common Purchaser Act, 47, 50, 67–68
Compact Board, 187
congressional authority, 186
Connally, Tom, 185
Connally Hot Oil Act, 185–87, 189, 191
Conroe field, 146
conservation: attitudes toward, 38–39; indifference to, 29; need for, 34; overproduction and, 25; Van unitization agreement and, 43
conservation efforts, 18–21
Conservationist, 100
conservation statutes, 34–35
Constantin, Eugene, 104
Constantin case, 104–108, 124, 128, 129–30, 168
Coolidge, Calvin, 19–20
correlative rights, 190
Cottrell, F. G., 9
Cranfill, Tom, 79, 121
Cranfill plan, 79, 80
crime, 76

Dallas Morning News, 139–40
Daly, U. de B., 67
Danciger, Joseph C., 61–64, 125, 126–27, 146, 177
Danciger case, 110, 112, 123
Dancy, Felix, 7–8
Dancy, Mattie, 7–8
Daugherty, W. H., 35–36

Dawes, Henry M.: Cole Committee and, 177; on Pure's need for oil, 118, 133; Pure's Van allowable and, 65–66, 68–69; on the rule of capture, 164
Deberry, Tom, 125
Dies, Martin, 170, 186
Dillon, John F., 33
dime barrel oil, 143–44
Disney, Wesley, 169
Doherty, Henry L., 18–19, 24, 25
Donnell, Otto D., 176
Donoghue, David, 114–15
Drake, Edwin L., 11
drilling leases, 5

Eagle, Joe, 169
East Texas field: abuses at, 89, 116, 135–36; allowable revisions at, 116–17; exceptions at, 59; hot oil at, 160; illegal production at, 139; martial law at, 93–94, 103–104; overproduction at, 57, 73, 77, 91–92, 98; proration orders for, 72; Red Scare at, 72–73; shutdown of, 130; size of, 57
East Texas Lease, Royalty and Producers Association, 58
East Texas oil boom, 56–57, 76
East Texas Oil Landowners' Association. *See* ETOLA
Elkins, James A.: Allred's antitrust investigation and, 88; on the Common Purchaser Act, 68; on federal control, 164; founding of Vinson & Elkins, 5; gratitude toward, 71; impact of, 73–74; influence of, 80, 89; on the legislative special session of 1931, 83–84; on the NRA, 156; prominence of, 65; prorationing and, 54; protest over committee appointments, 55–56; Pure's Van allowable and, 66–67, 69–71; at the TRC hearings, 114–16, 120, 121; Van allowable reduction and, 117, 118, 119, 120; on the Van unitization agreement,

42–43; Yates unitization agreement and, 31, 32
Ely, Northcut, 180
Emory, Don, 49
English common law, 10
Estes, Carl: on the Cranfill plan, 80; cooperation with Elkins, 113, 114, 117; on government regulation, 154; on hot oilers, 163–64; market-demand prorationing and, 126; at the 1931 legislative special session, 88; on prorationing, 72; at the Tyler meeting, 123; Van allowable reduction and, 117
ETOLA (East Texas Oil Landowners' Association), 144
Ex Parte Milligan, 105, 107

Farish, William S.: Anti-Market Demand Act and, 91; call for new laws, 99; Cole Committee and, 176–77; on the Common Purchaser Act, 47; conservationist stance of, 24; on East Texas field, 58; on overproduction, 30; on price-fixing, 157; on prorationing, 49; unitization and, 28, 29, 41; on waste, 27
Federal Oil Conservation Board. See FOCB
federal regulation: calls for, 141, 147; disagreement over, 149–50; need for, 149; opposition to, 188; results of, 163. See also government regulation
Federal Tender Board. See FTB
Ferguson, Miriam A., 141–42, 149, 167
field umpires, 52, 91, 95
Fischer, Fletcher: background of, 138; on NRA petroleum code, 181–82; in Panama case, 164, 165, 180; significance of, 184
flush production, 12, 18, 19, 20
FOCB (Federal Oil Conservation Board), 19–20, 21
Fourteenth Amendment, 22, 23, 33, 81, 107
Fouts, Elwood, 174

Francis, Charles I., 165
FTB (Federal Tender Board), 178–79
Funk v. Haldeman, 13

geophysical science, 18
German, W. P. Z., 175
Gladewater Gusher, 103
Glavis, Louis R., 167
gluts, 9
Godber, Frederick, 77
Golding & Murchison, 134
Gonzaulles, Manuel T., 76
government regulation: attitudes toward, 19; debate over, 20–21, 25, 98–103; need for, 9–10; precedent for, 22–23; public interest and, 23; of railroad rates, 33–34. See also federal regulation
Gray, Henry M., 100–101
Guiberson, S. A. Jr., 92
Gulf, 32

Hamer, Frank, 73
Hardwicke, Robert E. Jr., 101–102, 142, 161
Harrison Oil Company, 50
Hendrick oil field, 37–38
Herman v. Thomas, 35
Herndon, C. C., 153
Hogg, James Stephen, 33
Holliday, W. T., 176
Holmes, Ralph C., 139, 140, 144
hot oil: effect of FTB on, 178–79; elimination of, 155; oil prices and, 157; shipments of, 150, 151, 152
Hot Oil cases, 182–83
hot oilers: crackdown on, 144, 145; prosecution of, 158, 160, 161; techniques of, 160
House Bill 1052, 78–79
Hughes, Charles Evans, 20–21, 27–28, 129, 182–83
Humble Oil & Refining Company: circumvention of rule of capture by, 26–27; and Common Purchaser Act enforcement, 48; East Texas field and, 58–59; pipeline network

Humble Oil & Refining Company,
  (continued)
  of, 64; price cuts by, 46; unitization
  by, 25–26
Humphreys, Albert E., 5, 7–8
Hunt, H. L., 92–93, 145
Hunt case, 146
Hutcheson, Joseph C.: *Amazon* case
  and, 165–66; *Constantin* decision
  of, 106–107; *Hunt* decision of, 146;
  MacMillan decision of, 84–86;
  market-demand prorationing and,
  130–31; in the *People's* case, 120,
  122–23; *Rowan & Nichols* opinion
  of, 141

Ickes, Harold: appointment as
  petroleum administrator, 154–55;
  Cole Committee and, 178; denun-
  ciation of oil industry, 168; federal
  regulation and, 149–50, 151;
  formation of the FTB, 178; hot oil
  campaign of, 160; on price-fixing,
  158; Section 9(c) and, 152; on the
  Thomas-Disney bill, 187–88
Ickes Oil Dictatorship Bill, 169
Independent Petroleum Association of
  America. *See* IPAA
Independent Petroleum Association of
  Texas. *See* IPAT
Independent Petroleum Association
  Opposed to Monopoly. *See* IPAOM
interstate compact, 27, 179, 180
Interstate Oil Compact Commission,
  190
IOC (Interstate Oil Compact), 187,
  189, 190, 191
IPAA (Independent Petroleum
  Association of America), 40, 151
IPAOM (Independent Petroleum
  Association Opposed to Monopoly),
  150
IPAT (Independent Petroleum
  Association of Texas), 46, 100
Irish, W. M., 176

Johnson, Hugh S., 149, 153, 154
Joiner, Columbus M., 56–57

Keller, Morton, 60
Kelley, R. B., 115, 121
Kilgore, John, 127
Kleinstadtismus, 172
Knight, R. L., 138–39
Knox, K. M., 134

lease forfeiture clauses, 13
legal system: ideological decisions in,
  85, 86, 101, 130–31; slowness of,
  73, 97, 103
legislative special session of 1931, 81,
  82–84, 87–88
legislative special session of 1932,
  124–28
Lester, C. A., 140
Lewis, James O., 18
Liberty Pipe Line Company, 135
Lottery cases, 186
Luther v. Borden, 106, 107

MacMillan, Alfred E., 81
MacMillan case: appeal of, 124;
  Black's arguments in, 81;
  Champlin case and, 113; effect of,
  91–92; *Danciger* case and, 112;
  decision in, 84–86; influence on the
  Anti-Market Demand Act, 90;
  People's case and, 122
Manning, Van H., 9
Marginal Well Act, 136, 142, 143
marginal wells, 157
Margold, Nathan R., 155, 160, 168,
  170–71
maritime fuel oil, 4
Market Demand Act, 127–28
market-demand prorationing: fears
  of, 88; House Bill 1052 and, 78–79;
  legislative special session of 1931
  and, 81, 82; legislative special
  session of 1932 and, 125–27;
  MacMillan decision and, 86;
  physical waste and, 112; price-
  fixing and, 111, 126–27; Sterling's
  veto threat and, 86–87
Marland, Ernest W., 27, 180
Marland-Capper bill, 151–52

Marrs v. City of Oxford, 101
Marshall, J. Howard, 155, 173–74, 185, 190
martial law: declaration of, 92; defeat of, 129; effects of, 103–104; implementation of, 93–94; justification for, 103; legality of, 87, 105–108
Martin V. Mott, 106
McArthur, R. F., 49
McDonald, T. E., 127
McIlvain, R. W., 109
McKinney, W. E., 113
Methodist Episcopal Church, 109
Mexia land-title suits, 7–8
Meyers, Norman L., 173, 185
Minnesota Rate Cases, 168
Moody, Dan, 70, 71, 72, 88, 105–106
Moore, J. D., 72
Morris, W. C., 164
Moyer v. Peabody, 129
Munn v. Illinois, 101
Murray, William H., 87, 92

National Industrial Recovery Act. *See* NIRA
National Petroleum War Services Committee, 18
national regulation. *See* federal regulation
natural use doctrine, 10
Nazro, Underwood, 125–26
New Deal, 147
Nicholas, L. V., 176
Nickels, Luther, 127
NIRA (National Industrial Recovery Act), 148–49, 151, 152, 181–82, 183
Nye, Gerald P., 188

Ohio Oil v. Indiana, 23, 35, 36, 101
oil: mineral rights and, 11–12; as minerals *ferae naturae,* 13; ownership of, 11–15
Oil and Gas Journal, 138, 143, 152, 167, 189
oilmen: indifference toward conservation, 29; need for education, 27–28
oil shortages, 9, 21, 24–25
Oil States Advisory Committee (OSAC), 72
Oliver, Earl, 98, 171
O'Neal, J. E., 9
Orgain, Will, 55
overproduction: concern over, 72; conservation and, 25; at East Texas, 57–58, 77, 91–92, 98; effect of, on market price, 143; at Hendrick, 37; opinions on stopping, 27–28; per-well allowable and, 117; problems of, 30; unitization and, 19

PAB (Petroleum Administration Board), 155
Pace, Will, 145
Page, Paul, 105
Palmer v. Mulligan, 11
Panama Refining Company v. Ryan, 164, 165, 166, 169, 180–82, 183–84
Parker, Richard Denny, 37, 68
Parten, J. R., 100
Patten, Tom G., 104
Paul, Arnold M., 85
PCC (Planning and Coordination Committee), 154, 155
Peddy, George, 69
Penn, Robert R. (Dallas oilman), 48–49, 70, 79, 88, 100
Penn, Robert R. (wildcatter), 31
Pennsylvania Supreme Court, 12–15
People's case, 116, 120, 122–24
People's Petroleum Company, 116
per-well allocation formula, 94–95, 108, 109–10, 120, 122–23
petroleum: fugacious nature of, 12, 13–14; migration of, 14
Petroleum Administration Board. *See* PAB
petroleum code, 154–57, 161, 166–67, 189, 190
Petroleum Committee of the Texas Bankers Association, 160
petroleum conservation act of 1899, 34

petroleum conservation act of 1919,
36, 38
petroleum industry, 4
Pettengill, Samuel B., 170, 186
Pettus oil field, 50
Pew, J. Edgar, 66, 99, 176
Pew, J. Howard, 24–25, 176
Phillips, Frank, 177
Phillips, Nelson, 146
pipeline divorcement, 150–51, 175–76
Planning and Coordination Committee. *See* PCC
Platt v. Johnson, 11
Pogue, Joseph E., 9
Posner, Richard, 15
Pound, Roscoe, 168, 172–73
Powell, Ben, 56, 65, 68, 119
price cuts, 143–44
price-fixing, 111, 126–27, 153–54,
157–58
price-gouging, 132
priority doctrine, 10–11
Proctor, F. C., 29, 32
production control: advantages of, 77;
Ickes's confidence in, 155–56;
independents' view of, 46–47, 58;
need for, 18
prorationing: benefits of, 63; call for,
48; debate over, 49–50, 59; economic significance of, 133–34;
enforcement of, 52, 138–39;
implementation of, 52; legal battle
over, 62–64, 137–39; novelty of, 50;
protests of, 55; tensions in, 60
Pure Oil Company: allocation problems of, 64–69; effect of Common
Purchaser Act on, 50; effect of
prorationing on, 54; lawsuit of,
136–37; litigation against, 69;
market-demand prorationing and,
109; Mexia land-title suits and, 8;
production quota increase request,
56; reaction to first proration
order, 55–56; Yates unitization
agreement and, 31, 32
Pure-Van Pipeline, 54, 68
Pure Van Pipe Line Company, 135

railroad abuses, 32–33
*Railroad Commission of Wisconsin v.
Chicago, Burlington & Quincy
Railroad,* 168–69
railroad rates, 33–34
Rawlings, Frank, 87
Rawlings bill, 87–88
Rayburn, Sam, 170
reasonable use, 11
Requa, Mark, 19
Richards, Alvin, 88
Robert E. Hardwicke Legal Committee, 161
Roeser, Charles, 144, 145
Roosevelt, Franklin D.: appointment
of Ickes, 154–55; ban on hot oil
shipments, 152; Marland-Capper
bill and, 151–52; on price-fixing,
158; support for oil regulation,
188, 189; Washington conference
and, 149, 150
Ross, Sam, 144
Rowan, A. H., 137
Rowan & Nichols, 141
rule of capture: absolute ownership
and, 35–36; acceptance of, 14–15;
background of, 10; cases leading
up to, 12–14; circumvention of, 26–
27; criticisms of, 164, 172; effects
of, 17, 26; inadequacy of, 102;
problems with, 18, 21
rule of reasonableness, 86
Rule 37, 37

Saye, James N., 182
Schechter case, 189
Section 6 of the Common Purchaser
Act, 47
Section 9(c), 152, 164, 166, 181, 182–
84
Seubert, E. G., 176
Sharp, John H., 190
Shepherd, Robert A. Sr., 42, 50, 52,
82–83
Shorey v. Gorell, 11
Shreveport Cases, 168
shutdown movement, 92–93

slave marriages, 7
Smith, E. F., 105–106, 144
Special Order 48, 105
Spindletop, 3, 34
spoils system, 78
State v. Ohio Oil Company, 22–23
statute of 1917, 34
Stephens, Harold M., 180–81
Sterling, Ross: Anti-Market Demand
    Act and, 90; calling of legislative
    special session of 1932, 124–25;
    Cranfill plan and, 79–80; declara-
    tion of martial law, 93, 103; defeat
    of martial law, 129; on the People's
    case, 124; veto threat of, 86–87
Story, Joseph, 11
Strong, T. D., 49
Sweeton, Clyde, 7, 8, 136
Swift v. Tyson, 85

Teagle, Walter, 9, 20, 25, 27, 176
technological advances, 50, 52, 60–61
Tenth Amendment, 22
Terrell, C. V., 108, 123, 125, 126
Texas Company, 35–36, 139, 140
Texas Farmers' Alliance, 33
Texas Oil and Gas Conservation
    Association. See TOGCA
Texas Plan, 79
Texas Railroad Commission. See TRC
things ferae naturae, 23, 35, 36
Thomas, Elmer, 169
Thomas-Disney bill, 169–70, 171, 176,
    179, 187, 188–89
Thompson, Ernest O.: Cole Commit-
    tee and, 178; on duty of TRC, 139;
    on experimentation, 134; on
    gauging production, 118; on
    national production controls, 154;
    per-well allowable and, 116–17; on
    state control, 191; on TRC probe,
    135
Tilley, Rice M., 119, 137
titles, 4–5
Titus, Louis, 165–66
TOGCA (Texas Oil and Gas Conserva-
    tion Association), 100

Townes, Edgar E., 25–26
TRC (Texas Railroad Commission):
    adoption of Buck's formula, 128–
    29; authority of, 52, 54, 63; and
    Common Purchaser Act enforce-
    ment, 47, 48; corruption in, 95;
    criticisms of, 140–41; effect of
    patronage on, 78; erosion of power
    of, 77–78; favorable rulings for,
    146–47; Hendrick wildcatters'
    defiance of, 38; hesitancy of, 59;
    hot oil and, 160; legal troubles of,
    33–34; origins of, 32–33; petroleum
    conservation laws and, 34; probe
    of, 135; prorationing enforcement
    and, 52, 56, 123; proration orders
    of, 54–55, 80, 94–95, 133, 143;
    Texas House investigation of, 138,
    140; thirty-eight rules of, 36–37;
    Van unitization agreement and,
    43–44; Yates oil field and, 39
TRC hearings, 113, 114–16, 118–22,
    133, 134–35
Turlington, C. M., 135
Tyler v. Wilkinson, 11

United Mine Workers v. Coronado
    Coal Company, 170–71
unitization: benefits of, 28, 41, 43;
    debate over, 19–20; development
    of, 26–27; difficulties with, 28; lack
    of support for, 28–29; need for, 24;
    opposition to, 40; pilot of, 25–26;
    problems of, 48; prosecution and,
    156
University of Texas, 31, 50, 70

Van allowable increase: arguments
    for, 68, 70–71; debate over, 65–69;
    hearing on, 70–71; need for, 64, 66,
    67, 69; TRC's decision on, 71
Van allowable reduction, 117, 118
Van field, 41–42
Van unitization agreement, 42–43, 88
Veasey, James A., 22, 24
vice, 76
Vinson, William A., 5, 47

Vinson & Elkins: history of, 5–7; prorationing and, 50; role in Mexia land-title suits, 7–8. *See also* Elkins, James A.

Wagstaff, R. M., 82, 87
Wagstaff-Woodward bill, 82, 87
waste: Anti-Market Demand Act definitions of, 90; debate over, 20–21; government control and, 22–23; market-demand prorationing and, 112; Market Demand Act definition of, 127–28; as public nuisance, 22–23; scientific concern over, 17–18
water intrusion, 37
Weekly Digest, 179
Weimer v. Bunburym, 106

Westmoreland Natural Gas Company, 13–14
Wharton, Clarence, 124
Wheeler, Charles A., 63
White, Edward Douglas, 23, 36
wildcatters, 5, 38
Wilde, Claude, 49
Willis, J. Hart, 136
Wok, Hubert, 21–22
Wolters, Jacob F., 86, 93–94
Woodward, Walter C., 82
Wrather, Jack D., 104

Yates oil field, 31
Yates unitization agreement, 31–32, 39, 46
Young, J. S., 54

AFQ 3653 — 1

DATE DUE